Enhancing Instructional Problem Solving

The Guilford Practical Intervention in the Schools Series

Kenneth W. Merrell, Founding Editor
T. Chris Riley-Tillman, Series Editor

This series presents the most reader-friendly resources available in key areas of evidence-based practice in school settings. Practitioners will find trustworthy guides on effective behavioral, mental health, and academic interventions, and assessment and measurement approaches. Covering all aspects of planning, implementing, and evaluating high-quality services for students, books in the series are carefully crafted for everyday utility. Features include ready-to-use reproducibles, lay-flat binding to facilitate photocopying, appealing visual elements, and an oversized format.

Emotional and Behavioral Problems of Young Children:
Effective Interventions in the Preschool and Kindergarten Years
Gretchen A. Gimpel and Melissa L. Holland

Resilient Classrooms: Creating Healthy Environments for Learning
Beth Doll, Steven Zucker, and Katherine Brehm

Helping Schoolchildren with Chronic Health Conditions: A Practical Guide
Daniel L. Clay

Interventions for Reading Problems: Designing and Evaluating Effective Strategies
Edward J. Daly III, Sandra Chafouleas, and Christopher H. Skinner

Safe and Healthy Schools: Practical Prevention Strategies
Jeffrey R. Sprague and Hill M. Walker

School-Based Crisis Intervention: Preparing All Personnel to Assist
Melissa Allen Heath and Dawn Sheen

Assessing Culturally and Linguistically Diverse Students: A Practical Guide
Robert L. Rhodes, Salvador Hector Ochoa, and Samuel O. Ortiz

Mental Health Medications for Children: A Primer
Ronald T. Brown, Laura Arnstein Carpenter, and Emily Simerly

Clinical Interviews for Children and Adolescents: Assessment to Intervention
Stephanie H. McConaughy

The ABCs of CBM: A Practical Guide to Curriculum-Based Measurement
Michelle K. Hosp, John L. Hosp, and Kenneth W. Howell

Fostering Independent Learning: Practical Strategies to Promote Student Success
Virginia Smith Harvey and Louise A. Chickie-Wolfe

Helping Students Overcome Substance Abuse: Effective Practices for Prevention and Intervention
Jason J. Burrow-Sanchez and Leanne S. Hawken

School-Based Behavioral Assessment: Informing Intervention and Instruction
Sandra Chafouleas, T. Chris Riley-Tillman, and George Sugai

Collaborating with Parents for Early School Success: The Achieving–Behaving–Caring Program
Stephanie H. McConaughy, Pam Kay, Julie A. Welkowitz, Kim Hewitt, and Martha D. Fitzgerald

Helping Students Overcome Depression and Anxiety, Second Edition: A Practical Guide
Kenneth W. Merrell

Inclusive Assessment and Accountability:
A Guide to Accommodations for Students with Diverse Needs
Sara E. Bolt and Andrew T. Roach

Bullying Prevention and Intervention: Realistic Strategies for Schools
Susan M. Swearer, Dorothy L. Espelage, and Scott A. Napolitano

Conducting School-Based Functional Behavioral Assessments, Second Edition: A Practitioner's Guide
Mark W. Steege and T. Steuart Watson

Evaluating Educational Interventions: Single-Case Design for Measuring Response to Intervention
T. Chris Riley-Tillman and Matthew K. Burns

Collaborative Home/School Interventions: Evidence-Based Solutions for Emotional, Behavioral, and Academic Problems
Gretchen Gimpel Peacock and Brent R. Collett

Social and Emotional Learning in the Classroom: Promoting Mental Health and Academic Success
Kenneth W. Merrell and Barbara A. Gueldner

Executive Skills in Children and Adolescents, Second Edition: A Practical Guide to Assessment and Intervention
Peg Dawson and Richard Guare

Responding to Problem Behavior in Schools, Second Edition: The Behavior Education Program
Deanne A. Crone, Leanne S. Hawken, and Robert H. Horner

High-Functioning Autism/Asperger Syndrome in Schools: Asessment and Intervention
Frank J. Sansosti, Kelly A. Powell-Smith, and Richard J. Cowan

School Discipline and Self-Discipline: A Practical Guide to Promoting Prosocial Student Behavior
George G. Bear

Response to Intervention, Second Edition: Principles and Strategies for Effective Practice
Rachel Brown-Chidsey and Mark W. Steege

Child and Adolescent Suicidal Behavior: School-Based Prevention, Assessment, and Intervention
David N. Miller

Cognitive Therapy for Adolescents in School Settings
Torrey A. Creed, Jarrod Reisweber, and Aaron T. Beck

Motivational Interviewing for Effective Classroom Management: The Classroom Check-Up
Wendy M. Reinke, Keith C. Herman, and Randy Sprick

Positive Behavior Support in Secondary Schools: A Practical Guide
Ellie L. Young, Paul Caldarella, Michael J. Richardson, and K. Richard Young

Academic and Behavior Supports for At-Risk Students: Tier 2 Interventions
Melissa Stormont, Wendy M. Reinke, Keith C. Herman, and Erica S. Lembke

RTI Applications, Volume 1: Academic and Behavioral Interventions
Matthew K. Burns, T. Chris Riley-Tillman, and Amanda M. VanDerHeyden

Coaching Students with Executive Skills Deficits
Peg Dawson and Richard Guare

Enhancing Instructional Problem Solving: An Efficient System for Assisting Struggling Learners
John C. Begeny, Ann C. Schulte, and Kent Johnson

Enhancing Instructional Problem Solving

An Efficient System for Assisting Struggling Learners

JOHN C. BEGENY
ANN C. SCHULTE
KENT JOHNSON

THE GUILFORD PRESS
New York London

A Division of Guilford Publications, Inc.
72 Spring Street, New York, NY 10012
www.guilford.com

Printed in the United States of America

This book is printed on acid-free paper.

Last digit is print number: 9 8 7 6 5 4 3 2 1

The authors have checked with sources believed to be reliable in their efforts to provide information that is complete and generally in accord with the standards of practice that are accepted at the time of publication. However, in view of the possibility of human error or changes in behavioral, mental health, or medical sciences, neither the authors, nor the editor and publisher, nor any other party who has been involved in the preparation or publication of this work warrants that the information contained herein is in every respect accurate or complete, and they are not responsible for any errors or omissions or the results obtained from the use of such information. Readers are encouraged to confirm the information contained in this book with other sources.

Library of Congress Cataloging-in-Publication Data

Begeny, John C.
Enhancing instructional problem solving : an efficient system for assisting struggling learners / by John C. Begeny, Ann C. Schulte, and Kent Johnson.
pages cm. — (The Guilford practical intervention in the schools series)
Includes bibliographical references and index.
ISBN 978-1-4625-0477-0 (pbk.: alk. paper)
1. Response to intervention (Learning disabled children) 2. Learning disabled children—Education 3. Remedial teaching. I. Schulte, Ann C., 1955– II. Johnson, Kent R. III. Title.
LC4705.B45 2012
371.9—dc23

2012002509

To the hard-working educators around the world
who, through their persistent efforts, determination, and talents,
improve the lives of others and their communities

J. C. B., A. C. S., and K. J.

To my parents—
two truly committed educators, even if not by occupation

J. C. B.

About the Authors

John C. Begeny, PhD, is Associate Professor of School Psychology at North Carolina State University and a psychologist in North Carolina. He has had a variety of professional-practice experiences, having served as a school psychologist in elementary schools and a medical hospital, a classroom teacher in a school for students with learning difficulties, a paraprofessional for a public school, a school district consultant in academic instruction and assessment, and a clinician in a psychoeducational clinic. Dr. Begeny's current research examines academic consultation, methods to improve children's reading abilities, international education, and strategies to narrow the gap between research and practice in education. He has received several grants and awards for his teaching and research activities, including grants to improve literacy development for children nationally and internationally. In 2010, Dr. Begeny was the recipient of the Ernest A. Lynton Citation for Distinguished Engaged Scholarship, a nationally competitive award that recognizes an early-career faculty member who demonstrates exemplary integration of community-engaged teaching, research, and service.

Ann C. Schulte, PhD, is Professor of Psychology in the Department of Psychology at North Carolina State University. She has previously held appointments in the School of Education and at the Frank Porter Graham Child Development Institute at the University of North Carolina at Chapel Hill and at the Duke University Medical Center. Dr. Schulte serves on the editorial boards of multiple journals, including the *Journal of School Psychology, School Psychology Review,* and *Learning Disabilities Research & Practice.* Dr. Schulte's primary research interest is school-based services for children with disabilities and improvement of achievement outcomes for this population. She is a Co-Principal Investigator of the National Center on Assessment and Accountability for Special Education, recently funded by the Institute of Education Sciences. In addition to her research, Dr. Schulte continues to work with schools to respond effectively to struggling learners.

Kent Johnson, PhD, is founder and Executive Director of Morningside Academy, a laboratory school in Seattle, Washington, for elementary and middle school children and youth. Morningside Academy investigates effective curriculum materials and teaching methods, and it has provided training and consulting in instruction to over 125 schools and agencies throughout the United States and Canada since 1991. Dr. Johnson has published many seminal articles and books about research-based curriculum and teaching methods, including the book *The Morningside Model of Generative Instruction: What It Means to Leave No Child Behind* (with Elizabeth M. Street). The Morningside model focuses on foundation skills in reading, writing, mathematics, thinking, reasoning, and problem solving; studying core content; and project-based learning. Over 40,000 students and 1,000 teachers have used the Morningside model. Dr. Johnson is also a cofounder of Headsprout, Inc., a company that develops web-based, interactive, cartoon-driven instructional programs, including Headsprout Early Reading and Headsprout Reading Comprehension.

Acknowledgments

During our careers, we have worked with and learned from numerous educators who have helped to make the ideas and procedures presented in this book possible. We particularly thank the outstanding educators from the Wake County and Johnston County school districts in North Carolina with whom we have worked most recently. We are also grateful to Pam Bailey and Mary Bushnell for their advice about working with community volunteers. Given their many years of experience developing, coordinating, and sustaining an effective school volunteer program, their comments about Chapter 8 were invaluable. We acknowledge Scott Methe for his suggestions on many of the book's math intervention and assessment procedures. Finally, we extend our appreciation to the Helps Education Fund, a nonprofit organization, for sponsoring the companion website *www.sopaaforschools.org*, and for facilitating increased support to the educators who use the SOPAA consultation model.

Contents

APPENDICES

PART I

PREPARING FOR IMPLEMENTATION

CHAPTER 1

Introduction to the Systems-Oriented Plan for Academic Achievement

Most would agree that the primary mission of schools is to promote student learning. On a daily basis, the vast majority of school staff work hard to achieve this mission, often bringing work home, putting in extra hours, and worrying about those students who are experiencing difficulty. Yet it often seems that schools are struggling against the odds. They are asked to do more with less, for an increasingly diverse population of students.

Statistics also highlight this concern about student achievement and the difficulty schools face serving the needs of all children. The most recent National Assessment of Educational Progress (NAEP) data (U.S. Department of Education, 2010) indicate that only 33% of fourth graders score at or above the proficiency level in reading, and 34% score *below* the basic level. For eighth graders, 30% score at or above proficiency, and 26% perform below the basic level. Unfortunately, the NAEP figures are only slightly better in the area of mathematics, with only 39% of all fourth graders and 34% of all eighth graders scoring at or above proficiency.

Current education statistics in the United States reveal that *less than 40%* of fourth- and eighth-grade students score at or above the proficient level in reading and math.

For U.S. students living in conditions of poverty (i.e., the 41% of school-age children who are eligible for free or reduced-price lunch), the academic achievement statistics are even more concerning. For example, 81% of these fourth-grade students read below the proficiency level, and 49% read below the basic level. Figures from the *Condition of Education* (U.S. Department of Education, 2010) also report the diverse needs of American school children. For example, the percent of school-age children who speak a language other than English in the home has increased from 9 to 21% in the past 30 years. Also, nearly 13% of all U.S. children are identified as having a disability requiring special education services, and this figure excludes children who are referred for special education but then are not identified for services. In sum, although most schools aim to serve all students, they may fall short of that goal, simply because they are overwhelmed by the range of individual differences and needs of the children who attend school.

For decades many solutions have been to proposed the challenges faced by teachers and other educators in assuring that students master academic content. Often externally proposed (or imposed), these solutions are wide ranging. Some examples include new teacher education requirements, increased accountability for individual schools and teachers, more charter schools, universal preschool, parent outreach, and more technology in the classroom (Coplon, 2010; David & Cuban, 2010; McDonnell, 2004).

In addition, nearly all schools make at least some attempt to assist struggling learners before those students reach the upper elementary grades and/or are referred for special education services. In the most recent decades, problem-solving efforts such as prereferral intervention teams (Buck, Polloway, Smith-Thomas, & Cook, 2003; Graden, 1989), professional learning communities (PLCs; DuFour, Eaker, Karhanek, & DuFour, 2004), and more recently, multilevel models of response to intervention (RTI; Brown-Chidsey & Steege, 2010; Fuchs, Fuchs, & Stecker, 2010) have emerged as important advances in the ways educators try to remediate students' academic difficulties. However, despite some promising indicators of academic improvement as a result of these approaches (Burns, Appleton, & Stehouwer, 2005; Burns & Symington, 2002), many schools continue to face pragmatic challenges in applying these approaches to best assist struggling learners. For example, based on our research and years of work with teachers and schools (e.g., Begeny & Martens, 2006a; Johnson & Street, 2004; Osborne & Schulte, 2001), and based on the work of many others in the field of education (e.g., Coalition for Psychology in Schools and Education, 2006; Doll et al., 2005; Hirsch & Church, 2009), we suspect that most educators can relate to at least some, if not many, of the following 10 challenges associated with addressing students' learning difficulties.

1. There is an effective schoolwide system in place to identify students with learning difficulties, but most teachers in the school do not have the training and/or resources to select and use a research-based intervention.
2. Students with learning difficulties are identified with valid assessments, research-based interventions are available to teachers, but teachers do not have the time to learn or implement the interventions consistently and accurately (i.e., with integrity).
3. School-based teams *can be* effective in addressing students' learning difficulties, but often too much time elapses between the time the teacher raises the concern, the team meets to discuss it, the intervention is implemented, and the team can meet again to determine its effectiveness.
4. School-based teams have been developed to assist teachers with struggling learners, but no one educator in the school has the time, or perhaps sufficient knowledge, to ensure that the designed intervention plan is carried out by the teacher (or others) as it should be.
5. School-based teams have been developed to assist teachers with struggling learners, but they require too much time from too many educators. For example, the school does not always need a team of four or more educators to effectively develop an intervention plan for a struggling learner. Having too many educators spending time in meetings for which fewer persons are necessary to address the issue takes their time away from instruction or instructional planning.
6. Teachers are required to implement an intervention to assist a struggling learner before the student can be considered by a team or considered for special education, but the school does not have a system for helping the teacher accurately document the intervention provided, or for ensuring that the intervention is adequately carried out according to district or school policy (or according to what could be considered "best practice").
7. There is no established system in the school for identifying all students who struggle in

the core academic areas (reading, math, and writing), so some students continue to "fall between the cracks," with their problems unaddressed until their skill deficits are so severe that they require more resources and are harder to address.

8. There are insufficient resources within the school, or an insufficient system, for monitoring students' progress as a result of intervention. As a result, teachers experience great difficulty determining whether students receiving intervention are actually benefiting from it.
9. Educational leaders in the school have great ideas for addressing both systems-level and student-level challenges (such as those just described), but those leaders do not have the experience, time, and/or resources to integrate those ideas in a way that will be supported by other educators in the school, possibly including the school principal.
10. Educational leaders in the school have great ideas that will help to overcome challenges associated with addressing all students' learning needs, and teachers in the school would likely be supportive of the ideas, but the leaders are unsure how, when, and to what degree they should start implementing their ideas.

To further complicate these types of challenges, national data suggest that schools must increasingly do more with fewer resources. According to the Center on Budget and Policy Priorities (CBPP), the current U.S. recession resulted in substantial budget cuts to K–12 education in 2008 and 2009 in 29 states and the District of Columbia (Johnson, Oliff, & Williams, 2010). For example, Michigan's fiscal year budget for 2010 included a $165 per-pupil spending reduction from the previous year, Hawaii's 2009–2010 school year was shortened by more than 3 weeks, and Massachusetts enacted cuts to early intervention programs and K–12 funding, including cuts to teacher training and services for disabled students (Johnson et al., 2010). In North Carolina, a state not even designated in the 2010 CBPP report as a state with "substantial" cuts to K–12 education, a 2008 survey showed that 87% of North Carolina teachers indicated that K–12 educators desire more time and resources to meet the educational needs of their students (Hirsch & Church, 2009).

In sum, there have been important research, practice, and policy advances over the past several decades, all designed to move schools closer to the goal of effectively addressing the needs of all learners. However, many schools continue to struggle with how to move from where they are to where they want to be. They are interested in implementing innovative practices, but often lack a road map for change.

HOW THIS BOOK MAY HELP SCHOOLS MEET THE NEEDS OF STRUGGLING LEARNERS

This book does not propose any grand solutions to cure the woes of the U.S. education system. However, it does offer a pragmatic plan with which an educator or small group of educators at a single school can begin to systematically implement a number of innovations that have the potential to improve how their school responds to children encountering difficulty in the general education classroom. Our aim is to provide a comprehensive yet time-efficient, resource-efficient, and user-friendly approach to improving students' learning outcomes in reading, math, and writing. In addition, our approach and the materials presented throughout this book are designed to respond to recent changes in how schools are expected to document their efforts to assist struggling learners. For example, the 2004 reauthorization of the Individuals with Disabilities Education Improvement Act (IDEIA, 2004) requires that a special education referral for a learning disability include "data-based documentation of repeated assessment of achievement at reasonable intervals, reflecting formal assessment of student progress during instruction, which [should be] provided to the child's parents" (p. 34 CFR 300.309(b)(1–2).

Termed the Systems-Oriented Plan for Academic Achievement (SOPAA), this model is designed not only to put evidence-based interventions in the hands of teachers quickly, but also to move toward addressing needs of learners in a systemic, resource-efficient, schoolwide way. This academic consultation model integrates what is known to be effective through both organizational consultation and triadic consultation (both of these basic models of consultation are discussed in Chapter 2) to put into place a program for moving schools toward standardized and systemic procedures for serving all children. In using both organizational and triadic consultation, the SOPAA integrates six key components that should collectively improve how schools respond to the types of challenges described earlier in this chapter. A basic description of each component follows, with further discussion of each component in Chapter 2.

Introduction to the Six SOPAA Components

Targeted Assistance Program for Students

The Targeted Assistance Program for Students (TAPS) is a comprehensive but user-friendly approach to triadic, school-based consultation that is designed to identify and assist a struggling learner through systematic development of an intervention plan that is individualized, evidence-based, well-documented, and implemented with integrity and feasibility. The plan is developed by an expert consultant (i.e., a TAPS Support Teacher, a role described in subsequent chapters) and the classroom teacher. Parent support and/or input is also facilitated during each TAPS case. Also, to help teachers identify evidence-based programs to integrate into a TAPS intervention plan and target the student's specific academic deficit, Chapter 12 of this book provides several evidence-based and learner-verified intervention programs for teachers' consideration.

Assessment for Instruction

Strategies for simple, time-efficient methods to accomplish three assessment goals are provided as part of the SOPAA. Students assisted through the TAPS process receive a brief initial assessment to identify instructional needs and then are monitored with research-based and time-efficient assessment methods to evaluate their responsiveness to individualized TAPS intervention plans. Also, in order to best identify all struggling learners, schools not already using a brief, research-based, schoolwide screening assessment in reading and math are provided with information and resources to help develop such a system over time.

Maximized Intervention Personnel and Resources

This component of the SOPAA ultimately helps schools identify, train, and coordinate school personnel to assist classroom teachers during the TAPS process. Specifically, school personnel assist by occasionally implementing the evidence-based intervention program selected as part of the student's TAPS intervention plan. The school personnel involved in this way will differ depending on the characteristics of a particular school, but may include school volunteers and/or any other available school employee (e.g., teacher assistants, guidance counselors, librarians, and many others). Overall, this SOPAA component is designed to best maximize school personnel so that they can effectively assist classroom teachers with remediating students' learning difficulties.

Targeted Professional Development

Many classroom teachers are not adequately prepared to intervene with struggling learners, and many schools do not have a key leader who can always offer expert support and guidance for teachers who need assistance with improving a student's academic difficulty in reading, math, or writing. Targeted SOPAA professional development activities are therefore designed to address these challenges in a practical and systematic way. For example, aligned with SOPAA goals and procedures, professional development workshops are conducted for all teachers (e.g., classroom teachers, teacher assistants) involved with the TAPS process, typically one to three times throughout the school year. Also, systematic and ongoing professional development is feasibly integrated for the one to three specialized support teachers (i.e., the TAPS Support Teachers) within the school who are selected to manage and facilitate TAPS cases in reading, math, or writing.

Methods for Communication and Generating Support

Related to each of the preceding components, this book offers information, steps, and resources for successful communication among all individuals involved with SOPAA implementation (e.g., the school principal, classroom teachers, SOPAA lead facilitators). Through the recommended communication activities that occur at critical times throughout SOPAA implementation, this component is designed to maximize the effectiveness and time efficiency of starting and sustaining implementation.

Adaptable and Incremental Implementation

In developing this model, we recognize that schools operate differently and have varying strengths, needs, and weaknesses. Also, we recognize that systems-level change in schools will usually fail if proper infrastructure and timing variables are not considered well before implementation begins. Thus, this book describes how schools with varying characteristics can successfully implement the SOPAA in a way, and with a timeline, that is most fitting with the school's specific needs. For example, we describe how to (1) assess the needs, strengths, and characteristics of a school that will either support or prevent SOPAA implementation; (2) adapt SOPAA implementation based on the identified needs and strengths; (3) facilitate leadership of the SOPAA with multidisciplinary co-facilitators; and (4) select options for incrementally but systematically implementing SOPAA components and features over multiple school years.

A goal of this book is to describe how schools with varying characteristics can successfully implement the SOPAA in a way that fits with each school's specific strengths and needs.

IS THE SOPAA SUITABLE FOR YOUR SCHOOL?

When introducing the SOPAA to educators, there are five common questions they ask to determine the extent to which the SOPAA model might be useful for their respective schools. We present these questions and our answers here, knowing that readers may also have these initial questions.

Question 1: Given the six components of the SOPAA, how much time is realistically needed to use and actually benefit from this model?

The key feature of the SOPAA is the TAPS process, and if only one educator in the school serves as the primary facilitator of the SOPAA (and thus of TAPS), she should be able to manage six TAPS cases per month (one or two cases per week) in as little as 6.5 hours per week. Other SOPAA components (e.g., effective communication, training teachers in the school) will require additional time, but with the planning strategies described throughout this book, these tasks can be completed periodically throughout the academic school year so that the time needed to implement the SOPAA remains feasible.

Furthermore, as described in detail in other chapters, for many schools the SOPAA is best implemented by two to four primary facilitators. Thus, the total amount of time needed to implement all components of the SOPAA (including management of all TAPS cases) may require as little as 2–4 hours per week if multiple facilitators are involved. This model is specifically designed to maximize educators' time and resources, which is why it can be implemented in reasonable amounts of time.

The total time needed for SOPAA implementation also depends on the number of components and features integrated into the model during the initial years of implementation. That is, because the SOPAA allows for a systematic but incremental implementation plan, the total time needed for implementation can ultimately be adjusted to levels that are feasible for the school and those leading SOPAA facilitation, while also maintaining a model that will benefit the school in how it addresses students with learning difficulties. Chapter 2 and subsequent chapters explain in detail how much time is likely needed to successfully implement the SOPAA, as well as strategies and guidelines for successfully applying an incremental implementation plan.

Last, it is important to emphasize that the SOPAA is designed in a way that will eventually save schools time and resources once the model has been implemented for 1 or more years. Therefore, as educators throughout the school learn the model and improve their skills in addressing students' learning difficulties, the estimated times mentioned previously should decrease over time. Overall, then, even in the beginning years of SOPAA implementation, the model is designed in a way that is realistic for one to four educators to implement, and as the model is implemented over subsequent school years, implementation time should continue to decrease.

Question 2: Our school already uses a problem-solving model to address students' learning difficulties [e.g., RTI, PLCs, prereferral intervention teams], so how would we benefit from using the SOPAA?

As mentioned earlier in this chapter, one reason we developed the SOPAA was to help schools address the pragmatic types of challenges they often face even when they use (or attempt to use) a problem-solving model such as RTI, PLCs, or prereferral intervention teams to address students' learning difficulties. As such, the SOPAA model can be used in combination with another type of schoolwide problem-solving system. Using the SOPAA in this way should help schools address the issues presented in the previous list of 10 common challenges (pp. 4–5) schools face when addressing all students' learning needs. In short, some models of academic problem solving and school reform lack a clear step-by-step process; the SOPAA fills that gap by providing both specific procedures and material resources that can be used as part of a system for improving student learning outcomes.

Given the increasing popularity and use of RTI, a section in Chapter 3 also discusses more specifically how the SOPAA is aligned with principles of RTI, but how it differs from RTI and can be used to actually strengthen a school's model of RTI. That discussion should also have relevance for schools using a problem-solving approach other than RTI, such as PLCs or prereferral intervention teams. Related to these ideas, other chapters in this book should help educators understand that implementing the SOPAA should not be viewed as implementing a "new" model of problem solving. Rather, SOPAA implementation focuses on enhancing a school's existing practices for addressing students' learning difficulties and showing educators in the school how components of the SOPAA are likely to align well with existing practices.

Question 3: Our school has numerous challenges and needs and is probably not ready to use a systems-level model to address students' learning difficulties, so how can the SOPAA help our school?

Although the SOPAA was developed with the knowledge that many schools are already using a type of problem-solving model to address students' learning deficits, it was also developed knowing that many schools have not yet adopted (1) a schoolwide model of problems solving and/or (2) what many consider as best-practice in academic interventions, instruction, and assessment. Therefore, the SOPAA can be used just as effectively and meaningfully in schools without a current schoolwide system for improving students' learning deficits, because it describes a "ground-up" approach for initiating and then sustaining schoolwide change. In essence, as long as the school principal offers support for the SOPAA, this book is applicable because it describes realistic ways for any school to start and sustain SOPAA implementation. Chapter 9 is specifically devoted to helping educators communicate with and elicit support from school administrators such as the principal.

The SOPAA can be used in combination with another type of schoolwide problem-solving system, such as RTI), or in schools without a schoolwide system for improving students' learning deficits.

Overall, throughout the book the reader should understand how the SOPAA can be used in schools with varying characteristics and how Component 5 (methods for communication and generating support) and Component 6 (adaptable and incremental implementation) should be particularly relevant for schools that do not yet have a schoolwide system for instructional problem solving. In addition, for schools without a current school-wide problem-solving model, the SOPAA can be used as the model, and its sustained implementation may actually help the school later to add a model such as RTI so that a broader spectrum of students is served through an effective method of problem solving and data-based decision making.

Question 4: Is the SOPAA also designed to address student behavior problems?

The goal of the SOPAA is to improve learning outcomes for students who experience difficulties. Thus, although the SOPAA focuses primarily on resolving students' academic deficits, we recognize that student behavior challenges can sometimes exacerbate learning difficulties and/or prevent academic interventions from working most effectively. Although it is beyond the scope of this book to offer specific interventions that will help educators manage behavior problems that occur with students who also experience learning deficits, there are many useful resources already available to help teachers address such behavior problems (e.g., Alberto & Troutman, 2009; Jenson, Rhode, & Reavis, 1994; Shinn, Walker, & Stoner, 2002; Sprick & Howard, 1996; Steege, Watson, & Gresham, 2009). Also, determining whether a student has a behavior problem (and if so, how to address it) is integrated into the TAPS process, ultimately allowing the classroom teacher and the TAPS Teacher to develop an intervention plan that considers (and responds to) student behavior problems when applicable. Furthermore, the SOPAA model assists TAPS Teachers in handling potential behavior problems associated with a TAPS case through some of the targeted SOPAA professional development activities (discussed in Chapter 7).

Question 5: What are the primary advantages of using the SOPAA?

The specific advantages of using the SOPAA will differ across schools that have different needs and characteristics. For example, schools that do not maximize school volunteers and personnel to address students' learning needs would benefit much more from this SOPAA component, compared to schools that already make the most use of school personnel and volunteers. However, most schools should experience multiple advantages to using the SOPAA. Listed below are several possible advantages.

1. The SOPAA integrates a structured system of problem solving (i.e., through TAPS) and a plan for training and communicating with teachers and administrators about the system. By using a comprehensive, systems-level approach that incorporates research-based interventions, students' learning deficits are more likely to improve and the system for addressing their deficits is more likely to be implemented with consistency and integrity (Joyce & Showers, 2002).

2. The TAPS process allows for systematic implementation, documentation, and evaluation of academic interventions. Increasingly, state and federal agencies are requiring documentation of schools' efforts to assist individual students and the outcomes of those efforts. For example, IDEIA 2004 regulations require that before students can be eligible for special education, schools must document that the students' learning difficulties are not due to lack of appropriate instruction, and also that students' performance in general education were monitored. Schools that fail to provide good documentation of their efforts to serve students in general education may find themselves out of compliance with federal and state requirements, and out of step with the increased emphasis on early intervention that is reflected in recent legislation (Yell & Drasgow, 2007).

3. The SOPAA aims to maximize school personnel and community volunteers in an effort to address students' learning needs. This SOPAA component also helps to

   a. Empower community volunteers.
   b. Extend school resources.
   c. Demonstrate that all school personnel (e.g., school counselors, social workers) can help address the needs of struggling learners.

4. The SOPAA does not require that all educators have mastery-level knowledge of instructional interventions and consultation because:

   a. The model integrates numerous forms of ongoing professional development activities.
   b. This book provides easy-to-use resources for implementation, including suggestions for evidence-based intervention programs across the primary academic areas and subareas.

5. The SOPAA can be implemented by one school-based leader (e.g., administrator, school psychologist, special education teacher) or co-facilitated by two to four educators.

6. The SOPAA easily fits into other contemporary problem-solving models, such as RTI and problem-solving "teams," or it can be implemented without a school's adoption of a separate

problem-solving model. For schools that have not adopted a problem-solving model such as RTI, incremental implementation of the SOPAA may serve as a foundation for later adding an approach such as RTI.

7. The SOPAA is designed to be more time- and resource-efficient than an instructional problem-solving model that relies on school-based teams to address individual student problems. In Chapter 2, we highlight the typical amount of time needed to facilitate the SOPAA.

8. As needed, the SOPAA components can be implemented incrementally, and the model is designed to build upon a school's existing practices, rather than move a school toward completely "new" practices. This approach to implementation should:

a. Improve the overall success of implementation and sustainability.
b. Limit stressors and barriers associated with creating schoolwide procedural modifications.
c. Allow educators to progressively influence systemic change within a school.

FOUNDATIONAL PRINCIPLES OF THE SOPAA

Before proceeding to an extended discussion of each SOPAA component and how to effectively implement the SOPAA within a school, it is important to highlight the foundational principles embedded within this model. To effectively implement the SOPAA, the school principal and the primary SOPAA facilitators (i.e., the one to four educators in the school responsible for implementing the SOPAA) should endorse the following principles. Otherwise, strong differences in educational philosophy and/or principles may hinder effective implementation.

The SOPAA should be particularly effective when the school principal and SOPAA facilitators agree with the foundational principles of this model.

Principle 1: Use Student Outcome Data as an Important Basis for Instructional Decisions

Schools are sometimes characterized as "data rich, but information poor" (Miller, 2009, p. 1). This means that schools often have access to considerable data about student achievement, but do not use it to examine and improve school practices. Gut feelings, educational philosophy, or tradition may be the basis for instructional decisions, often because many educators lack experience in reviewing, manipulating, and interpreting data. A central focus in the SOPAA model is to collect data about students (both individuals and groups) and use the data as a basis for keeping or changing an existing practice. Schools that routinely evaluate what they do and how it is working are more likely to find and sustain practices that work for their student population.

Principle 2: Use Research to Guide Practice

Today, we have considerable evidence about what works and what doesn't work to improve achievement outcomes for students. For example, a number of websites and organizations (see Chapter 12) provides information about which instructional programs incorporate research-based practices or those that have been shown to result in achievement gains for learners. Increasingly, federal legislation and state regulations mandate the use of research-based practices in education (e.g., the

No Child Left Behind Act of 2001). Although there are still gaps in the research literature, using the available research findings in selecting programs increases the chances that effective programs will be selected, and that the programs can be defended if challenged. However, use of research evidence to select an intervention program does not mean that that program will work for every student. That is why routine use of data to examine the impact of instruction at the local school level is a key foundational principle.

Principle 3: Prevent Learning Problems by Ensuring Strong Core Instructional Programs

In 1895, Joseph Malins wrote a poem, "The Ambulance Down in the Valley" that has since been widely cited (e.g., Loeppke, 2008). The poem told the story of a village on a mountainside with a walkway next to a cliff. After many persons in the village had slipped off the cliff, the villagers began to take a collection to place an ambulance at the bottom of the mountainside to help those who had fallen. One wise villager suggested an alternative: building a fence at the edge of the cliff. How does this analogy apply to schools? Addressing children's learning problems is time consuming. If the core curriculum in a subject area is weak, many children will "fall off the cliff," and educators are likely to be overwhelmed by the task of trying to address these students' needs through targeted small group and individual interventions. Chapter 12 provides a comprehensive analysis of the subskills that should be addressed in a core curriculum for reading, math, and writing and also suggests some core instructional programs that we feel do a good job of targeting those key subskills. Also, the SOPAA model includes staff development to increase educators' knowledge about, and skills in, teaching the core academic areas.

Principle 4: Use a Structured and Standard Approach to Addressing Common Learning Difficulties

Having a structured and standard way of responding to common learning challenges increases the quality of interventions provided and minimizes time spent designing intervention plans. Even with the best core instruction, there are some skills for which a significant percentage of learners in a school are likely to need extra instruction and practice. For example, research estimates show that about 15–20% of early readers will experience difficulty with discriminating and manipulating phonemes, applying phonics rules to decode words, and acquiring a sizable sight-word vocabulary (Torgesen, 2000). Having standard intervention programs that are available at the school level to respond to common learning difficulties allows targeted help for students without asking each classroom teacher to find the time to learn and then deliver multiple interventions for her struggling or at-risk students. Also, having a structured way of getting these intervention programs into the hands of teachers and assisting teachers with using the programs further supports the challenging job of addressing all students' learning needs.

Furthermore, the use of standardized intervention programs delivered by educators who have a specific set of time slots built into their schedule for implementing small-group and one-on-one instruction increases the likelihood that an intervention will be implemented with sufficient integrity, and implemented often enough to have an impact on student achievement. Too many times, we have seen problem-solving teams enthusiastically devise a complex plan that is never implemented or implemented so infrequently that it does not improve student outcomes. Often, this problem emerges because it was falsely assumed that the classroom teacher would somehow find the time to learn and implement the intervention despite limited time and competing demands.

Principle 5: Integrate New Practices with Existing Procedures and Plan for Systems Support to Achieve Sustainability

Years of research show that many innovations, even if they are successful, are not sustained over time (Adelman & Taylor, 2003; Joyce & Showers, 2002; Rogers, 2003). Often, new practices are incompatible with existing organizational structures, making it easier for educators to return to previous practices even if they were less effective (e.g., Fuchs, Fuchs, Harris, & Roberts, 1996). New practices should be feasible to use within a school, and the effort involved in learning and implementing those practices should result in sustainability and improved learning outcomes for students. To achieve these goals, a system of implementing new practices should be, for example, (1) aligned with existing strengths and effective practices within the school; (2) valued by those involved with implementation; (3) strategically planned for long-term implementation, but responsive to evaluations of effectiveness and changing organizational structures; and (4) involve professional development and support from leadership (Adelman & Taylor, 2003; Durlak & DuPre, 2008; Furney, Hasazi, Clark-Keefe, & Hartnett, 2003; Gersten, Chard, & Baker, 2000).

OVERVIEW OF THE REMAINING CHAPTERS AND FEATURES TO SUPPORT SOPPA IMPLEMENTATION

In this chapter we sought to introduce the SOPAA model by providing an overview of its primary components and a general rationale for using it. We also commented on its potential advantages and compatibility within a given school, and highlighted five foundational principles embedded within the model. In the following chapter, we expand our description of the SOPAA by defining important terms, providing a historical context for the model, and more fully explaining the six SOPAA components and their interconnected relationship. The specific roles of the SOPAA facilitators are also defined and described in **Chapter 2**.

In **Chapter 3** readers begin to learn how to go about implementing the SOPAA, starting with some preliminary considerations before beginning actual implementation. For example, Chapter 3 should help readers consider a reasonable multiyear timeline for incremental SOPAA implementation, the time and resources needed for successful implementation, and the strengths and barriers within their schools that should influence key implementation decisions. Chapter 3 then concludes with a summary of step-by-step suggestions for using this book to implement the SOPAA. In reviewing these suggestions, readers should quickly understand that this book should be used as a resource or type of "manual" for implementation, rather than a book that can be successfully used after reading it once from start to finish.

Chapters 4–11 comprise Part II of this book and discuss in detail how and when to implement each of the SOPAA components, and a rationale for implementing each component is discussed throughout. More specifically, in **Chapters 4 and 5** we describe how TAPS Support Teachers and classroom teachers work through the TAPS process to assist struggling learners. Because TAPS is central to implementing the overall SOPAA model, information in these chapters is thoroughly detailed to provide educators with guidance and support for each of the steps in the TAPS process. Because assessment is an important feature of TAPS intervention plans, **Chapter 6** describes three places where brief academic assessments can help guide instruction or be used to evaluate student learning outcomes. For example, this chapter describes options for assessments that can be feasibly used as part of the universal screening in the SOPAA, or to evaluate student learning in reading, math, and writing in TAPS.

Although intervention and assessment practices are commonly discussed in books describing models of school-based consultation and schoolwide change, these practices are challenging, if not impossible, to implement without sufficient professional development and staff support. Therefore, in **Chapter 7** we describe a professional development plan that specifically aligns with the SOPAA components, as well as the assessment and instruction practices facilitated during TAPS cases. Throughout Chapter 7 readers will find numerous recommendations for facilitating a meaningful *and* feasible professional development plan for each educator involved with the TAPS process. In **Chapter 8**, we discuss how schools can increase their capacity for assisting struggling learners (and assisting those students' teachers) by including a systematic plan for soliciting and training school volunteers. Chapter 8 provides, for example, guidance for recruiting, training, coordinating, and sustaining school volunteers, as well as the rationale for including school volunteers as part of the SOPAA model. Other considerations for involving school volunteers are also discussed (e.g., screening school volunteers, the desired and reasonable role of school volunteers, and determining the appropriateness and feasibility of utilizing a school volunteer program to support the SOPPA).

As noted above, strong intervention, assessment, professional development, and staff resources are essential to a successful schoolwide model of academic support, but without effective communication with, and generating support from, school leaders and teachers about the model, implementation and sustainability of the model will likely fail. As such, **Chapters 9 and 10** are key features of this book and important resources for implementing the SOPAA model because they describe several aspects of effective communication with school leaders (e.g., the school principal) and teachers. In these chapters, numerous recommendations are provided to help SOPAA facilitators utilize effective communication procedures both prior to and during SOPAA implementation. **Chapter 11** concludes Part II by specifically highlighting how to successfully implement the SOPAA model with two to four co-facilitators. This chapter is important because, although the model can be initiated and directed by only one educator, Chapter 11 explicitly details the benefits and interacting roles that are associated with facilitating the SOPAA with more than one educator in the school.

As Chapters 4–11 discuss how and when to implement each of the SOPAA components, it is important to keep in mind that a key component of the SOPAA is *adaptable and incremental implementation* for each school, depending on the school's specific strengths and needs. Thus, throughout these "how-to" chapters, we describe how schools with varying characteristics can successfully implement the SOPAA in a way, and with a timeline, that is most congruent with the school's particular needs. Also, because the primary goal of this book is to assist educators in meaningfully improving student learning outcomes by initiating, implementing, and sustaining the SOPAA as a systems-level model of academic consultation, we include numerous reproducible resources throughout the appendices to support streamlined and systematic implementation.

Part III of this book offers additional information and guidance for SOPAA implementation, which is intended to supplement what readers learn in the preceding chapters. In **Chapter 12** we describe the key components and subcomponents associated with effective instruction in reading, math, and writing—information that is intended to help educators evaluate their core instruction and intervention programs. This chapter also describes dozens of evidence-based intervention programs (several in each of the three academic areas), which educators may consider using as part of their TAPS process. Overall, Chapter 12 is intended to be an important resource for identifying and implementing the most appropriate instructional programs and interventions in reading, math, and writing.

Throughout the book we offer several brief illustrations and examples of how the SOPPA components and features can be implemented in schools. However, more thorough case illustrations are reserved for **Chapter 13** so that readers can consider these examples after gaining a thorough understanding of each SOPPA component and feature, all of which are detailed in the preceding chapters. Thus, after discussing the relationships among SOPPA components and how they can often be adapted and implemented incrementally depending on a specific school's characteristics, Chapter 13 describes four schools with varying characteristics and needs, and how the SOPAA is implemented in those schools. There are, of course, no schools with the exact same characteristics, but the case illustrations in Chapter 13, along with the information from the preceding chapters, should further assist readers in recognizing how the SOPAA model could be implemented in their schools.

Finally, creating and sustaining systems-level change requires a relatively sophisticated repertoire of skills, and we believe that such skills should be acquired early in one's career as an educator—ideally as a college/university student. As such, in **Chapter 14** we provide a relatively detailed supplement for university teachers who are responsible for training our future educators. Within this brief chapter, university teachers should find feasible recommendations for how to use this book to help build, for example, the academic assessment, intervention, and consultation skills of soon-to-be educators.

Companion Website

To further support educators' use of the SOPAA model, a companion website is available. By visiting *www.sopaaforschools.org* educators will find various forms and related supplemental materials that, when specifically used with the information provided in this book, should assist them with implementing the SOPAA. Throughout the book several places direct readers to the website in order to access these supplemental materials, and each place is denoted with the icon shown immediately to the right of this text.

In addition to providing supplemental materials, the SOPAA website also serves as a venue on which educators can ask questions and get online support about SOPAA implementation. The SOPAA website is fully funded by the Helps Education Fund, a nonprofit organization that was founded by one of us (J.C.B.) and is devoted to improving educational outcomes for students nationally and internationally. Readers can learn more about each of the website support features by visiting *www.sopaaforschools.org.*

Authors' Note

Throughout this book, the use of masculine and feminine pronouns such as *he, she, his, hers, him, and her* are often used only to be succinct and to avoid the wordiness of overusing, for example, *he or she, him or her.* Text throughout this book that uses a masculine or feminine pronoun should not be interpreted as being relevant only to males or females. In all cases, the pronoun should be interpreted as a gender-neutral shorthand for *he/she, him/her, his/hers,* etc. For example, for consistency we typically refer to the SOPAA facilitators using only female pronouns, but we certainly acknowledge there are many male educators who will facilitate the SOPAA, and this book is equally applicable to educators of both genders.

CHAPTER 2

SOPAA Key Definitions, History, Components, and Roles

In this chapter we begin by describing key definitions relevant to the SOPAA, as well as some historical events in education that influenced the development of this model. Each of the six SOPAA components is then discussed in detail, including a description of how each component is related to the other and to the entire model. The five primary SOPAA roles are described, which include the SOPAA Lead Coordinator, the three TAPS Support Teachers (one for each of the academic areas of reading, math, and writing), and the TAPS Intervention Support Coordinator.

DEFINITIONS AND A BRIEF HISTORICAL OVERVIEW

School consultation does not have a neat, straightforward chronology. Sometimes fundamental tenets of consultation that dominated in one era or model have been abandoned as consultation has adapted to fit new circumstances and demands on schools. For instance, consultee-centered mental health consultation (Caplan, 1964, 1970) was one of the first models of consultation that was applied widely to schools. In that model, outside consultants worked with teachers one on one. Two major tenets of that model were that consultation was voluntary and that information exchanged between the consultant and consultee was confidential.

Today, if a special education teacher works with a general education teacher to develop and implement modified instructional support for a student with a disability, the special education teacher might describe that activity as *consultation.* However, unlike the conditions under which consultation originally developed, the special education teacher is a staff member in the same organization as the general education teacher, and they are expected to work together to benefit their mutual students. Their work together may even be mandated if it is included on the student's individualized education plan. In addition, special education legislation imposes many due-process and record-keeping requirements on schools that were not present when many consultation models were originally developed. As such, school consultation may no longer be voluntary or confidential (Erchul & Martens, 2010).

As a result of the continually evolving nature of schools and the services they provide, it is difficult, if not impossible, to find any universal characteristics that are common to all definitions of school consultation. In this book, we define *consultation* as a *role function* that multiple professionals may assume, including but not limited to special education teachers, school psychologists, reading specialists, regular education teachers, Title I teachers, and social workers. When professionals work in a consultative mode in schools, they are providing an *indirect service*. That is, the primary purpose of their actions is to help other professionals function better in their direct service roles or to help the system as a whole function better in promoting the academic, affective, and/or social development of students. Although a consultative role may involve some direct interaction with students (e.g., assessing a student to determine skill deficits, modeling a new instructional technique with a group of students, or occasionally implementing an intervention), the primary benefits to students are expected to accrue from changes in how direct service providers do their jobs when working with the student day to day.

Triadic and Organizational Consultation

A major distinction in the consultation literature is between triadic and organizational consultation. In *triadic consultation*, a consultant works with an individual teacher to address the needs of a student in her classroom. The consultant, the teacher, and the student form the triad for which this type of consultation is named. In *organizational consultation*, a consultant's activities are directed toward improving the functioning of an organization or system, not an individual.

The SOPAA model includes both triadic and organizational consultation. The TAPS component of the SOPAA fits the definition of triadic consultation. TAPS Support Teachers work with teachers to address individual students' difficulties in their classrooms. The steps we describe in the TAPS process draw heavily from a triadic consultation model originally developed by Bergan (1977). Bergan's model includes explicit problem-solving steps (problem identification, problem analysis, plan implementation, and evaluation) and a focus on changing the environment to change a student's academic or social behavior. We also borrow concepts from another problem-solving model used to address students' difficulties that developed in special education (Deno & Mirkin, 1977). Although we assume that triadic consultation involves some face-to-face interaction between the consultant and teacher, and continued interaction between parties throughout all stages of problem solving, the TAPS process within the SOPAA also uses written communication and forms to reduce the time teachers and consultants (i.e., TAPS Support Teachers) spend in meetings.

The SOPAA integrates both triadic and organizational consultation, with the TAPS component serving as the form of triadic consultation.

Organizational consultation components in the SOPAA model include (1) professional development for educators in evidence-based practices related to academic instruction; (2) recruiting and training school volunteers and assistive school personnel (e.g., teacher assistants, librarians, and/or others) to implement evidence-based intervention programs; and (3) schoolwide benchmark and progress monitoring assessment procedures. In each of these components, the focus is on improving how the organization or system (i.e., the school) functions as a whole. In addition, effective communication of SOPAA components and procedures, generating schoolwide support, and options for adaptable and incremental implementation (i.e., Components 5 and 6) help to support systematic SOPAA implementation throughout the school.

In both triadic and organizational consultation, we assume that professionals functioning as consultants *do not have supervisory authority* over the persons with whom they work. In that sense, consultants and consultees generally function as equals. However, it is assumed in our model that the consultant guides the problem solving during triadic consultation (i.e., the TAPS process), but in a way that supports the classroom teacher and involves consensus rather than unilateral decision making. In the organizational or systems-level consultation activities, the SOPAA facilitators (e.g., TAPS Support Teachers) are recruited from the educators in the school who have expertise in specific areas. As such, they may not have designated supervisory roles within the school, but they are assumed to be in a position to provide guidance to other educators in the school (e.g., regular education teachers) in areas related to their expertise.

Prescriptive Problem Solving

As stated above, the TAPS process is based on a problem-solving model of consultation. Within this kind of model a student's difficulties are specified as a discrepancy between desired and actual behavior, and then a plan is formulated and implemented to address this discrepancy. The success of the plan is evaluated in terms of whether the discrepancy between desired and actual behavior is reduced.

In the TAPS process, the "problem" is a discrepancy between grade-level expectations or standards and the student's skill level in an academic area. Problem analysis consists of pinpointing the subskill deficits that are likely contributors to the student's difficulty in meeting grade-level demands based on (1) what is known from research about which skills contribute to successful performance in specific academic areas (e.g., that word identification problems often contribute to poor reading comprehension); (2) examination of student work products; and (3) administration of brief, low-inference measures of the student's functioning on tasks that closely resemble classroom demands by the TAPS Teacher.

Following the problem analysis, one or more standardized, evidence-based interventions available at the school are matched with the student deficit(s), and the teacher selects the intervention(s). A plan is then developed for implementation of the selected intervention that is quite specific in terms of intensity (how often the intervention is offered), logistics (e.g., who provides the intervention), and integrity (how well the intervention matches the standards for implementation stated by the developer). We use the term *prescriptive problem solving* for our model because in most problem-solving models, unique interventions are collaboratively developed for each student referred as part of consultation. However, in the SOPAA model, interventions are selected from a limited set of evidence-based interventions that the school personnel have already been trained to provide. This strategy is based on a consultation approach developed by Fuchs, Fuchs, Bahr, Fernstrom, and Stecker (1990). In their test of a prereferral consultation model based on Bergan's (1977) work, these researchers found that having teachers choose from a limited set of interventions and eliminating multidisciplinary team participation during individual student problem solving resulted in more efficient problem solving, stronger intervention plans, and better outcomes for students. Fuchs et al. speculated that in schools with low stress and high expertise in consultation, a more collaborative, less prescriptive approach to consultation might be effective. However, when teachers are pressured for time or are inexperienced in intervention design, better results would be obtained when a consultant and teacher select from a limited range of already developed interventions that were based on sound research and instructional principles.

As an intervention is being implemented, the TAPS Support Teacher evaluates the integrity with which it is being implemented and meets with the classroom teacher briefly at regular intervals to review student progress. At a predetermined endpoint, the intervention and its impact on the target student's achievement are formally reviewed, and a decision is made about further actions needed (if any) to address the student's academic functioning.

A HISTORICAL OVERVIEW OF SCHOOL-BASED CONSULTATION AND PROBLEM SOLVING

A complete history of consultation and problem-solving approaches to addressing children's educational needs is well beyond the scope of this book. However, in this section we briefly trace the roots of contemporary consultation and schoolwide problem-solving models and then place the SOPAA model in this context.

In the 1960s, Gerald Caplan recognized the promise of public health methods for addressing a broad range of social problems. He had discovered the utility of an indirect approach to providing human services when he was in charge of mental health personnel serving large numbers of children who were in institutions in Israel after they had been orphaned prior to or during World War II and the events leading up to it. Rather than directly treating children who were having problems—an impossible task given the ratio of mental health personnel to children—he and the mental health professionals working with him found that they could address children's problems more efficiently by working with the orphanage staff to increase *their* effectiveness in working with children under their care.

Caplan wrote about how his method could be useful to professionals working with school staff to address children's learning and behavioral issues (Caplan, 1964, 1970). Then, as now, there were chronic shortages of specialists to help teachers address the needs of their students. His triadic consultation model (termed consultee-centered consultation) was seen as a promising solution because specialists could help more children and effect lasting change by improving teachers' functioning in the classroom. Many professionals working with schools used Caplan's ideas as the basis for developing their models of school consultation (e.g., Meyers, Parsons, & Martin, 1979).

After the passage of the Education for All Handicapped Children Act of 1975 (known in later reauthorizations as the Individuals with Disabilities Education Act or IDEA), consultation became one of the ways that services could be offered to students with disabilities. Two seminal works applying consultation methods to children's educational needs were published at about this time. Bergan (1977) published *Behavioral Consultation*, presenting in detail a behaviorally based problem-solving consultation model based on his work with Headstart, and Deno and Mirkin (1977) published *Data-Based Program Modification: A Manual*. This manual was written for special education teachers who were facing new demands to provide services to special education students in general education classroom.

Although outreach to identify students with disabilities was an initial concern after the passage of the Education for All Handicapped Children Act, less than a decade after its passage there were many concerns about how many children were being placed in special education, and who these children were. Large numbers of children were being referred for special education, and once they were tested, they were very likely to be found eligible and placed in special education (Algozzine, Ysseldyke, & Christensen, 1983). Other concerns included the overrepresentation of minority students in special education and the high cost of individual testing for children referred to special education (Shepard & Smith, 1983). Special education had been intended for a small proportion of students in schools, but the increasing numbers were quickly overwhelming the allotted funding.

Putting resources into consultation with general education teachers to help students *before* they were referred for special education seemed a good way to address these concerns about the growing number of special education students. Consultation emphasized prevention, efficient use of limited staff time, and increasing the skills of direct service providers—all highly pertinent to the problems now facing schools with overuse of special education. Several researchers adapted Bergan's (1977) behavioral model of consultation to fit their local or state context and examined whether implementing a modified version of behavioral consultation prior to testing a student for special education placement (i.e., a "prereferral" intervention) could reduce the number of students in special education. For example, Fuchs and Fuchs (1989) piloted a model in Nashville, Tennessee, and Reschly and Casey (1986) introduced a similar model in Iowa. Given the increased use of consultation to address students' academic difficulties, some consultation models developed during this time were more specific in how consultants should assess, analyze, and intervene with academic difficulties. For instance, Rosenfield (1987) developed one of the first consultation models that explicitly focused on examining and improving instruction.

As these models came into wider use in the 1990s, three developments began to influence the form of school-based consultation. First, a convincing body of evidence began to emerge about the sources of children's early reading problems, and the key components of a high-quality early reading curriculum. This research suggested that attention to the quality of the core curriculum in reading and addressing reading problems in the early grades could reduce the prevalence of reading disabilities by about half (Torgesen, 2000). These findings set the stage for whole-school, prevention-oriented approaches to providing educational services.

Second, assessment tools based on the early work of Lindsley (1972) and furthered by Deno and Mirkin (1977), which were both brief and sensitive to within-year growth, began to be widely available to monitor students' learning in reading and mathematics. These "curriculum-based" tools made it much easier to screen large numbers of students for academic difficulties and also to graph student progress in consultation cases to see how students were responding to any changes in instruction.

Finally, researchers in behavioral consultation began to raise intervention integrity as a critical issue in school consultation. Multiple studies documented that teachers often did not fully implement, or did not sustain their implementation of, the plans they developed with consultants. As the developers of consultation often had noted (Bergan, 1977; Caplan, 1970), minimizing the consultant's role during implementation increased the number of cases that consultants could address, but this new treatment integrity research made it apparent that this reduction in specialist time came at a high cost.

These developments made their way into subsequent education legislation. Responding to continued concerns about the numbers of students referred to special education, as well as broader concerns about students' reading and mathematics achievement, the No Child Left Behind Act (NCLB 2003) of 2001 contained many provisions that had implications for school-based consultation or problem-solving models. Its annual testing provisions and "adequate yearly progress" expectations put increased pressure on schools to address the instructional needs of low achievers. Influenced by the groundbreaking reading research in the 1990s, the law also required schools to document their use of programs with "scientific" evidence, and made available to schools more information about the scientific evidence to support various practices.

In the special education arena, the concerns raised about using ability versus achievement discrepancies to identify learning disabilities resulted in explicit permission for states to use the results of their efforts to address student learning problems in general education as a basis for placement in special education (as a student with a learning disability), as long as the placement involved the use of a research-based intervention process (Individuals with Disabilities Education Improvement Act of 2004 [IDEA, 2006]). Together, NCLB and the IDEA reauthorization provided the impetus for many schools to move toward a whole-school prevention framework for addressing children's learning problems with an emphasis on using instruction and intervention methods that had been validated through research.

This newer emphasis on the quality of core instruction, scientifically based interventions to help children with learning problems, and treatment integrity has led to changes in many models of consultation and problem solving. For example, the Heartland Area Education Agency in Iowa began using problem-solving consultation as a prereferral process in the late 1980s. It has recently added universal screening and progress monitoring to its framework, as well as incorporated a whole-school, three-tier prevention framework (core instruction, followed by strategic and then intensive intervention efforts) to the model. It also includes research-based instructional intervention packages and formal monitoring of treatment integrity (Grimes & Kurns, 2003; Grimes, Kurns, & Tilly, 2006).

As this brief chronology illustrates, consultation approaches have changed over the years in response to new legislation, research, and school needs. The SOPAA model incorporates what we perceive as some of the best of the old and new problem-solving and consultation approaches. It blends the efficiency of using a single consultant for initial student problem solving with a team approach to increasing the range and quality of instructional interventions available for the school as a whole. For many schools, consultation, progress monitoring, research-based interventions, and response to intervention are new. The SOPAA model offers a way to begin to implement research-based practices using an incremental change process that builds on the strengths and existing routines already present in the school. The SOPAA components can be implemented separately, giving schools time to adjust and increase staff expertise as changes are phased in over time.

The SOPAA offers schools a road map for implementing research-based practices efficiently and in a manner that builds on a school's existing strengths and routines.

THE SOPAA COMPONENTS

As we introduced in Chapter 1, there are six primary components of the SOPAA. Each is discussed within this section in more detail, and when applicable, we provide a reference to the chapter or chapters that provide extended information about the component. We acknowledge that readers will have a better context for understanding the SOPAA components if they are provided with descriptions of (1) the type of educator (or educators) within a school that might facilitate implementation of the SOPAA components, (2) the specific roles of the SOPAA facilitators, and (3) a case illustration describing how the components and roles are facilitated within a school. Later in this chapter, and throughout the book, we offer detailed information about the SOPAA facilitators and roles, and Chapter 13 presents several case examples to illustrate how SOPAA implementation might look in schools that have different characteristics. However, to provide a basic context for understanding the SOPAA components, we briefly discuss who the facilitators may be and the five SOPAA roles.

The SOPAA should be implemented by one to four facilitators, as we have mentioned. That is, in some schools the SOPAA may be best implemented with one facilitator, whereas in most schools it would be best implemented by two, three, or four facilitators. The exact number of facilitators needed depends on multiple factors, such as the school's needs, staff expertise, and preferences for implementing all or only some SOPAA components in a given school year. These factors are discussed throughout the book, but for now it is useful to highlight that facilitators would likely include special education teachers, school psychologists, reading specialists, curriculum specialists, Title I teachers, and/or speech–language pathologists, just to name some possibilities. Chapter 11 details the types of educators who would likely help to facilitate SOPAA implementation and how multidisciplinary facilitation may be advantageous.

To facilitate the SOPAA (and all of its components), there are five essential roles: the SOPAA Lead Coordinator, three TAPS Support Teachers (i.e., a TAPS Reading Teacher, a TAPS Math

Teacher, and a TAPS Writing Teacher), and the TAPS Intervention Support Coordinator. Because the SOPAA will be facilitated by one to four educators, facilitators obviously fulfill more than one of the five roles. The specific activities associated with each of the roles are described later in the chapter, but to understand the SOPAA components, it is worth noting here that the TAPS Support Teacher functions as the consultant when a classroom teacher needs assistance in addressing a student's learning difficulty. For example, if a teacher needs assistance addressing a student's reading difficulties, the consultant would be the TAPS Reading Teacher.

The sections described in this chapter provide a more complete understanding of how to implement the SOPAA and the reasons for doing so. For now, we offer greater detail about the six SOPAA components.

Component 1: TAPS

Instructional problem solving within the SOPAA relies on the TAPS process of triadic consultation, making it the central component of the overall model. Put simply, when a classroom teacher notes that a student in her class is experiencing learning difficulties, she works with the consultant (i.e., the TAPS Support Teacher) to pinpoint the student's learning difficulty, develop an intervention plan, implement the intervention plan, and evaluate the plan's effectiveness. In this basic way, TAPS works much like other consultation models (e.g., Bergan, 1977; Bergan & Kratochwill, 1990; Erchul & Martens, 2010), but the processes and materials associated with TAPS are intended to make it more systematic and time-efficient in addressing students' learning difficulties. As described later, there are also other components of the SOPAA designed to improve the effectiveness and efficiency of TAPS.

Chapters 4 and 5 explain the TAPS process in detail. They also refer readers to materials and forms that are used to improve (1) the speed in which struggling students are identified and assisted, and (2) the comprehensiveness in which the intervention plan is developed, implemented, evaluated, and documented. For now, we list the primary features and general sequence of the TAPS process:

1. The classroom teacher requests support from the respective TAPS Support Teacher (e.g., the TAPS Reading Teacher if the student's difficulty is with reading) by using a user-friendly form to explain the teacher's primary concerns.
2. The TAPS Support Teacher reviews the teacher's information, conducts a brief but targeted skills observation of the student (if needed), and based on all acquired information develops a list of evidence-based intervention programs likely to improve the student's academic deficit. Chapter 12 of this book is designed to assist TAPS Support Teachers with identifying an appropriate intervention program to target deficits in reading, math, and writing.
3. The TAPS Support Teacher meets with the classroom teacher for approximately 20 minutes to develop and document a targeted intervention plan, which includes a specified method for implementing an evidence-based intervention program and scheduled times to evaluate the effectiveness of that program with the student. The intervention plan also specifies how the classroom teacher will be supported during the intervention process (e.g., the TAPS Support Teacher and/or a teacher assistant will help with implementing the intervention program on certain days of the week) and how all implementers will be evaluated to ensure that the intervention program is implemented accurately.
4. As dictated by the timeline specified in the student's intervention plan, the TAPS Support Teacher meets again with the classroom teacher (usually 6 or more weeks following the

start of the intervention plan) to formally review, discuss, and reflect on the effectiveness of the intervention and to continue instructional problem solving on that TAPS case if needed.

Component 2: Assessment for Instruction

Evidence suggests that monitoring students' academic growth and then changing instruction if students are not making sufficient progress is a key factor in facilitating students' academic success, both at an individual and at a schoolwide level (Fuchs & Fuchs, 1986; Gersten (et al., 2008). For these reasons, an integral component of the SOPAA is monitoring students' academic progress (this topic is discussed in detail in Chapter 6). There are three primary aspects of this component, all of which are relevant to TAPS (Component 1).

First, a student referred for the TAPS process receives a brief initial assessment, or targeted skills observation, with low-inference academic measures. Drawing primarily on curriculum-based measures or curriculum-based evaluation procedures (described in Chapter 6), the TAPS Support Teacher collects brief samples of the student's academic performance in order to identify likely deficit areas where interventions should be targeted (e.g., whether the focus should be reading fluency or comprehension for a particular student) and to determine a baseline level of performance. Second, any student who receives intervention through the TAPS process must have his or her academic progress evaluated (i.e., monitored) throughout the intervention process so that the TAPS Support Teacher and the classroom teacher can identify the extent to which the student improved as a result of the intervention plan. Third, when possible, schools should use a system of schoolwide benchmark assessments in reading and math to evaluate all students' progress at least three times per school year (e.g., during the fall, winter, and spring). Sometimes referred to as universal screening, this schoolwide method of progress monitoring is related to the TAPS process because it helps TAPS Support Teachers and classroom teachers better select students who might benefit from receiving support through a TAPS intervention plan, and it also provides data to help evaluate core and supplemental instruction.

The targeted skills observation process and individual academic progress monitoring are both essential to SOPAA implementation. Schoolwide benchmark assessment will likely strengthen the implementation, but it is not imperative to include. Later in this chapter (e.g., see description of Component 6) and elsewhere in the book we discuss other situations in which the SOPAA components or their features may be appropriately excluded from implementation if that is best for a particular school at a given period of time.

As described in Chapter 7, the academic progress monitoring component is also supported by Component 4 (targeted professional development) because, in many cases, TAPS Support Teachers will improve their consultation outcomes by strengthening their knowledge about progress monitoring strategies and other forms of academic assessment. Academic assessment is not the only target area of professional development, but it is a core area given its importance to improving students' learning.

Component 3: Maximized Intervention Personnel and Resources

In many cases, schools are asked to do more with less (Hirsch & Church, 2009; Johnson et al., 2010). For example, one common barrier for many schools is not having sufficient personnel within the school who have the time and/or knowledge to implement evidence-based interventions for students who need them. For this reason, the SOPAA model integrates a system for training and coordinating educators who can implement targeted intervention programs with students. Chapters 7 and 8 offer specific recommendations and approaches to maximizing school personnel, including how to best utilize school volunteers (Chapter 8) and assistive school personnel such as teacher assistants. Also important, the system for training and coordinating educators is aligned with the TAPS process (Component 1) and with targeted professional development activities (Component 4).

Component 3 of the SOPAA is also designed to assist educators who struggle with (1) selecting intervention programs that should target and improve a student's deficit, and/or (2) identifying intervention programs that can be successfully implemented by school volunteers or others who may have little experience in using evidence-based instructional programs. Chapter 12 lists a number of evidence-based intervention programs, many of which can be implemented by school volunteers and/or teacher assistants. Chapter 12 also provides information for each listed intervention program regarding the skill area it targets (e.g., phonics, reading fluency, reading comprehension) and several other important characteristics to help educators select intervention programs that should improve student learning while also maximizing school personnel and resources.

Component 4: Targeted Professional Development

Professional development can be viewed as a centerpiece for successfully implementing and sustaining school-based models of prevention and intervention (Freeman et al., 2009; Furney et al., 2003; Kratochwill, Volpiansky, Clements, & Ball, 2007). Therefore, to continually strengthen the effectiveness of TAPS, the SOPAA model integrates a targeted plan of professional development activities for all educators involved in the TAPS process. The activities center around (1) using evidence-based intervention programs in reading, math, and writing; (2) conducting academic assessment; and (3) integrating concepts and principles associated with best practice in academic instruction.

There are three primary features of professional development within the SOPAA model. First, TAPS Support Teachers maintain ongoing professional development in a way that continually maximizes their effectiveness as consultants and is feasible to do considering their other job roles and responsibilities within the school. Second, classroom teachers (i.e., likely consultees during a TAPS case), as well as assistive school personnel and (if possible) school volunteers, will also be involved with SOPAA professional development activities by attending one to three workshops each school year. The focus of the workshops will vary, but at least some will be devoted to helping teachers learn the intervention programs that will be implemented during TAPS cases. Chapters 7 and 8 discuss the first two features of targeted professional development.

Third, embedded within the TAPS process (see Component 1, feature 4), each teacher involved with a TAPS case reflects on, documents, and discusses the case (e.g., aspects that were successful, unsuccessful, or improved over time) when evaluating the effectiveness of a student's intervention plan. During this process, the TAPS Support Teacher also helps the classroom teacher relate the TAPS case to prior experiences (e.g., information obtained during previous TAPS cases or during the SOPAA professional development workshops). The overall goal of this discussion is to help the TAPS Support Teacher and classroom teacher strengthen their applied and conceptual knowledge about all topics related to academic instruction, intervention, and assessment. Chapter 7 discusses each of the three SOPAA professional development features in greater detail.

Through a targeted professional development plan, classroom teachers and TAPS Support Teachers are likely to address students' learning needs more effectively and efficiently. For example, the targeted professional development activities increase the likelihood that the TAPS process will be maintained and become even more time-efficient across each school year because educators in the school will increasingly improve their understanding about academic intervention programs, assessment methods, and instructional best practices.

Component 5: Methods for Communication and Generating Support

Planning for implementing the SOPAA must begin by ensuring that the model is feasible, sustainable, and valued by those involved with its implementation (e.g., classroom teachers and the school principal). To achieve these goals, the SOPAA facilitators must effectively communicate a meaningful rationale for using the SOPAA to generate and maintain support from school leaders (e.g., the principal) and the teachers who will be involved with SOPAA implementation (Adelman & Taylor, 2003; Cherniss, 2006). Likewise, effective communication about SOPAA components and procedures is critical to ensuring and sustaining accurate implementation, as well as to producing the desired outcomes for students and teachers (Furney et al., 2003; McIntosh, Horner, & Sugai, 2009; Sindelar, Shearer, Yendol-Hoppey, & Liebert, 2006). For guidance, Chapter 9 offers numerous recommendations and resources for effective communication with the school principal, particularly as it relates to introducing the SOPAA and generating support and resources. Similarly, Chapter 10 describes specific methods and resources for introducing the SOPAA to teachers, both conceptually and procedurally. Chapter 10 also details how SOPAA facilitators should maintain ongoing communication about the model and how doing so should sustain and/or increase teacher and principal support.

Assuming that there is more than one SOPAA facilitator, communication and collaboration among the two to four co-facilitators is also vital to the effectiveness and efficiency of implementing this model. Several chapters discuss this topic, with Chapter 11 highlighting the multidisciplinary and collaborative relationships among the SOPAA facilitators.

Component 6: Adaptable and Incremental Implementation

Similar to the need for effective communication about the SOPAA procedures and rationale, Component 6 (adaptable and incremental implementation) is designed to strengthen the overall likelihood that the SOPAA procedures are implemented, valued, and sustained. More specifically, the adaptable and incremental options for implementation (including how to "scale-up" implementation over time) of SOPAA procedures make it more feasible to implement more accurately and with strong support from school leaders and other educators (Adelman & Taylor, 2003; Elias, Zins, Graczyk, & Weissburg, 2003; McIntosh et al., 2009). In this way, SOPAA implementation can be specifically tailored to each school's needs, strengths, characteristics, and resources.

Although approaches and options for adaptable and incremental SOPAA implementation are discussed throughout the book, Chapters 3, 11, and 13 particularly illustrate how the SOPAA can be successfully implemented in schools with few resources and little or no history with evidence-based intervention and assessment strategies, as well as how to use the model to improve schools that have ample resources and a long tradition of using evidence-based intervention and assessment strategies. Of course, most U.S. schools probably fall somewhere in the middle of this continuum, and there are certainly several school characteristics that must be considered before implementing a systems-level model to improve student learning.

Chapter 3, for example, offers guidance for SOPAA implementation that is relevant for schools with a wide range of characteristics. That chapter also describes how some SOPAA components, or features of a particular component, can be excluded during the initial years of implementation if a school is not ready to incorporate all SOPAA components. Chapter 11 describes how the

SOPAA can be adapted to allow for implementation by one to four multidisciplinary co-facilitators. Through case examples, Chapter 13 illustrates how the SOPAA can be adapted to work successfully in four different schools with varying characteristics.

Ultimately, the goal is for the SOPAA facilitators to incrementally expand implementation across school years until it is benefiting the most teachers and students in the school, across all academic areas (reading, math, and writing). To maximize implementation feasibility and to generate educators' support, incremental and adaptable implementation options should allow schools to use the SOPAA in the ways that fit best with each school's needs and characteristics.

Relationship of the Six SOPAA Components

To depict the relationship among the six SOPAA components, Figure 2.1 shows a diagram that illustrates how each of the components interact and contribute to the model as a whole. As shown, the diagram depicts *instructional problem solving* at the center of the SOPAA model because the ultimate goal is to successfully address students' learning difficulties through a systematic process of instructional problem solving. The diagram shows the SOPAA components that are designed to facilitate instructional problem solving. At the center is TAPS, which is the primary component (and process) by which a student's intervention plan is developed, implemented, and evaluated. To support the TAPS process, three components are needed: (1) assessment for instruction, (2) maximized intervention resources and personnel, and (3) targeted professional development. As shown in the figure (and described earlier), academic progress monitoring directly supports the success of TAPS (depicted by the arrow pointing to TAPS). Likewise, intervention resources and personnel directly support the success of the TAPS process. Targeted professional development supports TAPS, as well as intervention resources, personnel, and linking assessment with instruction. As was described previously, professional development helps to train personnel in the use of needed intervention resources. TAPS Teachers' ongoing professional development also supports

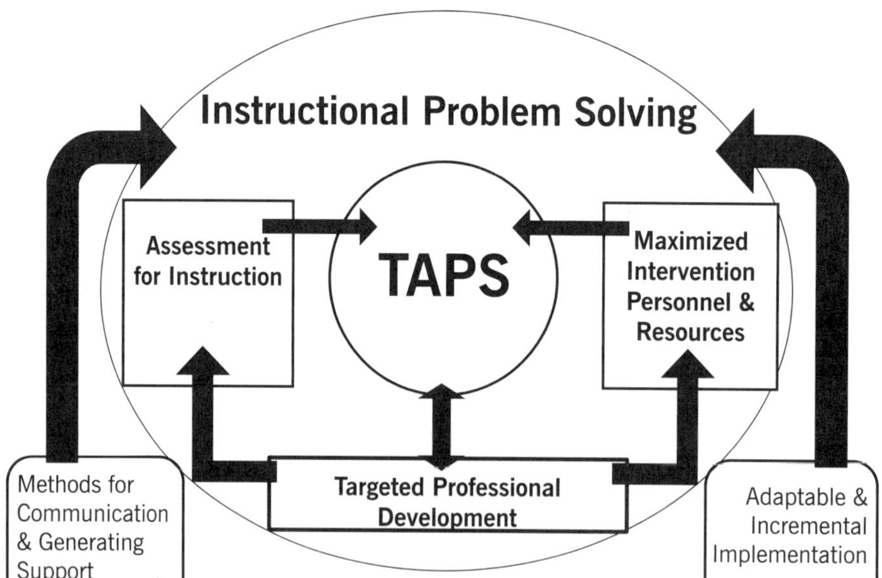

FIGURE 2.1. The SOPAA model.

their ability to link assessment with instruction because there are several professional development activities that help TAPS Support Teachers use assessment to best support TAPS cases. Last, the bidirectional arrow between TAPS and targeted professional development shows that each component supports the other. TAPS is supported by professional development because teachers are then better able to support students in the TAPS process. Professional development is supported by the TAPS process because a goal of finalizing a TAPS case includes discussion of what worked, what did not work, and how the case helped to build upon each participating teacher's previous SOPAA professional development activities.

Finally, within the SOPAA model but outside of the instructional problem-solving core, the final two components are presented: methods for communication and generating support (Component 5) and adaptable and incremental implementation (Component 6). These components are displayed outside of the *instructional problem-solving* core because they do not have a direct role in ensuring that the TAPS process results in improved student outcomes, especially as compared to the other SOPAA components. However, Components 5 and 6 are shown as *supporting* the instructional problem-solving process (as depicted with the arrows) because without those components, it is unlikely that this approach, including each of the components embedded within it, could be successfully facilitated. Also, a bidirectional arrow connects Components 5 and 6 because generating support for the SOPAA is largely facilitated by developing an adaptable and incremental implementation plan, and such a plan can be developed and implemented only through effective communication with the school principal, the participating teachers, and all SOPAA facilitators.

TAPS is only one component of the SOPAA, but it is the central component of the overall model.

DESIGNATED ROLES OF THE SOPAA

As we noted earlier in this chapter, the one to four facilitators in the school who are responsible for overall SOPAA implementation assume five essential roles. Each role is introduced in this section.

The SOPAA Lead Coordinator

Although the SOPAA can, and in many cases should, be facilitated by more than one educator in the school, one person, the SOPAA Lead Coordinator (or simply, the Lead Coordinator), should take the primary responsibility for overseeing and ensuring accurate implementation of the model and effective student outcomes. The Lead Coordinator's primary tasks are listed below, with chapters noted in parentheses to specify where we offer extended discussion about the task.

1. Oversee implementation of all SOPAA components to ensure that they are implemented with the greatest possible effectiveness (Chapter 11).
2. Introduce the SOPAA procedures and their rationale to all relevant school leaders, such as the school principal (Chapter 9).
3. Introduce the SOPAA procedures and their rationale to all relevant teachers in the school (Chapter 10).
4. Evaluate the effectiveness of all SOPAA components and student learning outcomes resulting from TAPS cases and facilitate procedural modifications to the model and/or TAPS process if necessary (Chapter 10).

5. Maintain ongoing communication of SOPAA outcomes, student learning outcomes, and procedural modifications with school leaders and all relevant teachers in the school (Chapter 10).
6. As applicable, develop and lead an incremental plan for SOPAA implementation (Chapter 3).
7. Serve as a TAPS Support Teacher in one or more of the three academic areas described below (Chapters 4 and 5).

As described in Chapter 11, SOPAA co-facilitators might assist with tasks 2–6, but the Lead Coordinator should maintain primary responsibility for overseeing and ensuring that the tasks are completed effectively. Of course, in a school in which there is only one SOPAA facilitator, the Lead Coordinator fulfills each of the five SOPAA roles. The time required of the Lead Coordinator, if she is the *only* SOPAA facilitator, is discussed in Chapter 3.

TAPS Support Teachers in Reading, Math, and Writing

Collectively, TAPS Support Teachers (whom we will now simply refer to as *TAPS Teachers*) represent three separate roles if a school plans to use the SOPAA to address learning difficulties in all three primary academic areas: reading, math, and writing. As such, the three TAPS Teacher roles include the TAPS Reading Teacher, TAPS Math Teacher, and TAPS Writing Teacher. In some cases, one individual may serve more than one of three TAPS Teacher roles. For example, if there are two educators facilitating the SOPAA, one may fulfill the Lead Coordinator, TAPS Math Teacher, and TAPS Intervention Support Coordinator (described below) roles, and the other educator would fulfill the TAPS Reading Teacher and TAPS Writing Teacher roles. The three TAPS Teacher roles are the same, except that each role is dedicated specifically to one academic area (i.e., reading, math, or writing). For clarity in understanding the total number of SOPAA roles, we separate the three roles according to each respective academic area.

The TAPS Reading Teacher

The TAPS Reading Teacher addresses all teachers' requests to help improve students' reading difficulties through the TAPS process. Starting from a teacher's initial request for support, the TAPS Reading Teacher's primary task is to assist the classroom teacher with developing, facilitating, and evaluating the student's intervention plan.

The TAPS Reading Teacher is also responsible for professional development activities in areas related to instruction, intervention, and assessment to address learning difficulties in reading. This includes her ongoing professional development, as well as hosting (or co-hosting) professional development workshops for classroom teachers in the area of reading. Chapters 4 and 5 provide detailed descriptions of the TAPS process and the TAPS Teacher's specific role throughout it. Chapter 7 describes professional development activities associated with the TAPS Teacher. Chapter 11 also describes how the TAPS Teacher works collaboratively with other SOPAA facilitators, if the school implements the SOPAA with more than one facilitator.

The TAPS Math Teacher

The TAPS Math Teacher fulfills the same role as the TAPS Reading Teacher, except TAPS cases and professional development activities are associated with math, rather than reading.

The TAPS Writing Teacher

The TAPS Writing Teacher fulfills the same role as the TAPS Reading Teacher and TAPS Math Teacher, except TAPS cases and professional development activities are associated with writing, rather than reading or math.

The TAPS Intervention Support Coordinator

The TAPS Intervention Support Coordinator (or simply, the TAPS Support Coordinator) is responsible for assisting each TAPS Teacher with identifying, training, and coordinating educators within the school (or school volunteers) who can assist in the TAPS process by implementing intervention programs for students who need them. In addition, the TAPS Support Coordinator sometimes assists the TAPS Teacher with monitoring the integrity of how educators implement intervention programs. The TAPS Support Coordinator's primary tasks are summarized below, with chapters noted in parentheses to specify where we offer extended discussion about the task.

1. Recruit school volunteers and/or other educators within the school (e.g., teacher assistants or other available staff) to implement intervention programs during TAPS cases (Chapters 7 and 8).
2. Assist TAPS Teachers with training school volunteers and/or other educators within the school to implement intervention programs during TAPS cases (Chapters 7 and 8).
3. Manage and coordinate the availability schedules of volunteers and other educators who can implement intervention programs during TAPS cases, and communicate this information to TAPS Teachers when requested (Chapters 5 and 11).
4. Sustain and evaluate a program for recruiting and training school volunteers (if possible and if needed) to implement intervention programs during TAPS cases (Chapter 8).
5. Assist TAPS Teachers with monitoring the integrity of educators' implementation of intervention programs that are delivered during TAPS cases (Chapters 5 and 11).

CONCLUDING COMMENTS

With a first reading, the SOPAA model may seem complex, with many components and many roles. However, the model is to be implemented in a componential fashion, so that educators can manage change and all are well prepared for its implementation. In the next chapter, we discuss preliminary steps in gathering support for school change. Appendix A summarizes the SOPAA components, the features within each component, and the SOPAA roles. It can serve as a "cheat sheet" that may be helpful in conceptualizing and communicating how the SOPAA components and roles are configured.

CHAPTER 3

Preliminary Considerations for SOPAA Implementation

Prior to implementing the SOPAA, the Lead Coordinator should consider (1) the types of evidence-based intervention programs the school has available (or needs) to facilitate TAPS cases, (2) a reasonable multiyear timeline for SOPAA implementation, (3) the time and resources needed for successful implementation, (4) the strengths and barriers within the school that should influence key implementation decisions, and (5) how the SOPAA can be used with or without other models of instructional problem solving, such as RTI. By first considering these preliminary aspects of the SOPAA, implementation planning should be better understood and organized, thereby allowing actual implementation to be more effective, accepted by educators in the school, and sustainable. As such, this chapter discusses these five preliminary considerations for SOPAA implementation and concludes with a summary of step-by-step suggestions for using the remainder of this book to implement the SOPAA.

SELECTING EVIDENCE-BASED INTERVENTION PROGRAMS TO USE WITH TAPS

As stated previously, a key feature of the TAPS process is ensuring that all struggling learners receive an intervention that is evidence-based, implemented for a suitable period of time, and implemented with integrity. There are multiple approaches to intervention in the primary academic areas, but we contend that most schools will best meet the needs of struggling learners by providing them with manualized intervention programs that offer teachers a specific set of procedures and materials that have been shown through research to improve students' learning.

Some definitions and an explanation may help readers understand our position. First, by *manualized* we mean that there is a clear statement of what comprises the intervention and detailed instructions for implementing it. This set of instructions should be sufficiently explicit that teachers and other instructional personnel know what they should and should not do, how often to implement the intervention, and with what materials. Ideally, there are tools (e.g., training materials, observation checklists) with the intervention that help teachers know how closely the instruction they provide matches what was intended by the program developers. By the time all these pieces are pulled together, they typically result in a book-sized manual for the intervention. The manual explains the rationale behind the intervention, how to prepare to use the intervention, and all the components just mentioned.

This explicit set of instructions makes it more likely that instructional staff will implement a program with integrity (i.e., as intended by its developers). Part of an intervention being "scientific," as required in federal law in the special education referral process, is that the intervention is replicable by others and actually has been replicated when it is used with a child by teachers. It is hard to replicate a program that is poorly described, which is why we recommend manualized interventions. Thorough descriptions, like those in a manual, also better facilitate use of the instructional procedures with high integrity by multiple educators in the school.

By intervention *program* we mean that the intervention has multiple evidence-based components or strategies within it. For example, the Helping Early Literacy with Practice Strategies (HELPS) Program is a reading fluency intervention that combines eight evidence-based instructional strategies, such as having the student reread instructionally appropriate text, practice reading words that were initially read incorrectly, and read along silently while an adult reads the text aloud. We recommend intervention *programs* to single intervention strategies because an intervention is likely to be more comprehensive when it packages together multiple evidence-based strategies.

Our final stipulation is that intervention programs have been shown through research to improve students' learning. We define our research criteria for a program in Chapter 12 and also provide detailed information about several evidence-based, manualized intervention programs a school may consider adopting for use with the SOPAA. The chapter also describes the key subskills for each of the three main academic areas: reading, math, and writing. Although manualized intervention programs can be expensive, there are many that cost very little. The cost of intervention programs should always be weighed against the likelihood that the intervention will be effective, well documented, and easily learned by those who will implement it.

In sum, for the sake of increased effectiveness, efficiency, and treatment integrity, as well as to assure compliance with legal mandates that may apply in some situations when interventions are used in schools, in this book we focus on schools' adoption and use of *manualized, evidence-based, intervention programs*. For simplicity, we typically refer to such interventions as *programs* or *manualized programs* throughout the remainder of the book. Although we provide much more detail later, in this chapter we simply emphasize that prior to starting implementation, the SOPAA facilitators should carefully consider which strategies or programs teachers in the school are currently using to address students' learning difficulties, and determine whether those interventions are manualized, have evidence of effectiveness, are implemented by all teachers who should use them, and are implemented by teachers with integrity.

Based on the SOPAA facilitators' assessment of intervention practices in the school, they should determine which academic areas and subskill areas might be better addressed by adopting one or more additional intervention programs. Therefore, before starting SOPAA implementation, intervention programs should be selected and available to target the subskills that will be addressed through the TAPS process. In some cases, an intervention program might successfully improve more than one subskill, but in other cases a more "targeted" intervention will be needed. A good example of this is in reading, where one program may successfully improve a student's difficulty with phonics and phonemic awareness, but a separate program would likely be needed if a student's specific deficit is in comprehension. Similarly, as described in Chapter 12, some intervention programs for math may be designed to improve both basic math facts *and* more advanced computation skills, but other interventions may be needed to target a more specific deficit.

To illustrate a school's selection of intervention programs prior to starting SOPAA implementation, suppose the school is starting Year 1 of implementation by trying to improve students' phonemic awareness, phonics, and fluency in kindergarten through second grade. Let us also suppose that a few teachers in the school have some successful strategies for improving students' phonics, but that there is an insufficient number of teachers using those strategies, assistive school personnel cannot assist with implementing those strategies (due to lack of training), and the strategies do not seem to improve students' phonemic awareness. Also, the teachers do not have much background with assisting students who have good phonics and phonemic awareness skills but struggle with text-reading fluency. In this example, the SOPAA facilitators (probably with support from the principal) could start their search for intervention programs that target phonemic awareness, phonics, and fluency by reviewing the information in Chapter 12 and, more specifically, looking into each of the programs listed across those three areas. Searching for additional intervention programs might also be useful.

Building upon this example, let us also suppose that the SOPAA facilitators have particular interests in identifying programs that have progress monitoring materials, and at least one program can be used by trained assistive personnel and school volunteers. Based on their review of the programs, the SOPAA facilitators might choose, for example, Sound Partners as the program to target students' phonics and phonemic awareness, and Read Naturally to target students' fluency.

In addition to determining which interventions will be used during TAPS cases, the TAPS Teachers, classroom teachers, and select assistive school personnel should know how to implement any intervention program they will be asked to use prior to starting SOPAA implementation. Recommendations and a process for ensuring that teachers know how to implement interventions are mentioned later in this chapter and discussed more thoroughly in Chapters 5 and 7. Although we highly recommend that teachers who will be involved with TAPS first know how to implement the intervention programs that will be used, Chapter 5 also describes options for training a small number of teachers just before beginning a studentc's intervention plan. As a way to summarize the selection of intervention programs and training plans for those interventions, SOPAA facilitators might use a format such as the one shown in Table 3.1.

TABLE 3.1. Example of an Intervention Program Menu Developed by a School Using TAPS to Target Phonemic Awareness, Phonics, and Fluency

Academic area and subskill	Intervention program selected	When will educators learn the program?	Can the program be used by assistive personnel and volunteers?
Reading—Phonemic awareness plus	Sound Partners	March 2013[a]	Yes
Reading—Phonics plus	Sound Partners	March 2013	Yes
Reading—Fluency	Read Naturally	August 2013	Yes

[a] Ideally, training in March 2013 means that the official start of SOPAA implementation will not occur until the beginning of the following school year (i.e., September 2013).

INCREMENTAL IMPLEMENTATION OF THE SOPAA WITH A MULTIYEAR PLAN

Full-scale implementation of the SOPAA means that *all* components are implemented for *each* of the three main academic areas, for *all* teachers, and for *all* grade levels throughout the school. However, in most cases the Lead Coordinator will recognize that full-scale implementation in the first school year would be very challenging and unlikely to work. As such, and as shown in the case examples described in Chapter 13, *incremental* SOPAA implementation will likely be the most feasible and successful. Prior to implementation, the Lead Coordinator should therefore consider how to implement the SOPAA across multiple school years and eventually generate a multiyear intervention plan with the principal and (if applicable) the co-facilitators.

Developing a clear plan for the SOPAA implementation should increase its likelihood of effectiveness and sustainability.

In establishing a multiyear implementation plan, the facilitators must keep in mind that the primary goals of implementing the SOPAA in the first year are to implement a version that (1) is feasible for the school given its existing resources and practices, (2) represents a meaningful change to what the school is currently doing to address struggling learners' needs, (3) should result in effective outcomes for students, and (4) should generate support for the model from teachers who use it. Overall, the decision about how to implement the SOPAA in the first year will depend on the school's specific characteristics, resources, and readiness for the model. Table 3.2 provides several examples of how the SOPAA can be appropriately modified in the first year to allow for more feasible and successful implementation.

As shown in Table 3.2, there are several ways in which the SOPAA can be modified to allow for more feasible implementation in the first year; but we must highlight more specifically what should be considered acceptable SOPAA modifications. First, schools should only modify the SOPAA according to the ways listed in Table 3.2. For example, schools should not start implementation in the middle of a school year, nor should schools exclude SOPAA components unless it is specified as acceptable in Table 3.2. Second, the right-hand column of Table 3.2 shows some *examples* of acceptable modifications. In other words, a school may modify implementation in any way that is consistent with the acceptable modifications listed on the left-hand side of Table 3.2.

Third, the modification options listed in Table 3.2 can also be used in combination. For example, consider a K–5 elementary school we will call Franklin Elementary School for the purposes of this illustration. At Franklin Elementary School, the principal and Lead Coordinator decide that the first year of the SOPAA implementation will occur only with first-, second-, and third-grade classrooms, and as part of that initial implementation year, only reading (specifically, phonics, phonemic awareness, and fluency) will be addressed during TAPS cases. Also during that first year, the school decides that volunteers should not yet be recruited or trained to implement evidence-based intervention programs, but teacher assistants, two special education teachers, and the school's art teacher will serve as assistive school personnel to support the TAPS process. With these modifications, the school has appropriately modified a full-scale implementation plan because each modification appears on the left-hand side of Table 3.2.

The top portion of Table 3.3 (Example 1, pp. 35–36) illustrates this implementation plan for the first school year, as well as an implementation plan across multiple school years. Referring to Appendix A (the summary of SOPAA components and features) might also help with interpreting Table 3.3.

The bottom portion of Table 3.3 (Example 2, p. 36) illustrates a different school's implementation plan across several school years. In that example, the K–6 grade Oakland Elementary

TABLE 3.2. Acceptable Modifications to the SOPAA Prior to Implementing It at Full Scale

Acceptable modification	Examples of modification
Implement all components of the SOPAA with only some grade levels in the school.	If the SOPAA is being implemented in a K–6 elementary school, implement it with only some grade levels (e.g., first, second, and third grades).
Implement all components of the SOPAA with only some teachers in the school.	Implement the SOPAA with half of the teachers in the school (e.g., those who are randomly selected, selected by the principal and Lead Coordinator, or volunteer to be involved). Or, implement the SOPAA with half of the teachers per grade level.
Implement all components of the SOPAA in only one or two of the academic areas.	Implement the SOPAA only in reading or only in reading and writing.
Exclude the SOPAA component related to recruiting and training school volunteers.	Train selected assistive school personnel (e.g., teacher assistants) to help with intervention implementation, but do not train or recruit school volunteers for this purpose.
Reduce the recommended number of staff development workshops for teachers.	Hold only one staff development workshop (rather than two or three) that targets teachers' greatest need in an area of academic instruction or intervention. *Note:* The 1-hour meeting devoted to introducing the SOPAA to participating teachers, as described in Chapter 10, must be done during the initial year of implementation. This introductory meeting for teachers is not considered a staff development workshop. Staff development workshops are described in Chapter 7.
Exclude or reduce schoolwide benchmark assessments in reading and/or math.	Use schoolwide benchmark assessments in reading only, use reading and math benchmark assessments only for classroom teachers who are involved with the SOPAA, or only use ongoing progress monitoring (including benchmark assessments) for students receiving intervention support through TAPS.

School plans to implement the SOPAA only with teachers who express interest in the model and volunteer to take part in its implementation. Also, Oakland Elementary School only uses the model with math because that is the academic area with which students struggle the most. This school also decides to exclude using schoolwide benchmark assessments in math during the first year and instead integrates that feature during the second year of implementation. Later in the implementation process, Oakland Elementary also begins to address students' reading difficulties through the TAPS process and selects the Title I teacher in Year 4 to begin preparing as the TAPS Reading Teacher.

Using a format like the case illustrations in Table 3.3, the Lead Coordinator should benefit by preparing a SOPAA implementation timeline and then propose that timeline during the initial meeting with the principal (a process that is discussed in Chapter 9). Being able to develop a 4- or 5-year timeline may be challenging because of unknown circumstances associated with the school's functioning, but having an overall vision of how incremental implementation might work is useful, even if that original plan must be modified later.

TABLE 3.3. Examples of Incremental Implementation of the SOPAA in a Timeline Summary

School year (implementation year)	Primary modifications from full-scale SOPAA implementation	Components or features to exclude	Components and features to implement
	Example 1 (a hypothetical illustration of SOPAA implementation at Franklin's K–5 Elementary School)		
2012–2013 (Year 1)	1. Implement the SOPAA only with first-, second-, and third-grade classrooms; include *all* teachers from these grades. 2. Only target phonics, phonemic awareness, and fluency with the TAPS cases. *The SOPAA will be facilitated by two individuals: the school's reading specialist (serving as Lead Coordinator and TAPS Reading Teacher) and the school psychologist (serving as TAPS Support Coordinator).*	1. For Component 3 (*maximized intervention personnel and resources*) school volunteers will not be trained or recruited to implement intervention programs selected for TAPS cases.	1. All features of the TAPS process. 2. All features of Component 2 (assessment for instruction), including targeted skills observations, progress monitoring with curriculum-based measurements of reading during TAPS cases, and universal screening with passage for oral reading fluency. 3. Train all grade 1–3 teacher assistants, two special education teachers, and the art teacher to assist with implementing the selected intervention programs to use with TAPS cases. 4. Conduct ongoing professional development with the TAPS Reading Teacher. 5. Conduct two SOPAA professional development workshops (both will include teachers and assistive personnel). 6. Facilitate all methods for communication and generating support (Component 5).
2013–2014 (Year 2)	1. Begin implementation with K so that SOPAA is now implemented with K, first-, second-, and third-grade classrooms. 2. Begin implementation with writing, so that the SOPAA is now implemented with reading and writing.	Same as Year 1	Continue plan from Year 1, plus designate the school psychologist as the TAPS Writing Teacher and allow him or her to complete ongoing professional development; also, use early reading measures for universal screening with K.

(cont.)

TABLE 3.3. *(cont.)*

School year (implementation year)	Primary modifications from full-scale SOPAA implementation	Components or features to exclude	Components and features to implement
2014–2015 (Year 3)	Begin implementation with fourth and fifth grade so that SOPAA is now implemented with all K–5 classrooms in reading and writing.	None	Continue plan from Year 2; in addition, the TAPS Support Coordinator will facilitate a SOPAA volunteer program and help to train all fourth- and fifth-grade teacher assistants to implement intervention programs.
2015–2016 (Year 4)	Begin implementation with math so that SOPAA is now being implemented full-scale.	None	To support full-scale implementation, recruit additional school volunteers.
	Example 2 (hypothetical illustration of SOPAA implementation at Oakland's K–6 Elementary School)		
2012–2013 (Year 1)	1. Implement the SOPAA only with teachers who express interest and volunteer to take part in TAPS. 2. Only target math with the TAPS cases. *The SOPAA will be facilitated by two individuals: a special education teacher (serving as Lead Coordinator and TAPS Math Teacher) and the social worker (serving as TAPS Support Coordinator).*	For Component 2 (assessment for instruction), schoolwide math benchmark assessments will not be used.	1. All features of the TAPS process. 2. All features of Component 2 (assessment for instruction) except universal screening in math. 3. Train at least six teacher assistants and the school's music teacher to assist with implementing the selected intervention programs to use with TAPS cases. 4. Conduct ongoing professional development with the TAPS Math Teacher who will also host each professional development workshop for teachers and school volunteers because the social worker is not familiar enough with math intervention programs. 5. Conduct two SOPAA professional development workshops (both workshops will include all teachers and teacher assistants, and both workshops will train teachers to use math intervention programs). 6. Begin SOPAA volunteer program and recruit at least three school volunteers to assist. 7. Facilitate all methods for communication and generating support (Component 5).

2013–2014 (Year 2)	No changes, but encourage more teachers in the school to take part in TAPS.	None	Continue plan from Year 1, plus start doing schoolwide benchmark assessments in math. For the two SOPAA professional development workshops, devote at least one to training teachers to use the math benchmark assessments.
2014–2015 (Year 3)	1. Implement with all teachers of grades K–3 plus all teachers of grades 4–6 who express interest and volunteer to take part in TAPS. 2. Continue to target only math with the TAPS cases.	None	Continue plan from Year 2, plus start doing schoolwide benchmark assessments in reading. For the two SOPAA professional development workshops, devote one to training teachers to use the reading benchmark assessments and the other to training teachers to use a selected intervention program for reading.
2015–2016 (Year 4)	1. Implement with all K–6 teachers in the school. 2. Continue to target only math with TAPS cases.	None	Continue plan from Year 3. For the two SOPAA professional development workshops (including teachers, assistive personnel, and school volunteers), devote both workshops to training teachers to use a selected intervention program for reading. Start preparing the Title I teacher to serve as the TAPS Reading Teacher (she should begin ongoing professional development this year and meet with the other co-facilitators).
2016–2017 (Year 5)	For all K–6 teachers, start targeting reading with TAPS cases, in addition to math. *The SOPAA will now also be officially co-facilitated by an additional educator: a Title I teacher (serving as the TAPS Reading Teacher).*	None	Continue plan from Year 4. *Note: In this school, teachers are effective in addressing students with writing difficulties, so there is no plan to integrate the TAPS process for writing.*

SOPAA Implementation Requirements

We highlight again that the examples in Table 3.2 represent each of the *acceptable* modifications for initial SOPAA implementation. In other words, successful outcomes of the SOPAA will likely be compromised if the plan is modified in ways not explicitly stated in the left-hand column of Table 3.2. For clarity, the list below describes each primary component and feature of the SOPAA that must be implemented.

1. The Lead Coordinator must effectively communicate the SOPAA procedures and rationale and ultimately generate principal and teacher support for the plan, as described in Chapters 9 and 10.
2. For each of the academic areas the school addresses through SOPAA implementation (i.e., reading, math, and/or writing), the TAPS Teacher(s) must complete each step of the TAPS procedures for instructional problem solving, as described in Chapters 4 and 5.
3. Implementing the TAPS procedures also includes 8–10 hours per month of professional development for the TAPS Teacher (part of Component 4, targeted professional development), as discussed in Chapter 7.
4. The TAPS Support Coordinator (perhaps in collaboration with other SOPAA facilitators) must train at least some available assistive school personnel (e.g., teacher assistants, librarians, or any other educators who can assist periodically) to implement appropriate evidence-based intervention programs, as described in Chapter 7. Although support for classroom teachers is needed to periodically implement intervention programs during each year of the SOPAA implementation, *initial* implementation might exclude school volunteers from this role, as shown in Example 1 of Table 3.3. Chapter 8 further discusses how, when, and whether to include school volunteers as intervention assistants.
5. The TAPS Support Coordinator must coordinate assistive personnel to support TAPS cases, as described in Chapters 5 and 11.

Potential Need for a SOPAA Preparation Year

Considering the requirements for SOPAA implementation and the options for incremental implementation, it is possible that some schools would benefit most by starting with a SOPAA preparation year *prior* to starting Year 1 of the implementation plan. To be clear, a preparation year should be planned and facilitated *after* generating the principal's support, selecting SOPAA co-facilitators (if there will be multiple facilitators), and determining a multiyear implementation plan. Thus, the preparation year would occur throughout the school year immediately *before* Year 1 of the established implementation timeline.

During the preparation year, the primary goal would be to ensure that all TAPS Teachers have access to, and experience using, the evidence-based interventions that would be selected for TAPS cases. For example, if a school has a limited number of intervention programs that have been used to assist struggling readers, and Year 1 of the implementation plan will target reading, the preparation year should be used for the TAPS Reading Teacher to acquire, learn, and use at least one intervention program that targets each subskill (e.g., phonics, fluency, comprehension). Again, Chapter 12 of this book can be used as a resource for the Lead Coordinator and TAPS Teachers to identify and possibly select evidence-based intervention programs if there are no such programs available in the school to target a particular subskill.

When possible, the preparation year should also be used to achieve one or more secondary goals or tasks, assuming that the school has not already achieved those tasks. For example, the TAPS Teacher(s) involved with Year 1 of implementation should learn and begin using the assessment methods described in Chapter 6. This preparation could include using the assessments with a small number of students receiving intervention, or if feasible, at a class-, grade-, or schoolwide level. The preparation year could also allow the SOPAA facilitator(s) to begin training at least some teachers and other school personnel in the intervention programs that will be considered during TAPS cases once Year 1 of implementation begins. In essence, TAPS is best facilitated when there are multiple educators who have at least some training with the available intervention programs, and the preparation year is an ideal time to train teachers in at least one or two intervention programs. Likewise, if Year 1 of the implementation plan will include school volunteers as possible implementers of the intervention programs, the preparation year could be used to train those volunteers.

To further facilitate a smooth transition into Year 1 of the school's implementation plan, the preparation year could also allow the TAPS Teacher or Teachers to get experience using the TAPS process. Even if teachers in the school do not yet know how to request support through the TAPS process, the TAPS Teacher could begin managing her consultation cases by using the TAPS process and forms if she already serves in some capacity as a consultant prior to SOPAA implementation. This initial use of the TAPS process with a small number of consultation cases during the preparation year should help the TAPS Teacher become more fluent with the process and forms, as well as help to introduce the process to the few teachers whom the TAPS Teacher assists through consultation. We want to highlight here that managing consultation cases using the TAPS process may be one initial activity that could be tried without having explicit support for the SOPAA from the school principal, particularly if a similar form of consultation is already in place. Likewise, "trying out" the TAPS process would not require identifying SOPAA co-facilitators or outlining a multiyear implementation plan.

Last, if possible, the preparation year might include having the TAPS Teacher start with at least some portion of the ongoing professional development (e.g., 4–5 hours per month). Of course, learning and using new intervention programs will likely make up a large part of the TAPS Teacher's professional development during the preparation year. However, by taking part in some other professional development activities (i.e., those described in Chapter 7), the TAPS Teacher will start Year 1 of implementation with a stronger knowledge base and a potential routine for ongoing professional development.

The Lead Coordinator, principal, and possible SOPAA co-facilitators must ultimately determine whether the school would benefit from a preparation year prior to Year 1 of implementation, and this decision will be influenced by multiple school, teacher, and student factors. For guidance, however, the SOPAA leaders might consider the following questions to determine whether a preparation year is needed.

Of the TAPS Teacher(s) who will use TAPS during Year 1 implementation:

1. Do those TAPS Teachers have access and experience implementing the selected evidence-based intervention programs?
2. Do the TAPS Teachers have adequate knowledge and experience using academic assessments to monitor intervention effectiveness?
3. Do the TAPS Teachers have adequate experience following a systematic approach to academic consultation and instructional problem solving?
4. Do classroom teachers and other school personnel who will be involved with the SOPAA during Year 1 have experience implementing the selected intervention programs?

If the general response to most of the above questions is "no," a preparation year should ease the implementation and enhance effectiveness during Year 1 of the plan. To summarize, the preparation year should include, if needed, as many of the following activities as possible:

1. Ensure that all Year 1 TAPS Teachers have access to, and experience using, the evidence-based interventions that would be selected for TAPS cases.
2. Allow Year 1 TAPS Teachers to learn and use academic progress monitoring strategies.
3. Train school personnel (including teachers, teacher assistants, and possibly school volunteers) to use one or more intervention programs that will be considered during TAPS cases in Year 1.
4. Allow Year 1 TAPS Teachers to use the TAPS process and forms.
5. Allow Year 1 TAPS Teachers to begin a routine of ongoing professional development.

Most of these activities should occur only after there is support from the principal for the SOPAA and at least a Year 1 plan for implementation. However, readers may also consider engaging in some of these activities (e.g., activity 4) to get a better sense for TAPS and the potential benefits of the SOPAA. With this information, securing support from others (e.g., the principal, classroom teachers) may be easier.

TIME AND MATERIAL RESOURCES NEEDED FOR SOPAA IMPLEMENTATION

Lack of time and access to the resources that are needed to create schoolwide change are among the key reasons why attempts for schoolwide innovations often fail (e.g., Latham, 1988). For this reason, it is essential that the Lead Coordinator generate sound support for the SOPAA from the principal and is candid in stating what time and resources will be needed to implement the plan effectively. Although each school is unique in its current resources, and each Lead Coordinator will have differing levels of availability to implement SOPAA components, the information below should help the Lead Coordinator determine the approximate amount of time and resources she will need to implement the model.

Typically, the time invested in developing an efficient system for assisting struggling learners will ultimately help more students and save educators considerable time and resources.

Time Needed Weekly for SOPAA Implementation

We have not yet detailed the specific tasks associated with the TAPS process, as these are described mainly in Chapters 4 and 5. However, enough information about TAPS has thus far been presented for us to now turn to the amount of time that would be needed weekly to facilitate this core component of the SOPAA.

Table 3.4 illustrates the approximate amount of time one person (i.e., the Lead Coordinator, who also serves as the TAPS Teacher) would need weekly to implement the *full-scale* SOPAA. These approximations are based on the TAPS Teacher receiving one or two teacher requests for academic support each week. Assuming that one or two requests occurred per week from September through March of a typical school year (i.e., approximately six requests across each of the first seven months of the school year), 42 students each school year would be assisted with the TAPS process. Depending on the size of the school and the needs of its students, this number may reflect an over- or underestimate of the number of students who would need such assistance, but it nonetheless provides a meaningful gauge by which to estimate time costs for using the TAPS process. As discussed previously, implementation in the initial years will likely *exclude* some features of the SOPAA (e.g., TAPS will be used only in one academic area); therefore, initial implementation should require less time than what is presented in Table 3.4.

TABLE 3.4. Estimates of Time Needed by a SOPAA Facilitator to Process TAPS Cases When Using the SOPAA at Full Scale

General description of activity and relevant SOPAA component	SOPAA role	Approximate amount of time needed per TAPS case	Approximate amount of time needed per month
Process teacher's Request for TAPS Form (e.g., conduct targeted assessment, develop list of intervention options, develop follow-up questions and prepare for planning meeting); Components 1 and 2	TAPS Teacher	25–55 minutes	2.5–5.5 hours
Identify and coordinate assistive school personnel (or volunteers) who can assist the teacher with intervention implementation; Components 1 and 3	TAPS Teacher and TAPS Support Coordinator	10–15 minutes	1–1.5 hours
Develop an intervention plan during a meeting with the classroom teacher requesting support; Component 1	TAPS Teacher	20–30 minutes	2–3 hours
Conduct initial follow-up meeting to discuss the student's intervention plan; Component 1	TAPS Teacher	5–15 minutes	0.5–1.5 hours
Conduct periodic follow-up meetings; Component 1	TAPS Teacher	~5 minutes every 2 weeks = 10 minutes monthly	1 hour
Assist with implementing the selected intervention program; Component 1	TAPS Teacher	15–30 minutes every 2–3 weeks = ~40–50 minutes monthly	4–5 hours
Facilitate academic progress monitoring; Components 1 and 2	TAPS Teacher (if not completed by classroom teacher)	~5 minutes every week = 20 minutes monthly	2 hours
Observe each implementer's implementation integrity; Components 1 and 3	TAPS Support Teacher and/or TAPS Support Coordinator	~10–30 minutes every 2 weeks = 20–60 minutes monthly	2–6 hours
Facilitate formal review of intervention effectiveness during a meeting; Component 1	TAPS Teacher	20–45 minutes [a]	2–4.5 hours
Maintain ongoing professional development in academic assessment, intervention, and related concepts and principles; Components 1 and 4	Each TAPS Teacher		8–10 hours
Meet with all SOPAA facilitators, possibly including the school principal, for planning, review, and organizing; Component 1	All SOPAA facilitators		1 hour
Estimated total amount of time needed each month to support six TAPS cases (and estimated amount of time needed each week to support one or two TAPS cases)		*26–41 hours per month (~6.5–10 hours per week)*	

Note. TAPS, Targeted Assistance Program for Students. *TAPS Teacher* is a broad term for the TAPS Reading, Math, and Writing Teachers. The time associated with TAPS activities assumes two new requests for academic support per week (across the three academic areas). The estimated times shown in the table should decrease with continued implementation of the SOPAA over time.
[a]During initial months of the school year, formal review meetings are unlikely to take place because students will have not yet received the intervention plan that is discussed during this meeting.

The approximations in Table 3.4 reflect the amount of time *one* facilitator might need to use the TAPS process. As shown, TAPS requires approximately 6.5–10 hours per week to support one or two cases per week. One must keep in mind, however, that the SOPAA would probably be even more effective by involving more than one facilitator, which would meaningfully reduce the weekly time demands for any one educator. Also, a long-term goal of implementing the SOPAA (and using TAPS) is to ultimately reduce the amount of time and resources educators need to expend to successfully address students' learning difficulties. The Lead Coordinator should highlight this fact when generating support for this model from school leadership (e.g., the principal). By doing so, the principal (and others) should understand that the first year or two of implementing the SOPAA will be the most time consuming, but eventually the SOPAA model should become more effective and time efficient. For example, across one or more school years, classroom teachers will have fully learned the TAPS process and several evidence-based intervention programs; community volunteers will become more helpful with implementing intervention programs; multiple staff development workshops will be developed; and TAPS Teachers will become increasingly more knowledgeable and efficient with their consultative support.

Additional Time Needed for SOPAA Implementation

Although Table 3.4 provides weekly estimates of time needed for SOPAA implementation, it excludes the time needed to implement other features of the model. For example, it excludes the time needed to recruit and train school volunteers, create professional development workshops for classroom teachers, and coordinate schoolwide benchmark assessments in reading and math. As such, Table 3.5 describes all other features of the SOPAA that will require time for implementation and provides comments and suggestions about each of the activities (e.g., recommendations about when to implement each feature during the school year).

Because the activities described in Table 3.5 will require variable amounts of time, we do not provide time estimates for each activity. For example, if a school already uses a system for benchmark assessments in reading and math, the TAPS Teachers will spend much less time facilitating benchmark assessments throughout a school year compared to a school that does not currently use a system for benchmark assessments; in this latter situation, the TAPS Teachers will probably need to spend relatively more time training school staff to administer benchmark assessments. Similarly, different Lead Coordinators will require different amounts of time to prepare for the initial SOPAA meetings with the principal and teachers (discussed in Chapters 9 and 10).

As stated previously, by utilizing a preparation year before Year 1 of SOPAA implementation, the time needed for the activities listed in Table 3.5 can be better dispersed across the preparation year and Year 1 of implementation. Likewise, the options for adaptable and incremental SOPAA implementation mean that the time required for many of the activities listed in Table 3.5 can be dispersed across multiple years, depending on the school's incremental implementation plan. Further, as stated in the table (and discussed in detail in Chapter 11), most of these activities can be completed by more than one SOPAA facilitator, thereby reducing the time commitment of any one educator.

Material Resources Needed for Implementation

In addition to the time needed by the Lead Coordinator and potential co-facilitators, SOPAA implementation will require some material resources. Table 3.6 provides a list of potentially needed materials, a brief rationale for needing those materials, and (when applicable) some suggestions for how to potentially save costs for the given resource. Overall, schools should not need to spend a

TABLE 3.5. Additional Activities Associated with Full-Scale Implementation of the SOPAA

General description of the SOPAA activity and relevant component of the SOPAA	SOPAA role[a]	Notes and comments about the activity
Prepare for initial meetings to discuss the SOPAA with the principal and the introductory presentations for classroom teachers who will use TAPS; Component 5	All SOPAA facilitators, led by the Lead Coordinator	This activity should occur prior to implementing the SOPAA at the beginning of the school year. Meeting with principal in detail about the SOPAA may only need to occur in the first year of implementation. Depending on the incremental nature of implementation, the SOPAA facilitator(s) may need to hold an introductory presentation with teachers each year. See Chapters 9 and 10 for details.
Acquire needed resources for SOPAA implementation; related to all SOPAA components	All SOPAA facilitators, led by the Lead Coordinator	As resources are acquired each year, this activity will be minimized greatly. Chapter 3 describes resources likely needed for SOPAA implementation, and Chapter 9 describes the process of requesting resources from the school principal.
Design and facilitate schoolwide progress monitoring assessment system in reading and math; Component 2	All TAPS Teachers, led by the Lead Coordinator	The time needed for this activity will vary depending on the approach used to facilitate the assessment system, and will require differing levels of time for reading and math. This topic is discussed in detail in Chapter 6.
Prepare and deliver workshops for classroom teachers and others in school; Components 3 and 4	All SOPAA facilitators, led by the Lead Coordinator	This activity should occur one to three times per school year. The focus of these workshops in early stages of SOPAA implementation should be to train teachers to use the evidence-based intervention programs they will likely implement as part of TAPS cases. See Chapter 8 for additional details.
Train educators in the school (e.g., classroom teachers, assistive school personnel, school volunteers) on a case-by-case basis to implement intervention programs; Components 3 and 4	TAPS Teachers and TAPS Support Coordinator	As discussed in Chapter 5, it is not ideal to train teachers on a case-by-case basis, but in some schools, this may sometimes be necessary to do before starting a student's intervention plan. This activity should be minimized with systematic and incremental implementation of the SOPAA.
Recruit and train school volunteers to implement intervention programs; coordinate volunteers' availability; Components 3 and 4	TAPS Support Coordinator, with input from the Lead Coordinator	The time needed for this activity will vary depending on the availability of, and necessity for, school volunteers. Not all schools will include school volunteers as part of implementing students' intervention plans, but many schools will benefit from volunteers' support. This topic is discussed in detail in Chapter 9.
Communicate with teachers to provide reminders and updates regarding the SOPAA implementation; Component 5	Lead Coordinator	As discussed in Chapter 10, the Lead Coordinator will want to remind teachers to request academic support through SOPAA and possibly to update them with midyear data related to the model.
Conduct formal and informal evaluation of the SOPAA to determine its strengths, weaknesses, and needs; Component 5	All SOPAA facilitators, led by the Lead Coordinator	At the end of the school year, the SOPAA facilitators should develop an end-of-year evaluation and summary of the model's strengths, limitations, and needs. This topic is discussed in Chapter 10.

[a] In most cases, the activities described in the table can facilitated by multiple leaders of the SOPAA team (e.g., the Lead Coordinator, the TAPS Support Coordinator). Chapter 11 describes the collaborative work of the SOPAA co-facilitators in detail.

TABLE 3.6. Likely Material Resources Needed to Implement the SOPAA

Type of material resource	Rationale for need	Possible ways to save costs
Intervention programs that will be used as part of TAPS intervention plans	As described in Chapter 3, there are several good reasons for using manualized intervention programs. These programs are an essential component to the TAPS intervention process.	• Through a detailed evaluation of each program (and the available research), determine whether inexpensive programs will be as effective as more expensive programs. From our perspective, of the programs we list in Chapter 12, there appears to be no relationship between quality and cost. We provide multiple options for programs because there are strengths and limitations to each. • If necessary, schools may save costs by targeting academic areas and/or subskills with TAPS incrementally, thereby acquiring only one to three new programs per academic year. • With each program that seems beneficial to the school, determine whether the materials are free to reproduce for multiple teachers.
Academic assessment materials	Low-inference measures that reflect the curriculum and are sensitive to within-year growth at the individual student level are needed to match student needs with interventions, and to evaluate whether the intervention is working for the student.	• Many of the options we provide for assessment are free or inexpensive. Schools may want to begin with the least expensive options and only move to more expensive options if there is a clear advantage (e.g., better match with state achievement standards).
Books and related print materials covering educational best practices and related topics	As part of the SOPAA professional development activities, resource books on topics such as academic instruction, academic assessment, and instruction for English language learners will help TAPS Teachers improve their effectiveness.	• Check with educators in the school to see if they own a needed book or resource and if possible, borrow from that person. • Utilize school or public libraries. • Borrow books from those who may have access to more extensive resource libraries (e.g., colleges and universities). • Buy used versions of books. • Share books (and costs) with teachers within the same school or across other schools in the district.
Conference and workshop attendance for TAPS Teachers	Professional development will sometimes be best facilitated by attending local, state, or national conferences or workshops. Workshops to learn instructional programs may help to improve TAPS Teachers' use and training of those programs.	• Seek out conferences and workshops that are of high quality but lower cost (e.g., attend state conferences instead of national conferences) • Apply for local grants that may support teachers' professional development through conferences and workshops. • Attend only those conferences and workshops that are sure to have a direct impact on SOPAA professional development. • Rotate turns among SOPAA facilitators to attend beneficial conferences.

(cont.)

TABLE 3.6. *(cont.)*

Type of material resource	Rationale for need	Possible ways to save costs
Printing and photocopying needed materials	To facilitate several SOPAA components (e.g., using the TAPS process, hosting professional development workshops), paper materials will be needed.	• Use (or create) electronic versions of materials as long as they do not violate copyright restrictions or compromise functionality and purpose. • Plan carefully to determine exactly how many copies are needed and reuse paper copies of materials when possible (e.g., volunteer recruitment flyers posted in school). • Share paper copies of materials among teachers as long as doing so does not compromise functionality and purpose.

great deal of money on new materials to implement the SOPAA, but implementation will be more effective if key resources are acquired. As described in Chapter 9, when introducing the SOPAA and generating support for it from the school principal, the Lead Coordinator will share information about needed materials.

IMPLEMENTATION READINESS ASSESSMENTS

In an earlier section we offered a rather straightforward and basic approach to considering a multiyear timeline for SOPAA implementation. In this section, we describe how the Lead Coordinator (likely with assistance from co-facilitators) can consider the implementation readiness of her school in more detail. Specifically, after the Lead Coordinator reads the subsequent chapters in this book, generates a more complete understanding of the SOPAA model, and potentially identifies SOPAA co-facilitators (discussed in Chapter 9), the facilitator(s) should review the instructions and questions posed in Appendix B (Schoolwide Capacity Assessment of Relevant Characteristics). As stated in the instructions, the goal of this assessment is *not* to specifically answer each and every question. Instead, the SOPAA facilitators should consider the questions in broad terms, as prompts that should help them think more carefully about characteristics, strengths, and barriers within their school that should be considered prior to initiating SOPAA implementation. By considering the many questions that are embedded within seven primary topics, the SOPAA facilitators should be capable of responding to the 13 rating scale items that appear at the end of the assessment. After completing these items, the team should have a clearer picture about how SOPAA implementation may be launched most effectively and how to provide a rationale for using the SOPAA to other educators in the school. We return to each of these topics in subsequent chapters; we recommend using the schoolwide assessment during implementation conceptualization because the assessment results should strengthen later implementation planning and activities.

A central task in preparing to use the SOPAA is determining the school's implementation readiness.

In addition to completing the Schoolwide Capacity Assessment, each TAPS Teacher identified for initial SOPAA implementation should review the instructions and questions posed in Appendix C (TAPS Support Teacher Self-Assessment of Relevant Characteristics and Experiences). The goal of this self-assessment is to assist all TAPS Teachers in thinking carefully about their own strengths, weaknesses, and overall experiences with triadic consultation. The self-assessment is designed to help each TAPS Teacher consider the types of skills that he or she will need to target and learn (e.g., mastery in more academic intervention programs, more experience using academic progress monitoring) prior to facilitating TAPS cases during SOPAA implementation. Like the Schoolwide Capacity Assessment, the questions in the TAPS Teacher Self-Assessment should be considered broadly (rather than answered in detail) so that each TAPS Teacher can most accurately respond to the 10 likert-scale items at the bottom of the assessment. After each one completes the self-assessment, all TAPS Teachers should meet and discuss their responses.

Last, Appendix D (SOPAA Implementation Planning Summary Checklist) can be used by the SOPAA facilitators to summarize their discussion following the Schoolwide Capacity Assessment and the TAPS Teacher Self-Assessment. As shown, this planning checklist allows the SOPAA facilitators to discuss and establish some consensus about which SOPAA features are likely to be implemented with success during the initial year of implementation. In essence, discussing and completing the checklist should serve as a general guide to help facilitators better determine how to plan and proceed with implementation, as well as to create the most feasible implementation timeline. For example, responses to the checklist may help guide decisions about whether to have a SOPAA preparation year, initiate implementation with only some components, or implement the full model with only a small number of teachers, and how to address the other planning considerations discussed earlier in the section about incremental implementation.

USING THE SOPAA WITH OR WITHOUT OTHER MODELS OF PROBLEM SOLVING, SUCH AS RTI

Recently, whole-school problem-solving models and prevention frameworks, typically containing a multi-tiered approach to addressing children's learning and behavioral needs, have been a focus in education research, policy, and practice. Multi-tiered models, often referred to as RTI, incorporate many of the features of previous problem-solving and school improvement models (e.g., prereferral problem-solving teams, PLCs), but have added a focus on core instruction and sequential decision making as students move up and down a continuum of increasingly intense interventions (Brown-Chidsey & Steege, 2010; Fuchs et al., 2010). Given the current focus on multi-tiered models, readers might wonder whether the SOPAA is compatible with prevention and problem-solving models such as RTI, and if so, how?

The SOPAA is quite consistent with the core principles of RTI, and there are several possible ways that the SOPAA can align with RTI, ranging from using the SOPAA model's incremental approach to school change as a means to moving a school to RTI, to using the TAPS process as one tier of problem solving in an existing RTI model. We elaborate on these points below, starting with a very brief overview of RTI.

There is no unitary RTI model. Instead, there are multiple models with important commonalities and differences (Fuchs et al., 2010). Commonalities in all RTI models are a focus on improving core (or Tier 1) instruction, more intense services when students encounter difficulty in core instruction, a focus on evidence-based instruction and treatment integrity, universal screening, and data-based decision making (Batsche et al., 2005). Models differ in (1) the number of tiers (some models have three, some have four); (2) whether both academic and behavioral concerns are addressed in the model (sometimes only academic concerns are addressed); (3) whether special education is a tier in the RTI model or separate from it; and (4) the use of individualized versus standard protocol approaches to developing interventions after the first tier.

For a school that does not have an RTI model in place and has no plans to move in that direction, the SOPAA, and in particular the TAPS process, is meant to help the school improve the problem-solving process that is already in place to address student learning difficulties. For example, as stated in Chapter 2, many schools have an existing prereferral or student assistance process wherein educators design and implement an instructional intervention in general education. One of the purposes of this problem-solving process is to confirm that a student's educational difficulty cannot be solved with a brief but high-quality instructional intervention before the student is assessed for possible special education placement. However, in our experience, this prereferral problem solving at individual schools often is not implemented as was intended by policymakers. The interventions and the documentation to support their implementation are usually weak, as is any impact on student outcomes. Our perception has been confirmed by others (e.g., Doll et al., 2005; Flugum & Reschley, 1994). The TAPS process is meant to assist educators in strengthening this problem-solving process, but also making it more efficient by providing structure, standardization, and professional development to support the process.

For schools that are contemplating moving to an RTI approach, the SOPAA offers a means to begin systematically and incrementally changing from current school problem-solving structures to the broad outlines of an RTI model. For instance, if the SOPAA were fully implemented at school, then strong core instruction in reading and mathematics would be in place, universal screening would be under way, and there would be a range of standardized interventions for students who were not responding to core instruction. There would also be a process in place for assuring that these standardized interventions were implemented with integrity and a process for documenting students' responses to intervention. These components would constitute the first tier of RTI, core instruction, and a second tier of specialized interventions for students who are not making sufficient progress when provided only with core instruction. For RTI models in which there are three tiers of intervention (exclusive of special education), converting to a three-tier model would likely involve examining the interventions available through TAPS, differentiating them into second- and third-tier interventions, and likely adding interventions to assure a full range of interventions at the second and third tiers. Second-tier interventions would typically consist of standardized group-based or brief one-on-one interventions administered by a range of personnel, including volunteers. Third-tier interventions would consist of TAPS interventions that were more intensive, more individually tailored, and typically provided only by a teacher. Therefore, beginning RTI implementation after experience with SOPAA would likely smooth the transition to RTI, as universal screening would already be in place and school staff would have experience with both progress monitoring and interventions. With the transition from SOPAA to RTI, placement of students into interventions at the second tier could begin to be based on decision rules (e.g., using scores on the universal screening instruments), and second-tier intervention plans would likely be well developed and implemented properly, based on teachers' earlier experience with TAPS and SOPAA professional development activities. With teacher-led development and implementation of Tier 2 interventions (i.e., the TAPS Teacher would not need to be involved or only minimally involved), the TAPS process, with its individualized approach to problem solving and teacher consultation, could then begin to take place primarily at the third tier.

Finally, for schools with RTI currently in place and no prior experience with the SOPAA, adding components of the SOPAA may be helpful in assuring that the RTI process runs more smoothly. For example, the recruitment and training of community-based volunteers would likely increase the number of second-tier interventions available, or free up educators to conduct complex interventions for which trained volunteers are not appropriate and credentialed teachers or specialists are required. Also, developing and documenting interventions may be more systematic and time-efficient through using the TAPS process, and clear documentation would provide a means of evaluating the efficacy of all interventions developed and implemented. Further, targeted professional development activities and TAPS Teachers' ongoing professional development might better facilitate the intervention and assessment practices embedded within the RTI model. Finally, the SOPAA includes a structured system of evaluating the TAPS problem-solving process and communicating with teachers about the effectiveness and potential changes in that process, which is not always explicit within an RTI model.

Collectively, the SOPAA model shares characteristics of other problem-solving models, such as RTI, but SOPAA implementation can be used concurrently with a model such as RTI because it may improve the efficiency, documentation, and evaluation of the interventions implemented with struggling learners. In schools without an RTI model, the SOPAA can also be used and in some cases may help schools move toward it.

STEP-BY-STEP SUGGESTIONS FOR USING THIS BOOK TO IMPLEMENT THE SOPAA

To conclude this chapter we list a step-by-step framework for using this book. Some educators may find that SOPAA implementation will be successfully carried out using a slightly different sequence than the one listed below, but in most cases the following sequence should move readers from first exposure to this book through actual implementation. The specific steps are also provided because the interrelated SOPAA components described throughout this book cannot be presented in a perfectly linear way; therefore, a more linear representation of SOPAA implementation may be useful to some readers.

1. Read this book to acquire a primary understanding of the model and the resources provided within the book. *Note:* It will be impossible to read all chapters of this book and then successfully implement the SOPAA without ever returning to the book for recommendations and resources. As such, the goal of the first read of this book should be to gain a full understanding of the SOPAA model and to know which resources are available to assist with implementation, including the companion website *www.sopaaforschools.org*.

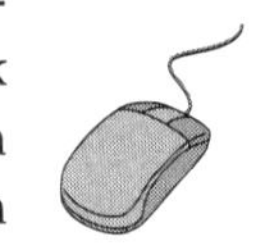

2. If appropriate, and using Chapters 9 and 11 for guidance, generate potential interest from a small number of other educators within the school who may be able to serve as SOPAA co-facilitators.
3. Read Chapter 3 again and complete The Schoolwide Capacity Assessment, the TAPS Teacher Self-Assessment, and the Intervention Planning Summary Checklist.
4. With the SOPAA facilitators, generate a basic plan for how implementation might occur and prepare to discuss the plan with the school principal, if this has not been done earlier.
5. Communicate ideas with the principal in order to develop an implementation and evaluation plan and ensure that implementation time and resources can be acquired (use Chapter 9, in particular, for guidance).
6. As needed and determined by the implementation timeline, facilitate a SOPAA preparation year (use Chapter 3, in particular, for guidance).
7. At the beginning of Year 1 of implementation, introduce the SOPAA to the teachers in the school who will be involved with implementation that year (use Chapter 10, in particular, for guidance).
8. Using this entire book for guidance and resources, implement the SOPAA as dictated by the Year 1 implementation plan that was developed, and using guidance from Chapter 10, evaluate SOPAA implementation at specified times during the year.

9. Using the SOPAA implementation plan that was developed, yearly program evaluation data to guide effectiveness and possible modifications of the plan, and this book as a regular resource, maintain and incrementally increase SOPAA implementation during subsequent school years.

SUMMARY

SOPAA facilitators must consider several factors as part of implementation planning and organization. Specifically, prior to initiating SOPAA implementation, the following questions must be adequately addressed:

- What evidence-based intervention programs does the school have available (or need) to facilitate TAPS cases?
- What is a reasonable timeline for implementing the SOPAA and is there a need for a preparation year?
- What time and material resources are needed for successful implementation?
- What are the strengths and barriers within the school that should influence implementation?
- If the school currently uses a model of instructional problem solving, how can the SOPAA model be used in concert with the existing model?

To further support implementation planning and organization, we concluded this chapter with a summary of step-by-step implementation suggestions that SOPAA facilitators can use as a guide to both using this book and implementing the model.

PART II

THE SIX SOPAA COMPONENTS

CHAPTER 4

Initial Steps of the TAPS Process

Requests for Academic Support and Preparation for the Intervention Planning Meeting

Component 1 of the SOPAA is TAPS, designed to be a systematic and time-efficient process for prescriptive, instructional problem solving and triadic consultation. This chapter describes the initial steps of the TAPS process. Specifically, we discuss how classroom teachers request academic support from a TAPS Teacher, as well as the rationale for this process. We also describe how the TAPS Teacher and classroom teacher should prepare for the intervention planning meeting, which follows a request for academic support and serves as the meeting to develop a student's TAPS intervention plan. For brevity, we henceforth refer to classroom teachers as *teachers*.

REQUESTING ACADEMIC SUPPORT

To initiate the TAPS process, a teacher identifies a student with a learning difficulty and determines the primary academic area with which the student needs assistance (i.e., reading, math, or writing). The teacher then completes a Request for TAPS Form (Appendix E, described below) and submits the form to the specific TAPS Teacher who supports the respective academic area. For example, if a student is identified with difficulties in math, the teacher submits the Request for TAPS Form to the TAPS Math Teacher; if a student is identified with difficulties in reading, the teacher submits the request form to the TAPS Reading Teacher.

Figure 4.1 shows an example of a completed Request for TAPS Form. Reviewing the example should illustrate how the form is used and the information that should be included. We encourage the reader to photocopy Appendix E in order to have the Request for TAPS Form easily viewable while reading the remaining portion of this chapter and others. Also, for teachers and TAPS Teachers who prefer to use an electronic version of the Request for TAPS Form, the companion website *www.sopaaforschools.org* offers a downloadable electronic version so that teachers can type information directly into the form.

Teacher's Name: J. Metcalfe Student's Name: Stuart Dent Student's Grade: 3rd Date: 10/11/13

(1) Describe your primary concern as specifically as possible. For example, if you have concerns about reading, specify the reading skill(s) (e.g., phonics, fluency, comprehension) the student struggles with most.

Stuart's reading skills are far below average for his grade. During class read-alouds Stuart reads slowly, and when he reads independently he struggles with comprehension. It seems to me he struggles most with fluency and comprehension.

(2) How long have you had the primary concern?
Since the beginning of the school year. I talked with Stuart's 2nd-grade teacher from last year and she thought he might show more progress after the first couple weeks of school, but he continues to struggle and I want to get him proper assistance soon.

(3) Briefly describe and/or attach evidence that supports your primary concern. For example, you may want to write down classroom observations, student grades/progress reports, scores from relevant assessments, and/or attach relevant documents such as assessment forms or student work samples.

I am not attaching any reading assessments because I have not formally assessed his fluency or comprehension. However, as noted above, I have observed him reading slowly and not being able to answer comprehension questions. I have some worksheets in which he is asked to answer comprehension questions, but his answers are not reflective of his independent abilities because my teacher assistant (TA) has been working with him to answer comprehension questions.

(4) If applicable, briefly describe strategies that have been used to address your primary concern.

I have identified reading books that are below a 3rd-grade level and have asked Stuart to read these books during independent reading times. I have also had my TA work with him on comprehension activities and worksheets. I know he needs more practice reading, but I am not sure how to incorporate practice strategies into his everyday instruction.

(5) If you responded to item 4, how successful were those strategies (e.g., what were strengths and/or weaknesses of the strategies used)? If applicable, attach relevant documents such as assessment forms or student work samples that help to show the effects of the strategies used.

I don't see any improvements in Stuart's reading skills based on these strategies. However, he does like reading with my TA.

Note: if you are submitting this referral electronically, please check one of the boxes below:

☐ I am also submitting hard copies of evidence (e.g., assessment forms, work samples) to support Items 3 and/or 5.

☑ I am NOT submitting hard copies of evidence (e.g., assessment forms, work samples) to support Items 3 and/or 5.

(6) Describe any secondary concerns that may be related to your primary concern (e.g., student behavior, motivation, related academic skill deficits).

Stuart is a very quiet and sweet little boy. He tries very hard with all of his academic skills, but I know he is embarrassed about not being able to read well. As a result, sometimes he tries to leave the classroom (such as asking to use the bathroom) when students are asked to read aloud.

(7) Provide any additional information that may be relevant to your concerns. For example, are there factors that may complicate intervention development or implementation (e.g., English language learner, scheduling logistics, behavioral concerns, presence of a medical condition, frequent student absences)?

None

(8) Specify the student's strengths (academic and/or other).

Stuart is kind and tries very hard. I think he feels very good when he is successful and adults tell him he is doing a good job. Although he is quiet, he has many friends in the class and generally gets along well with everyone.

(cont.)

FIGURE 4.1. Sample Request for TAPS (Targeted Assistance Program for Students) Form.

(9) Based on the information described in Item 1, are there other students in your class who exhibit the same types of academic difficulties at approximately the same level of severity? If so, write the name(s) of the student(s) and provide any additional information about the other student(s) if you would like.

There are two other students in the class who struggle with reading, but they are not struggling as much as Stuart, and unlike Stuart, one of the students seems to have the skills but because of behavior does not always try to do his best.

(10) Indicate days and times you are generally available and can meet for a 20- to 30-minute intervention planning meeting. This meeting will likely be scheduled 1–3 weeks from today's date.

I am happy to meet any day during my planning period (10:00–10:45) or after school on T, W, or TH.

(11) Indicate days and times during the next two weeks that the TAPS Teacher can meet briefly (5–20 minutes) with the student. When possible, the Support Teacher will conduct a brief observation and/or assessment of the student before meeting with you for the intervention planning meeting.

It would be best to meet with Stuart in the morning during our language arts period (8:15–10:00). You may also be able to meet with him before school on T or W because his father drops him off early those days.

FIGURE 4.1. *(cont.)*

How Classroom Teachers Should Request Support

All teachers will first be exposed to the request process (and the items on the Request for TAPS Form) during the Lead Coordinator's introductory presentation of the SOPAA to teachers (discussed in Chapter 10). Without knowing the details of the process before requesting support, teachers are unlikely to provide the information the TAPS Teacher will need to most effectively prepare for the intervention planning meeting. In addition, teachers may become frustrated with completing the Request for TAPS Form if they do not know (1) the type of information they should include, (2) the amount of detail they should provide, and (3) the time it will take to complete the form (typically 15–20 minutes). Chapter 10 describes when and how to explain the Request for TAPS Form to teachers.

Information That Should Be Provided in the Request for Academic Support

The Request for TAPS Form specifies all information the teacher should provide for the TAPS Teacher. Each item on the form is designated with a number (1–11) and asks teachers to provide the needed information. Although the items on the form are relatively straightforward, Table 4.1 offers explanation and details about some items, as well as some suggestions for TAPS Teachers who interpret teacher responses on the request form. The suggestions for teachers outlined in Table 4.1 should be shared with teachers during the introductory SOPAA presentation so that they are more likely to provide thorough and accurate information when they eventually do need to use the request form. For further guidance in understanding the Request for TAPS Form, recall that Figure 4.1 shows an example of a completed request form.

In many cases the Request for TAPS Form will be completed only by the classroom teacher. However, teachers should also be encouraged to seek and incorporate input from any teacher assistant who works regularly with the target student. For example, in classrooms where a teacher assistant works daily with the target student (e.g., assists the student with independent seatwork, works with the student in small-group instruction), the teacher assistant may meaningfully add to the classroom teacher's responses on the Request for TAPS Form (e.g., helping to describe secondary concerns and the student's strengths). In addition to possibly providing the classroom teacher

TABLE 4.1. Request for TAPS Form Explanations and Suggestions for TAPS Teachers

Request for TAPS Form Item No.	Suggestions for teachers when completing the item	Suggestions for TAPS Teachers when interpreting teacher responses to the item
1	The teacher should carefully consider each of the subskills in the academic area (as described in Chapter 12) and specify the skill(s) with which the student struggles the most.	Examine the teacher's comments in collaboration with data provided by him or her. The student's primary skill deficit should also become clear during the brief student observation.
2	The teacher should specify approximately when he or she *first* noticed the student's academic difficulty.	Understanding the approximate amount of time the student struggled could influence both assessment and intervention planning (e.g., intervention intensity might be greater if the student was clearly having difficulty for a long time).
3	The teacher should be encouraged to describe and submit as much *relevant* information as possible, but not so much information that the concern is less clear to the TAPS Teacher. During the SOPAA introductory presentation with teachers, the presenter should describe good examples and nonexamples of information to share.	All information presented by the teacher should be considered, but the most objective forms of evidence will likely provide the best information for understanding the student's primary deficit.
4	No suggestions.	No suggestions.
5	No suggestions.	Even if a teacher indicates that he or she tried a particular strategy and it did not work, this should not automatically preclude using the strategy as part of the intervention plan. Sometimes a strategy could be effective, but may need to be implemented more often or as one part of a more comprehensive intervention.
6	The teacher should indicate *any* additional concern that may influence the primary concern.	When considering intervention options, also consider how the additional concerns might impact intervention effectiveness and/or might also be targeted through the intervention plan. For example, if the teacher reports that the student has low levels of confidence, the intervention plan should integrate components such as high levels of specific praise and feedback for successes.
7	The teacher should indicate *all* additional information that may influence the primary concern.	Similar to interpreting information in Item 6, consider how the additional information might impact intervention effectiveness and/or might also be targeted through the intervention plan
8	The teacher should indicate at least one to three student strengths, particularly if they may have some relevance to intervention planning (e.g., the student works very hard for a particular teacher, likes to be a classroom leader).	Similar to interpreting information in Items 6 and 7, consider how information about student strengths might influence intervention planning.

(cont.)

TABLE 4.1. *(cont.)*

Request for TAPS Form Item No.	Suggestions for teachers when completing the item	Suggestions for TAPS Teachers when interpreting teacher responses to the item
9	The teacher should be encouraged to think about this item in terms of identifying whether a small-group intervention might be used with multiple students, including the target student.	Consider possible small-group (or even whole-class) interventions when a teacher identifies multiple students with the same difficulties. It is beyond the scope of this book to describe small-group interventions, but some of the interventions listed in Chapter 12 can be implemented with small groups, if needed.
10	No suggestions.	No suggestions.
11	No suggestions.	No suggestions.

with meaningful information to include on the Request for TAPS Form, involving the teacher assistant during the early stages of the TAPS process is important because it is likely he or she will be involved with the target student's intervention plan (as discussed in Chapters 5 and 7).

When Classroom Teachers Should Request Support

Teachers should request academic support when they (1) have a concern that a specific student is not performing at grade level in an academic area; (2) have at least some evidence (e.g., classroom assessment data, schoolwide assessment data, student work samples) indicating that the student is performing below grade level; and (3) would likely benefit from intervention planning assistance (from the TAPS Teacher) and/or assistance with intervention implementation (e.g., the TAPS Teacher can assist with finding others in the school to help implement the intervention by monitoring the student's progress during intervention and monitoring implementation integrity).

The best time for teachers to request TAPS support varies depending on school or teacher preferences, teachers' experiences with successfully addressing student learning difficulties through intervention, and many related factors. For example, teachers might be encouraged to request TAPS support (1) immediately upon recognizing that a student is struggling academically; (2) following a certain period of time (e.g., 2–4 weeks) after first recognizing the student's deficit, which may help the teacher better understand how (or if, in fact) the student is struggling academically; or (3) after the teacher spends a certain period of time (e.g., 2–4 weeks) trying to address the skill deficit without assistance from the TAPS Teacher.

Although the exact timing and circumstances in which a teacher should request TAPS support will vary depending on the school, we suggest the following three guidelines to better ensure that students' academic difficulties are appropriately addressed as early as possible.

- First, during at least the first 2 years of SOPAA implementation, teachers should be encouraged to request support immediately upon recognizing (and having at least some evidence to support) that a student is struggling academically. After 2 or more years of being involved with the TAPS process and the associated professional development workshops discussed in Chapter 7, teachers may have acquired the needed skills for addressing student learning difficulties and monitoring intervention effectiveness without the assistance of a TAPS Teacher. At that point, if the Lead Coordinator feels confident that teachers can successfully intervene without support from a

TAPS Teacher, teachers might be encouraged to request TAPS support only after they have implemented an intervention for 2–4 weeks and find that their concerns about the student remain.

• Second, the expectation for teachers to request TAPS support should be consistent across all teachers who are eligible to request this support, particularly in the first 2 years of SOPAA implementation. This consistency will better ensure an effective, clear, and efficient TAPS process. Also, if all teachers are expected to request support under the same circumstances and timing, teachers throughout the school should feel a better sense of equity with the TAPS request expectations. In contrast, if some teachers are encouraged to request support immediately, and some are encouraged to intervene for a period of time before requesting support, teachers encouraged to request support immediately may perceive this as an implicit indicator that they are less trusted or competent with their academic intervention and assessment skills.

• Third, after multiple years of SOPAA implementation and when the Lead Coordinator finally encourages teachers to implement academic assessment and intervention prior to seeking TAPS support, teachers should also be encouraged to (1) request support more immediately if they feel it would be beneficial; and (2) make brief contact with the respective TAPS Teacher to inform her about the key aspects of the intervention plan (e.g., which intervention is being implemented, why, with which student, how often, who is implementing it, and how intervention effects are being monitored). By having the teacher inform the TAPS Teacher about the teacher-developed intervention plan, the TAPS Teacher can still stay abreast of academic interventions being implemented in the school and, as needed, check with teachers periodically to discuss intervention effectiveness and the possible need to support teachers with implementation. To facilitate this process, the Lead Coordinator may create a simple form teachers can use to share information about the intervention being implemented. Using such a form would also help the school maintain documentation of all academic interventions being implemented.

The TAPS request for support process is designed to gather and document, in the most time-efficient way, all the key information needed for intervention planning.

THE TAPS SUPPORT TEACHER'S PREPARATION FOR THE INTERVENTION PLANNING MEETING

As stated previously, after the teacher requests academic support from the TAPS Teacher, an intervention planning meeting will occur between the two teachers in order to develop an intervention plan for the student. However, before this planning meeting occurs, the TAPS Teacher must do several things to prepare for the meeting. This section of the chapter describes these preparation activities.

After the TAPS Teacher receives and reviews the completed Request for TAPS Form from the teacher, she should develop a TAPS file folder for the target student. This folder should contain all paper copies of information collected for that student throughout the TAPS process. Also, Appendix F (TAPS Case Tracking Form) could be stapled to the inside cover of the folder and used by the TAPS Teacher to track the occurrence of each step in the TAPS process. Next, the TAPS Teacher should complete the following steps, as numbered:

1. Conduct a targeted skills observation with the student.
2. Develop a list of potential intervention options that will target the teacher's primary concern (if multiple options are available).

3. Share the list of intervention options with the teacher before the intervention planning meeting.
4. Prepare a list of clarification questions to pose during the intervention planning meeting.
5. Begin thinking about how to develop and facilitate the student's intervention plan.

Each of the five steps is described below.

Conduct a Targeted Skills Observation

In order for the TAPS Teacher to feel reasonably confident that the teacher's primary concern (i.e., the concern reported in Item 1 of the Request for TAPS Form) is, in fact, the student's primary difficulty, the TAPS Teacher should conduct a 5- to 20-minute targeted skills observation. Coordinating a time for this observation is facilitated by the information provided by the teacher about availability in Item 11 of the Request for TAPS Form.

By a *targeted* observation we mean that the TAPS Teacher should observe the specific and related skills identified by the teacher as the primary concern. Completing this skills observation can take two basic forms. First, if the TAPS Teacher received clear and detailed supporting evidence from the teacher to document the primary concern, he or she may simply complete a brief, informal observation or assessment of the child performing the skills associated with the primary concern. For example, if the teacher's primary concern is the child's phonics skills, the TAPS Teacher may simply have the student read grade-appropriate text aloud and listen carefully for the student's decoding skills. If the teacher's concern is with spelling and grammar usage, he or she may simply ask the student to write a story for 3–5 minutes and observe as the student writes the story. In both cases, quickly and informally observing the student's work and skill level should help the TAPS Teacher better understand the student's ability level, strengths, weaknesses, academic motivation, and related characteristics.

Through a brief targeted skills observation, the TAPS Teacher better ensures that the process results in an intervention plan that will be most appropriate for the student.

The other approach to a targeted skills observation is to have the TAPS Teacher conduct a brief but more formalized assessment of the student engaging in all skills related to the teacher's primary concern. For example, if the teacher reports a primary concern with a sixth-grade student's reading comprehension, the TAPS Teacher could use one of the brief reading comprehension assessments described in Chapter 6, as well as one or more other measures to determine whether comprehension deficits may actually result from skill deficits in more basic areas of reading (e.g., decoding or text reading fluency). Of course, in this example, if the student shows significant deficits in decoding, intervention planning would likely start by addressing decoding rather than comprehension. Chapter 6 describes some brief assessments that might be used during the targeted skills observation.

Another goal of the targeted skills observation is to obtain a brief but psychometrically sound baseline measure of a student's academic functioning so that the impact of the intervention can be assessed later. For example, as described in Chapter 6, the TAPS Teacher could administer three curriculum-based measurement probes in an academic area and then use the median score as an estimate of the student's level of academic functioning before any intervention. In schools that have universal screening programs in place, a baseline level of performance for the student may already be available when the teacher submits the Request for TAPS Form, and provided the skills that need to be targeted are clear, the TAPS Teacher would not need to conduct any additional assessments during the targeted skills observation. As is described in Chapter 6, this same type of assessment will also be completed at the very end of the student's intervention plan (i.e., several weeks later), which allows for one method of evaluating the student's academic skill before and after intervention.

Overall, given the TAPS Teacher's level of expertise in her specific academic area, a brief but targeted assessment, whether formal or informal, should help her achieve four primary goals: (1) confirm and/or better understand the student's primary skill deficit; (2) obtain additional information about the child's strengths and weaknesses; (3) obtain a brief but formal assessment of the student's skill level as a "preintervention" evaluation if such data do not already exist; and (4) interact with the child, which should benefit the upcoming intervention planning meeting with the teacher. Of course, prior to receiving the teacher's Request for TAPS Form, if the TAPS Teacher already has experience with and data about the student, she can skip the targeted skills observation and explain to the teacher that this step in the TAPS process is not needed. Again, the primary purpose of the targeted skills observation is for the TAPS Teacher to feel confident that the teacher's primary concern is truly the student's primary difficulty and to ascertain formal data about the student's performance prior to implementing the intervention.

Last, it is important to highlight that, although improbable, it is possible that the teacher's primary concern may be addressed with an instructional modification that is easier to implement than the types of intervention plans typically developed through the TAPS process. For example, by conducting a brief observation and/or assessment of the student, the TAPS Teacher may realize that the student's perceived reading difficulties are primarily a result of visual impairments or perhaps an inability to understand the directions of language arts assignments. In this case, intervention planning would be different than the type of planning for a student who has difficulties due solely to reading skill deficits.

Develop Intervention Options

After reviewing the information on the Request for TAPS Form and completing a skills observation with the student, the TAPS Teacher should next develop a short list of no more than two to four potential intervention options that will target the student's specific academic deficit. For example, if the student is primarily struggling with phonics skills, TAPS Teachers should develop a short list of evidence-based intervention programs that are available in the school and that specifically target phonics instruction. Chapter 12 of this book provides a list and description of possible interventions to target deficits in the various subskills in each academic area. Although the list of interventions in Chapter 12 is not exhaustive, it should assist TAPS Teachers with selecting evidence-based interventions that target specific academic deficits. In addition to using the tables of intervention programs summarized in Chapter 12, the TAPS Teacher should also consider other interventions the school has successfully used to address the targeted academic deficit.

When a teacher expresses multiple academic concerns about a student within the same general area (e.g., math fact computations and word-based problem solving), and the TAPS Teacher observes those same deficits, the TAPS Teacher should consider intervention options that might address more than one skill deficit. In other words, if there are evidence-based intervention programs available in the school that can target multiple skills, these programs may be preferable to interventions that target only one or a smaller set of skills. However, in many cases targeting the primary deficit (e.g., math-fact computational fluency) will often improve students' performance in related academic areas (e.g., word-based problem solving). Therefore, targeting one primary subskill deficit can be quite beneficial in helping the student improve with other skills. Chapters 6 and 12 of this book provide additional information about assessment and intervention, which should assist the TAPS Teacher with using assessment to determine the most suitable options for intervention.

It is also important to highlight two additional aspects of developing intervention options. First, the selected intervention options should be familiar to the TAPS Teacher, and ideally she should have at least some experience implementing each program. In essence, she should know the strengths and possible weaknesses of the proposed intervention programs and should be familiar enough with each program to describe it for the teacher during the intervention planning meeting. Increasing each TAPS Teacher's knowledge of intervention programs is a central topic of Chapter 7 and is described as part of her need for ongoing professional development.

Second, many schools will not have access to (or teachers trained to implement) more than one intervention program to target the student's specific skill deficit (e.g., phonics). In this situation, until teachers have training in, and access to, various intervention options to target the skill, the "list" of intervention options may simply reflect the one intervention program available within the school. The availability of only one option for an intervention program is acceptable as long as the intervention program has been effective for other students in the school and teachers are willing to use the program. A program that is not effective or is considered unacceptable by teachers indicates to the TAPS Teacher that additional intervention options are needed within the school to target the specific skill.

In conclusion, the TAPS Teacher should develop a short list of intervention programs that (1) should target the student's specific academic deficit (e.g., phonics, vocabulary); (2) have evidence of effectiveness within the school and/or in the research literature, such as those described in Chapter 12; and (3) are familiar to the TAPS Teacher. The classroom teacher, and possibly assistive school personnel, should also be familiar with the selected intervention program options; but when they are not, Chapter 5 offers ways to address this scenario.

Share Intervention Options with the Teacher

Once the TAPS Teacher develops a list of possible intervention options that should address the teacher's target concern, he or she should share the list with the teacher (e.g., through e-mail or a note in the teacher's school mailbox). Ideally, the list should be shared at least 5–7 days before the intervention planning meeting. The following text represents a template the TAPS Teacher might use to communicate with the teacher about the list of intervention options.

> Dear [**insert teacher's name**].
>
> Based on the information that you provided on the Request for TAPS Form and the information I obtained from my targeted observation, I believe the following intervention programs will be most likely to improve [**insert student's name**] difficulties with [**insert primary target concern; e.g., phonics**]:
>
> [**List the intervention programs identified and provide a one- to three-sentence description of each listed program.** ***Chapter 12 provides brief descriptions that can be used.***]
>
> On [**insert <u>day</u>, <u>date</u>, and <u>time</u> of the intervention planning meeting, *which should correspond with the teacher's response to Item 9 of the Request for TAPS form***], we will discuss the above intervention programs to determine which would be best for [**insert student's name**]. Before our meeting, if time permits in your schedule, I encourage you to review the above intervention programs. Program materials for each intervention are located in [**insert location where intervention programs are kept; e.g., the school's resource library or a specific teacher's classroom. Also,**

the TAPS Teacher might specify an Internet address that provides brief, online descriptions of each program]. Also, if you have ideas for intervention options I did not specify above, please let me know before our intervention planning meeting, or we can simply discuss your ideas during the meeting.

I look forward to working with you in an effort to improve [**insert student's name**] [**insert target concern; e.g., phonics**].

Sincerely, [**insert TAPS Teacher's name**]

There are four main reasons for sharing the list of intervention options and using the above form of communication with the teacher. First, it demonstrates (and documents) that the TAPS Teacher started assisting the teacher through the TAPS process. Second, it allows the teacher to know which intervention programs will be discussed during the upcoming intervention planning meeting, and that one of those programs will likely be selected as part of the student's intervention plan. As such, the teacher will also have time (if desired and possible) to examine the intervention programs on the list and begin thinking about which intervention program is best suited to the student and his or her difficulty. Third, the correspondence reiterates to the teacher that her ideas for intervention options are welcome and will be considered, in addition to the intervention programs listed by the TAPS Teacher. Fourth, it reminds (or informs) the teacher about the day, date, and time of the intervention planning meeting. If the TAPS Teacher has only one suitable option for an intervention program, she should still inform the teacher about that option and encourage the teacher to recommend other options, if possible.

Prepare Clarification Questions

Based on the information obtained from the Request for TAPS Form and the targeted skills observation, the next step in preparing for the intervention planning meeting is for the TAPS Teacher to develop a list of possible clarification questions she will pose at the beginning of that meeting. Depending on the information obtained by the TAPS Teacher thus far, the type of academic referral made (reading, math, or writing), and the specificity of the teacher's concern, the TAPS Teacher may benefit by asking questions about some or all of the subskills within the academic area, the answers to which should ultimately help to confirm or elucidate the student's academic difficulty. We describe academic subskills in Chapter 12, and the information in that chapter may help the TAPS Teacher develop possible clarification questions.

For example, if the teacher's primary concern about a student is in the area of reading, and the specific concern is with vocabulary, the TAPS Teacher may wish to ask the teacher whether she has similar, lesser, or greater concerns in the other key areas of reading (i.e., phonics, fluency, comprehension, and spelling). Asking the teacher for evidence to support her response to the questions may also be worthwhile. For instance, the teacher may indicate that she does not have concerns about phonics because student work samples indicate phonics skills that are average or above average. Of course, teacher responses to clarification questions should be interpreted in light of the targeted skills observation and other forms of data available to the TAPS Teacher. Again, the goal of posing these questions during the intervention planning meeting (if needed) is to confirm or clarify the student's academic deficits and improve the likelihood of developing a targeted and effective intervention plan.

The TAPS Teacher may wish to ask the teacher questions about two additional areas to better understand the extent of the student's difficulty and the options for intervention: (1) the extent to which this difficulty is a classwide problem, and (2) the potential for a home–school collaborative intervention. Regarding the classwide question, if there are multiple students in the class who struggle with the specified area of concern, a classwide or small-group intervention may be appropriate and more time-efficient. This follow-up question is particularly relevant if the teacher identifies students with similar difficulties on Item 9 of the Request for TAPS Form.

With respect to a home–school collaborative intervention, obtaining background about the student's parents may lead to strengthening the school-based intervention by linking it with a home-based component (e.g., having parents reward student progress made in school and/or ensure that the student practices the target skill deficit at home). For example, the TAPS Teacher might ask the teacher (1) Do you have a good relationship with the student's parent(s)?; (2) How regularly are you in contact with the student's parent(s)?; (3) Have the parents ever assisted with a school-based intervention by supporting it at home (and if so, how)?; and (4) Have the parents expressed any concerns about the student's academic skills? In short, with background about the student's parents and their communication with the teacher, it may be possible to strengthen the school-based intervention by including a home-based component.

Begin Thinking about How to Develop and Facilitate the Intervention Plan

In Chapter 5, we introduce the TAPS Intervention Planning Form, which is completed during the intervention planning meeting and serves as the primary tool for developing and documenting the student's intervention plan. In this section, we simply point out that the final step in preparing for the intervention planning meeting is to begin considering how the student's intervention plan could be developed and facilitated. By considering these points before the planning meeting, the amount of time and discussion needed should significantly decrease.

The following list of questions presents the items the TAPS Teacher should consider prior to entering the intervention planning meeting (these same items appear on the TAPS Intervention Planning Form described in Chapter 5).

1. Who will implement the intervention program (e.g., the classroom teacher, a teacher assistant, a school volunteer)?
2. How will intervention implementers get trained, or are they already trained?
3. Where will the intervention be implemented and at what time(s) of day?
4. On what date should implementation begin and what days per week will the intervention occur?
5. How will implementation integrity be evaluated, by whom, and when?
6. How will the student's progress be monitored (e.g., with what form of assessment, how often, by whom)?
7. How many full intervention sessions should be implemented before the TAPS Summative Review of Intervention Effectiveness is conducted, and by what date should all sessions be implemented?
8. What is a realistic and objective goal the student should meet as a result of intervention (e.g., improve oral reading fluency to 120 words correct per minute on grade-level text)?
9. How will periodic "follow-ups" of intervention success occur (e.g., who will initiate them, approximately how often)? (Note: Periodic follow-ups are discussed in Chapter 5.)

By considering these questions and recording possible responses to them prior to the intervention planning meeting, the TAPS Teacher will more efficiently and effectively facilitate the meeting. This is not to suggest that the TAPS Teacher's responses to each question will constitute the final intervention plan. Each of the questions should be discussed with the teacher during the planning meeting, and a collectively agreed-upon response to each question should constitute the final intervention plan. However, because of the TAPS Teacher's experience with assisting other teachers, as well as her knowledge of the intervention program options, appropriate assessment methods, procedures for monitoring implementation integrity, and personnel resources within the school, the TAPS Teacher should begin considering responses to the questions because the planning meeting will otherwise be much too long and potentially inconclusive. For example, during the planning meeting both teachers must agree when the intervention plan should begin, but the TAPS Teacher should have an idea about appropriate dates for initiating the plan because a start date should take into consideration the type of intervention program being implemented, the number of sessions likely needed for the student to improve, and related information the classroom teacher may not be able to fully consider.

Related to the first question (Who will implement the intervention program?), prior to the intervention planning meeting the TAPS Teacher will also need to access information from the TAPS Support Coordinator about school volunteers or assistive school personnel who can potentially help implement the possible intervention programs. However, we describe how the TAPS Teacher and TAPS Support Coordinator correspond about this topic in Chapter 5, because that chapter provides greater detail about facilitating the intervention planning meeting and the role of the TAPS Support Coordinator.

RATIONALE FOR THE TAPS REQUEST FOR SUPPORT PROCESS

The rationale for the TAPS request for support process—including the TAPS Teacher's preparation activities after receiving a request for support—is that it offers a time- and resource-efficient process for (1) documenting a teacher's primary academic concern about a student, (2) facilitating clear communication about the concern with an expert consultant (i.e., the TAPS Teacher), (3) initiating a series of activities the TAPS Teacher can follow to confirm and clarify the teacher's concern, and (4) aggregating the most relevant information needed to develop an academic intervention plan for the target student. There are, of course, many approaches and strategies that can be used to collect information about a student needing academic assistance (e.g., one-on-one problem identification interviews with the teacher, extensive assessment of the student's academic skills, team meetings to discuss the student's strengths and weaknesses), but the TAPS request for support process is designed to gather all the needed information for intervention planning in what should be the most time-efficient way.

The TAPS forms assist educators with preparing for, facilitating, and documenting the complete TAPS process in a consistent way for all students who receive TAPS support.

For example, with the TAPS process, extensive amounts of time and multiple educators are not needed to interview the teacher about her concerns because the teacher is taught (during the SOPAA introductory meeting) how to specify her concerns on the Request for TAPS Form. Similarly, the extensive resources required of team meetings are minimized in the TAPS process because only two educators (the classroom teacher and the TAPS Teacher) are needed to pinpoint the student's primary academic deficit. Further, the time needed to coordinate team meetings is eliminated in the TAPS process, as are possible delays in developing and implementing an intervention that can result from trying to involve multiple educators in a meeting.

SUMMARY

In this chapter we introduced the initial activities that should occur as part of the TAPS process. Information and guidance were provided with respect to how and when teachers should request academic support through TAPS, as well as how the TAPS Teacher should prepare for the intervention planning meeting (which is discussed in greater detail in the following chapter). The rationale for the TAPS process was also summarized. Because TAPS represents the core component of the overall SOPAA model, TAPS Teachers should gain strong familiarity and ideally some practice with each of the steps and forms associated with the TAPS process prior to starting SOPAA implementation; and like learning any new procedure, TAPS Teachers should gradually become more skilled and efficient as their experience with TAPS cases increases.

CHAPTER 5

Secondary Steps of the TAPS Process

Intervention Planning, Follow-Ups, and Summative Reviews of Intervention Effectiveness

Expanding on the information discussed in Chapter 4, this chapter continues the description of steps that occur as part of the TAPS process (i.e., Component 1 of the SOPAA). Specifically, this chapter discusses the intervention planning meeting, brief follow-up meetings that occur during implementation of the intervention plan, and the meeting that occurs to formally review the effectiveness of the intervention plan. (We continue to refer to classroom teachers as *teachers*, and to TAPS Support Teachers as *TAPS Teachers*.)

THE INTERVENTION PLANNING MEETING

If the TAPS Teacher prepares for the intervention planning meeting according to the suggestions described in Chapter 4, a high-quality intervention plan can be developed in no more than 20–30 minutes.

After a teacher requests academic support and the TAPS Teacher begins the initial steps for processing the request (all described in Chapter 4), the two teachers will get together for the intervention planning meeting. This meeting typically lasts no more than 20–30 minutes and should occur within 1–3 weeks from the date that the teacher submits the Request for TAPS Form.

Prior to the intervention planning meeting, the TAPS Teacher should encourage the teacher to invite any teacher assistant to the meeting who works regularly with the target student. As discussed in Chapter 4, a teacher assistant who works frequently with the target student may add important input when the classroom teacher completes the Request for TAPS Form and should therefore be involved with key stages of the TAPS process. As such, when possible and beneficial, the teacher assistant should attend the intervention planning meeting. The classroom teacher, rather than the teacher assistant, should be the primary collaborator with the TAPS Teacher when determining the student's intervention plan; however, the teacher assistant may have meaningful input and suggestions to share during the intervention planning meeting.

There are three primary goals of the intervention planning meeting. The first goal is for the TAPS Teacher to confirm the teacher's primary concern and obtain teacher ratings regarding the severity of her concern. Goal two is to discuss the predeveloped list of evidence-based intervention programs and select the most suitable program that will address the primary concern. Goal three is to develop a comprehensive intervention plan for the target student. Each goal is highlighted directly on the TAPS Intervention Planning Form and Record, henceforth referred to simply as the *Intervention Planning Form*, or IPF. Appendix G shows a blank copy of the IPF and Figure 5.1 shows a sample of a completed IPF. Each goal and its correspondence with the IPF are described throughout this chapter. We encourage the reader to photocopy Appendix G in order to have the IPF easily viewable while reading the remaining portion of this chapter and others. Also, the companion website *www.sopaaforschools.org* offers a downloadable electronic version for teachers and TAPS Teachers who prefer to use an electronic version of the IPF, so that they can type information directly into the form.

Goal 1: Share Results of Skills Observation, Confirm Teacher's Concern, and Determine Severity of Student's Deficit

As shown toward the top of the IPF, the TAPS Teacher starts by briefly summarizing the results from her targeted skills observation and asking any needed follow-up questions that will help to confirm the teacher's primary concern. Usually this step can be accomplished quickly because the TAPS Teacher (as described in Chapter 4) has already completed the skills observation with the student and prepared clarification questions to ask the teacher. Once the TAPS Teacher feels certain about the student's primary deficit (e.g., decoding, reading comprehension, poor early numeracy skills), the primary concern should be recorded on the space provided on the IPF.

Next, to determine the severity of the student's academic deficit, the TAPS Teacher should ask the teacher to respond to the items on the TAPS Case Rating Scale (Appendix H). These items should be asked verbally by the TAPS Teacher so that the teacher (and the teacher assistant, if applicable) can provide a numerical response on the 1–5 rating scale, as well as elaborate verbally on any given item. As shown on the TAPS Case Rating Scale, the teacher is asked to respond to questions about (1) the severity of the student's deficit in the specific skill(s) listed as the primary concern, (2) the severity of the student's deficit in the respective academic area, (3) the likelihood that the concern can be addressed through typical instruction, and (4) the student's overall academic progress at the present time. As we describe later, this same rating scale will be completed again after the student receives the determined intervention plan.

Through Goal 1 of the intervention planning meeting, the TAPS Teacher should further understand the extent of the student's academic difficulty, and through gathering this information, the TAPS Teacher may also recognize aspects of the case that will influence the success of the intervention plan (e.g., frequent student absences, difficulties with student behavior in small-group settings). When applicable, such information should be written on the IPF within the Goal 1 section (see the line starting, "Write additional notes . . . "). Last, after the teacher finishes responding to all TAPS Case Rating Scale items, the TAPS Teacher should check the corresponding box on the IPF. Completing the steps for Goal 1 of intervention planning meeting should take approximately 4–7 minutes.

Goal 2: Select an Intervention Program to Implement

As discussed in Chapter 4, the TAPS Teacher will prepare a list of no more than two to four intervention programs that should address the teacher's primary concern, and share this list with the

Teacher's Name: J. Metcalfe Student's Name: Stuart Dent Student's Grade: 3rd

TAPS Support Teacher's Name: I. Brock Date of Planning Meeting: 10/28/13

Goal 1: Share results from skills observation, ask follow-up questions to specify the teacher's primary concern, and get ratings on the TAPS Case Rating Scale.

Write primary concern here: Reading fluency and comprehension. Deficits in reading fluency likely hinder Stuart's comprehension.

Write additional notes that may be relevant to intervention implementation and success: Stuart likes working with adults.

☑ Check this box to indicate that the TAPS Case Rating Scale has been completed.

Goal 2: Discuss the list of feasible evidence-based intervention programs and select the most suitable program that will directly address the primary concern.

Write the selected intervention program here: The HELPS Program

Goal 3: Develop the Intervention Plan.

1. Who will implement the intervention program? J. Metcalfe (teacher) 1 day per week and A. Ponte (school volunteer) 2 days per week; with implementation support from I. Brock (TAPS Teacher) approximately once every 2 weeks.
2. Will a predeveloped intervention protocol be modified in any way, and if so, how and why? No.
3. How will intervention implementers get trained (if applicable)? All implementers have been trained and verified to implement HELPS with integrity.
4. Where will the intervention be implemented and at what times of day? Implementation will occur in the classroom or at a desk just outside the classroom. Intervention will ideally occur: Mon, 8:45–9:00 (J. Metcalfe); Wed, 8:15–8:30 (A. Ponte), Fri, 8:15–8:30 (A. Ponte).
5. How many minutes of intervention (and/or lessons) will occur each day, and how many days per week will intervention occur? Intervention sessions will last 10–15 minutes per day (until that day's lesson is complete); sessions will occur 3 days per week.
6. On what date will implementation begin and what days per week will the intervention occur? Implementation will begin no later than 11/8/13 on M, W, and F.
7. How will implementation integrity be evaluated, by whom, and when? I. Brock and J. Metcalfe will each monitor implementation integrity (of each other and take turns monitoring A. Ponte), and each implementer's integrity will be evaluated at least once every 2 weeks until the implementer shows 100% implementation integrity for two consecutive sessions. At that point, integrity will be monitored no less than every 4 weeks.
8. How will student progress be monitored (e.g., with what form of assessment, how often, by whom)? An oral reading fluency assessment was completed by I. Brock during the targeted skills observation and will be completed again by I. Brock just prior to the Summative Review of Intervention Effectiveness meeting. Progress will also be monitored through the HELPS program because each session will indicate whether Stuart met his Reading Goal. As specified through the HELPS Teacher's Manual, if Stuart does not meet his goal as would be expected, modifications will be made to his intervention plan.
9. Who will contact the student's parent(s) to inform him or her about the intervention plan, seek parent input, and seek possible support? J. Metcalfe
10. When will the parent(s) be contacted: 10/29/13 (If a parent offer objections, input, or support that prompts a change in the intervention plan, this should be communicated between the classroom teacher and TAPS Teacher immediately; if applicable, changes should be made to the intervention plan.)
11. Date for initial review of intervention plan and signatures (this meeting must occur no more than 1–2 weeks after the date specified in Item 6): 11/18/13.
12. How many weeks of intervention will occur before the TAPS Formal Review of Intervention Effectiveness? At least 9 weeks, assuming that there is no compelling evidence that the intervention must stop earlier.

(cont.)

FIGURE 5.1. Sample TAPS Intervention Planning Form (IPF) and Record.

13. Specify an objective goal the student should meet, resulting from the intervention: Based on the pre–post oral reading fluency assessment, Stuart should increase his oral reading fluency by at least 11 words correct per minute (WCPMs an average of more than 1.2 WCPM per week).
14. By approximately what date will the intervention period (specified in Item 12) be completed? 1/17/14
15. Specify the date for the Summative Review of Intervention Effectiveness meeting (must be within 2 weeks of the date specified in Item 14): 1/24/14
16. How will periodic "follow-ups" of intervention success occur (e.g., who will initiate them, approximately how often)? Follow-ups will occur at least once every 2 weeks with I. Brock checking in with both J. Metcalfe and A. Ponte during one of her implementation times. Implementation integrity will also be evaluated just prior to the follow-up. J. Metcalfe will also check in periodically with A. Ponte to ensure that things are going well and answer any questions she may have. J. Metcalfe and A. Ponte will contact I. Brock by e-mail if there is a more immediate question or concerns regarding Stuart's intervention plan.

Signatures below specify an agreement on the intervention plan and that both parties agree to fulfill their roles unless extenuating circumstances arise. Signatures also specify that the student's parent(s)/guardian(s) was contacted to obtain verbal consent for this intervention plan. Signatures should occur during the meeting date specified in Item 11.

Classroom Teacher: ______________ Date: ________ TAPS Teacher: __________ Date: __________

Student's parent/guardian gave verbal consent for plan (check one): ☐ **Yes** ☐ **No** ☐ **No reply**
(List all dates parent[s] was called: ____)

Intervention Follow-Up Information

	Date of follow-up:	**Notes from follow-up (e.g., implementation difficulties/successes, minor changes to intervention plan, need for extended meeting):**
1.	________	________________________________
2.	________	________________________________
3.	________	________________________________
4.	________	________________________________
5.	________	________________________________
6.	________	________________________________
7.	________	________________________________
8.	________	________________________________
9.	________	________________________________
10.	________	________________________________
11.	________	________________________________
12.	________	________________________________
13.	________	________________________________

FIGURE 5.1. *(cont.)*

teacher at least 5–7 days before the intervention planning meeting. With this preparation, selecting an intervention program to implement as part of the student's overall intervention plan should not require more than 5–10 minutes, unless for some reason a substantially different concern or student skill deficit emerges during the discussion of Goal 1 in the intervention planning meeting.

Assuming that the teacher's primary concern remains aligned with the TAPS Teacher's predeveloped list of intervention options, the TAPS Teacher should begin this phase of the meeting by asking the teacher whether she (1) has additional ideas for intervention that should be added to the list of options, (2) had the opportunity to review (or previously use) any of the interventions from the list, and (3) has strong preferences for or against any of the listed intervention programs. If the teacher is generally unfamiliar with the intervention options, the TAPS Teacher may spend a couple minutes per intervention describing its basic features (e.g., what the intervention targets, how long it takes to implement in a single intervention session) and its relative advantages and/or disadvantages.

At this point the teacher should have at least some familiarity with each intervention option, and the TAPS Teacher should lead a discussion that ultimately establishes which intervention program should be used to improve the student's target academic deficit. Of course, the selected intervention option should be feasible for the teacher to implement with integrity, but the final decision about which intervention to use should also be based upon its likely effectiveness with the specific student. Once the intervention program is determined, the TAPS Teacher should record its name on the corresponding line of the IPF. Although there are advantages to using structured intervention programs (see discussions in Chapters 3 and 12), if the intervention selected is not a specific manualized program or the intervention program will be used in addition to other procedures, all procedures should be recorded on this line of the IPF.

As discussed in Chapter 4, many schools do not have multiple options for intervention programs to target each specific academic subskill. If this is the case, this portion of the planning meeting will not require a discussion of intervention options, but the TAPS Teacher should still discuss the one intervention program with the teacher and ensure that she agrees it should be implemented. Also, a goal of the SOPAA (through Components 3 and 4) is to train teachers to use as many as possible of the evidence-based intervention programs that will be selected for TAPS cases, so that over time it is unlikely that the TAPS Teacher will need to spend much time discussing intervention programs during the planning meeting.

Goal 3: Develop a Comprehensive Intervention Plan

Selecting an intervention program that is evidence-based, targets the student's primary deficit, and is likely to be implemented with integrity is one primary feature of the student's overall intervention plan. However, there are several details related to implementing the selected intervention program, which, once determined, collectively embody the student's comprehensive intervention plan. Therefore, Goal 3 of the intervention planning meeting is to determine each of the details associated with implementing the selected intervention program.

The IPF specifies 16 questions/items that must be discussed and agreed upon by the TAPS Teacher and classroom teacher during the intervention planning meeting. The majority of these items should be straightforward for those with experience developing intervention plans, but the table shown in Appendix I offers comments and suggestions associated with each specific item. The TAPS Teacher should be highly familiar with the ideas in Appendix I so that decisions made about the student's intervention plan reflect feasibility and a high likelihood for effectiveness. Because Appendix I is fairly comprehensive, we recommend that the TAPS Teacher review this information both before and during the intervention planning meeting, and for convenience in reviewing this resource, we encourage TAPS Teachers to have a photocopied version of this table. In addition to using Appendix I as a resource for understanding and completing the IPF, Items 1, 3, and 7 of the IPF are described below to offer greater detail and clarification about each item.

Extended Comments for Item 1 of the IPF

The TAPS Teacher must consider Item 1 of Goal 3 on the IPF before the intervention planning meeting because she must enter the meeting knowing whether there are individuals within the school who are capable of implementing (or learning how to implement) the intervention program options that will be discussed during the meeting. This preparation is important because it facilitates the intervention planning meeting (i.e., reduces time spent in meeting) and helps the classroom teacher feel supported by others who can help her implement the intervention plan, if needed and possible.

The classroom teacher should serve as a regular intervention implementer, and in this way would ideally implement the intervention at least once or twice per week. The TAPS Teacher should also assist with implementation on occasion because doing so is likely to enhance her success with supporting the TAPS case and show the classroom teacher that she is not only there to offer advice, but also to assist with implementing the plan. As shown in Chapter 3 (Table 3.4), the TAPS Teacher will likely be available to implement the intervention program only once every 2–3 weeks, but this level of support should still meaningfully assist the teacher and provide the TAPS Teacher with important information about intervention effectiveness. Because the classroom teacher and TAPS Teacher are the key educators making decisions about the student's instruction and academic progress, it is important that both are involved with implementing the intervention program.

However, assuming that the intervention program selected is conducive to implementation by more than one implementer, the TAPS Teacher should enter the intervention planning meeting having identified others within the school who are able to help with the intervention program. For example, a regular school volunteer or one of the assistive school personnel staff members (e.g., teacher assistant, librarian, intervention specialist) may be a good person to select as an implementation assistant. Chapters 7 and 8 discuss considerations for recruiting and training individuals within the school to implement intervention programs.

When determining who within the school could assist with intervention implementation, the TAPS Teacher should communicate with the TAPS Support Coordinator. As discussed in Chapter 2, the primary responsibilities of the TAPS Support Coordinator are to (1) recruit school volunteers and identify assistive school personnel who may be able to implement interventions when needed; (2) train or facilitate training so that volunteers and/or assistive personnel can implement interventions; (3) manage implementation support availability and schedules, and provide this information to TAPS Teachers when requested; and (4) assist with measuring intervention implementation integrity. Given these responsibilities, the TAPS Support Coordinator should be able to identify individuals within the school who might assist with implementing the intervention program options prepared by the TAPS Teacher.

To facilitate communication, the TAPS Teacher should provide the TAPS Support Coordinator with all relevant information that will allow the Support Coordinator to identify individuals within the school who may assist with intervention implementation for that particular TAPS case. This communication can occur in a brief, informal meeting, or it can be accomplished by exchanging the following types of information forms. Appendix J (Request for Information from the TAPS Support Coordinator) shows a form that the TAPS Teacher might complete and give to the TAPS

Support Coordinator, and Figure 5.2 shows a completed sample of this form. We recommend that the TAPS Teacher gets this form to the TAPS Support Coordinator at least 1 week before the intervention planning meeting, and request a response from the coordinator at least 2 days before the intervention planning meeting.

Appendix K (Intervention Support Options Identified by the TAPS Support Coordinator) shows a form that would be completed by the TAPS Support Coordinator and given to the TAPS Teacher in response to the request for information. As shown in the form, the TAPS Support Coordinator will supply the TAPS Teacher with up to three names of educators within the school (possibly including school volunteers) who could implement the intervention programs listed by the TAPS Teacher in her request for information. In addition, details about each educator's role in the school, availability, and experience and training with the intervention program are provided. This form, along with the TAPS Support Coordinator's responses on the request for information form, should be given to the TAPS Teacher prior to the intervention planning meeting. With this information, the TAPS Teacher will know whether individuals within the school can assist with intervention implementation. This will also inform the TAPS Teacher about the potential need to train implementation assistants. More specific instructions for how the TAPS Support Coordinator should complete Appendixes J and K are provided in Chapter 11.

When the TAPS Teacher and classroom teacher decide who will implement the intervention program, they should keep in mind that too many implementers may decrease intervention effectiveness, feasibility, or communication among them. As such, a general rule of thumb is for the classroom teacher and one other support person (e.g., a teacher assistant, school volunteer, or special education teacher) to implement the intervention regularly, with the TAPS Teacher implementing an intervention session once every 2–3 weeks.

Extended Comments for Item 3 of the IPF

Ideally, when the TAPS Teacher and classroom teacher meet for the intervention planning meeting, both will already have acquired training and experience with the intervention program selected during the meeting. This state of affairs is common particularly if the SOPAA is implemented incrementally over multiple school years and perhaps includes a preparation year for training teachers to use intervention programs eligible for TAPS cases (as discussed in Chapter 3). Chapter 7 also describes the importance of training teachers within the school to implement relevant intervention programs. However, until all teachers have a broad range of training and experiences with the evidence-based intervention programs selected to address students' academic difficulties, the TAPS Teacher, on a case-by-case basis, may sometimes need to provide or facilitate training so that the teacher—and perhaps another intervention implementer—are capable of implementing the selected intervention.

Training one or more teachers on a case-by-case basis just before starting a student's intervention plan can be accomplished in a variety of ways. Two primary approaches are described below. As the TAPS Teacher decides the most effective, feasible, and time-efficient approach for case-by-case training, it is important to keep in mind the overall goal of this training: to ensure that all implementers are able to implement the intervention procedures accurately and consistently.

One basic approach to case-by-case training is for the TAPS Teacher to facilitate training before the student's intervention plan officially begins (i.e., before the start date written on the IPF, Goal 3, Item 6). Using this approach, an educator in the school who has experience accurately implementing the selected intervention program (e.g., the TAPS Teacher, the TAPS Support Coordinator, another teacher or assistive personnel in the school) should work with the implementer(s) as quickly as possible so that she learns how to accurately and consistently implement the interven-

Dear TAPS Support Coordinator:

Please see the information below to determine whether there is one or more educators within the school who can assist with implementing an intervention program as part of this TAPS case.

Name of student: Stuart Dent Student's grade: 3rd

TAPS Teacher: I. Brock Classroom teacher: J. Metcalfe

Academic subskill we plan to target during the TAPS case: Reading fluency

Date of intervention planning meeting: 10/28/13

Date this request was submitted to TAPS Support Coordinator: 10/18/13

Intervention programs that are currently being considered for this TAPS case:

1. HELPS
2. Great Leaps
3.
4.

Questions for TAPS Support Coordinator (Please respond to the questions below and attach this form to your Intervention Support Options Form.)

- If needed, are you available within the next 2 weeks to train one or more educators to implement any of the above intervention programs (check one)? ☐ Yes ☐ No
- If you can assist with training, please specify any of the above intervention programs you do not feel comfortable training others to use, and make any additional comments as needed.

  ____

  ____

  ____

- If needed, are you available to monitor implementation integrity with the selected intervention program (check one)? ☐ Yes ☐ No
- If you can assist with monitoring implementation integrity, please specify any of the listed intervention programs you do not feel comfortable monitoring, and make any additional comments as needed.

  ____

  ____

  ____

If you can assist with monitoring implementation integrity, please specify days and times you are likely available:

____

It would be greatly appreciated if you can reply to this request by: 10/25/13.

Please remember to reply by submitting your responses to this form along with your completed Intervention Support Options Form.

FIGURE 5.2. Sample Request for Information from the TAPS Support Coordinator.

tion program. During this training, the trainer should first provide the trainee with access to all needed resources (e.g., the teacher's manual of the program, training videos) and instructions for how to best use the resources. Next, trainees should have multiple opportunities to practice the implementation procedures while receiving feedback from the trainer. Because training others to implement new instructional practices requires a notable level of sophistication, the TAPS Teacher (if she is not the trainer) should ensure that the trainer is following the aforementioned practices effectively. The TAPS Teacher should also ensure that training is complete within 1–2.5 weeks of the intervention planning meeting, so that the student's intervention plan can begin immediately afterward.

The second basic approach to case-by-case training is for the TAPS Teacher to facilitate most of the training once the student's intervention plan officially begins. The TAPS Teacher should use this approach only if she is certain that all implementers identified in the plan can realistically learn how to implement the intervention program within 1–1.5 weeks of beginning the plan. If training takes longer, the student's intervention plan could be compromised because the student may not be receiving the intervention program accurately and consistently. Some intervention programs may be conducive to this approach, but some certainly will not. Based on the TAPS Teacher's experience with each of the intervention programs, she should ultimately decide how realistic it is to train teachers using this approach.

Although the TAPS Teacher should decide whether this second approach to training should be used, it is reasonable that another educator (e.g., the TAPS Support Coordinator, another teacher in the school) actually facilitates the training. In the following example, however, we will consider the TAPS Teacher as the trainer.

To facilitate this second training approach, the basic procedures described in the first case-by-case training approach should be used, but the time to achieve this training will be more limited. As such, we suggest that the TAPS Teacher begin by asking the trainees to read relevant implementation materials (e.g., material in a teacher's manual), watch demonstration videos or other teachers implementing the program, and then start practicing the procedures with an adult. These tasks should be accomplished within 2–4 days, and then the trainees should observe the TAPS Teacher as she implements the first (and if helpful, second) intervention session with the student. During the observation the TAPS Teacher should address trainee questions and/or provide comments as needed. During the next few intervention sessions, the TAPS Teacher will observe the trainees as they implement the intervention and provide feedback about their strengths and weaknesses. Ultimately, all trainees should be observed until they can implement the procedures with 90–100% accuracy across at least two consecutive sessions, or at another criterion that is specified in the teacher's manual of the intervention program. With this training criterion, the first approach to case-by-case training may require less overall time from the trainer, but the second approach will likely get the student's intervention plan started more quickly. Again, the goal of training is to ensure that all implementers are able to implement the intervention procedures accurately and consistently; with this goal in mind, the TAPS Teacher must determine a case-by-case training approach that will maximize resources and effectiveness in the most time-efficient manner.

Using either of the above training approaches, it is also important to highlight the following considerations. First, it is possible that a classroom teacher will know how to implement the selected intervention program, but that there will be no other educators in the school who can assist with regular implementation. In this case, the teacher and TAPS Teacher may decide that the teacher would be the best person to train an implementation assistant (using either of the above approaches to training). Second, if there are too few educators in the school who know how to implement the intervention program, the TAPS Teacher and classroom teacher might decide it would be more resource-efficient if multiple educators in the school were trained at that time to implement the program. Even if only one or two educators are needed more immediately to implement the intervention program for that specific TAPS case, training multiple educators at once would likely benefit the school and the TAPS process during subsequent cases.

Last, we want to emphasize that case-by-case training is not a goal of the SOPAA and that this form of training would be minimized or all together unnecessary if the SOPAA were implemented systematically and incrementally. For example, if the first year of SOPAA implementation will occur only for some grade levels and for one academic area (e.g., reading), the Lead Coordinator can ensure that all teachers receive training in two or three of the key intervention programs that will be used to target students' reading difficulties (e.g., Sound Partners to target basic decoding, Great Leaps to target fluency, and Headsprout Reading Comprehension to target comprehension). As described within this section, however, TAPS Teachers may encounter situations in which the most appropriate intervention for a student is not one with which the classroom teacher or others in the school are familiar. The aforementioned suggestions provide some guidance for TAPS Teachers who encounter this situation.

Extended Comments for Item 7 of the IPF

During the intervention planning meeting, while discussing who, how, and when to evaluate the implementation integrity of each implementer, the TAPS Teacher must keep in mind that some implementers may feel uncomfortable being observed in this way and/or may not understand the need to be observed for implementation integrity. Accordingly, the TAPS Teacher should ensure that all implementers understand the purpose and importance of evaluating implementation integrity and be able to address any possible questions or concerns that arise during the discussion. The following paragraph highlights some key reasons for monitoring teachers' implementation integrity.

The importance of implementation integrity and providing feedback to implementers is well documented in the research, which shows that implementation integrity and feedback are likely to improve intervention outcomes (Noell et al., 2005; Roach & Elliott, 2008). Also, if implementation integrity is poor and students do not show improvement at the end of the intervention process, educators cannot be sure whether lack of progress is due to poor alignment of the intervention procedures with the student's academic deficit, poor student response to the intervention, an otherwise ineffective intervention, failure to implement the intervention as it is designed, or a combination of these factors. Observing and documenting implementation integrity during each TAPS case helps educators improve (or ensure) their implementation accuracy and consistency, as well as inform their interpretations and decisions about the effectiveness of the intervention plan (described in detail later in this chapter).

For the decision to allocate more intervention resources to a student to be valid, there must be a system to determine that the interventionist used the intervention as planned.

In terms of who should monitor implementation integrity, the TAPS Teacher and/or the TAPS Support Coordinator will likely take primary responsibility for this task. Communication with the TAPS Support Coordinator about monitoring implementation integrity will occur, at least partially, through the Request for Information from the TAPS Support Coordinator (Appendix J). Detailed information about this communication is discussed in Chapter 11.

If there are other educators in the school who have documented accurate and consistent implementation of the intervention program, any one of these educators might also assist with monitoring implementation integrity when needed. Of course, as more teachers in the school gain experience with implementing a broader range of intervention programs, the TAPS Teacher's options for recruiting others to assist with implementation integrity monitoring will increase. If other educators assist with this task, the TAPS Teacher should ensure that they know how to record implementation integrity for each specific intervention and how to provide feedback to implementers.

The implementers associated with a specific TAPS case might also monitor each other's implementation integrity (including monitoring the TAPS Teacher's implementation). For example, after all implementers have been shown to implement the intervention program with 90–100% accuracy across two consecutive sessions, the implementer may then be taught to monitor others' implementation integrity.

With respect to the frequency of monitoring implementation integrity, we offer the following suggestions. At the beginning of the student's intervention plan (e.g., weeks 1–4), an implementation integrity check (of all implementers) should occur at least once every 1–2 weeks to ensure that all implementers are adhering to the intervention procedures. Once the TAPS Teacher has evidence that all implementers are implementing the program with strong integrity, observations can occur less frequently (e.g., once every 3–4 weeks). Because the TAPS Teacher presumably has both prior evidence of implementing the program with high integrity and will likely implement the program only every 2–3 weeks, someone should monitor her implementation integrity one to three times during the entire TAPS case. Similarly, if other implementers already have used the intervention program previously and showed accurate and consistent implementation, those implementers can be evaluated once every 3–4 weeks as long as their implementation integrity remains high (e.g., above 90% or a similar criterion that may be specified in the teacher's manual of the intervention program).

The timing for monitoring implementation integrity will vary depending on each monitor's schedule. As long as each implementer is evaluated (1) throughout the entire intervention session, (2) according to the frequency suggestions just discussed, and (3) using a consistent set of instructions for how to monitor implementation integrity, the days for monitoring implementation integrity can be determined according to each monitor's schedule. For the TAPS Teacher, monitoring implementation integrity may be best scheduled immediately before or after designated follow-up meetings, as is discussed later in this chapter.

Last, to facilitate implementation integrity monitoring, materials must be available for each monitor to record whether the implementer is following the intervention procedures as directed. Many manualized intervention programs have, for example, a list of procedures or even a checklist of procedures that can be used by a monitor to evaluate an implementer's integrity.

However, if a clear list of procedures or checklist does not exist for the respective intervention program, the TAPS Teacher should create a simple checklist of intervention procedures that can be used to evaluate whether implementers are adhering to the procedural protocol. It would be beyond the scope of this book to provide specific directions for creating procedural checklists, but the companion website *www.sopaaforschools.org* has supplemental information and materials that will assist TAPS Teachers who need to develop implementation integrity materials and checklists for programs that do not offer these materials.

Completing the Intervention Planning Meeting

Because the TAPS Teacher will enter the intervention planning meeting having already considered items 1, 3–8, 12–14, and 16 of Goal 3 on the IPF (as described in Chapter 4), this preparation should decrease the amount of time and discussion needed during the planning meeting. On average, determining responses to Items 1–16 on the IPF should take 10–20 minutes, but the amount of time will depend on the TAPS Teacher's level of preparedness, the complexity of the TAPS case, the extent to which the classroom teacher and TAPS Teacher agree about the intervention plan, and several related factors.

Once Items 1–16 on the IPF are completed, two steps should occur: (1) Implementation of the plan should begin by the date specified in Item 6 on the IPF, and (2) the TAPS Teacher and classroom teacher should meet again (on the date specified in Item 11) for an initial review of the intervention plan and to sign the IPF. This initial review of the plan, as well as subsequent follow-up meetings between the TAPS Teacher and the intervention plan implementers, is described in detail next.

FOLLOW-UP MEETINGS THROUGHOUT INTERVENTION PLAN IMPLEMENTATION

After developing the IPF, the TAPS teacher will facilitate two primary types of follow-up meetings with the teacher and, if applicable, other implementers of the student's intervention plan. The first type of follow-up meeting (i.e., the initial review of the intervention plan) includes the TAPS Teacher and all other key implementers of the plan, and should occur after the intervention plan has been implemented for 1–2 weeks. The second type of follow-up meeting (i.e., periodic follow-up meetings) should occur every 2–3 weeks following the review of the intervention plan and generally requires only a few minutes of discussion between the TAPS Teacher and other implementers of the plan. Each type of follow-up meeting is described in detail below, but the overall goals of the follow-up meetings are for TAPS Teachers to ensure that the intervention plan is being implemented as intended, that teachers are supported in their implementation of the plan, and that the intervention plan appears to benefit the target student.

Initial Review of the Intervention Plan

As stated above, the initial review of the intervention plan should occur on the date specified on Item 11 of the Goal 3 on IPF, which takes place no more than 1–2 weeks after the intervention plan has been implemented. This meeting should include the TAPS Teacher, classroom teacher, and all other individuals who are implementing the intervention program with the student (e.g., a teacher assistant, a school volunteer). To facilitate the meeting, the TAPS Teacher should arrive with the student's original IPF and copies of the IPF for all meeting attendees. The meeting is then conducted by having the group review each item of the student's IPF.

Typically, the meeting can be completed within 5–15 minutes. The goals of the meeting are for the TAPS Teacher to (1) ensure that intervention implementation has started; (2) review the intervention plan and address any possible problems or concerns from all implementers; (3) determine whether the student's parent(s) provided any input or suggestions that should influence the originally designed intervention plan; and (4) obtain signatures on the original IPF from the teacher and TAPS Teacher, after they agree on all parts of the intervention plan and make any necessary modifications. If the student's parent(s) has still not provided consent for the plan because he or she did not respond to teachers' multiple attempts for communication, the TAPS Teacher should ensure that continued attempts are made to discuss the plan with the parents (for additional details, see Items 9 and 10 in Appendix I).

Assuming that the intervention planning meeting resulted in a well-designed intervention plan supported by the teacher and TAPS Teacher, the review of the intervention plan should be brief, confirm that the plan is appropriate, and allow the teacher and TAPS Teacher to make minor changes if needed. If more substantial changes to the plan are required, such changes should reflect an even stronger plan to address the teacher's primary concern; even substantial changes to an intervention plan represent a positive feature of the TAPS process, because the changes should reflect a plan that maintains likelihood for success while also increasing implementation feasibility.

Periodic Follow-Up Meetings

Periodic follow-up meetings should occur every 1–3 weeks and usually last no more than 2–5 minutes. In Item 16 of Goal 3 on the IPF, the teacher and TAPS Teacher should determine who will initiate the meetings and how often they will occur. For example, it may be determined during the intervention planning meeting that every 2 weeks the TAPS Teacher will go to the location where the intervention program is being implemented with the student and plan for a brief meeting with that day's implementer, before or after the implementer completes the intervention. If this plan is made, the TAPS Teacher should make sure that she follows up with *each* implementer every 1–3 weeks. In addition, it might be decided during the intervention planning meeting (and documented on Item 16 of the IPF) that periodic follow-up meetings/discussions can be initiated via e-mail by any one of the intervention implementers.

Brief "checkups" are integral to the TAPS process because they allow for ongoing review and communication about the effectiveness and feasibility of a student's intervention plan.

The purpose of the periodic follow-up meetings are for the TAPS Teacher and implementer (e.g., classroom teacher, teacher assistant) to (1) ensure that all parts of the intervention plan are being implemented as intended, (2) quickly review intervention data and progress, (3) address any concerns or questions, and (4) determine whether to make any minor changes to the intervention plan (e.g., add one additional intervention session per week, change the start times of the intervention sessions, change the implementers' schedule to better facilitate the intervention plan). On the area provided toward the bottom of the student's official IPF, the date and all relevant notes (e.g., minor changes to the intervention plan) from each periodic follow-up meeting should be documented by the TAPS Teacher.

In general, because the intervention planning meeting should result in a feasible intervention plan with likelihood for success, minor changes to the intervention plan should not occur all that frequently when holding periodic follow-up meetings. When minor changes are made, the appropriateness of those changes should be documented and confirmed by the teacher and TAPS Teacher. If a follow-up meeting results in a proposal for substantial changes to the intervention plan (e.g., modifying the intervention protocol, decreasing the number of days per week allotted to the student for intervention), these proposed changes should be discussed in a lengthier meeting among all implementers, and if needed, a new draft of the IPF should be developed and attached to the original IPF for documentation purposes. Again, major modifications to the intervention plan should be minimal or nonexistent across TAPS cases because a sound intervention plan should be developed during the intervention planning meeting.

Maximizing Time during Periodic Follow-Up Meetings

In addition to the above reasons for holding periodic follow-up meetings, these meetings are also beneficial because they present good opportunities for the TAPS Teacher to achieve two other key components of the intervention plan: (1) to collect progress monitoring assessment data, and/or (2) to monitor implementation integrity of the implementer. For example, if the IPF specifies that the student will receive a brief (1- to 3-minute) assessment once per week, the TAPS Teacher might plan periodic follow-up meetings by first assessing the student's progress, then holding the brief follow-up discussion with the implementer, then observing (and recording the implementation integrity of) the teacher implementing the intervention, then providing the teacher with implementation integrity feedback and related discussion. There is no one particular order for facilitating each of these tasks on a given day, but the above example should illustrate one approach to helping the TAPS Teacher maximize her time with a TAPS case.

THE TAPS SUMMATIVE REVIEW OF INTERVENTION EFFECTIVENESS

After completing the specified number of weeks of the student's intervention plan (see Goal 3, IPF Item 12, which should also coincide with the date indicated on IPF Item 14), the TAPS Teacher should facilitate a meeting on (or very close to) the date specified on IPF Item 15 in order to formally review the effectiveness of the student's intervention plan. Attendees of this meeting must include the TAPS Teacher and classroom teacher, but may also include other implementers of the intervention plan (e.g., a teacher assistant), the student's parent(s) or other legal guardian(s), the school principal, and any other key stakeholder in the target student's educational progress. Determining who should attend the Summative Review of Intervention Effectiveness meeting (henceforth referred to as the *summative review meeting*) will likely be up to the TAPS Teacher, Lead Coordinator, classroom teacher, and school principal. If parents are not included in the summative review meeting, they should be invited to attend another meeting that allows for discussion of their child's progress during implementation of the intervention plan.

The three primary goals of the summative review meeting are to determine (1) the extent to which the intervention was effective; (2) the extent to which the intervention plan was carried out as planned, and (if applicable) how poor implementation of the plan may have compromised intervention effectiveness; and (3) what should occur next to ensure that the student maintains or increases progress in the targeted academic area and/or subskill. To facilitate these goals, at least 1 week prior to the summative review meeting, the TAPS Teacher should complete another academic assessment of the student's skill(s) that was targeted during the intervention. Specifically, the same type of assessment that was used as a "preintervention" assessment (likely conducted during the targeted skills observation) should be administered. The "postintervention" assessment will serve as one key source of information for determining intervention effectiveness.

Furthermore, to facilitate the summative review meeting, the Summative Review Form (SRF) should be completed by the TAPS Teacher in collaboration with all implementers of the student's intervention plan, particularly the classroom teacher. Appendix L shows a blank SRF, and Figure 5.3 shows an example of a completed SRF. Recommendations for completing the SRF and facilitating the summative review meeting are discussed next according to the three primary goals of the meeting. We encourage readers to photocopy Appendix L in order to have the SRF easily viewable while reading the remaining portion of this chapter and others. Also, the companion website *www.sopaaforschools.org* offers a downloadable electronic version for teachers and TAPS Teachers who prefer to use an electronic version of the SRF, so that they can type information directly into the form.

Goal 1: Summarize Intervention Effectiveness

The TAPS Teacher should arrive at the summative review meeting having already completed the basic background information requested at the top of the SRF (e.g., student name, number of

Student name: Stuart Dent Date of meeting: 1/24/14

Individuals present during the meeting: J. Metcalfe (teacher), I. Brock (TAPS Teacher), B. Dent (student's father), S. Spadowski (principal)

Is date of meeting within 2 weeks of the date specified on Item 14 of Goal 3 on the TAPS IPF? (check one): ☑ **Yes** ☐ **No**

If the response above is "No," state why:

Academic area targeted for intervention (check one): ☑ **Reading** ☐ **Writing** ☐ **Math**

Primary skill(s) targeted during intervention (and name of intervention program, if applicable): Reading fluency (the HELPS Program)

Number of intervention sessions implemented up to this date: 25

Number of weeks student was in school since intervention start date: 9 weeks

Indicate the student's goal (specified in Item 13 of the IPF) and student's current academic performance related to that goal: Based on the pre–post oral reading fluency assessment, the goal was for Stuart to increase his oral reading fluency by at least 11 words correct per minute (WCPM; an average of more than 1.2 WCPM per week). Stuart increased his oral reading fluency by 18 WCPM since the start of the intervention (an average of ~2 WCPM per week).

Intervention Effectiveness Summary

1. The intervention successfully addressed the primary concern (check one and then describe details and relevant assessment data to support your response):

☐ 1–Strongly Disagree ☐ 2–Disagree ☐ 3–Neither Agree nor Disagree ☐ 4–Agree ☑ 5–Strongly Agree

Stuart's pre–post scores (a gain of 18 WCPM) exceeded his goal, and his progress monitoring via the HELPS system showed that Stuart regularly met his reading goal after one or two sessions practicing a given passage.

2. The student should receive additional services in the same academic area subskill(s) targeted for intervention (check one and then describe your rationale):

☐ 1–Strongly Disagree ☐ 2–Disagree ☐ 3–Neither Agree nor Disagree ☑ 4–Agree ☐ 5–Strongly Agree

Although Stuart has been making meaningful progress, his oral reading fluency is still below average (as measured by the posttest assessment), and he would benefit from additional intervention in this area.

3. The student should receive additional intervention services in the same academic area, but different subskill(s) (check one and then describe your rationale):

☐ 1–Strongly Disagree ☐ 2–Disagree ☐ 3–Neither Agree nor Disagree ☑ 4–Agree ☐ 5–Strongly Agree

Classroom observations suggest that Stuart still struggles with reading comprehension, but comprehension seems to be improving as he improves his reading fluency.

4. Students with the same skill-area deficit would likely benefit from the same intervention program (check one and then describe your rationale):

☐ 1–Strongly Disagree ☐ 2–Disagree ☐ 3–Neither Agree nor Disagree ☑ 4–Agree ☐ 5–Strongly Agree

Other students with reading fluency deficits should also benefit from this intervention, but students in older grades may respond differently to the motivational component of HELPS. If used with older students, the motivational system might be adapted to make it completely age-appropriate.

☑ **Check this box to indicate that the TAPS Case Rating Scale has been completed.**

Intervention Implementation Summary

5. Average implementation integrity of the intervention program across all sessions and implementers: 96.2% (Write "NA" if not applicable.)

(cont.)

FIGURE 5.3. Sample TAPS Summative Review of Intervention Effectiveness Form (SRF).

For Items 6–12, rate the degree to which the component of the overall intervention plan was implemented according to the student's TAPS IPF. If your rating is not "Agree" or "Strongly Agree," indicate the reason(s) for this using the following list, "Reasons for deviating from the intended intervention plan," and write comments as needed.

Reasons for deviating from the intended intervention plan, as specified in the student's TAPS IPF:

a) Plan described in the TAPS IPF was unclear to one or more individuals implementing the component.
b) Due to school and/or classroom scheduling challenges, there was insufficient time to always complete the component.
c) Student needed academic or behavioral support beyond expected levels, which minimized opportunities to always complete the component.
d) Implementer had insufficient training or knowledge to always complete the component.
e) High level of student or implementer absences—specify number of absences and who (implementer or student) had the high level of absences.
f) Inadequate space and/or resources within the school to always complete the component.
g) Other reasons—explain the reason(s) on the respective lines.

6. Intervention program procedures were implemented with integrity (if rating = 3 or less, write corresponding number[s] for reason[s]:______).

☐ 1–Strongly Disagree ☐ 2–Disagree ☐ 3–Neither Agree nor Disagree ☐ 4–Agree ☑ 5–Strongly Agree

Explain reason if needed:

7. All Implementers were well trained, as intended (if rating = 3 or less, write corresponding number[s] for reason[s]:______).

☐ 1–Strongly Disagree ☐ 2–Disagree ☐ 3–Neither Agree nor Disagree ☐ 4–Agree ☑ 5–Strongly Agree

Explain reason if needed:

8. Intervention program was implemented the minimum number of weeks stated (if rating = 3 or less, write corresponding number[s] for reason[s]:______).

☐ 1–Strongly Disagree ☐ 2–Disagree ☐ 3–Neither Agree nor Disagree ☐ 4–Agree ☑ 5–Strongly Agree

Explain reason if needed:

9. Per day, the intervention program was implemented the minimum number of minutes stated (if rating = 3 or less, write number[s] for reason[s]: b).

☐ 1–Strongly Disagree ☐ 2–Disagree ☑ 3–Neither Agree nor Disagree ☐ 4–Agree ☐ 5–Strongly Agree

Explain reason if needed: *On 4–5 of the days the intervention had to be stopped early because of an unexpected event (e.g., school fire drill) or there was insufficient time to complete the intervention before needing to move Stuart to a new learning activity.*

10. Implementation integrity of intervention program was evaluated as intended (if rating = 3 or less, write corresponding number[s] for reason[s]:______).

☐ 1–Strongly Disagree ☐ 2–Disagree ☐ 3–Neither Agree nor Disagree ☑ 4–Agree ☐ 5–Strongly Agree

Explain reason if needed:

11. Progress monitoring assessments occurred as intended (if rating = 3 or less, write corresponding number[s] for reason[s]:______).

☐ 1–Strongly Disagree ☐ 2–Disagree ☐ 3–Neither Agree nor Disagree ☐ 4–Agree ☑ 5–Strongly Agree

Explain reason if needed:

12. Periodic follow-up meetings occurred as intended (if rating = 3 or less, write corresponding number[s] for reason[s]: b).

☐ 1–Strongly Disagree ☐ 2–Disagree ☑ 3–Neither Agree nor Disagree ☐ 4–Agree ☐ 5–Strongly Agree

Explain reason if needed: *On three occasions the TAPS Teacher did not arrive on time to conduct a periodic follow-up meeting or had to leave before completing the follow-up meeting. However, when these instances occurred, she follwed up with both teachers by e-mail to see if they had questions or concerns.*

(cont.)

FIGURE 5.3. *(cont.)*

13. Deviations of the intervention plan (such as deviations possibly noted above) weakened the success of the plan (check one and describe, if needed):

☐ 1–Strongly Disagree ☑ 2–Disagree ☐ 3–Neither Agree nor Disagree ☐ 4–Agree ☐ 5–Strongly Agree

Although there were a few deviations from what was stated in the IPF (see items 9, 10, and 12 above), these deviations did not seem to reduce the effectiveness of the intervention plan because Stuart still made meaningful progress with his oral reading fluency.

14. Describe successes related to implementing the intervention plan:

Student made meaningful improvements in his oral reading fluency; there was strong implementation integrity for each of the implementers; J. Metcalfe reported that she improved her knowledge and use of HELPS; the intervention plan was generally implemented as intended; Stuart seemed to like working with each of the implementers, and his confidence as a reader seemed to improve.

Summary of Next Steps

What steps should now be taken? Check all that apply and write additional information that describes how the classroom teacher, the TAPS Teacher, and/or other school professionals will proceed to ensure positive learning outcomes for the student.

☐ 1. Discontinue all intervention program(s) described in TAPS IPF.

☑ 2. Monitor student's academic performance every 15–18 week(s) with assessment (specify frequency on the given line).

☑ 3. Continue implementing the intervention program(s) described in the current TAPS IPF; on lines below, specify frequency, duration, etc.

☐ 4. Modify the intervention program(s) described in the TAPS IPF; on lines below, specify how the program will be modified.

☐ 5. Begin a new intervention program that addresses the same skill; on lines below, specify the new intervention program and its rationale.

☑ 6. Modify the intervention plan (other than the specified intervention program); on lines below, specify how the plan will be modified.

☐ 7. Develop and implement an intervention that specifically addresses student behavior/motivation; on lines below, describe basic aspects of the intervention.

☐ 8. Seek additional problem-solving support from other school staff; on lines below, specify who, how, why, and related details.

☐ 9. Conduct a thorough student assessment to improve instructional problem solving; on lines below, describe details (when, what assessments, why, etc.).

☐ 10. Have classroom teacher request assistance regarding a different academic area or subskill; on lines below, describe the teacher's new concerns.

☐ 11. Other; describe on lines below.

Stuart should continue receiving HELPS but should receive it 4 days rather than 3 days. J. Metcalfe will now implement HELPS on M and T, and A. Ponte will implement HELPS on W and F. In addition, the TA in J. Metcalfe's class will work with Stuart at least 2–3 days per week to ensure that he is independently answering his comprehension questions successfully during independent reading times. J. Metcalfe will check with the TA at least twice per week to assess Stuart's ability to answer his comprehension questions and will report his progress to I. Brock. If comprehension does not seem to improve over the next 3–4 weeks, a comprehension intervention may be added to Stuart's intervention plan.

In terms of monitoring Stuart's academic performance, an oral reading fluency benchmark assessment will also occur in the spring and should occur during the fall, winter, and spring of the subsequent school year in order to continue evaluating Stuart's reading progress.

FIGURE 5.3. *(cont.)*

intervention sessions implemented), as well as Item 5 (average implementation integrity) of the form. The TAPS Teacher should have also examined all data collected during the TAPS case and attempted to make some preliminary interpretations (e.g., determine whether the data seem to show meaningful student improvement, or at least some improvement). Ultimately, however, the TAPS Teacher must facilitate the summative review meeting by soliciting input and impressions from all members of the implementation team. To start the meeting, the TAPS Teacher should solicit team input regarding overall intervention effectiveness (i.e., Items 1–4 of the form).

To establish the most accurate responses for Items 1–4 of the SRF, the TAPS Teacher ought to begin the discussion by objectively describing all quantitative achievement data collected throughout the TAPS case. For example, the TAPS Teacher should verbally summarize and show the team the pre- and postintervention assessment scores, progress monitoring assessment scores, possible trends in the student's progress, and anything else that offers an objective account of student achievement in the targeted academic area. While describing the student's achievement data, the TAPS Teacher should avoid interpretive statements (e.g., "Look how great [or poorly] the student did"), as these types of statements may influence the team's overall impression of intervention effectiveness and may ultimately prevent the team members from providing their true impressions of intervention effectiveness. Instead, the TAPS Teacher should use more objective statements, such as, "During this progress monitoring assessment day the student scored 3 points higher than he did the previous 2 weeks." Using objective statements, followed by subsequent team discussion of the data, should also help the TAPS Teacher understand the extent to which team members use the objective data to determine their views of overall intervention effectiveness. This understanding is important because, in most cases, the team will benefit most by interpreting intervention effectiveness according to objective data collected throughout the TAPS process.

After objectively describing the data acquired throughout the case, the TAPS Teacher should ask for each team member's overall impression of intervention effectiveness, allow for any needed discussion, and ultimately ask the team to make a decision about how they would rate Item 1 of the SRF, ranging from Strongly Disagree through Strongly Agree. The team's response to Item 1 should also reflect the TAPS Teacher's interpretations of intervention effectiveness, and if necessary, the TAPS Teacher should guide the discussion about Item 1 in a way that other team members recognize both the strengths and possible weaknesses of the objective and subjective data obtained throughout the TAPS process. After discussing Item 1 and determining a rating, all relevant details supporting the rating should be written in the space provided below Item 1. The TAPS Teacher should then facilitate team responses for Items 2–4 on the SRF and, like Item 1, write supporting details for each respective item.

There are clearly many possible outcomes for intervention effectiveness that may occur during a TAPS case, ranging from the student increasing performance consistent with grade-level expectations in the target area to the student performing even further below grade-level expectations in that area. Of course, TAPS is designed to improve student performance and help students achieve at levels commensurate with grade-level expectations. However, depending on many factors (e.g., the student's level of performance prior to starting TAPS, the duration of implementing the intervention plan, the type of intervention program used in the plan, the targeted skill for intervention, the quality of intervention programs available to address the targeted skill), it is unrealistic to expect the TAPS process to always produce student improvements that reflect grade-level standards in the core area or even the subskill area targeted during intervention. Because each of these factors should be understood by the classroom teacher and TAPS Teacher prior to starting the process, the ratings of intervention effectiveness should also reflect this understanding and ultimately correspond with the stated intervention goal in Item 13 of the IPF. For guidance, Table 5.1 offers suggested criteria for using the SRF rating scale with Item 1 of the form. By using these

TABLE 5.1. Suggested Guidelines for Using the SRF Rating Scale with Item 1 of the Form

General description of intervention effectiveness	Suggested rating
Preintervention assessment scores reflect stronger performance compared to postintervention scores, progress monitoring assessment data show a flat or decreasing trend over time, *and* all implementers of the intervention plan feel that the student did not improve at all in the targeted skill area.	1—Strongly disagree
Postintervention assessment scores do not show improvement in student skill level compared to preintervention scores, *or* progress monitoring assessment data show a flat or decreasing trend over time. Also, all implementers of the intervention plan feel that the student did not make expected improvements in the targeted skill area.	2—Disagree
According to all implementers of the intervention plan, the student appeared to show meaningful signs of improvement, but improvement was not detected with pre- to postintervention assessments or progress monitoring assessments (i.e., assessments showed no improvement or slight decrease in the skill level compared to grade-level expectations).	3—Neither agree nor disagree
According to all implementers of the intervention plan, the student appeared to show meaningful signs of improvement, and improvement was detected with pre- to postintervention assessments (e.g., student improved at or above the expected rate according to normative progress with the assessment) *or* progress monitoring assessments (i.e., assessments showed student performing at or nearly at the selected goal for intervention).	4—Agree
According to all implementers of the intervention plan, the student appeared to show meaningful, important signs of improvement, and improvement was detected with pre- to postintervention assessments (e.g., student improved at or above the expected rate according to normative progress with the assessment) *and* progress monitoring assessments (i.e., assessments showed student performing above or at the selected goal for intervention)	5—Strongly agree

suggested guidelines, the TAPS Teacher should also be able to develop a heuristic for the remaining rating-scale items on the SRF.

After completing SRF Items 1–4, the TAPS Teacher should have the classroom teacher once again use the TAPS Case Rating Scale (Appendix H) to evaluate her current impressions of the student's academic abilities. This is the same rating scale that was used at the beginning of the intervention planning meeting, and should therefore reflect the teacher's potential change in perceptions since starting the student's intervention plan. Having answered similar items as part of the SRF, completing the TAPS Case Rating Scale should not require a great deal of time. When having the teacher respond to this scale, the items should be presented exactly as they were during the intervention planning meeting, but she should not be able to review her responses from the planning meeting, as this may bias her current perceptions.

Goal 2: Summarize Intervention Implementation Integrity

The next major goal of the summative review meeting is to summarize and evaluate the extent to which the student's intervention plan was implemented according to the student's IPF. To facilitate this goal, Items 5–13 in the SRF should be discussed and ultimately answered by the implementation team. Similar to Goal 1 of the summative review meeting, the TAPS Teacher should start the discussion about intervention implementation by objectively describing all relevant data (e.g., average implementation integrity of the intervention program across all implementers, average implementation of the intervention program per week, the number of times each implementer was observed for implementation integrity, the number of periodic follow-ups that occurred and a summary of with whom they occurred). Related to preparing data to share with the team, recall that the TAPS Teacher should enter the summative review meeting having already entered the correct value into Item 5 of the SRF (assuming this is applicable, as is discussed next).

To illustrate correct computation for Item 5, suppose in one TAPS case there are three implementers of the student's intervention program: the classroom teacher, a teacher assistant, and the TAPS Teacher. For each of those implementers and throughout the duration of the TAPS case, implementation integrity was observed and recorded at least three times using a checklist of implementation steps that correspond with the intervention procedures. The checklist would specify each step the teacher completed and did not complete during each observation. If, for example, the classroom teacher's implementation integrity (computed as percentage of implementation steps completed accurately) was 88%, 94%, 98%, 100%, and 100% across the five sessions she was observed, her average implementation integrity would be: (88 + 94 + 98 + 100 + 100) ÷ 5 = 96%. Let's now suppose that the average implementation integrity for each implementer was as follows: the classroom teacher = 96%; the teacher assistant = 94%; and the TAPS Teacher = 96%. Given these values, the score reported on Item 5 of the SRF should be 95.3% (i.e., [96 + 94 + 96] ÷ 3).

When the TAPS Teacher discusses implementation integrity data during the summative review meeting, it may be best *not* to share average implementation integrity scores for each implementer if there are one or more implementers who have substantially lower scores. Major discrepancies between scores should be rare, however, because the TAPS Teacher should be helping to improve implementers' integrity (as needed) during the TAPS process. In either case, reporting discrepancies across implementers during the summative review meeting may make some team members feel uncomfortable. However, if there are major discrepancies between implementers' integrity, the TAPS Teacher might present this information tactfully and professionally, given that discrepancies in implementation integrity could have influenced the student's degree of improvement during the intervention plan.

Although the information elicited by Item 5 could be useful for the team to understand the extent to which the intervention program was implemented with integrity, we must offer some caveats and urge the TAPS Teacher to be mindful of these points when interpreting the average score obtained for Item 5. First, if the intervention program does not provide a specific form for monitoring implementation integrity, a checklist developed by others may not produce the most valid means of monitoring the program's implementation integrity. Also, computing a general percentage of steps implemented versus those not implemented does not account for the possibility that (1) some implementation steps are more important than other steps (which again relates to appropriate development of the checklist), and (2) variations in implementation frequency occur across implementers (e.g., one implementer's low integrity score, which would bring down the group average, would be particularly important if that person implemented the program often but perhaps less important if the person implemented the program rarely). Finally, some intervention programs use rating scales to capture an overall level of implementation integrity rather than try to record implementation of each step in the program's procedures. As such, these types of rating scales cannot be averaged or interpreted in the ways just described. For this reason, the TAPS Teacher may simply record "Not Applicable" for Item 5 and instead present any other data obtained about implementers' integrity.

Similar to the summative review meeting procedures for Goal 1, after objectively describing the relevant implementation data acquired throughout the case, the TAPS Teacher should ask for each team member's input and generate an agreed-upon team response for Items 6–12 of the SRF. As with responses to Items 1–4 of the form, responses to Items 6–12 should reflect objective data and all implementers' input, including that of the TAPS Teacher. Unique to Items 6–12, however, is the need to discuss and record an explanation for any item that is not rated as "Agree" or "Strongly Agree" (i.e., items rated 3 or less). As shown in the SRF, there are six listed common reasons that the implementers may have deviated from the intended intervention plan (e.g., the plan was unclear, there was insufficient time, there were high levels of absences) and an "Other" option shown as reason 7 in the list. When "Agree" or "Strongly Agree" is not the team's response for any item, the reason(s) for plan deviation should be recorded on the corresponding item's line, with additional explanation (if needed) written below the item in the space provided. There are four main rationales for explaining deviations from the implementation plan: (1) to document the information as part of the student's record of intervention services; (2) to use the information for better understanding the effectiveness of the intervention plan; (3) to facilitate discussion, feedback, and learning among members of the implementation team; and (4) to identify barriers of the implementation plan that may be prevented during future TAPS cases.

After completing Items 6–12 of the SRF, the TAPS Teacher should review the identified deviations from the intervention plan and discuss with the team whether those deviations meaningfully weakened the success of the intervention plan. Based on the team's discussion, a response should be determined and recorded for Item 13. Next, the TAPS Teacher should discuss successes related to the team's implementation of the plan and write those for Item 14. Successes might include implementation of the intervention program for the predetermined number of days and weeks (as indicated on the student's IPF); teachers making some useful modifications to the intervention plan during periodic follow-ups; all implementers implementing the plan with at least high (e.g., 90%) integrity; or any other success that can be documented. One goal of noting implementation successes in writing (or typing) is to help ensure that the team recognizes both student-level and implementation-level successes that occurred as part of the TAPS process. Chapter 10 provides further discussion about this topic within the subsection "Case-by-Case Reviews."

Goal 3: Summarize Upcoming Instructional Plans

The final goal of the summative review meeting is to determine what should happen next in the student's instructional program to ensure continued academic success and, if needed, further remediation. Once again, the TAPS Teacher should facilitate discussion regarding the next steps for the student's instructional plan, but all others at the meeting should contribute to the discussion so that a strong, collective decision is made. To assist the TAPS Teacher with facilitating Goal 3 of the summative review meeting, the SRF offers a list of 10 common options that may constitute a logical next step in a student's instructional programming (e.g., continue to monitor the student's academic progress, modify the student's intervention plan, seek additional problem-solving support from other educators in the school). If helpful to the discussion, the entire team should review this list of options; in nearly all cases more than one option from this list will be selected and built into the student's instructional program. Likewise, it is possible and appropriate for the team to develop and integrate instructional plans not specified within the list (as shown in Item 11, "Other").

> **Following implementation of a student's TAPS intervention plan, important decisions must be made to determine what should happen next to best support the student.**

Of course, there are many factors that the team must consider when determining next steps for the student's instructional program, but the items previously discussed and rated as part of the summative review meeting should assist the team with deciding appropriate next steps. In particular, responses to Items 1, 2, 3, and 13 of the SRF, as well as the teacher's current responses to the TAPS Case Rating Scale, should help the team determine further plans for the student's instructional program.

The summative review meeting should be used to determine a strong plan for next steps, and the SRF should be used as a method to document the steps and strategies that will become part of the student's instructional program. As shown on the SRF, the TAPS Teacher should check the boxes that correspond with the team's decisions, and details for each decision should be written on the lines below the checklist. For example, details may include dates, timelines, and descriptions that will improve clarity and implementation of the next steps. When appropriate, the team may also decide to create a new or heavily modified IPF for the student.

Collectively, the summative review meeting should serve as an integral piece of the TAPS process. Put simply, the meeting should assist all implementers of the student's intervention plan to review the success of the plan and determine what further steps should be taken to maintain or improve the student's academic success. Furthermore, the summative review meeting should be used as an opportunity for all implementers—particularly the classroom teacher and, if applicable, a teacher assistant—to reflect upon (1) the strengths and weaknesses of the intervention plan, and (2) what they learned throughout the TAPS implementation process. Chapter 7 also describes how the TAPS Teacher can help other teachers connect learning that occurs throughout a TAPS case with learning that occurs during other components of the SOPAA. For a summary of the primary TAPS activities and the estimated time needed for the TAPS Teacher to complete the activity per TAPS case, see Appendix M.

SUMMARY

Using triadic consultation, the TAPS process is the core component of the SOPAA model, and following the systematic steps of the process is integral to ensuring that teachers have the knowledge and support to help each of their students meet their learning goals. Through the TAPS process, structured documentation of intervention development, implementation, and evaluation also occur, and the process concludes with a systematic approach for determining what should happen next for a student supported through TAPS.

CHAPTER 6

Assessment for Instruction

From the perspective of many school staff, the thought of more student assessment is enough to draw groans and protests of "Leave us alone to teach!" This response is not unreasonable. Assessment takes professional time and resources away from instruction, and students' achievement is much more likely to be improved by professional time devoted to instruction than assessment.

However, assessment can serve useful purposes, and for this reason assessment for instruction is Component 2 of the SOPAA. This chapter discusses three places where assessment is used within the SOPAA model. In each case, the focus is on using brief, low-inference measures to guide low-stakes instructional decision making. By *low inference* we mean that the connection between what is assessed and what is to be taught is very easy to discern (i.e., the teacher does not have to infer the meaning of the assessment results). Two examples of low-inference measures are the number of words read correctly per minute as a measure of reading fluency, and the number of addition problems computed correctly as a score for a measure of addition skills. By *low stakes* we mean that the assessments are used to make instructional decisions that can be easily modified (e.g., placing a child in a supplemental reading intervention, altering instruction if a student is not making progress).

The first time assessment is used in SOPAA is during the targeted skills observation the TAPS Teacher conducts after a classroom teacher has turned in a Request for TAPS Form. As discussed in Chapter 4, the TAPS Teacher conducts a 5- to 20-minute assessment or skills observation to (1) verify that the referred student is experiencing difficulty in an academic area, (2) gather enough evidence of likely skill-area deficits to suggest intervention options to the classroom teacher, and (3) gain some personal experience with the student.

Another time assessment is used within the SOPAA model is during intervention implementation. When the TAPS Teacher and classroom teacher select an intervention and plan for its use, they decide how the child's response to the intervention will be monitored while instruction is taking place (i.e., progress monitoring). Two ways to monitor progress during intervention implementation are discussed: mastery measurement using some type of curriculum-embedded assessment, such as unit tests in a curriculum, and individualized progress monitoring with curriculum-based measurement (CBM). Mastery measurement involves breaking a curriculum into an instructional sequence and then assessing students' mastery of successive objectives.

The final way in which assessment is used in the SOPAA model is for universal screening of student achievement. Universal screening is a form of assessment wherein all students in a grade or school (hence the term *universal*) are assessed with brief measures to identify which students are progressing well and which may need a closer look at how they are doing in a subject area. Assessment decisions generally involve a tradeoff between the amount of assessment conducted and the accuracy of the results. In screening, poor results flag a student for a closer look rather than definitively indicating the presence of a problem. The approach allows many students to be assessed in a minimal amount of time.

The type of universal screening included in the SOPAA model involves assessments of academic achievement three to four times within a school year. The results are examined to determine whether students are performing as expected for the time of year (i.e., performing at benchmark), as well as whether they are making progress from where they started at the beginning of the school year. This type of universal screening is a key component in RTI models of academic instruction (Burns & Gibbons, 2008; Gersten et al., 2008), but can also be used independent of an RTI model to identify students at risk.

Suggestions for how to use assessment data for each of these purposes (the initial skills observation in TAPS, progress monitoring for students in TAPS, and universal screening in reading and mathematics) are described in separate sections in this chapter. Unfortunately, it is not possible to provide a detailed "how to" for each of these topics in a single chapter. Instead, our goal is to provide an orientation to the changes that are occurring in assessment in schools, introduce readers to some of the new types of assessment tools that are becoming widely available to educators (and the issues involved in their use), and then discuss how these tools might be used in the three assessment situations described in the SOPAA. Our primary focus in the chapter is on CBM, but we also describe some other types of assessment tools that are useful in guiding instruction at the individual or group level.

STANDARDS-BASED SCHOOL REFORM AND ASSESSMENT IN SCHOOLS

Norm-Referenced Assessment

Until recently, the dominant approach to assessment in public schools has been a norm-referenced approach. Assessment tools constructed within a norm-referenced model are designed to provide information about how a student compares to other students in some reference group. For example, if we give a norm-referenced reading test and a student scores at the 10th percentile, we know that the student is not doing very well in reading compared to peers. This information is useful for some purposes, such as indicating that we should probably be concerned about this student. However, we have little information about what the student can and can't do and what to do to improve this student's skill level. Tests designed primarily for norm-referenced assessment are constructed in ways that ensure that they do what they were intended to do. For example, a good norm-referenced test will have items that cover a wide range of skills in a subject area so that it is possible to accurately describe all students' skill levels relative to peers. Items are included on this type of test even if almost all of the students in the norm group could not answer them correctly. After all, in order to accurately say that a student scored at the 99th percentile, we must have test items that only 1% of the same-age peers could answer!

Although norm-referenced tests typically serve their intended purpose quite well, they are not useful for some of the most important questions that educators and others ask. For example, if we wanted to know whether all students in the nation were improving in achievement, a norm-referenced test would do a poor job of answering this question. Because norm-referenced scores are relative, we would never know it if all students in the nation improved (given that national norms were up to date). Half the students would score above the 50th percentile, and half the students would score at or below the 50th percentile.

Norm-referenced tests do not do a good job of telling educators if an individual student's skill level has changed from one point in time to another for multiple reasons. First, most norm-referenced tests do not have enough items at each skill level to be sensitive to anything but large changes in achievement. Second, to see a score change on a norm-referenced test, a student must not only make enough gains in achievement to answer more items correctly, but the change also must be big enough to affect the student's standing relative to peers. A student scoring at the 25th percentile in fourth grade who achieves a year's improvement will still be at the 25th percentile in fifth grade, even though she answered more items correctly in fifth grade. Of course, sometimes we do want to know about a student's standing relative to a national peer group, and in these situations a norm-referenced test is quite useful.

Assessment for Instructional Decision Making

In the 1990s, many states began to move toward a standards-based model of education. Rather than evaluating students and schools with norm-referenced tests, states began to articulate grade-level standards that described what students should know or be able to do at each grade level in an academic area. With these standards in place, states then constructed tests that provided information to schools about whether or not students met those standards and used results from these tests to report outcomes for classroom, schools, and districts in terms of the percent of students meeting these standards.

This approach to assessment is called *criterion-referenced assessment*. These types of assessments provide information about whether or not a student has reached a performance standard or criterion. Criterion-referenced testing therefore addresses the problem identified earlier with using norm-referenced tests to evaluate improvement for a group. That is, if the number or percent of students performing on grade level improves, a criterion-referenced test results will show this change.

Particularly for struggling learners, meaningful and ongoing assessment is critical to maximize learning outcomes.

By 2000, 49 out of the 50 states had established content standards in one or more academic areas (Schulte & Villwock, 2004) and most had large-scale testing programs to evaluate students' performance relative to these grade-level standards. The passage of the No Child Left Behind Act in 2001 put the force of federal policy behind this standards-based accountability movement. States were mandated to develop grade-level standards in reading and mathematics and to test all students in grades 3–8 annually relative to these standards. Regardless of whether a student was in general education or special education, or spoke English or another language, this legislation put the onus on schools to prove that students were meeting these performance standards or moving toward mastery.

For any educator involved in assessment, these reform efforts have brought dramatic changes. Because schools are judged on how well students perform relative to state performance standards, schools often want information on how students are doing relative to the skills reflected in the standards. There is interest in knowing whether students are making progress toward year-end standards even early in the year. If a student is not meeting an established standard, educators want information about the skills the student lacks that should be targeted to meet the performance standard.

These new questions have led to changes in assessment tools. Although some instructionally focused assessment tools have been available for decades, their use on a wide scale and in relation to state-level performance standards is new. Many educators find themselves unfamiliar with the new assessment tools currently available or unsure how to use them to answer the questions schools and teachers are asking about students.

THREE INSTRUCTIONALLY ORIENTED ASSESSMENT APPROACHES

In this section, we provide overviews of three instructionally oriented assessment approaches that are in wider use with the advent of standards-based accountability and schoolwide approaches to providing core and supplemental instruction so that all students meet grade-level standards. We refer to these three approaches later as we discuss how educators can find tools to help them match students with interventions, monitor student progress, and implement a universal screening program. The first assessment approach is CBM. The description we provide of CBM is lengthy because in each of the three circumstances where assessment is used within the SOPAA, CBM is a primary assessment option, and considerable background knowledge is needed to understand and use CBM effectively.

Following the description of CBM, we briefly describe task analytic approaches to academic assessment, wherein informal assessments are used to identify the prerequisite skills a student lacks to perform an expected task. This assessment approach is used in the TAPS targeted skills observation. Finally, we introduce computerized testing systems with criterion-referenced scoring systems that link student scores with specific-skill levels or state performance standards. This new type of assessment approach is becoming more common for universal screening.

Curriculum-Based Measurement

In this section, we provide an overview of CBM and describe typical features for reading, mathematics, and written expression.

History of CBM

CBM had its start over 30 years ago in work by Stan Deno and his doctoral students at the University of Minnesota. In a small manual for teachers serving students in special education, Deno and Mirkin (1977) gave this advice to teachers:

> At the present time we are unable to prescribe specific and effective changes in instruction for individual students with certainty. Therefore, changes in instructional programs which are arranged for an individual child can be treated only as hypotheses which must be empirically tested before a decision can be made on whether they are effective for that child. (p. 11)

Considerable research has borne out the wisdom of Deno and Mirkin's (1977) advice (e.g., Arter & Jenkins, 1979; Fuchs & Fuchs, 1986). Regardless of how much initial assessment is conducted to match an instructional program to a student's unique needs and strengths, knowing what program will be effective for an individual student before it is implemented is still a professional "best guess" (Arter & Jenkins, 1979; Stanovich & Stanovich, 2003). Although the use of research-based programs for core instruction and supplemental interventions increases the likelihood that students will benefit from the instruction, it is not a guarantee.

Given that we cannot tell ahead of time whether an instructional approach, curriculum, or intervention will work for a particular student, an important component of effective teaching is having access to a means to verify that the instruction is effective *while it is being implemented.* The realization that we can't predict a student's response to instruction ahead of time has been part of the rationale to move away from a "front-loaded" assessment approach where an intensive case study, often taking hours of assessment time, precedes actual assistance for a student with difficulty. Instead, many educators have moved toward an approach in which the initial assessment to place a student into an intervention is quicker and more informal, but there is more ongoing assessment to see if the instructional program is actually working. This approach is incorporated into SOPAA, and it is the reason we devote so much time to CBM in this chapter.

CBM was born out of the desire to have a quick, accurate, and easy-to-use tool for deciding whether instruction is resulting in educational gains while instruction is under way (Fuchs & Fuchs, 2002a). Thirty years ago, as today, many of the assessments developed in education were not sensitive to within-year gains in achievement, and they were so lengthy that daily, weekly, or monthly use was impractical. Experimenting with assessment methods developed within precision teaching (Lindsley, 1972), a behavioral analytic approach to instruction, Deno and his colleagues (Deno, 1985; Fuchs, Deno, & Mirkin, 1984) found that repeated administration of brief tests, of equal difficulty, on a daily or weekly basis, could indicate in a matter of weeks whether an instructional approach was working for an individual student. Deno and his colleagues did not claim that these tests were measuring everything a student was learning. They saw these brief tests as indicators of learning. Just as medical staff monitor pulse or temperature as "vital signs" or indicators related to other important aspects of health, CBMs were meant to be vital signs of underlying learning, showing that growth was occurring in the targeted achievement area.

Key Features of CBM

CBM has three key features. One is the repeated use of short tests, or *probes*, that are of equal difficulty (Fuchs & Fuchs, 2002). Each probe is constructed so that students have the opportunity to make many responses in a short period of time. Making many responses in a short period of time increases CBM's sensitivity to student progress. A second key feature of CBM is emphasis on technical adequacy (Stecker, Fuchs, & Fuchs, 2005). CBM probes typically have standardized administration and scoring procedures, produce consistent results across alternate forms, and have evidence to support that they are valid measurements of the construct being assessed (e.g., reading or math achievement). This focus on technical adequacy increases the confidence we can have in CBM results, especially relative to informal ways of deciding if instruction is working.

The final key feature of CBM is the graphical depiction of data (Stecker et al., 2005). CBM results are almost always presented as graphs, with the number of correct items per unit of time (usually per minute) on the vertical axis and weeks of instruction on the horizontal axis. This feature helps make the results of CBM probes more easily interpretable to teachers, parents, and students.

The most well-known type of CBM is the one used to determine passage reading fluency. A typical passage reading fluency probe set consists of 20–30 short reading passages, each at the same reading level. Each passage constitutes a probe. In a probe administration, a teacher reads a student a standard set of instructions that directs the student to read the passage aloud for 1 minute. The teacher follows along, marking words read incorrectly on a separate copy of the reading passage. The teacher stops the student after a minute and then records the number of words read correctly and incorrectly. The primary measure of interest is the number of words read correctly, although the number of errors and the student's ability to summarize what he or she read may also be of interest.

Although the results depend, to some extent, on the reading level of the student and the quality of the probe set, multiple research studies have shown that this 1-minute "test" is strongly correlated with well-established and much longer measures of reading skills, including measures of decoding, fluency, and reading comprehension (Wayman, Wallace, Wiley, Ticha, & Espin, 2007). Furthermore, when three oral reading probes are administered at one time (requiring about 5 minutes of testing time), the use of the median or middle score results in an even more reliable and valid measure of reading. Thus, in 5 minutes, educators can complete a reading assessment that tells them much about a student's current level of reading skill. Studies have also documented that it is possible to construct similar CBM probes in other achievement areas, such as mathematics and spelling. These probes correlate with much longer, more comprehensive measures of the same subject area, and unlike most norm-referenced tests, are sensitive to change over short time intervals (Foegen, Jiban, & Deno, 2007).

Uses of CBM and the Research to Support Them

The use of CBM has expanded from its original application for progress monitoring. In this section, its use for progress monitoring, skills analysis, and universal screening are briefly reviewed.

As part of the SOPAA model, CBM might be used for progress monitoring, skills analysis, and/or universal screening.

PROGRESS MONITORING

CBM was originally used to examine whether an instructional program was working for an individual student. In multiple studies, several researchers documented that use of CBM improved student outcomes (e.g., Fuchs et al., 1984; Fuchs, Fuchs, Hamlett, & Stecker, 1991). The typical procedures used in these studies included (1) CBM probes administered at least two times per week and an intervention of at least 7 weeks; (2) establishment of a baseline score for a student through the administration of multiple probes; (3) representation of data in graphical form; (4) use of goal setting in the form of an endpoint the teacher thought was ambitious yet achievable for an individual student and a line connecting the baseline level of achievement to the endpoint (an aim line); (5) comparison of the rate of progress reflected by the aim line with how the student was actually doing, and use of this information to guide instruction and adjust the aim line; and (6) some sort of instructional consultation to help the teacher decide how to change instruction. Figure 6.1 illustrates a typical CBM progress monitoring graph, including the collection of baseline data, an aim line based on setting an outcome goal and drawing a line between baseline and the goal, and the implementation of a teaching change when the current program did not appear to be meeting the student's needs.

Although this list of the typical procedures is rather long, it is important to make its components explicit because if CBM is implemented without these features, there is little, if any, research to suggest it will improve outcomes for students. It *may* improve achievement; we simply don't have research data to demonstrate it. However, much of the current advice promoting the use of CBM to improve achievement—and citing the research base to support its use—fails to note the way in which progress monitoring was used in the original research. Many of the suggestions in the literature, such as the one for monthly progress monitoring of students who are scoring below a specified level, have never been tested formally in an experimental study to verify whether they improve achievement (Gersten et al., 2008). The suggestions are extrapolations from the existing database to new situations. They are logical extrapolations, and it costs schools little in terms of

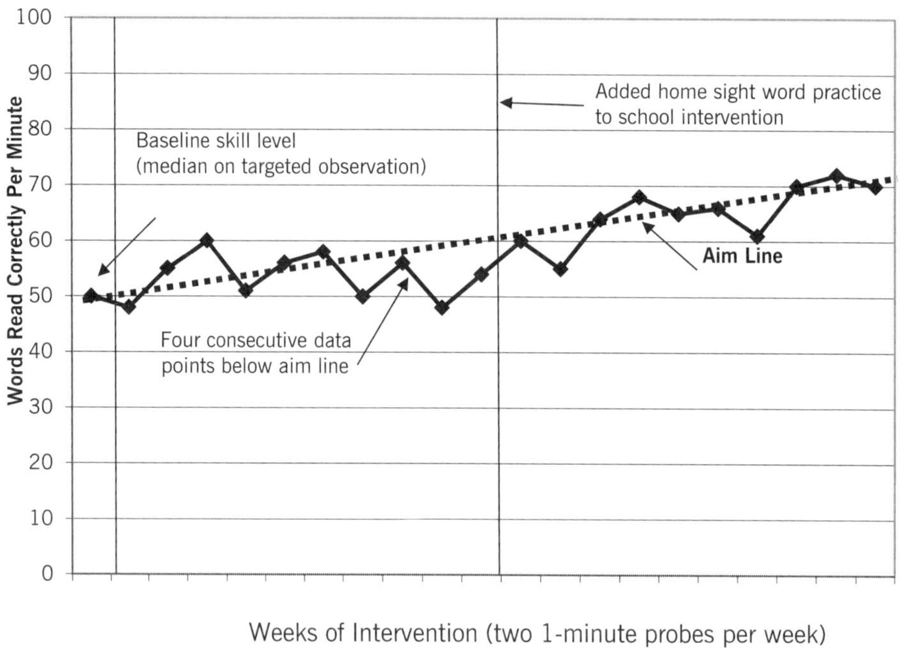

FIGURE 6.1. Progress monitoring with CBM.

time to complete these brief assessments, but they do not have the strong research base that is otherwise associated with CBM. We think this information is important to emphasize to TAPS Teachers and other educators because it helps explain why there is conflicting information about how to do progress monitoring in the literature. There are multiple extrapolations of how the CBM progress monitoring literature applies to schools, and each school will need to determine what works best for its needs. However, the closer one adheres to using CBM the way in which it was used in the research that demonstrated its positive effects, the more likely it is that those positive effects will be achieved.

SKILLS ANALYSIS

After CBM's role in improving outcomes through progress monitoring was established, researchers began to explore ways to expand its use, such as analyzing student response patterns on CBM probes, or using probes that assessed different skills (e.g., letter–sound fluency, passage reading fluency) to decide where remedial instruction should be targeted. For example, Fuchs et al. (1990) developed mathematics computation probes that tested multiple grade-level computation skills and a program that informed educators as to which skills students had mastered and not mastered (e.g., mastered multiplying by one digit; inconsistent performance on two-digit multiplication). They found that students in classes where teachers were given skills analysis information outperformed students in classes where teachers used CBM, but were not given skills analysis information.

These results and the desire of researchers to develop CBMs that tell teachers not just *when* to make a teaching change but that provide information about *what* to change, have led researchers to experiment with different decision rules and ways to use CBM to provide educators with additional instructional guidance. Some of these ways, such as the skills analysis program for mathematics developed by the Fuchs, have been validated in experimental studies. Other techniques are less formal, have limited research to support them, but are probably reasonable for use in low-stakes instructional decision making. For example, several researchers (Hintze, Christ, & Keller, 2002; Shapiro, 2011a) have outlined ways to use CBM probes from multiple grades (1) to assess in what grade-level material a student is able to read accurately and fluently, and (2) to identify the likely skill deficits that account for poor performance on a set of CBM probes. These approaches are called *survey-level assessment*. We provide some suggestions for using CBM for this type of skills analysis later in this chapter.

UNIVERSAL SCREENING AND BENCHMARKING

As noted earlier, one of the key characteristics of CBM probes is that they are technically sound. That is, although they are brief, they are designed to be reliable and correlate well with much longer, more comprehensive measures of the academic areas they are designed to assess. Given this important characteristic, and the sensitivity of CBM probes to within-year change, it should be no surprise that as early intervention and prevention of children's academic difficulties became a focus in school accountability, CBM probes began to be used to easily and quickly identify children who were experiencing academic difficulty.

One of the earliest examples of the use of CBM for universal screening is the set of CBM probes developed by Kaminski and Good (1996), the *Dynamic Indicators of Basic Early Literacy Skills* (DIBELS). With the universal screening component of this assessment system, a team of educators could individually administer a set of CBM probes to all students in a class in a matter of hours and identify students who were not mastering the basic skills related to learning to read with a high degree of accuracy. Because of the low-inference nature of the data, the screening results were easily interpretable and had clear instructional implications. Not only could educators identify individual students in need, but looking at results across all students allowed educators to identify areas in which many students were struggling, suggesting areas of the core curriculum that needed to be modified (e.g., Simmons et al., 2002). Although DIBELS is still available, a revised version of it, entitled "DIBELS Next," is just being introduced (Good & Kaminski, 2011). It moves even more toward the criterion-referenced approach to testing discussed earlier, tying benchmark scores to later reading outcomes.

Currently, multiple CBM probe sets are available for universal screening (as well as for progress monitoring). In the section of the chapter on implementing universal screening on pages 119–121, we offer guidance and resources for selecting, and beginning to implement, a reading or mathematics universal screening program.

Is the use of universal screening with CBM or other types of screening measures a research based practice? Both of the IES practice guides for assisting students who are struggling in reading and mathematics (Gersten et al., 2008, 2009) identify universal screening, if it is accompanied by interventions for students identified as at risk, as an educational practice with moderate research support. Although there is research to support the use of universal screening in reading and mathematics, the specific cutoff scores for benchmarks used in many of the systems have been set on a rational basis rather than on the basis of a statistical relationship between the benchmark cutoffs score and a criterion (what the scores are predicting, such as later reading failure). For example, many systems still use students' standings compared to a norm group (e.g., scoring below the 10th percentile) to identify which students are at risk for reading difficulties. For the reasons we have stated earlier, this practice presents difficulties. Ideally, benchmark expectations for students in a criterion-referenced system are based on a known relationship between a cutoff score (benchmark) on the screening measure and an external performance criterion, not solely on norms (Silberglitt & Hintze, 2005).

However, even if the benchmark cutoff score is based on statistical relationship with a criterion, the criterion used to set the benchmark scores may be different than the criterion the school is trying to predict. For example, the benchmark cut-off score for a first grader on a passage-reading fluency probe may predict below grade-level reading on a third-grade end-of-year assessment in one state, but not in another. States may have different expectations for student achievement by the end of third grade, and these differences affect the accuracy of the benchmarks for CBM probes.

Table 6.1 shows the progress monitoring benchmarks at each grade level that different publishers and researchers have suggested for passage reading fluency CBM probe sets. The numbers are similar, but they do differ. The message here is that there is some judgment involved in interpreting the meaning of different score levels on CBM probes. It may take some direct experience with a CBM probe set, as well as knowledge of the extent to which testing error affects individuals® scores (i.e., the test's standard error of measurement), to understand what the scores from a CBM probe or set of probes mean in the context of a school's performance expectations for stu-

TABLE 6.1. Range of Benchmark Values[a] and Rates of Improvement[b] for Selected Passage Reading Fluency CBM Probe Sets

Grade	Benchmark period	AIMSweb	DIBELS Next	EasyCBM[c]	Hasbrouck & Tindal[d]
1	Fall	12	—	7	—
	Winter	31	23	27	23
	Spring	62	47	54	53
ROI[b]		1.4	1.3	1.3	1.7[c]
2	Fall	60	52	52	51
	Winter	85	72	78	72
	Spring	102	87	97	89
ROI		1.2	1.0	1.2	1.0
3	Fall	83	70	83	71
	Winter	106	86	114	92
	Spring	121	100	115	107
ROI		1.1	.8	.9	1.0
4	Fall	104	90	105	94
	Winter	119	103	132	112
	Spring	133	115	138	123
ROI		.8	.7	.9	.8
5	Fall	117	111	145	110
	Winter	134	120	153	127
	Spring	149	130	169	139
ROI		.9	.5	.7	.8

[a]Benchmarks are based on 50th percentile for CBM probe set, except for DIBELS Next, which based benchmarks on the relationship of scores at each testing period to a criterion measure. The 2009–2010 values were used for AIMSweb and DIBELS Next.
[b]Rates of improvement (ROI) calculated by subtracting fall benchmark from spring benchmark score and then dividing by 36.
[c]Easy CBM provides CBM probe sets for reading and math and is discussed later in this chapter.
[d]Hasbrouck and Tindal (2006) provided average weekly improvement values (same as ROI) in their publication that were based on a 32-week interval between fall and spring assessments. These were converted to 36-week ROIs for comparison purposes.

dents. Because of this issue some CBM systems (e.g., AIMSweb) include analysis tools that allow schools to set their own benchmarks that relate to high stakes tests or performance expectations in their district.

CBM Progress Monitoring Options for Reading, Mathematics, and Writing

Since CBM was developed in the 1970s, several researchers and/or publishers have developed CBM probe sets. These probe sets vary in multiple ways, including administration format (computerized, individually administered, group administered), which skills are assessed, the extent to which the developer provides information to document the technical quality of the probe set, and the actual technical qualities of the probe set (e.g., reliability, validity). Some CBM probe sets are free, and some must be purchased. Some researchers and publishers have developed complete systems that provide CBM progress monitoring probes, universal screening probes, computerized entry, graphing, analysis systems, and intervention guidance tied to results. Others CBM probe sets consist only of the probes themselves.

In this section, we describe some common types of CBM that have been developed in reading (including early reading), mathematics (including early numeracy), and writing. We discuss commonly used types of CBMs, but not specific products. For example, there are passage reading fluency probe sets from different developers that are quite similar in content and format, although they differ somewhat in their technical characteristics (e.g., AIMSweb, DIBELS, and EasyCBM). Readers who wish to compare different probe sets can consult the developers' websites (listed in Figure 6.2), and Table 6.2 provides basic information on examples of probe sets for each type of CBM. Another useful source is the website of the National Center for Response to Intervention (*www.rti4success.org*). A national panel of experts has articulated standards for progress monitoring and universal screening measures, reviewed individual measures submitted by their authors in relation to these standards, and then summarized these results in chart form. Readers can refer to these charts for extensive information on the technical characteristics of different CBM options in reading and mathematics, as well as their cost. However, not all available CBM options are listed in this chart because developers have to submit their measures for evaluation. Additional resources for all the types of assessment discussed in this chapter are provided in Figure 6.2 (pp. 100–102).

CBM EARLY READING AND READING MEASURES

A number of CBM probe sets are available for assessing early reading and reading.

Early Reading. Although passage reading fluency was one of the first CBM measures developed, passage reading fluency will not be a sensitive measure of reading skill development until children have enough phonics skills and sight words to read connected text. Most students are expected to acquire phonemic awareness skills and learn to associate letter names, sounds, and graphemes (written letters) in kindergarten and the first months of first grade. Typical CBM early reading measures in kindergarten include tasks for which children are asked to separate spoken words into phonemes (phoneme segmentation), identify letter names, or identify the sounds associated with written lists of individual letters (letter–sound fluency) or with nonsense words (consonant–vowel–consonant, or CVC, and vowel–consonant, or VC, combinations). There is a substantial body of research to support the technical characteristics of early reading CBMs and their ability to predict later reading outcomes (e.g., Fuchs, Fuchs, & Compton, 2004).

Some of these same early reading measures may be useful for first graders, depending on their level of skill development. For example, nonsense word fluency CBM can be a useful for monitor-

TABLE 6.2. Examples of Published CBM Probe Sets by Type

Probe set type	Available from	Number of probes for progress monitoring, grade levels offered	Graphing and data display resources?
	Reading		
Phoneme segmentation fluency	AIMSweb	33, K–1	Yes
	DIBELS/DIBELS Next	20 total	Yes
	EasyCBM	17, K-1	Yes
Letter naming fluency	AIMSweb	33, K–1	Yes
	DIBELS/DIBELS Next	3, K	Yes
	EasyCBM	17, K–1	Yes
Letter–sound fluency	AIMSweb	33, K–1	Yes
	Curriculum-Based Measurement in Reading (CBM-R)	5	No
	EasyCBM	17, K–1	Yes
Nonsense word fluency	AIMSweb	33, K–1	Yes
	DIBELS/DIBELS Next	20	Yes
Word identification fluency	CBM-R	30, 1	No
	EasyCBM	17, K–3	Yes
Passage reading fluency	AIMSweb	23, K–1 33, 2–8	Yes Yes
	CBM-R	30, 1—7	No
	DIBELS/DIBELS Next	20, 1–6	Yes
	EasyCBM	17, 1–6 14, 7 16, 8	Yes
	System to Enhance Educational Performance (STEEP)	50, 1–5	Yes
Maze passage fluency	AIMSweb	23, K–1 33, 2–8	Yes
	CBM-R	30, 1—7	Yes
	DIBELS Next	20, 3–6	Yes
	Mathematics		
Oral counting	AIMSweb	Only 1 form needed, counting 1–100	Yes
Number identification	AIMSweb	33, K–1	Yes
Quantity discrimination	AIMSweb	33, K–1	Yes

(cont.)

TABLE 6.2. *(cont.)*

Probe set type	Available from	Number of probes for progress monitoring, grade levels offered	Graphing and data display resources?
Mathematics computation	AIMSweb	33, K–8	Yes
	Monitoring Basic Skills Progress (MBSP)	30, 1–6	No
Mathematics concepts and applications	AIMSweb	33, K–8	Yes
	MBSP	30, 2–6	No
	Writing and spelling		
Prompts for writing stories	AIMSweb	94, grade independent	Yes
Spelling	AIMSweb	33, 1–8	Yes

Note. This table presents a sampling of CBM probe sets. Each individual probe set identified in the table has administration and training materials that accompany it, and score interpretation information related to use of the probe set for universal screening and progress monitoring.

ing students who are receiving help learning to associate graphemes (written letters) and sounds and to blend sounds. However, if the intervention program includes phonics skills beyond those used to blend CVC and VC combinations, nonsense word fluency is not likely to reflect changes in children's skill level when they progress beyond CVC words (McMaster, Fuchs, Fuchs, & Compton, 2005).

For this reason, one of the most useful measures for monitoring intervention programs targeted at skills to be mastered in the first grade is word identification fluency (Fuchs et al., 2004). Each probe in a word identification fluency CBM contains a list of words encountered across the year in first-grade reading instruction. The range of words increases the likelihood that the measure will be sensitive to increases in phonics and sight word skills for the entire first-grade year, unlike nonsense word fluency. However, the easier words on the word identification probes mean that the measure can be used before first graders acquire enough reading skills to allow use of a passage reading fluency CBM.

Passage Reading Fluency. When using passage reading fluency CBMs (described earlier) for progress monitoring, a set of CBM probes at the student's instructional level is used to gauge progress. Although passage reading fluency probes are a good general outcome measure of reading for students who are reading at the late first- to third-grade level, it is important to consider the time-limited relationship between passage reading fluency and reading comprehension. Passage reading fluency is more strongly related to reading comprehension in early grades than upper grades (Wiley & Deno, 2005). As students become skilled decoders of text (e.g., by fourth grade for an average or above-average reader), the relationship between comprehension and oral reading fluency becomes less strong (Paris, 2011). Switching to a reading CBM that more directly taps reading comprehension skill, such as the next type of probe to be described, may be desirable in fourth grade and above (Hosp, Hosp, & Howell, 2007). However, there are many situations where passage reading fluency probes may provide useful information in the upper grades, particularly

Described below are key resources that should be useful for learning more about the three types of assessment featured in SOPAA or for getting more information about specific tools mentioned in the chapter. Full references for books and articles are provided in the references section at the end of this book.

General Sources to Learn More about (and How to Use) CBM and Other Assessment Options

Websites

National Center on Response to Intervention (*www.rti4success.org*)

This center's website provides extensive information on the use of CBM and other types of measures for progress monitoring and universal screening. Training resources, implementation resources, and research summaries are available at this site. Important tools for any school considering progress monitoring or universal screening on this site are the two "Tools Charts" that rate assessment tools for universal screening and progress monitoring on multiple dimensions and provide detailed information about each tool (information about each tool can be found in pop-up menus activated by clicking on the name of the measure in the Tools chart).

National Center on Student Progress Monitoring (*www.studentprogress.org*)

This center's website provides extensive information on the use of CBM, including specific training in using CBM for progress monitoring in reading, math, and writing.

Intervention Central (*www.interventioncentral.org*)

This website has many resources relevant to progress monitoring, universal screening, and identifying intervention targets for an individual student. It provides the resources to generate CBM probes and for easy charting of CBM results. However, unless educators have sufficient measurement and research background to evaluate the technical adequacy of the CBM probes they create, we recommend use of assessment tools with published technical characteristics. Using established CBM probe sets provides educators with key information about the instruments' general strengths and shortcomings.

IRIS Center (*http://iris.peabody.vanderbilt.edu*)

This website is designed to provide information on special education scientifically validated and evidence-based instructional strategies that promote inclusion. Several modules on assessment provide free training on progress monitoring.

Print Resources

The ABC's of CBM: A Practical Guide to Curriculum-Based Measurement (Hosp, Hosp, & Howell, 2007)

This paperback book is a simple introductory guide to CBM that provides step-by-step instructions for using CBM for progress monitoring, universal screening, and survey-level assessment in reading, math, and writing (including spelling). Although easy to read, the book provides an excellent introduction to many of the issues involved in planning, implementing, and using CBM for many purposes.

Academic Skills Problems and *Academic Skills Problems Fourth Edition Workbook* (Shapiro, 2011a, 2011b)

This book and workbook provide a broad view of assessment for instruction that includes CBM and resources for low-inference assessment of student skills in reading, math, and writing (including spelling). These two books are written at a more advanced level than the *ABC's of CBM* resource mentioned above.

Assessing Reading: Multiple Measures (2nd ed.; Diamond & Thorsnes, 2008)

This book contains a range of low-inference measures of different reading skills and guidance in linking assessment results to areas where intervention should be focused. This chapter discusses the CORE Phonics Survey in the most depth, but this book provides other assessment instruments that may be useful for educators.

(cont.)

FIGURE 6.2. Key resources and information about assessments that can be used with the SOPAA.

Best Practices in School Psychology 5th edition (Vol. 2; Thomas & Grimes, 2008)

The second volume in this five-volume set addresses data-based decision making and accountability. Several of the chapters directly address curriculum-based evaluation and using low-inference data to decide what type of intervention is needed to address a student's achievement difficulty. Chapters 20–25 deal exclusively with curriculum-based evaluation.

Sources for Specific CBM Probe Sets Mentioned in Chapter 6

Websites

AIMSweb (*www.aimsweb.com*)

AIMSweb is a benchmark and progress monitoring system published by Pearson. It provides benchmark and progress monitoring probe sets in early reading and numeracy, reading, math, and writing (including spelling). In addition to probe sets, the site provides many resources with which to train and guide users in the application of the probe sets in AIMSweb for universal screening, progress monitoring, and survey assessment. There is a charge for using AIMSweb, although sample materials can be downloaded from the site for examination at no charge.

Dynamic Indicators of Basic Early Literacy Skills (DIBELS) and DIBELS Next (*dibels.uoregon.edu and www.dibels.org/next*)

DIBELS and DIBELS Next are CBM probe sets that provide information about key skills in early literacy. The materials can be downloaded free of charge, but there is a cost to access the data system. Video demonstrations and quick-start guides are available at the website, as well as resources on reading instruction and schoolwide models for reading instruction.

EasyCBM (*www.easycbm.com*)

EasyCBM provides probe sets for early reading and mathematics. Its developers describe it as a "next generation" CBM set, and they provide some of the more widely known probe sets (e.g., letter–sound fluency, passage reading fluency) described in the chapter and referenced in Table 6.2, and also some newer probe sets. For example, EasyCBM provides probe sets that are aligned with the National Council of Teachers of Mathematics focal points in mathematics (grades K–8) and a set of reading comprehension multiple-choice items (grades 2–8). These newer probe sets can be administered on the computer. Web-based training videos demonstrate how to administer probe sets, with quizzes to assess mastery of administration procedures. Classroom-level use of EasyCBM is free; there is a charge for additional features that may be useful at the school or district level.

STEEP (*www.isteep.com*)

STEEP (System to Enhance Educational Performance) is a comprehensive RTI system. CBM probes are sold only to registered users of the company's data system, and there is a charge for use. Probe sets for early literacy and numeracy, mathematics, and reading are available, along with a system for directly linking CBM results to specific interventions and for prioritizing intervention needs.

Print-Based CBM Probe Sets

Curriculum-Based Measurement in Reading (CBM-R)

CBM-R has probe sets available for sound identification, word identification, passage fluency reading, and maze passage fluency. Training manuals and interpretive information are available. There is a small charge for the probe sets. CBM-R is available from Vanderbilt University, Peabody #228, 110 Magnolia Circle, Suite MRL418, Nashville, TN 37203-5721; Phone: 615-343-4782; e-mail Flora Murray (*flora.murray@vanderbilt.edu*) to order this tool and to answer any questions.

Monitoring Basic Skills Progress (MBSP; *www.proedinc.com*)

MBSP is a master set of the mathematics concepts and applications and computation probes used in much of the Fuchses' mathematics research that has been cited in the chapter. A kit that includes the master sets for both types of probes and a manual and answer key can be purchased. MBSP is available through ProEd.

(cont.)

FIGURE 6.2. *(cont.)*

Computerized Assessment Tools Mentioned in Chapter 6

The assessment tools in this section are more expensive than CBM probe sets. However, they require less staff time to administer, score, interpret, and summarize results. In most cases, results can be reported on a developmental scale (a single scale to track growth in a subject area across grades) so that growth in achievement can be tracked across multiple years. Publishers often provide information about how these developmental scores are related to, and can be used to predict, states' large-scale assessment results. With the exception of Yearly Progress Pro, these instruments are not designed for weekly progress monitoring, but are more appropriate for tracking universal screening or benchmarking.

Websites

Accelerated Math (*www.renlearn.com/se*)

Accelerated Math is a software program that provides students with practice in mathematics skills as well as assesses students' mastery of specific mathematics skills, and also provides developmental scores that reflect students' mastery of mathematics content across grades. An unlimited number of forms can be generated, so that this tool can be used for progress monitoring, as well as for screening of students in mathematics. Accelerated Math is published by Renaissance Learning.

Scholastic Reading Inventory (*teacher.scholastic.com/products/sri_reading_assessment/index.htm*)

The Scholastic Reading Inventory assesses reading comprehension. Scores are provided in Lexiles,[R] (an approximation of test difficulty) which can be used to place students in reading material that they can comprehend. Students must be able to read noncontrolled text, so the test may not be sensitive for poor readers in the lower grades (K–3). The test has been evaluated for progress monitoring by the National Center on Response to Intervention. However, recommended use is three to four times per year, so it is not appropriate for weekly progress monitoring. The inventory is published by Scholastic.

STAR Early Literacy, Reading, and Mathematics (*www.renlearn.com/se*)

STAR Early Literacy, Reading, and Mathematics tests are computer-adaptive tests that can be administered in 15 minutes or less and provide within-year and across-year assessments of students' achievement. Benchmarks, aligned to state standards, are available, as well as a variety of reports at the individual student, class, and school level. The tests are published by Renaissance Learning.

Yearly Progress Pro (*www.ctb.com/ctb.com/control/productFamilyViewAction?productFamilyId=591&p=products*)

Yearly Progress Pro is a set of computerized curriculum-based assessments in reading and mathematics. The probes can be adapted to states' reading and mathematics standards, and specific information on mastery of skills within each area is provided. Yearly Progress Pro is published by CTB/McGraw-Hill.

FIGURE 6.2. *(cont.)*

if information about students' decoding skills remains of interest (e.g., passage reading fluency probes may be useful for older students who need remedial instruction in word mechanics, decoding, or passage reading fluency).

MAZE PASSAGES

CBM probes for maze passages consist of reading passages of equivalent difficulty in which every seventh word has been omitted and replaced with a number of alternate word choices (typically three). Students are given a short period of time (typically 2.5 minutes) to read through the passage, selecting the correct word to complete the sentence for each omitted word. In essence, the student encounters a multiple-choice item every seventh word.

One advantage of maze passages is that they can be administered in a group setting, eliminating the need for individual student assessment. Thus, this type of probe is particularly useful for universal screening where large numbers of students are assessed. There are also computerized versions of maze passage CBM probes available (e.g., Yearly Progress Pro). Stecker et al. (2005) have noted that teachers tend to respond more favorably to computerized probes because of the ease of administration and scoring. Use of maze passages for assessing reading is most helpful in grade 4 and above and in situations where information is needed specifically about reading comprehension, not about decoding speed and accuracy.

CBM EARLY NUMERACY AND MATHEMATICS MEASURES

Although mathematics measures are less widely used than reading CBM probe sets, there are several types of CBM probe sets available in the area of mathematics.

Early Numeracy. Early numeracy CBMs can be helpful in identifying children who are not acquiring basic mathematics knowledge and understanding prior to formal instruction in this area. Some typical early numeracy CBMs for use in kindergarten and first grade are oral counting, wherein a student counts sequentially for 1 minute while pointing on a sheet to the numbers from 1 to 100, written sequentially; number identification, wherein a child orally reads numbers written on a sheet; and quantity discrimination, wherein a child is given a series of number pairs and identifies which one is larger (Clarke & Shinn, 2004). Although there is a substantial body of research showing the utility of mathematics computation CBMs (see Foegen et al., 2007, and Hosp et al., 2007, for summaries), there is a less developed body of research to support early numeracy CBMs (Hosp et al.). Nevertheless, research on key early numeracy skills is growing (e.g., Lago & DiPerna, 2010), and reliable measures of early numeracy are available that show strong relationships with more comprehensive measures of mathematics (Foegen et al., 2007).

Mathematics Computation. CBM probes for math computation typically present a series of grade-appropriate computation problems and ask children to complete as many problems as possible within 2 minutes. Some sets of CBM computation probes cover problems for an entire grade. Others sample a narrower range of computation problems (e.g., addition only). For example, AIMSweb (*www.aimsweb.com*) has single-operation and mixed-operation probe sets available in its set of CBM mathematics probes.

There are multiple ways of scoring CBM computation probes. For example, some probe sets have scoring procedures wherein each digit completed correctly is counted, even digits written when working out a problem. Other probe sets have simplified scoring procedures. The advantage of counting each digit correct is that the measure is likely to be more sensitive to small changes in student skills (Hosp et al., 2007). On the other hand, simplified scoring systems can speed up the time it takes to score CBM probes and reduce errors.

Mathematics Concepts and Applications. CBM probe sets also assess mathematics concepts and skills (e.g., word problems, graph reading, money). Individual probes tend to be longer (e.g., 6–8 minutes) than those used to assess computation because students must apply their skills in a specific context, such as a word problem. These probe sets offer the advantage of assessing a wider range of mathematics content than computation probes. However, because the test items take longer to complete, there are less items, and the probes can be less sensitive to short-term improvement in a student's skill level.

New Mathematics Probes. Early CBM research in mathematics began with a focus on computational fluency and then expanded to the assessment of mathematics concepts and applications.

However, there are other ways to conceptualize the structure of mathematics skill development and appropriate foci for assessment. For example, the National Council of Teachers of Mathematics (2006) describes mathematics instruction in terms of five content strands: (1) number and operations (understanding numbers, comparing quantities, and fluency with computational procedures), (2) algebra, (3) geometry, (4) measurement, and (5) data analysis and probability. Some of the newer CBM probe sets parallel these content strands (e.g., EasyCBM), or allow school districts to select a set of probes that matches the content of the curriculum and the performance standards set for students by schools or states (e.g., Yearly Progress Pro).

In reading, passage reading fluency and maze probe sets do a good job of assessing reading development across a relatively wide range of curricula and grade levels. For this reason, they are often referred to as "general outcome measures." However, the structure of mathematics knowledge is different, and CBM probe sets in mathematics are more sensitive to differences in curriculum (Hosp et al., 2007). Therefore, it is important that educators examine the match of the content in different CBM probe sets with state grade-level mathematics standards as well as the intervention and/or instruction that students are provided. If not, the scores will not be accurate, and the probes will be less sensitive to changes in students' skill level.

One positive aspect of most mathematics CBM probe sets is that they can be administered to a group, as long as students have the reading skills to understand instructions and word problems. In addition, some CBM probe sets in mathematics provide information about the types of problems that present difficulty for students (e.g., Monitoring Basic Skills Progress computation probes and Yearly Progress Pro mathematics probes). This characteristic makes it easier for educators to look for student skill deficits that can be targeted during instruction.

CBM WRITING MEASURES

There is far less consensus in the research literature on what constitutes skilled writing and how it is best measured. As a result, development of CBM measures in writing lags far behind that for reading and mathematics, and there is little research demonstrating that the use of CBM writing measures for progress monitoring or screening improves student outcomes (McMaster & Espin, 2007). However, some writing CBMs have been developed, and they are briefly mentioned here.

Early Writing. A limited body of research is available on CBM probes for early writers (McMaster, Du, & Petursdottir, 2009). However, for first graders, one promising CBM probe set is sentence copying (McMaster et al., 2009). It may be surprising that for early writers, simply copying a sentence appears to be a sensitive measure of writing skill. However, students must be able to form letters and words with speed and automaticity to put their thoughts onto paper, and this simple task appears to be a sensitive indicator of early writing development (Berninger, Yates, Cartwright, Remy, & Abbott, 1992). Instructions for constructing sentence copying prompts and a summary of their technical characteristics can be found in McMaster et al. Story prompts are also sometimes used with first graders and are described below.

Spelling. Monitoring of students' spelling skills with CBM can be helpful in assessing phonics knowledge and mastery of common spelling patterns or for monitoring students' response to intervention in this area. CBM spelling probes have typically been scored by counting the number of correct letter sequences students produce so that small changes in students' spelling skill can be detected. Spelling CBM probe sets should be constructed or selected to reflect the spelling rules taught to students, and they can be useful in monitoring students' generalization of the spelling rules taught across a school year (Hosp et al., 2007). They can also be used diagnostically (Fuchs, Fuchs, Hamlett, & Allinder, 1991).

Writing. A commonly used type of writing CBM probe begins with a story prompt (e.g., "If I had a million dollars I would . . ."). Students are given 30 seconds to plan and then write in response to the prompt for 3 or 5 minutes. Multiple ways of scoring these probes have been examined, included counting the number of words written, the number of words written correctly, and number of correct writing sequences. Scoring correct writing sequences provides a count of the number of adjacent, correctly spelled words acceptable within a written phrase (Hosp et al., 2007) and takes into account whether punctuation, spelling, and language use are correct in the writing sample. Each of these types of scoring is sensitive to change over time and moderately related to broader measures of writing (Foegen et al., 2007).

At present, the limited research on writing CBMs is likely to make it difficult for educators to use and interpret CBM results in this area. However, at least one CBM developer, AIMSweb, provides a set of story prompts and norms for grades 1 through 8 for correct writing sequences. A set of story prompts is also available at *www.interventioncentral.org/index.php?option=com_content&view=article&id=194.*

CBM Summary and a Caveat

This section provides a brief snapshot of what CBM is, why it was developed, and some of the typical tasks that are used in CBM probes. It provides a context for more specific information in the next sections about how CBM can be used within SOPAA for assessing students' skill deficits, progress monitoring, and universal screening.

CBM is a powerful yet simple tool. Although use of CBM has been reported in the research literature for years, only recently have the availability of computer and web-based CBM applications, as well as changes in federal policy, led to widespread availability and use of CBM in schools. Like any new assessment tool, time, training, and experience are needed to use the tool to its full advantage and to understand what the results mean. Some professional development resources for CBM are provided in Chapter 7 and at the end of this chapter.

Mastery Measurement/Task Analytic Approaches to Assessment

As stated earlier, one of the defining characteristics of CBM probes is that all probes in a probe set are meant to sample the same set of skills and be of equal difficulty. That way, if a student's skill level improves, his or her score improves. Another approach to assessing students' skill development is to break down a complex task into necessary subskills, arrange the subskills into a hierarchy, and then construct measures of each subskill. With this approach, test content changes across time, and students' mastery of an academic area is demonstrated by reaching a performance criterion on a series of increasingly complex tasks. For example, in reading, we might start by teaching, and then assessing, students' mastery of letter–sound sequences. If the students masters letter–sound sequences, we would then teach and assess blending skills for CVC combinations, before moving onto teaching and assessing how to decode a different type of syllable.

This type of assessment is an alternative to CBM. Like CBM, it provides instructionally useful information, particularly if the assessments are very closely aligned with what it being taught. For the TAPS targeted skills observation, mastery measurement can help identify which skills a student lacks in order to match him or her with an intervention. Many research-based interventions (see Chapter 12) have built-in mastery measures for progress monitoring, with assessment content closely aligned to the skills being taught in the intervention. When used for universal screening, mastery measurement tests can identify which students are having difficulty, and also which skills they have not mastered. A disadvantage of mastery measurement is that mastery tests tend to be longer because there need to be a sufficient number of items assessing each skill to be certain that a student has, or has not, mastered it.

One area in which mastery measures are often used is in an instructional problem-solving and decision-making model called *curriculum-based evaluation* (Howell, Hosp, & Kurns, 2008; Howell, 2000; Howell & Nolet, 2000). Howell and his colleagues have developed very useful task analyses and associated low-inference measures for many academic areas as part of the development of curriculum-based evaluation, and these task analyses and measures are useful tools that play a central role in some RTI models, such as the Heartland model (Grimes & Kurns, 2003; Kurns & Ikeda, 2008).

Computer-Adaptive Criterion-Referenced Testing

We introduce computer-adaptive criterion-referenced testing in this chapter because this type of testing is coming into wide use in the schools for universal screening. In computer-adaptive criterion-referenced testing, students respond to an individually tailored set of items (items get easier or harder depending on whether each student answers an item correctly or incorrectly) that then provides information about skills the students have mastered.

Tests of this type span multiple grade levels, so that students who are functioning above or below grade level are presented with items that are appropriate for their skill level. The primary scores yielded from these tests describe where students fall on a skills continuum, rather than how they compare to students their age. Thus, these tests are like mastery tests because they tell educators which skills a student has mastered, but they only sample skills close to where the student appears to be functioning. Students are assumed to have mastered skills far below their current skill level and not to have skills far above their skill level. Unlike most mastery tests, the scores on computer-adaptive tests are on a multigrade continuous scale (called *vertical scaling* or a *developmental scale*). This means that if a student's skill level goes up, the student's score also goes up. One advantage of this type of test is that it is sensitive to growth both within grade and across grades.

Many of the publishers of this type of test also have linked their tests to state standards. This characteristic means that the relationship of the benchmark scores on within-year assessments with these tests to year-end standards-based assessments is known. Examples of this type of test include the Star Reading and Mathematics tests (*www.renlearn.com*) and the Scholastic Reading Inventory (*http://teacher. scholastic. com/products/sri_reading_assessment/index. Htm*).

ASSESSMENT STRATEGIES FOR THE TAPS TARGETED SKILLS OBSERVATION

When a TAPS Teacher receives a student referral, one of the first steps in the TAPS process is to review the classroom teacher's characterization of the problem and the information she has supplied to support it. Review of this information helps the TAPS Teacher decide what further information (if any) is needed verify that a problem exists and to characterize the problem accurately. As is discussed more extensively in Chapter 12, it is important to remember that sometimes the problem that presents is not the problem to solve. For example, a teacher may refer a child for poor reading comprehension, but a poor performance in reading comprehension often is due to difficulties with decoding or fluency.

Framework Guiding Assessment in the Targeted Skills Observation

In the targeted skills observation, the goal of assessment is to match a student with an intervention that will address the skill deficits that appear to be the reason for the student's classroom difficulty. The assessment procedures we describe for the targeted skills observation generally fit broadly within the curriculum-based evaluation framework (Howell et al., 2008). Curriculum-based evaluation is a problem-solving technology that makes use of CBM, but also employs other types of low-inference assessment strategies. The general approach is to evaluate what a student can and can't do compared to what the teacher would like him to do. The central focus of assessment is clearly specifying a task that a student does not perform in the classroom, and then identifying and verifying the task subskills or prerequisites that the student lacks (Howell & Morehead, 1987).

The search for missing task subskills and prerequisites is generally guided by the curriculum scope and sequence for a particular academic area, as well as by logical or empirical analyses of the skills that must be present for a student to perform the targeted task. An example of a prerequisite identified on a logical basis is the "tool skill" of writing digits quickly. Logically, if a student is to be able to write the answers to math computation problems at a rate of 40 or more digits correct per minute, he must first be able to write or copy digits at the same or a faster rate (with no computation required). Digit writing speed places a "cap" on how quickly a student can respond to computation problems.

An example of an empirical prerequisite is the finding that rapid retrieval of basic math facts or number combinations appears to facilitate acquisition of higher mathematics, such as developing an understanding of algebraic equations (Gersten, Jordan, & Flojo, 2005). The critical role that fluency in addition, subtraction, multiplication, and division play in the development of mathematical knowledge and skill explains the inclusion of these skills as curriculum focal points by the National Council of Teachers of Mathematics (2006).

The instructional hierarchy delineated by Haring, Lovitt, Eaton, and Hansen (1978) is a heuristic that has proved useful in curriculum-based evaluation as well as in instructional design (Codding et al., 2007; Deno & Mirken, 1977; Martens & Eckert, 2007). This model proposes that skill development progresses through four stages that require different kinds of instructional support. During *acquisition*, students are just learning a skill. They are slow and make many errors. In this stage, teachers need to demonstrate, model, scaffold, provide cues, and require repetition of the skill under the controlled conditions until the student can successfully perform the skill. This stage ends when the student has acquired the skill, but performance is still effortful, prone to errors, and somewhat slow. In the *fluency or proficiency* stage, the student is learning to perform the skill more automatically and effortlessly. The instructional emphasis is on increasing the student's speed and varying the conditions under which he is asked to perform the skill (e.g., mixing newly learned multiplication facts with addition and subtraction facts), as well as ensuring sufficient motivation for the student to continue practicing the skill. When speed and accuracy in the skill reach a critical level (which varies for different skills), learning moves to the *generalization* stage where the student must learn how to apply the skill in novel situations and also learn when the skill is not useful. In the final stage, adaption, the student learns to respond flexibly and can independently adapt the skill or change tactics when monitoring indicates that the skill is not yielding the intended result (Hansen & Eaton, 1978).

For assessment, the instructional hierarchy suggests that assessing a student's accuracy and fluency is helpful in deciding what type of instruction will be beneficial. Students who are in the acquisition stage (low accuracy, low fluency) are said to be at the frustrational level in the skill and likely to need comprehensive and explicit instruction to learn to perform the task, as well as instruction in prerequisites they may not have acquired. Students who are in the proficiency stage (higher accuracy, low fluency) may need instruction in some component skills, but they also need fluency practice so that the skill becomes rapidly and accurately executed. Students who are in the generalization or adaption stage are at the mastery level in the skill. They are ready to move onto the next skill in a curriculum sequence and to use the skill in broader contexts.

The Targeted Skills Observation

Given the focus on a curriculum's stated scope and sequence, logical and empirical skill prerequisites, and the instructional hierarchy, the TAPS Teachers should have good knowledge of the skill sequence and performance standards in each grade for an academic area, as well as understand how each classroom teacher in the school structures her core curriculum to teach children the performance standards. Ideally, a school's core curriculum is implemented in a way that is consistent across teachers of the same grade level, and is systematically aligned from one grade level to the next. But this ideal is not always the reality in some schools, so the TAPS Teacher must carefully consider the skills a student has or has not been taught as part of the core instruction. In addition, the TAPS Teacher must know how specific interventions available at her school map onto grade-level performance standards and which interventions are available for strengthening particular skills. Collectively, this knowledge provides the link between assessment and intervention.

The work samples and information provided by the teacher with a TAPS request for support should be the starting point for the TAPS Teacher's targeted observation. These work samples and the classroom teacher's description on the Request for TAPS Form may provide enough information to suggest where intervention efforts should be directed. If the school has a universal screening program in place, the TAPS Teacher can also use those results to help guide intervention selection.

Even if the TAPS Teacher believes that the information provided by the teacher, work samples, and a thorough records review allows her to suggest one or more possible intervention programs, having some time directly interacting with the student, one on one, or observing the student during instruction in the area of difficulty is an important piece of the targeted skills observation. Direct interaction or observation of the student helps assure that the TAPS Teacher is familiar with the student. This personal experience with the student is an important basis for teachers' and parents' confidence in the insights and suggestions the TAPS Teacher provides about the child.

A TAPS teacher's expertise should extend to the use of brief assessment methods in her academic area (or be developed during the SOPAA implementation planning year). Some suggestions for brief assessments when conducting the targeted skills observations in reading, mathematics, or written expressions are provided here.

Prereading and Reading Skills

One of the key goals for the targeted skills assessment in reading is to identify the areas in which the TAPS student is struggling from among the five key areas of reading (phonemic awareness, phonics, fluency, vocabulary, and reading comprehension). A useful construct for guiding this type of assessment is the *simple view of reading* (Catts, Adolph, & Weismer, 2006; Gough & Tunmer, 1986), which postulates that reading comprehension is the product of two separate skill strands: translating written text into its spoken equivalent, and language comprehension skills. What this means for assessment is that first we want to assess students' phonemic awareness, phonics, and sight word skills to identify potential deficits that are interfering with rapid word recognition and fluent reading of text. Research has suggested that students with reading difficulties are often deficient in one or more of these areas, and that addressing these deficits improves reading skill

(Stanovich, 1986). However, we also want to assess vocabulary and overall language skills to determine if once a student's word recognition difficulties are addressed, the student has the language skills to be able to comprehend grade level text. If not, we may want to include an intervention that targets vocabulary or language as part of the student's intervention plan, either simultaneously or following an intervention targeting decoding and fluency skills.

Phonemic Awareness, Phonics, and Decoding Assessment

Two useful tools for assessing students' decoding and reading fluency skills are a survey-level assessment with CBM and the diagnostic plan and related measures outlined by the Consortium on Early Reading (CORE; Diamond & Thorsnes, 2008). Both are described here.

SURVEY-LEVEL ASSESSMENT WITH PASSAGE FLUENCY CBMs

Although the specific methods for survey-level assessment with CBM differ somewhat by source (e.g., Hosp et al., 2007; Shapiro, 2011a, 2011b; Shinn, 2002), the general principle of survey-level assessment in reading is to administer passage reading fluency probes at the student's present grade level, and then at each grade level below the student's placement until a grade level is identified where the number of words read correctly and number of errors made by the student on CBM probes fall in the instructional range for children at that grade level. Even if an instructional level is identified, assessment continues until the student reaches a grade level where the number of words read correctly and the number of errors made falls in the mastery range.

The underlying assumption in this type of assessment is that the student's accuracy and error rates in passage reading fluency (and in some survey-level CBM approaches, the student's ability to answer comprehension questions on those passages) are indicators of whether or not instruction is needed on skills targeted at that grade level in a curriculum's scope and sequence. If the student scores at the mastery level in curriculum material at a particular grade, interventions for the skills targeted at that grade in the curriculum scope and sequence are unlikely to be needed. If the student scores at the frustrational level, it is likely that he has not mastered necessary skills at a lower grade level. If the student scores at the instructional level, then the skills targeted in the curriculum at that grade level are likely to be the ones to target in an intervention. However, since this premise is only an assumption, it is important that the TAPS Teacher also carefully look at the student's performance on the survey-level probes to verify that this method matches interventions to student needs.

If a school or district has already adopted a CBM system with probes and benchmarks at multiple grade levels, then when doing a survey-level assessment with CBM probes, those probes should be used, as well as the survey level procedures described for that system (if they are provided). For example, schools already using AIMSWeb (*www.aimsweb.com*) should use the CBM probe sets and reading benchmarks in that system and refer to their detailed training manual for conducting survey-level assessments (Shinn, 2002). If a school does not have a standard set of CBM probes in use, then educators may want to experiment with using the survey-level assessment described here, based on a technique described in Shapiro (2011a), with one of the CBM systems that is available free of charge (e.g., DIBELS, EasyCBM).

One method for survey-level assessment suggested by Shapiro (2011) is basing instructional level on local or national norms in passage reading fluency. A student's instructional level is the level closest to his or her own grade level where the median words read correctly per minute fall within the 25th to 75th percentile range. With the general approach to survey-level reading assessment outlined here, the TAPS Teacher should begin by asking the student to read three passage reading fluency probes at his or her present grade level. These probes should be administered and scored for the number of words read correctly per minute and for errors, according to the directions for the particular passage reading fluency probe set. Then, the median score on the three grade-level probes (middle score when the scores are rank-ordered) should be compared to the percentile ranges for the appropriate time of year (fall, winter, or spring).

For example, consider assessing a fourth grader in December: Three fourth-grade passage reading fluency probes would be administered. Using Hasbrouck and Tindal's (2006) passage reading fluency norms (available at *www.readnaturally.com/howto/orftable.html*), if the student's median words read correctly per minute were between 87 and 139 words, he or she would be considered correctly placed. If the number of words read correctly was below this level, the TAPS teacher would work backward until the number of words read correctly by the student fell between the 25th and 75th percentiles for the spring reading norms for that grade level.

This survey-level assessment gives the TAPS Teacher an idea of the grade level in which the student's reading would be comparable to children achieving as expected. If the TAPS Teacher knows the curriculum well in her area (and the way the student's teacher actually uses the curriculum), this information should provide an indication of the skills to be targeted in an instructional intervention. It also suggests which grade-level probes should be used if CBM is used for progress monitoring when an intervention is implemented.

Listening to the student read aloud when administering these probes can provide the TAPS Teacher with additional information to pinpoint likely skill deficits to be targeted in intervention. For example, what strategies does the student use to decode unknown words? Does the student try to sound out the word? Does he or she try to use context to supply a word that makes sense in the sentence, but contains none of the letters or sounds in the correct word? Is the child reading accurately but slowly, or quickly and making many errors?

If a child does not score at the instructional level for third grade, or is not yet in the third grade, the TAPS Teacher should administer CBM probes that assess sight words (word identification fluency), basic phonics (nonsense word fluency or letter–sound fluency), and phonemic awareness (phonemic segmentation). If scores for these probes fall below the benchmark level for the grade assessed, they are indicators that those skills should be targeted when selecting an intervention.

CORE'S READING MEASURES AND DIAGNOSTIC PLAN

The CBM survey-level procedures just described provide one approach to deciding which areas of reading should be targeted during instruction. If the TAPS Teacher is not familiar with CBM or wants to explore alternate measures and procedures for deciding which areas to target in a TAPS intervention, the book *Assessing Reading: Multiple Measures* (Diamond & Thorsnes, 2008) may be useful. This inexpensive book contains multiple assessment measures for evaluating phonological awareness, decoding, word attack, spelling, fluency, oral vocabulary, and reading comprehension. It also includes measures for students whose first language is Spanish, as well as reproducible test protocols to go with each of the measures. There are reading diagnostic plans for grades 2–12 with guidance about what to assess, in what sequence, and decision rules for linking test results to the areas that should be targeted for intervention.

One of the most useful measures in this book is the CORE Phonics Survey. The survey begins with items assessing students' knowledge of letter names and sounds and ends with items assessing students' skills in decoding multisyllabic words. The items link well with many phonics programs, so that an educator can identify not only that a student needs assistance in phonics, but which phonic skills are mastered and which need more instruction (e.g., it provides information on students' mastery of different syllable types). Although the entire test is not available online, the CORE Phonics Survey record form can be downloaded (*www.scholastic.com/dodea/Module_2/resources/dodea_m2_tr_core.pdf* to allow readers to evaluate its content.

VOCABULARY AND READING COMPREHENSION ASSESSMENT

In the early grades, difficulty comprehending grade-level text is usually a decoding or fluency problem. The language level of early reading texts is so basic, it is rare that children would have difficulty comprehending if they are able to decode (unless they are English language learners). However, when the vocabulary and syntactic structures in reading material become more complex, it becomes more likely that students will have reading comprehension difficulties that are not related to their difficulty in decoding.

If a teacher expresses concern about a student's reading comprehension in the TAPS referral, the targeted skills observation should start with decoding skills (as described above). At the grade level where the child scores in the instructional range, a reading comprehension probe can be administered. For example, EasyCBM provides reading comprehension probes that consist of a passage and multiple-choice comprehension questions. In that system, comprehension probes are available for grades 2 and above, and score interpretation guidelines are provided. If a student meets passage reading fluency and accuracy guidelines, but does not score above the 20th percentile in reading comprehension, then the TAPS Teacher should consider a vocabulary or reading comprehension intervention. A useful way to discern whether the problem is due to poor reading comprehension or poor language skills, regardless of whether the language is presented in written or oral format, is to administer some of the reading probes orally by reading both the passage and the questions to the student. If the student is not able to answer more questions orally, then vocabulary or background knowledge may need to be increased to improve both reading and listening comprehension.

Two other options for assessing students' reading comprehension skills are CBM maze reading comprehension probes and asking students to do an oral retell. If students are able to score at grade level for passage reading fluency, but below grade level on maze passages, this pattern indicates that they may benefit from reading comprehension instruction. In an oral retell, a student is asked to tell the TAPS Teacher a summary of what he just read. The summary is evaluated in terms of how much information the student is able to provide. Inadequate oral retells across multiple reading passages are another indication that reading comprehension is a problem. Shapiro (2011b) provides instructions for conducting and scoring oral retells of narrative and expository text.

Early Numeracy and Mathematics Assessment

In reading, our ultimate objective is for students be able to comprehend grade-level text. In mathematics, our ultimate objective is for students to understand the properties of numbers and to be able to apply mathematics concepts and computation skills to solve complex problems involving numbers. However, just as in reading, where addressing a reading comprehension deficit may require intervention for a lower level skill (e.g., decoding), in mathematics, deficits in these higher-level skills may need to be addressed by instructing students in one or more component skills. As such, the TAPS Teacher's goal in a targeted skills observation in mathematics is to determine which areas of mathematics skill deficits should be addressed in intervention efforts.

A careful assessment of a student's strengths and weaknesses is important because the problem that presents itself may not be the main problem to solve.

Two useful tools for determining a student's level of functioning in mathematics and areas of need are a survey-level assessment with mathematics CBM probes and the Number Knowledge Test (*http://clarku.edu/numberworlds/nw_TestInfo.htm#*), which measures a student's conceptual understanding of mathematics (Okamoto & Case, 1996).

Survey-Level Assessment with Mathematics CBMs

As with survey-level assessment in reading with CBM probes, there are several different procedures for mathematics survey-level assessments described in the literature (e.g., Hintze, Christ, & Keller, 2002; Hosp et al., 2007; Kelley, 2008; Shapiro, 2011a, 2011b). The common element in these survey-level procedures is to begin assessment with CBM mathematics probes at the student's current grade placement and then to continue to assess at successively lower grade levels until the student is performing at or above the end-of-year benchmark score (i.e., at mastery level). The procedure described below is consistent with Kelley's (2008) recommendations for survey-level assessment in mathematics, and includes administration of CBM probes to examine a broad array of mathematics skills, observation of student strategies used while solving probe items, and conversation with the student about specific items to examine the student's knowledge of basic mathematics concepts, algorithms for performing calculations, and strategy in answering the item. In Kelley's system, the goal of CBM probe administration is to examine the student's skills relative to grade-level expectations for early numeracy, computation, and concepts and application. If a student is not at mastery level for a grade level, then error analysis should be used to determine the source of the student's difficulty.

In this discussion, we use the suggested mathematics CBM benchmark assessments (as well as CBM mathematics benchmarks for other grade levels) from AIMSweb. We selected AIMSweb because this assessment system has probes for computation, mathematics concepts and applications, and early numeracy (if needed). This approach could be used with other systems that have probes for both mathematics computation and applications (e.g., Monitoring Basic Skills Progress [MBSP] Basic Math Computation). Another option is to create an assessment tool matched to the curriculum (see Kelley, 2008) or purchased (e.g., both Yearly Progress Pro and Accelerated Mathematics computerized assessments can be matched to state grade-level curriculum objectives).

First, the TAPS teacher should administer and score a set of grade-level benchmark assessments in mathematics (assuming that they have not already been administered in a universal screening program). For example, in fourth grade in the AIMSweb system, the recommended CBM probes for universal screening are a mathematics concepts and applications probe lasting 8 minutes, and three mathematics computation probes lasting 2 minutes each.

Next, the scores should be examined relative to the benchmark cutoff scores that are closest to the time the student was assessed. If these scores do not fall within the instructional range (25th to 75th percentile), then the TAPS teacher should work backward, administering a benchmark set of assessments for each grade until the student scores above the year-end benchmarks for students at that grade level. The grade-level curriculum 1 year past the CBM probe set where all benchmarks were met should be the focus for further follow-up to identify the skills that will be targeted in an intervention.

Developing hypotheses about skills in need of further instruction can begin with a review of the items missed on the CBM probes where the student's scores fell at the instructional level. Once the hypotheses are developed based on the CBM probes completed in the survey level assessment, additional, more focused CBM probes, work samples, or a student interview should be used to gather further evidence to verify or disconfirm the hypotheses. For example, the test blueprint for

AIMSweb's third-grade computation CBM probes indicates that the probes examine basic facts (0–12) in addition, subtraction, multiplication, and division as well as complex computations in these areas. After administering the three computation probes, the TAPS Teacher can look for consistent patterns of errors on these four types of items to discern areas of difficulty. For example, if a student consistently gets addition and subtraction items correct, but misses multiplication and division items, this pattern suggests that the student's difficulties are in that multiplication and division. The student's attempts at those items can be examined for clues to the source of difficulty, or she can be asked about the strategies used to solve the problem.

If the student does not score above the 25th percentile on the second-grade computation and concepts and applications probes, or if the TAPS Teacher has concerns that the student is missing some fundamental skills, then early numeracy CBM probes should be administered and examined relative to the kindergarten and first-grade end-of-year benchmarks. If these fundamental skills are missing, then they should be a focus of intervention.

Students who are able to do computation problems but perform poorly on the mathematics concepts and applications probes may be unable to read the test items. This hypothesis can be verified by reading the items aloud on a different CBM probe and seeing if the student's score improves substantially. Alternately, the student may need instruction in specific applications, vocabulary, or in completing word problems. Because there are few items of each type in a concepts and applications probe and only one is administered per grade-level benchmark, the TAPS Teacher may want to give an additional CBM probe so that a more reliable assessment of the types of the items with which the student has difficulty can be confirmed. Other confirmation strategies include reviewing work samples, teacher interview, or student interview.

A study by Codding et al. (2007) provides verification of the need to consider the fluency and accuracy level of students' computation skills when considering interventions. They found that students in the acquisition stage for subtraction, with low accuracy and low fluency (less than 10 digits correct per minute), benefited little from an intervention to improve fluency, whereas students in the instructional range did benefit from a fluency intervention.

Number Knowledge Test

If the TAPS Teacher is concerned about a student's early numeracy skills and understanding of whole numbers, a useful assessment is the Number Knowledge Test (Griffin, 2005; Okamoto & Case, 1996) available at *www.clarku.edu/numberworlds/nw_TestInfo.htm*. This assessment is a series of simple counting and computation tasks with whole numbers that children are asked to complete without pencil and paper. Props are used, and the tasks are developmentally sequenced to provide the TAPS Teacher with an opportunity to interact with the student and observe the child's facility with counting and problem-solving strategies for simple questions about quantity discrimination, number sequencing, addition, and subtraction. There are four levels corresponding to skills typically mastered at 4, 6, 8, and 10 years of age (although the first three levels are the ones most appropriate for assessing early numeracy and number sense).

The scoring system places the child at a developmental level in terms of his or her knowledge of whole numbers and number sense. The test has been found to be reliable, and scores are highly correlated with later mathematics achievement (Gersten et al., 2005). Research suggests that students who do not perform at mastery on the skills tapped at a particular developmental level are not likely to acquire mathematics concepts and skills taught in subsequent grades (Griffin, 2005). The Number Worlds early mathematics instructional curriculum, mentioned in Chapter 12, is an intervention program tied to the skills targeted in this assessment (*www.sranumberworlds.com*).

Written Expression Assessment

As noted previously, the state of the art for brief, low-inference measures of written expression or early writing lags well behind assessment in reading and mathematics (McMaster & Espin, 2007). In part, this lag may be due to the complexity of written expression and the number of skills that must be in place for a child to write competently. First, the student must have the language skills and vocabulary to formulate the ideas or content that is to be conveyed. Second, she must have sufficient knowledge of spelling to translate these ideas into written form, and the transcription skills to rapidly put these ideas into written form (handwriting or typing). Third, she must have enough knowledge of language conventions to produce grammatically and syntactically correct word sequences; punctuate them correctly; and organize these thought units into longer, coherent sequences of writing, including paragraphs and essays. Finally, the student must have the reviewing and editing skills to consider whether the information provided is adequate for the reader to understand the intended meaning, to consider word choice and options that better convey meaning, and to correct errors in all of these domains.

To complicate matters further, expectations for acceptable performance vary with the intended purpose. For example, descriptive, expository, persuasive, or narrative writing (four genres that are commonly taught in school) pose unique demands for writers. In addition, skilled writing is usually conceived of as a process that requires multiple phases, including prewriting (planning), composing, editing, and publishing (Graves, 1983). The number of skills involved in writing and its iterative, time-intensive nature make it difficult to develop valid measures of writing skill, let alone develop brief, countable CBM writing probes that are reliable and valid.

Nevertheless, the three types of writing CBM probe sets described earlier (sentence copying, spelling, and story starters) can help the TAPS Teacher identify areas to be targeted for intervention. However, unlike in the other achievement areas where survey-level assessment begins with CBM probes, writing assessment starts with a review of a student's written products from the classroom, followed up by CBM probes, as needed, to provide a quantitative index of student functioning.

What Are the Expectations?

Many states and districts have very prescriptive rubrics for evaluating writing, with particular types (e.g., narrative, expository) assessed at different grades. Therefore, the starting point for any writing assessment is an understanding of the areas of emphasis in writing, grade-level expectations, and the conditions under which writing products are typically produced (e.g., multiday writing process, daily journaling) at the school site. Asking the student's teacher to provide work samples from children who are functioning above, at, and below grade level can provide a good overview of the normative expectations in the classroom.

If the district has a writing rubric, it is helpful to see how the work samples the teacher has provided have been, or would be, scored with the rubric. Ultimately, intervention will be aimed at helping the student meet grade-level standards, so knowledge of the scoring rubric for writing and its application is critical for intervention.

If the district does not have a writing rubric, then the 5-point beginning writing rubric available from Education Northwest (*www.educationnorthwest.org/webfm_send/772*) may be a helpful for characterizing the writing samples as well as the referred student's writing. The Education Northwest rubric provides descriptive anchors at 5 points along a continuum: *experimenting* (little to no mastery on that dimension) to *emerging, developing, capable,* and *experienced* (highly skilled on that dimension). Writing dimensions include (1) ideas, (2) organization, (3) voice, (4) word choice, (5) sentence fluency, (6) conventions, and (7) presentation.

Survey-Level Assessment

Review of sample writing products from the class (or entire grade) and comparison with the referred student should help the TAPS Teacher narrow down the problematic areas. For many children experiencing writing problems, simply producing enough text may be the most salient problem. If the work samples for the referred student are markedly shorter than those of other students, then administering a sentence copying CBM and story starter CBM can provide additional evidence that production is a significant problem. A comparison between the number of words written when copying sentences versus planning and writing a story can help discern whether fluency of handwriting may be an issue, or if the child struggles in thinking of and then developing an idea. To check that underlying language issues are not causing difficulties, asking a child to tell a story from a story starter rather than to write it may also provide clues about whether it is transcription or language that poses the problem.

If local norms are available or a CBM system with norms for story starters is in use in the school, the number of correct word sequences can be compared to grade-level and lower grade-level norms to ascertain how the TAPS student is functioning compared to other students. If spelling is problematic and should be a focus of intervention, then three spelling CBM probes (with the median used as the initial score) can be used as the baseline level for progress monitoring. Error analysis on the three probes can help identify spelling rules that the student has yet to master.

PROGRESS MONITORING IN TAPS

One of the key decisions the TAPS and classroom teachers make in this process is deciding on a method of monitoring a student's progress while the student receives the intervention. There are different ways to conduct progress monitoring. A widely used option, with considerable research to support it, is the use of CBM probes on a weekly basis. This approach has been described earlier; its specific application in TAPS is discussed here.

A second type of progress monitoring involves mastery assessment of successive objectives in a curriculum. Many research-based curricula or intervention programs include embedded assessments that can be used to examine whether a student has mastered the content that has been presented (for intervention programs with embedded progress monitoring systems, see Tables 12.2–12.4 in Chapter 12). Unlike CBM probes, where there is an emphasis on evaluating technical qualities of the probes, the reliability and validity of these embedded assessments are rarely evaluated. Instead, the overlap between the content of the measure and the curriculum is assumed to result in a valid assessment. Unit tests from a mathematics curriculum are an example of this type of progress monitoring. With embedded assessments, the tasks on the mastery tests change as the content of instruction changes. As a result, graphing or summarizing results across time is not as easy as it is with CBM; however, given that the assessment method is part of the intervention, it is an efficient and very targeted way to accomplish progress monitoring.

Using one or both types of progress monitoring are TAPS options. If an intervention program has embedded assessments, then these should be used. For example, Sound Partners, one of the interventions mentioned in Chapter 12 for phonics intervention, has mastery tests after each 10 lessons. If a student does not reach the stated mastery levels for the skills just taught, the educator is instructed to reteach the content until the student has mastered it before proceeding to the next set of 10 lessons.

However, not all research-based programs have embedded assessments. If a program does not, then the TAPS and classroom teachers should look for CBM probes that are a good match with the intervention and make plans to use those to monitor the student's progress.

The ideal situation is to use both forms of progress monitoring. The embedded assessments give very specific information about the skills the student is mastering. But progress monitoring with CBM, if used as outlined earlier (weekly probes, use of an aim line, and changes in instruction based on monitoring results), has been shown to result in improved outcomes for students (Fuchs & Fuchs, 1986; Stecker et al., 2005), and this positive effect argues for its use whenever possible. Progress monitoring with CBM probes also provides a formal means of documenting that a student is, or is not, making progress. It allows a teacher to provide objective data that others can examine and make their own determination of a student's progress. This feature is quite useful in communicating with parents and other educators, and is also required if interventions are being implemented while students are being evaluated for learning disabilities (Individuals with Disabilities Education Improvement Act, 2006). A final advantage of using CBM probes for progress monitoring is that by looking at CBM results across students, the overall effectiveness of an instructional intervention can be evaluated. For example, if a particular intervention seems to consistently produce positive results for students, then that intervention should be continued as an option in the school. Cumulating data across students helps a school pinpoint successful ways of responding to student need and to identify practices that are not working. In Chapter 5 we discuss how the TAPS Teacher might consider collecting and using data from progress monitoring systems embedded within an intervention program, as well as from a separate system, such as CBM.

Progress Monitoring in TAPS with CBM

Although progress monitoring with CBM can have substantial benefits and is conceptually simple, deciding which probe to use, how to set goals, understanding the procedures, finding time to do the progress monitoring, and graphing and interpreting the results can be challenging. Just like using a new teaching technique, the understanding and use of progress monitoring increase with practice, but the tool can be more cumbersome until one is familiar with it. The brief description here is not sufficient to begin implementing progress monitoring. Unless at least one educator at the school is very familiar with the use of CBM for progress monitoring and can provide assistance to others, training will be needed to use CBM. Early in its use, CBM progress monitoring should be completed or overseen by TAPS Teachers. After experience using it and with additional staff development, other educators in the school may be able to assist TAPS Teachers. Some good training resources for learning how to do progress monitoring with CBM are presented in Figure 6.2. A general set of steps for implementing CBM progress monitoring in the TAPS process is provided here.

Step 1: Decide What Probe Set to Use for Progress Monitoring

Once the TAPS and classroom teachers have decided upon a skill area to focus for intervention and picked out a specific intervention program, then they will need to choose a CBM probe set. An important aspect of this decision is making sure that the CBM probe set is sensitive to improvements in the primary skill(s) targeted with the intervention. A selected CBM probe set should either be a general outcome measure appropriate to the grade-level skills being taught or a skills-based CBM or mastery CBM assessing skills that closely match the content taught in the intervention. For example, if a fifth-grade student is receiving instruction in rapid recall of addition and subtraction facts, then one should use CBM probes that assess these skills. Two possibilities are CBM mathematics computation probes at the second-grade level, as they typically have many items per probe tapping these skills, or probes constructed specifically to assess addition and subtraction (e.g., AIMSweb's Math Facts CBM probe sets).

Step 2: Administer CBM Probes to Get a Baseline Skill Level

The goal in this step is to establish an accurate measure of the student's skill level before he starts intervention. How many probes are needed to get an accurate measure varies with the student and the measure. For example, if 1-minute CBM probes are used, the median of three probes administered at one time likely provides a good estimate of the student's starting skill level, and could be done in one 5-minute session with the student. With longer CBM probes (e.g., reading maze probes), administering three probes in one sitting may be unrealistic, whereas two probes in 1 week may be realistic. A general rule is to give at least two, preferably three, CBM probes before intervention starts, to have some basis for feeling confident that the baseline results are reasonably accurate. For example, CBM probes are designed to be of equal difficulty. If a TAPS Teacher administers two probes and the student receives very different scores on the two probes, we would be less confident that we really knew what the student's true skill level is; therefore, we should administer at least one other probe.

Ideally, we would be very confident that we have an accurate measure of the student's functioning before an intervention is started. After all, it is hard to judge improvement if one isn't really sure about the student's skill level when intervention started! However, accuracy in measurement should be balanced with time spent assessing versus intervening. CBM was developed to allow assessment to be streamlined, particularly initial assessment.

Step 3: Set an Outcome Goal

An outcome goal that specifies a CBM performance level and the endpoint when that goal should be reached should be set before beginning an instructional intervention. There are many different approaches to setting an outcome goal. In each case, the outcome goal set should be ambitious—pushing the student and educators to move as quickly as possible to help the student catch up, but also realistic enough that reaching the goal is conceivable. Some sources of information to use in setting a goal are established benchmark levels of performance for the CBM probe set and grade, if they are available, or published tables of typical rates of improvement on CBM probes. The endpoint should be at least 6 weeks away, given that 6 weeks of implementation are recommended as the minimal duration of a TAPS intervention. For example, consider a student who is in second grade and is about to begin an intervention to increase her decoding skills. The TAPS teacher administered three passage reading fluency probes in January from DIBELS Next as part of her targeted skills observation, and the student's median score was 50 words read correctly per minute. One way to set an outcome goal would be to consider typical rates of improvement and the duration of the intervention's implementation. A typical rate of improvement for DIBELS Next (based on the information in Table 6.1) in the second grade is 1.0 word per week. The TAPS Teacher and classroom teacher decide to aim for an improvement of 2 words per week, or a gain of 20 words read correctly per minute during a 10-week intervention period, because they are planning to provide the student with one-on-one tutoring with a volunteer, for 20 minutes a day, and they think that this is a realistic yet ambitious goal. As such, the student outcome goal would be set at 70 correct words per minute at the end of 10 weeks of intervention (Figure 6.1 depicts the student's baseline median score of 50, an outcome goal of 70, and an aim line).

Good and Kaminski (2011), in discussing goal setting for DIBELS Next, have provided another method for setting outcome goals using two simple rules. First, if the student is being monitored in grade-level materials, use the score for the next benchmark period as a target, and use the time when the next benchmark would be administered as the time frame for the outcome goal. Thus, in our example with the student reading 50 words per minute, we would select an outcome goal of 87 words correctly read per minute as the target (DIBELS Next Spring benchmark for second grade in Table 6.1) and the end of the school year as the time frame. Second, if the student is being monitored with below grade-level CBM probes, use the Spring benchmark score for that grade as the outcome goal, and set the time frame for achieving it as half the time expected for a student who was actually placed in that grade. Applying this rule in our example, if the second-grade student was reading at the first-grade level in January when the TAPS Teacher did the targeted skills observation (e.g., 35 words per minute in first-grade reading passages), we would set the target goal at 47 words per minute (the DIBELS Next first-grade Spring benchmark in Table 6.1) and then aim to accomplish this goal in 6 weeks instead of the 12 weeks that separate the winter and spring benchmarks. Although not empirically validated, Good and Kaminski's simple pair of decision rules seems to be a reasonable option to consider when trying to decide what a reasonable outcome goal and time frame would be for an intervention.

Once an outcome goal and endpoint date are established, whatever the method used to establish them, a line is drawn between the baseline and the outcome goal. Ultimately, it is the aim line that is of most interest in progress monitoring, because judgments of progress will be based on how CBM probe data, collected weekly, fall in relation to the aim line.

Step 4: Collect CBM Probe Data

Each week, one or two probes should be administered as the intervention is under way and graphed. If weekly data collection is not possible, the TAPS Teacher should keep in mind that a minimum of 4 data points after baseline are required to have a reasonable level of certainty that the results show how the student is responding, versus just reflecting testing error.

Step 5: Compare the CBM Probe Results to the Aim Line and Decide If Action Is Needed

When the intervention is under way and 4 data points have been collected (not counting the baseline data), compare the results to the aim line. We recommend what Hosp et al. (2007) term *data point analysis,* not a trend line or slope analysis. That is, the data points should be examined relative to where they fall in relation to the aim line. If 4 points in a row fall below, or above, the aim line, then the TAPS Teacher, classroom teacher, and educator implementing the intervention need to consider making a change. If four scores fall below the aim line, then possible reasons for this negative pattern need to be considered. Do other data, such as the embedded assessments, confirm that student is making poor progress in the intervention? Is the intervention being implemented correctly, or does the educator implementing it need some additional training? Does the student lack a prerequisite skill that was overlooked? If the student shows improvement over baseline, but his four scores are below the aim line, perhaps the original outcome goal and the aim line drawn based on it were unrealistic, and an alternate outcome goal needs to be considered. Sometimes, a simple change can be all that is needed to bring the student's scores back above the aim line, such as drilling the student on some minor skill that he is having difficulty mastering.

If 4 data points are above the aim line, the outcome goal might be raised, or if the outcome goal has been met, perhaps the student should be exited from the intervention. Decisions like these will be based on knowledge and judgment about the case from the TAPS Teacher and classroom teacher, as well as guidance from the intervention program's manual. If no clear pattern is evident when the data are compared to the aim line, then the intervention and CBM data collection should continue. Once 8 data points have been collected, examining whether 6 out of 8 data points fall above or below the aim line can be substituted for the "four in a row" rules just discussed.

The data point analysis procedure we recommend differs a bit from some recommendations for deciding whether an intervention is working that involve trend line analysis, where the slope of the CBM scores (calculated by computer or hand) is compared to the aim line. Recent research has suggested that despite developers' best efforts to make CBM probes of equal difficulty, there is still considerable "bounce" in scores from probe to probe that is related to error, not actual change in students skill (Christ & Silberglitt, 2007). The amount of bounce can vary by probe set and also by student.

The TAPS assessment process should include assessments embedded within the intervention as well as an occasional "outside" form of assessment (e.g., CBM) that is relevant to the skills targeted during intervention.

That is, some developers have done a better job than others of producing probes of equal difficulty, and some students do not respond consistently day to day, perhaps because of fluctuations in the attention and effort they devote to the task. (The practice of taking the median score of three CBM probes is one suggestion that CBM developers have used to reduce this bounce.) Bounce in scores that is not due to real changes in student skill causes particular problems with the accuracy of slope calculations for individuals (but less so with larger groups of students), especially when few data points are used to calculate the slope. For example, an ambitious goal for a gain per week in passage reading fluency for a second grader is two words (Hosp et al., 2007). With moderate levels of error in testing conditions, it would take 20 data points (10 weeks with two CBM probes per week) to get the error band around a slope narrow enough to be confident that the student's slope was between one and two words read correctly per week instead of zero words per week (i.e., no gain). This issue may explain the problems some educators have in getting interpretable results using CBM progress monitoring for individuals: They are not waiting long enough (or more realistically, do not have sufficient time) to get stable data. The "above the aim line" or the "below the aim line" approach does not involve getting an accurate estimate of slope. It involves deciding if probe scores are falling above or below the score on the aim line for that week. This different measurement approach helps lessen the effect of score bounce. Concerns about the error in slopes has led to recent recommendations for more research before using slopes in decision making with CBM (e.g., Wayman et al., 2007).

To use CBM progress monitoring most effectively, educators should follow each of the five aforementioned steps.

UNIVERSAL SCREENING

Universal screening is one component of the SOPAA and also a component of current multi-tiered RTI models for preventing and addressing children's learning problems. The form of universal screening included in the SOPAA model is the same one contained in most RTI models. It involves administration of brief assessments in reading and mathematics three to four times a year. Typical universal screening tools provide educators with periodic scores for students, as well as classifications of risk that place students into a limited number of categories that characterize student functioning relative to grade-level expectations (e.g., "at grade-level benchmark," "needs strategic intervention," and "needs intensive intervention").

Universal screenings serve multiple purposes. First, they provide schools and teachers with information about how well their students are doing as a group. When a high percentage of students is meeting grade-level expectations (e.g., 85%), it signals that core instruction is working reasonably well. Results that are not as positive signal the need for a closer look at the school's core instructional program and some investigation of the possible reasons for so many students experiencing difficulty. For example, a high rate of students scoring below benchmark levels may signal that the core curriculum is problematic, that professional development may be needed to make sure teachers are implementing the curriculum with integrity, or perhaps one teacher may need some assistance with a particularly challenging group of students.

Second, universal screening data can serve as a means for targeting students or groups of students for extra help and identifying the areas where targeted intervention programs are most needed. TAPS Teachers rely on teacher referral/requests as the basis for providing extra help to students. However, if a universal screening program is in place, scores from the universal screening can be used as (1) a basis for identifying students who should benefit from a TAPS intervention plan, (2) additional information for the TAPS teacher, or (3) the baseline measure for beginning progress monitoring if an intervention is put in place.

Third, because universal screening measures are administered more than once a year, changes in students' scores across benchmark screening can be used to evaluate within-year efforts to address learning difficulties, either at the individual or group level, and help teachers decide what to do next.

Universal screening can provide much useful information for schools, but unless a program is carefully planned and educators are adequately trained to interpret and use the results, it can become just another set of test results that are put in a file drawer that contributes little to improving student achievement outcomes. Thus, an important first step in beginning a universal screening program is examining options for universal screening and planning how the data will be used at a school.

Two useful resources for reviewing the evidence for universal screening and then moving toward implementing it in a school are the IES practice guides for implementing RTI models in reading and mathematics (Gersten et al., 2008, 2009). Another very useful resource, mentioned earlier in the chapter, is the website of the National Center for Response to Intervention (*www.rti4success.org*). Experts from the center have articulated a set of standards for evaluating screening tools and then reviewed a number of universal screening instruments that publishers have submitted. Readers who visit this website will note that a different set of standards is applied to tools that are used for screening versus progress monitoring, even though some of the same tools appear on both charts. When achievement measures are used for different purposes, different test characteristics become more or less important. For example, when using a measure for progress monitoring on a weekly or biweekly basis, it is important that the measure be very sensitive to change over short periods of time and also that there are many alternate forms of a test available. However, for universal screening, the number of forms is less important, but how well the tests align with the general education curriculum and predict students' achievement in later grades is particularly important. The charts reviewing tools for progress monitoring and screening reflect these different purposes.

The IES practice guide for reading (Gersten et al., 2008) provides specific recommendations for areas to target in universal screening programs for grades K–2. For kindergarten, recommended measures test letter naming fluency and phoneme segmentation. Although letter naming fluency is not a skill that should be targeted for intervention in most cases, it is a brief and sensitive measure that predicts a student's future achievement in reading. Recommended universal screening measures for first grade are phoneme segmentation, nonsense word fluency, and word identification fluency. Word identification and passage reading fluency measures are recommended for second grade.

In addition to CBM probe sets, computer-adaptive criterion-referenced tests in reading and mathematics are an option for screening. These tests typically take longer to administer than CBM probes, but they can be done in groups and are scored automatically. These features save educators considerable time. Another advantage is their potential for more specific skill assessments and scores because the tests are longer. However, there are also some disadvantages to these measures. They are more costly and are easiest to use in a school where there is a computer classroom where all students in a class can be administered the test at one time. The tests also cannot be used for frequent progress monitoring, which means that for students in the TAPS program, CBM probes would need to be administered for a baseline assessment relevant to progress monitoring. Lastly, in our experience, some students do more poorly on computerized tests and benefit from the presence of an examiner who monitors and maintains their attention while they complete an assessment. We have found that test results on the computer can vary widely from testing occasion to testing occasion for some students with attentional difficulties, making it difficult to document whether a student is making progress across the testing sessions.

Considerations for Using Universal Screening

Schools contemplating the use of universal screening will face many decisions. To help schools plan ahead for implementing universal screening, this section explores some of the questions schools will face as they implement the measures.

TAPS First or Universal Screening?

This issue has been discussed earlier. TAPS provides instructional support for students, and our overall preference is that developing instructional support for students be given priority over more assessment when schools cannot initiate time and resources for both at the same time. However, a universal screening program and the results it provides can give schools useful information about where intervention options are most needed. It can also motivate educators to action (i.e., poor results can lead to quicker actions, and changes in schoolwide results on universal screenings can reinforce educators' change efforts). Another advantage to starting with universal screening is that school- or gradewide results provide valuable information about how particular CBM probe sets or other assessment measures align with other school measures. When CBM probe sets are used for only a small number of students, as in TAPS, it can take longer for educators to understand scores and see how scores reflect their own classroom appraisals of students.

What Grades, What Areas?

Schools may want to experiment with universal screening when starting to use it by limiting the grades and achievement areas where it is used. More research has been conducted on early literacy and reading universal screening, so schools may want to begin with measures in this area. Early mathematics screening is still in the early stages, and educators may find less guidance with newer measures. Chapter 13 presents an illustration of a school starting with universal screening in one grade and in one area, and how it had a marked effect on student achievement.

Which Measures?

Once grades and area (reading or mathematics) are selected, educators must decide which particular measures offer an appropriate fit with their needs. Some of the criteria to consider in making choices include technical adequacy, cost, ease of use (including scoring and entering results), and professional development resources available. One important consideration for technical adequacy is whether a particular set of measures aligns with the school's curriculum or state standards. Some test publishers have conducted linking studies so that it is possible to interpret screening results with reference to predicted scores at the end of the year on some state's accountability measure (e.g., STAR Reading and Mathematics), and others provide instructions and tools for schools to generate their own norms or investigate relationships between screening and outcome measures (e.g., AIMSweb). Talking to local school staff where measures are in use can provide insight on the strengths and weaknesses of measures relative to the needs of a particular school.

What Kind of Professional Development Is Needed?

Chapter 7 suggests sources for professional development pertinent to progress monitoring and universal screening. An educator or group of educators knowledgeable about testing and data entry at a school will be important for starting a universal screening program and for troubleshooting its initial implementation. Unless the universal screening is administered by computer, examiners will be need to be trained. There also will be broader needs for professional development to help teachers understand the measures, interpret test results appropriately (e.g., take into account test error), and then take instructional action based on those test results. The Lead Coordinator and TAPS Teachers may have, or be able to acquire, the range of expertise needed to provide this professional development to other educators at the school, but if not, there must be a plan to help school staff members learn how to understand assessment results and use them responsibly.

Who Will Administer the Screenings and When?

A team of examiners can administer CBM-based probe sets to an entire grade in a matter of hours. However, they must be trained ahead of time in administration and scoring. Generally, all screening should be done within a 2-week period, and there should be a plan for dealing with students who were absent when their class was tested. In many cases, universal screening occurs three or four times per school year (e.g., once in the fall, winter, and spring), with approximately the same number of weeks between the assessment periods.

Who Will Interpret the Screening Results?

Benchmark cutoff scores are helpful in deciding whether screening results merit action, whether that action is taking a closer look at a student's performance or some kind of instructional intervention. Particularly in the early years of a screening program, it is important for SOPAA facilitators to help teachers decide the instructional implications of test results.

How Will Quality Control Be Maintained?

Even if all staff in a given school year receive professional development in universal screening and a team is trained to give universal screening measures in a standardized manner, staff turnover and changes in screening measures are likely to create a need for continuing professional development and monitoring to see that the quality of the screening program is maintained.

How Will Results Be Compiled and Distributed?

Some universal screening tools have computer- or web-based programs that provide many types of graphs or ways of presenting data (e.g., AIMSweb, Scholastic Reader Interactive). Other systems do not provide such services, or the services are provided at an extra charge. If reporting tools are not part of the universal screening method, then the school will need to find a staff member skilled in a spreadsheet program or who can use one of the web-based programs available to graph results (e.g., Chart Dog; *www.jimwrightonline.com/php/chartdog_2_0/chartdog.php*). In addition to the format for presenting results, decisions need to be made about who has access to data, how it will be shared with parents, and how results will be reported (e.g., by grade or class).

As this list of points for consideration makes evident, universal screening merits careful planning to implement correctly. However, resources are available to help schools plan for using this beneficial set of assessment tools. The reward for the time and effort involved can be a powerful system for examining schoolwide outcomes and tracking progress of individual students and groups.

CHAPTER 7

Maximizing Implementation through Targeted Professional Development

Ongoing professional development is an integral facet and common goal across all disciplines within education (e.g., National School Psychology Certification Board, 2010). In essence, all educators have a professional responsibility to stay abreast of developments in research, practice, and conceptual frameworks that will ultimately help to serve students, families, schools, and/or their communities. Professional development can also be viewed as a centerpiece for successfully implementing and sustaining school-based models of prevention and intervention (Freeman et al., 2009; Furney et al., 2003; Kratochwill et al., 2007). In addition, professional development opportunities that occur at the individual school level can establish a strong sense of community among teachers within the school and are pivotal to improving instruction (Hausman & Goldring, 2001; Louis, Marks, & Kruse, 1996).

Therefore, to continually strengthen the effectiveness of a school's approach to instructional problem solving (via TAPS), SOPAA Component 4 integrates a targeted plan of professional development activities for all educators involved in the TAPS process. The activities center around (1) using evidence-based intervention programs in reading, math, and writing; (2) conducting academic assessment; and (3) applying concepts and principles associated with best practice in academic instruction. Overall, through a targeted professional development plan, classroom teachers and TAPS Teachers should be able to address students' learning needs more effectively and efficiently.

The three primary features of professional development in the SOPAA model are discussed in this chapter. First, TAPS Teachers maintain ongoing professional development in a way that is feasible but will continually maximize their effectiveness as consultants during the TAPS process. Second, classroom teachers (as well as assistive school personnel and school volunteers, if they are part of the school's SOPAA implementation plan) attend one to three targeted inservice workshops each school year. The focus of the workshops will vary from year to year, but at least some will be devoted to helping teachers learn the intervention programs selected to be used during TAPS cases.

A well-aligned and systematic plan for professional development is one feature of the SOPAA model that often distinguishes it from existing models of instructional problem solving.

Third, embedded within the TAPS process, case discussions help to enhance professional development for the classroom teacher and TAPS Teacher.

ONGOING PROFESSIONAL DEVELOPMENT FOR EACH TAPS TEACHER

To successfully facilitate the TAPS process, ongoing professional development for each TAPS Teacher (i.e., the TAPS Reading, Math, and Writing Teacher) is particularly important because that individual must serve as the school's primary expert in assessment and instruction within the specific academic area. To illustrate the importance of having highly skilled TAPS Teachers, when a classroom teacher requests academic support, the TAPS Teacher must be fully prepared to do the following:

1. Confirm the nature and severity of the student's specific academic difficulty (which occurs during the targeted skills observation).
2. Determine one or more intervention options that will likely address the student's difficulty.
3. Lead in developing a comprehensive intervention plan (which occurs during the intervention planning meeting).
4. Assist the teacher, and perhaps a teacher assistant or school volunteer, if necessary, with learning how to implement the intervention with integrity.
5. Develop and/or facilitate a system for monitoring the effectiveness of the intervention and the degree to which it is implemented with integrity.
6. Link progress monitoring assessment data with other information (e.g., teacher reports, implementation integrity data, severity of the student's deficit) to determine the overall effectiveness of the intervention plan.
7. Understand all aspects of the case to help facilitate ongoing instructional decisions that will maximize the student's academic success.

To achieve success with each of these complex tasks requires a thorough conceptual understanding of the academic area and all its relevant subskills. Likewise, success requires knowledge and experience to facilitate assessment and intervention for each struggling student. For instance, knowledge of, and experience with, assessment requires the TAPS Teacher to utilize psychometrically appropriate formal and informal assessment methods. Knowledge of, and experience with, academic instruction requires the TAPS Teacher to know how to implement evidence-based intervention strategies (and to train others), anticipate the possible strengths and limitations of various intervention strategies, and potentially modify intervention programs to best meet the student's specific needs.

Upon starting SOPAA implementation within a school, each TAPS Teacher will possess many of the skills needed to successfully facilitate each TAPS case. In fact, the TAPS Teacher's relative expertise, compared to other educators in the school, is a key factor the school principal and Lead Coordinator must consider when determining which educator(s) in the school should be a TAPS Teacher (also discussed in Chapter 11). However, it is improbable that any TAPS Teacher will start the role having the maximum level of expertise in each aforementioned area. This is improbable because academic instruction and assessment, as well as the related variables that influence instruction and assessment (e.g., student behavior, student's history of instruction, classroom teacher's knowledge and experience), comprise a complicated mix of factors that likely require extensive and focused training, knowledge, and experience before one can most successfully address *all* student learning difficulties in the specific academic area. Furthermore, research, best-practice guidelines, and conceptual understandings of each academic area continually advance, thereby requiring ongoing professional development to stay abreast of those advancements.

Developing Expertise within an Academic Area

Although developing expertise in most tasks requires substantial time and effort, most of us would agree that there are meaningful reasons to develop such expertise. With respect to TAPS Teachers specifically, there are three key reasons for developing expertise in academic instruction, assessment, and concepts related to their target academic areas.

First, increased levels of expertise should result in increased success when supporting classroom teachers through the TAPS process. Of course, increased success with TAPS cases ultimately means that the school more effectively addresses its students' learning needs.

Second, teachers who receive guidance from an expert in the core academic area should facilitate more time-efficient and effective support compared to teachers who receive assistance from an educator without strong knowledge in the area, and/or from a team of educators in which no one person possesses strong knowledge in the given area. This is not to suggest that multiple educators cannot influence intervention planning for a TAPS case. However, for purposes of time efficiency and overall effectiveness, we believe that it should be left to the one expert (i.e., the TAPS Teacher in the respective academic area) to seek input and information (e.g., from printed resources and/or other educators within the school) to facilitate intervention planning for a struggling student. This overall approach of having one expert in the school facilitate key decisions is analogous to a knowledgeable and experienced school principal who ultimately makes decisions about best practice for a given school. In such situations, the principal will make a decision relevant for the school; however, difficult decisions will likely be influenced by consultation with other educators in the school, and perhaps scholarly literature related to the topic.

Third, establishing an expert within the school in each core academic area should eventually facilitate prevention as much as it does intervention. More specifically, the expert TAPS Teacher will not only help to facilitate intervention planning and implementation on a case-by-case basis, she will also help other educators throughout the school improve their knowledge and experiences with academic assessment and instruction. Such dissemination of knowledge and expertise is integrated within the SOPAA plans to (1) host inservice workshops for teachers, and (2) help teachers connect current knowledge and workshop experiences with knowledge obtained during each TAPS case (both topics are discussed later). Through these knowledge dissemination practices, it is likely that classroom teachers will become better skilled at assessing and instructing students, and therefore preventing student learning difficulties (Kratochwill et al., 2007).

Comparative Forms of Professional Development

The primary reason the SOPAA requires each TAPS Teacher to maintain ongoing professional development (in the ways highlighted later in this chapter) is because typical forms of professional development are unlikely to generate the level of expertise a TAPS Teacher needs to maximize her success. That is, compared to the SOPAA activities, professional development requirements from national education organizations typically do not require (1) as much professional development activity; (2) the same level of intensity (e.g., national organization standards may require only one to three professional development activities per year); or (3) the degree of linkage among professional development activities (e.g., national organization standards generally encourage breadth of knowledge rather than expertise in, for example, reading assessment and instruction practices).

To be clear, we fully agree that an educator's overall professional development must involve a wide variety of learning activities across the range of topics relevant to that profession—and in this way we support the professional development activity guidelines espoused by national education organizations with which we are most familiar. However, we believe that there are strong advantages of establishing, within each school, an expert educator to facilitate instructional problem solving and consultation in the core academic areas. In this way the SOPAA requires professional development for TAPS Teachers that extends *beyond* the continued professional development that most educators complete as part of their professional organization's standards.

SOPAA Professional Development Activity Recommendations for TAPS Teachers

In this section we describe (1) the number of hours each TAPS Teacher should commit to SOPAA professional development activities, (2) the general methods by which TAPS Teachers should complete SOPAA professional development activities, (3) the specific areas that should be targeted during SOPAA professional development and resources related to those areas, (4) how to develop a personal plan for SOPAA professional development activities during a given school year, (5) how to document professional development activities, and (6) how a team of TAPS Teachers within a school might work together to strengthen their SOPAA professional development activities. Henceforth, the term *professional development activities* refers specifically to SOPAA professional development activities, unless otherwise stated.

Hourly Commitment to Professional Development

As described in Chapter 3 (Table 3.4) the TAPS Teacher in each academic area should maintain an average of 2–3 hours per week of professional development activities, for a total of at least 8–10 hours per month. The distribution of professional development activity may vary according to each TAPS Teacher's preferences and demands. For example, it would be appropriate to complete 4–5 hours of activity in 1 day, every 2 weeks; or it would be appropriate to complete all 8–10 hours one day per month. However, for consistency, 8–10 hours of professional development should occur *each month* (i.e., the TAPS Teacher should not skip 1 month and then accumulate 16–20 hours during the next month).

For clarity, it is important to emphasize that an educator serving as a TAPS Teacher in more than one academic area should complete professional development activities for each area. Ideally, professional development would occur 8–10 hours per month in each academic area, but if necessary, some multiple-role TAPS Teachers may have to divide professional development time between the areas. For instance, for an educator who serves as the TAPS Teacher in two academic areas, we recommend at least 12–16 hours of professional development per month (i.e., 6–8 hours per academic area). For an educator who serves as the TAPS Teacher in all three academic areas, we recommend at least 16 hours of professional development per month (i.e., 5–6 hours per academic area). As described in Chapter 11, however, it is unlikely a school will benefit most by only having one educator serve as the TAPS Teacher for all academic areas.

There are no known standards designating how much professional development is needed in a core academic area for one to become "expert" in assessment, instruction, and concepts related to that area. The number of study and practice hours is likely to be well into the thousands, and of course, TAPS Teachers will start SOPAA professional development activities with many (but varied) hours of relevant training and experience. By our best current estimate, we suspect that most TAPS Teachers will need to continue our recommended professional development plan for at least 2–3 years (depending on the SOPAA implementation plan and the number of SOPAA co-facilitators). At that point, some TAPS Teachers may begin to decrease the number of hours, if desired. With this said, our hourly recommendations are meant to be feasible yet meaningful. For instance, they should be feasible because, for a typical 40-hour per week job in a school year that lasts approximately 10 months (resulting in approximately 1,500 total work hours per year), completing 10 hours per month of SOPAA professional development results in less than 7% of the TAPS Teacher's total work hours. Yet, 10 months of professional development at 8–10 hours per week are meaningful and should result in a substantial increase in knowledge and expertise.

Methods for Completing Professional Development Activities

Consistent with many national education organizations' standards and recommendations for professional development, SOPAA professional development activities can and should occur in a variety of ways. For example, similar to the National School Psychology Certification Board (2010), we agree that "membership in professional organizations, attending professional conferences [and/or workshops], reading professional literature, and discussing professional issues with colleagues are all essential components of any [educator's] overall professional development" (p. 3). As such, we recommend that TAPS Teachers complete the targeted SOPAA professional development activities using any of the aforementioned methods.

In fact, because it is important that each TAPS Teacher maintain consistent professional development each month, it is unlikely that all professional development activities can come from any one of the above methods. For example, because it is unlikely that a TAPS Teacher will have the availability and resources to attend a professional conference or workshop 8–10 hours per month, she will likely need to spend some of her yearly professional development activities reading professional literature and discussing professional issues with colleagues. At the same time, although there may be a convenience to acquiring all professional development activities from reading professional literature and discussing the literature with colleagues, this approach would prevent the TAPS Teacher from learning directly from experts who present workshops and papers in professional settings. Overall, each TAPS Teacher should utilize a range of professional development opportunities to maximize learning and eventual expertise in her specific academic area.

SOPAA Professional Development Target Areas and Learning Resources

An educator's overall professional development must involve a wide variety of learning activities across the range of topics (e.g., student learning, student behavior, academic assessment, working with English language learners [ELLs]) relevant to the profession. However, to become an expert TAPS Teacher, each one needs a targeted professional development plan in her relevant academic area. Appendices N, O, and P outline key topics and subtopics that all TAPS Teachers should study and understand in their pursuit of expertise in the given academic area. As shown, topics are categorized according to three broad areas that all TAPS Teachers should master: (1) evidence-based instruction and intervention, (2) academic assessment and data-based decision making, and (3) academic subskills and conceptual foundations. Thus, in addition to learning the procedures associated with the TAPS process, a TAPS Teacher's effectiveness should improve with increased knowledge in these three broad areas.

Within each of the three broad topics, Appendices N–P show the integral subtopics that should be the focus of professional development, with each appendix specific for the particular

TAPS Teacher (i.e., reading, math, and writing). As shown, subtopics include areas such as implementing evidence-based intervention programs, implementing interventions with integrity, progress monitoring assessment, and knowing the key subskills within an academic area. Overall, in order for TAPS Teachers to most effectively facilitate TAPS cases, the focus of professional development during the early months of SOPAA implementation (and perhaps during a planning year, as discussed in Chapter 3) should be on acquiring knowledge about the subtopics listed in the TAPS Teacher's respective appendix (e.g., Appendix O for the TAPS Math Teacher).

In particular, before facilitating a TAPS case, the TAPS Teacher must have knowledge of, and experience with, the intervention programs that were selected during SOPAA implementation planning to be used during TAPS cases. Likewise, he or she must be familiar with using progress monitoring assessment methods related to the academic area, as well as how to monitor teachers' implementation integrity of selected interventions. Although facilitating TAPS cases necessitates knowledge of how to use intervention and assessment in the pertinent academic area, the skill of selecting intervention programs and assessment methods will be strengthened by a thorough understanding of the academic area subskills and, with reading and math, the school's core curriculum and state's standards. Again, based on the skills and experiences the TAPS Teacher has acquired prior to assuming the role, there will be a need to prioritize one or more of the subtopics listed in the pertinent appendix to most effectively facilitate TAPS cases.

USING THE SUGGESTED PROFESSIONAL RESOURCES

Because we suspect that each TAPS Teacher will complete at least some professional development activities by reading pertinent literature, Appendices N–P provide one to four key references related to each subtopic. These references should not be viewed as the only or the absolute "best" source about these topics for all audiences or purposes. However, all references were selected based on (1) a thorough review of the existing literature, (2) recommendations from educational experts associated with the topics, and (3) our own familiarity with, and use of, the resources. We also attempted to select references that should be easily accessible to most educators, including several free, Internet-based resources. Further, we sometimes selected book chapter references that are available within the same book or set of materials so that TAPS Teachers can obtain information about multiple topics from the same set of materials.

Across the varying resources suggested, it is possible a TAPS Teacher will find inconsistencies in terminology and/or recommendations. However, such inconsistencies are inevitable because the field of education will never be directed by only one educational approach or set of perspectives. In fact, if inconsistencies are identified across different resources, TAPS Teachers can use this opportunity to discuss those inconsistencies, broaden their knowledge of the area, and determine which educational practices are most compatible for their school and for their overall SOPAA implementation plan.

ACCESSING PROFESSIONAL RESOURCES

If TAPS Teachers (or other educators) within a given school do not have access to the recommended books or chapters shown in Appendices N–P, the Lead Coordinator might include these in the list of needed resources that are discussed with the school principal (described in Chapter 9). Alternatively, TAPS Teachers may be able to access some resources by sharing costs and resources with colleagues, and/or locating the resource at the local public library (and if applicable, requesting that the library purchase the resource). An examination of Appendices N, O, and P will reveal that some resources appear in all three appendices. As such, sharing resources will be cost-effective and facilitate collaborative professional development (discussed later in this chapter).

For reasons of accessibility, we recommended only a small number of literature resources from peer-reviewed professional journals because many educator practitioners have difficulty accessing a range of different journals. However, we do encourage TAPS Teachers to seek out relevant literature from peer-reviewed journals, as such literature represents a primary source of information that is regularly advancing and often relevant to research, practice, and concepts in the core academic areas. To identify potentially useful information from journal articles, the TAPS Teacher will likely find pertinent references to journal articles within the sources recommended in Appendices N–P. Thus, as needed, TAPS Teachers should determine how to get access to peer-reviewed journals from their place of employment. For example, some professional organizations offer their members online access to multiple professional journals, or there may be opportunities for TAPS Teachers to access journals through local college or university libraries.

TAPS Teachers are also encouraged to find additional literature and resources related to the SOPAA target topics for professional development. There are many reasons to do so. For example, the listed references in Appendices N–P should be relevant and useful, but they do not represent an exhaustive or authoritative list. Also, the reference lists were created in spring 2011; thus, as years pass, TAPS Teachers should explore similar resources that may be more updated. Recall also, to stay abreast of contemporary research and practice, they should engage in professional development activities by attending workshops and conference presentations, which may be hosted nationally, regionally, within the state, and/or within the school district.

OTHER PROFESSIONAL DEVELOPMENT TARGET AREAS

As we highlighted earlier, one's professional development will ideally cover a range of topics, including but not limited to the subtopics listed in Appendices N–P. For example, related only to academic instruction, intervention, and assessment, the following topics are also important:

- Conceptual frameworks for teaching and learning (e.g., the learning hierarchy, Bloom's taxonomy of learning domains, increasing students' opportunity for active engagement)
- General principles of effective teaching (e.g., differentiated instruction, modeling, practice, promoting skill generalization)
- Single-case experimental designs or case study data to more systematically evaluate intervention outcomes (see companion website *www.sopaaforschools.org* for a related online resource)
- Topics of cultural awareness and diversity (e.g., valid academic assessment with ELLs, increasing teachers' cross-cultural competence).

Indeed, such a list could continue for many pages.

In addition, as noted in Chapter 1 about using the SOPAA to address student behavior problems, professional development for TAPS Teachers might also include activities that will ensure that TAPS Teachers can effectively assess and improve student behavior problems that may interfere with learning and academic interventions (e.g., identifying skill versus motivation deficits, using rewards to improve a student's motivation). This area of professional development is particularly important in schools where one or more TAPS Teachers repeatedly find academic interventions ineffective (or difficult to implement) because of challenges related to student behavior. It would be beyond the scope of this book to detail fully how to assess and intervene with a student who simultaneously presents significant behavior and learning difficulties, but there are several excellent resources available to assist teachers (including TAPS Teachers) with addressing student behavior (e.g., Alberto & Troutman, 2009; Jenson et al., 1994; Shinn et al., 2002; Sprick & Howard, 1996; Steege et al., 2009). Also, as described in Chapter 5, the TAPS process helps teachers address student behaviors that may interfere with academic intervention. In situations in which the TAPS process and relevant professional development activities do not allow the TAPS Teacher and classroom teacher to effectively intervene with a struggling learner, an additional form of intervention support may be warranted. For example, some schools may designate one educator to serve as a TAPS Behavior Specialist. The TAPS Behavior Specialist's primary role would be to consult with the TAPS Teacher and classroom teacher during a TAPS case in which student behavior problems significantly reduce the teacher's ability to effectively implement an academic intervention.

Overall, as important as the "other professional development target areas" are for ongoing professional development, they are not specified in the list of subtopics shown in Appendices N–P because we feel that the listed subtopics are those that TAPS Teachers should prioritize to successfully facilitate TAPS cases, especially in the early years of SOPAA implementation. As those subtopics are mastered and the TAPS process works efficiently, devotion to any one of the "other" areas may eventually become a focus of professional development to further improve the effectiveness of TAPS and/or the school's approach to core instruction. Of course, TAPS Teachers will also recognize when professional development in a given area must be prioritized to improve the success of TAPS. For example, if TAPS is used with a large number of ELLs and the TAPS Teacher has little knowledge of evidence-based assessment and instruction with ELLs, professional development targeting this area would become a priority, along with the subtopics listed in Appendices N–P. Because effective instruction involves a large range of interrelated topics and variables, one of our recommended resources is a six-volume set of books that includes more than 100 chapters covering an extensive range of educational topics. Thus, as SOPAA professional development activities go beyond those subtopics listed in Appendices N–P, this set of books may be useful as a starting point for professional development in other areas related to effective instruction.

Developing a Personal Professional Development Plan

As already noted, professional development in the SOPAA targeted areas should occur 8–10 hours per month (for each TAPS Teacher) and should include a range of professional development activities (e.g., reading professional literature, attending workshops and conference presentations). To maximize one's professional development, each TAPS Teacher should develop and follow a personal professional development plan. The plan should specify the topics that will be covered, the type of professional development activity (e.g., reading literature, attending workshops), resources that will be used to increase knowledge about the topics, the reasons for covering those topics (e.g., TAPS Teacher needs to learn intervention programs to better facilitate TAPS process), and the dates and times set aside for professional development each month.

Appendix Q shows a blank Yearly Professional Development Planning Guide that can be used by a TAPS Teacher to create her development plan. This form also includes a column for the TAPS Teacher to indicate whether the professional development activity occurred as intended (by circling *yes* or *no*). Figure 7.1 shows a sample Yearly Professional Development Planning Guide that is completed by a TAPS Reading Teacher at the beginning of the school year during Year 1 of SOPAA implementation. This sample is provided because it not only shows how one might complete the Planning Guide, but it also shows a plan for consistent professional development (at least 8–10 hours per month), a range of activities and resources, and logical reasons the TAPS Teacher wants to prioritize learning about particular topics. Of course, prioritizing some topics over others will be determined by each TAPS Teacher and will largely depend on what he or she needs to learn most to improve her effectiveness with the TAPS process.

TAPS Teacher's Name: I. Brock **School year and (SOPAA Implementation Year):** 2013–2014 (Year 1)

TAPS Teacher's Target Area (circle one): (Reading) Math Writing

Topic(s) to Cover	Type of Activity	Resources Needed	Reasons to Cover the Topic	Dates and Times to Cover Topic	Topic Covered as Planned?
Evidence-based intervention in reading fluency (the HELPS program)	Read Teacher's Manual and complete training exercises in order to learn and implement HELPS.	HELPS Teacher's Manual, curriculum of passages, and online training video	I need to learn this program because HELPS will be used in the current academic year to assist students struggling with reading fluency, and a workshop on HELPS will be hosted for teachers in October.	September 6 (6 hours) September 13 (3 hours)	Yes No
Components of a good core reading curriculum and the state's standards for core reading curricula	Read literature related to core reading curricula and review and evaluate the school's core.	—Chapter 12 of this book —Dewitz, Leahy, Jones, and Sullivan (2010) —Simmons and Kame'enui (2003) —State's standards for reading	Communication with teachers and facilitating TAPS cases will be improved with increased knowledge of state standards and components of core curricula.	October 11 (4 hours) October 18 (4 hours)	Yes No
Components of a good core reading curriculum and the state's standards for core reading curricula	Same as above	Same as above	Same as above	November 1 (4 hours) November 15 (4 hours)	Yes No
Best practices and concepts related to monitoring implementation integrity	Attend district workshop on the topic, then review materials provided by district.	Materials provided by school district	Increase knowledge about monitoring implementation integrity so that monitoring practices during TAPS cases can be conducted most effectively and efficiently.	December 2 (attend full-day district workshop) December 6 (2–3 hours to review literature)	Yes No

*Best practices and concepts related to progress monitoring in reading	Read literature related to progress monitoring.	—Chapter 6 —Resources provided by the National Center on Student Progress Monitoring (www.studentprogress.org)	Although I have experience using progress monitoring assessments in reading, reviewing this literature will help me update and improve my knowledge of the topic so that progress monitoring during TAPS cases is best facilitated.	January 10 (4 hours) January 17 (4 hours)	Yes No
Various areas related to reading and effective instruction and assessment	Attend national conference in education.	Funds to attend conference (paid for through district stipend and out-of-pocket costs)	Attending presentations from national scholars in areas related to reading instruction and assessment will strengthen my knowledge about the topics and perhaps influence positive changes in how I facilitate TAPS cases.	February 20–23 (more than 10 hours over the course of the conference)	Yes No
Universal screening in reading	Read literature related to universal screening and plan for universal screening practices.	—Chapter 6 of this book —Johnson, Mellard, Fuchs, and McKnight (2006) —Ikeda, Neesen, and Witt (2008)	In the following school year the SOPAA implementation plan will include universal screening in all grades K–3; thus professional development activities are needed to prepare and facilitate this universal screening.	March 14 (5 hours) March 21 (3 hours)	Yes No
Universal screening in reading	Same as above	Same as above	Same as above	April 4 (4 hours) April 11 (4 hours)	Yes No
Evidence-based intervention in reading comprehension (the Reading Success Program)	Read teacher's materials and complete training exercises in order to learn and implement Reading Success.	Reading Success Teacher's Manual and training video	In the following school year the SOPAA implementation plan will include Reading Success as an intervention program and will be primarily used when the SOPAA implementation plan begins to include grades 3–6 in reading; thus professional development activities are needed to learn Reading Success.	May 9 (5 hours) May 16 (5 hours)	Yes No

*With the Lead Coordinator, remember to review your professional development plan during the middle of the school year.

FIGURE 7.1. Sample Yearly Professional Development Planning Guide.

This sample of the Professional Development Planning Guide was written by a TAPS Teacher who already has a good working knowledge of the key subskills in reading (as discussed in Chapter 12) and has experience using (1) the TAPS process, (2) two of the three intervention programs selected for TAPS cases (an intervention targeting phonemic awareness and another targeting phonics), and (3) progress monitoring assessment strategies in reading. Note also that, although the sample Professional Development Planning Guide does not specify the professional development that occurs through collaboration and discussion with other TAPS Teachers, it is assumed that this type of collaboration will occur each month, in addition to the hours listed in the personal plan. The topic of collaborative professional development is discussed later in this chapter.

Before any TAPS Teacher begins her personal professional development plan, the plan should be discussed with the Lead Coordinator and modified if needed. Occasionally the Lead Coordinator will have recommendations for professional development that reflect school needs a particular TAPS Teacher may not recognize. Furthermore, the Lead Coordinator (who, as the reader should recall, is also a TAPS Teacher in at least one academic area) may benefit from ensuring continuity between each TAPS Teacher's professional development plan so that learning for all TAPS Teachers works most efficiently toward overall success with SOPAA implementation. For example, if the school does not have a strong system for monitoring progress in any academic area, it may be best for each TAPS Teacher to first prioritize learning about progress monitoring in her academic area. Then, TAPS Teachers can work collectively to develop a progress monitoring plan that is consistent across the academic areas. As noted in the Professional Development Planning Guide, all TAPS Teachers and the Lead Coordinator should collectively review their individual professional development plans during the middle portion of the school year (e.g., December or January for schools who follow a traditional academic calendar) to determine whether any of their plans should be modified. As SOPAA implementation evolves, school needs change, and TAPS Teachers continue to gain expertise in their respective areas, it is possible that modifying the professional development plan will maximize TAPS Teachers' success with facilitating the TAPS process.

Last, it is critical to emphasize again that professional development during the initial year (or years) of SOPAA implementation should prioritize successful facilitation of the TAPS process. Namely, TAPS Teachers must have knowledge of, and experience with, TAPS procedures (e.g., facilitating the intervention planning meeting), as well as the intervention programs and progress monitoring assessments that will be used during TAPS cases. Because this knowledge and experience are critical to facilitating TAPS, we recommended in Chapter 3 that a planning year might be used prior to starting Year 1 of SOPAA implementation, and during that planning year TAPS Teachers take the time to learn the process and use one or more of the intervention and assessment tools that will be integrated within TAPS cases. During this planning year classroom teachers and assistive personnel might also begin to learn the intervention programs that will be used in the cases (thereby minimizing the type of case-by-case intervention program training discussed in Chapter 5). However, in some schools a planning year may not be needed because the TAPS Teacher and classroom teachers will already be familiar with evidence-based intervention, assessment, and consultation procedures related to TAPS. Our key point here is that without prioritizing certain knowledge and experience early in SOPAA implementation, the model may be less successful because TAPS Teachers may not be able to effectively facilitate most cases.

Documenting Professional Development Activities

Each TAPS Teacher must document her professional development activities because the documentation (1) helps to show others in the school (e.g., the principal, the Lead Coordinator) that meaningful and ongoing professional development occurred as intended and should benefit the overall goals of the school; (2) serves as a summary and reminder of what was learned, which may be useful as a reference for the TAPS Teacher during subsequent months of professional development, TAPS case management, and/or meetings with the other TAPS Teachers; and (3) may sometimes be needed to verify professional development activities that can count toward maintaining one's national certification or credentials. In addition, documentation may help TAPS Teachers to prepare professional development workshops for classroom teachers and/or help to someday train a new TAPS Teacher within the school.

Appendix R shows an example of a Professional Development Documentation Form. For clarity in using this type of form, the TAPS Teacher should note the following:

1. "Topic(s) Covered During Activity" should state the primary *and* subtopic description that aligns with the SOPAA professional development target areas (e.g., academic assessment and data-based decision making—progress monitoring).
2. "Type of Activity" should state the ways in which professional development occurred (e.g., attended district workshop, read professional literature, attended national conference).
3. "Resources Used and/or Sponsor of Activity" should state all resources used and/or a sponsor (e.g., Chapter 3 of Shapiro [2011a] book: *Academic Skills Problems*; Wake County Public Schools district-sponsored workshop).
4. "Description of What You Did and Learned and How You Might Use the Information" should clearly state what was done (e.g., spent 3 hours reading the chapter and reflecting on how the information aligns with my current progress monitoring assessment practices), the key information learned, and how the information could reasonably be used in practice, particularly with respect to work with TAPS cases.

Strengthening Personal Professional Development through Collaboration

This section describes how all TAPS Teachers within a school can work together to ensure that individual professional development plans are the most meaningful and, when beneficial to SOPAA implementation, consistent for all TAPS Teachers. The collaborative nature of professional development consists of three primary tasks.

First, each TAPS Teacher develops her own professional development plan by prioritizing the target topics that will most meaningfully improve her success with facilitating TAPS cases. For example, knowing how to implement a range of intervention programs in the academic area, how to monitor student progress during intervention implementation, and how to evaluate implementers' integrity likely serve as foundation skills for facilitating the TAPS process. Based on her current knowledge and experience as a TAPS Teacher, she would likely prioritize one or more of those topics early in her professional development plan.

Second, as stated earlier, before any TAPS Teacher begins a personal professional development plan at the beginning of the school year, the plan should be discussed with the Lead Coordinator. Ideally, during a meeting with all TAPS Teachers, the group should review each others' personal professional development plans. The Lead Coordinator should suggest ways to modify personal plans if she feels a TAPS Teacher would be more successful by prioritizing topics in a different manner, and/or feels that TAPS Teachers would collectively benefit from professional development plans that are more congruent (e.g., during month 1, all TAPS Teachers learn how to implement two new intervention programs specific to their academic area; during month 2, they review best practices for monitoring intervention implementation; during month 3, they review best practices for academic progress monitoring). This is not to suggest that all TAPS Teachers' plans must be completely aligned by topic. However, early in Year 1 of SOPAA implementation (or perhaps as part of the preparation year), aligning the professional development plans may help to ensure that each TAPS Teacher has the foundational knowledge needed to consistently facilitate the TAPS process.

Third, at the end of each month the Lead Coordinator should arrange for a discussion (lasting from 15 to 60 minutes) among all TAPS Teachers to communicate what each TAPS Teacher learned during her monthly professional development activities. The primary goals of that discussion are to help all TAPS Teachers strengthen and confirm each others' knowledge of the topics learned, offer practice-oriented suggestions and feedback based on the learning that occurred, and (when applicable) develop strategic practice plans that are consistent among the TAPS Teachers.

To facilitate these goals, every discussion should allow each TAPS Teacher to summarize what she learned and how she plans to integrate that knowledge into her practice. From there, TAPS Teachers should discuss the knowledge they have generated and work collectively to offer feedback and develop practice-oriented plans related to the SOPAA. This discussion should also help the Lead Coordinator ensure that all TAPS Teachers benefit from the professional development activities and the group discussions, and as needed the Lead Coordinator can propose modifications to the professional development activities. Because there are many benefits to collaborative professional development (Hausman & Goldring, 2001), we encourage this form of professional development, and TAPS Teachers will recognize some overlap across suggested resources in Appendices N–P.

Through targeted professional development for TAPS Teachers, each school is sure to have a knowledgeable leader to help guide difficult instruction and assessment decisions for reading, math, and writing.

INSERVICE SOPAA PROFESSIONAL DEVELOPMENT FOR TEACHERS

The second primary feature of SOPAA Component 4 (targeted professional development) is for teachers to participate in one to three inservice workshops per year that relate to topics that will help to facilitate the SOPAA, and more specifically, the TAPS process. Particularly in the early years of SOPAA implementation, training teachers to use intervention programs available for TAPS cases should be a priority for SOPAA-related inservice training. (Henceforth, reference to workshops and other forms of inservice training within a school are to SOPAA-related training and workshops, unless stated otherwise).

As discussed in Chapter 11, inservice training is generally hosted by one or more of the SOPAA facilitators. Although workshop attendees might include classroom teachers, assistive school personnel (e.g., teacher assistants), and possibly school volunteers (as described in Chapter 8), we refer to this entire group of potential attendees simply as teachers. Although each school's yearly plan for workshops and inservice training will differ depending on the school's SOPAA implementation plan, the number of years the SOPAA has been implemented in the school, and teachers' particular needs and preferences for training, this chapter offers some guidance and information related to hosting teacher workshops and other forms of inservice professional development. For example, we discuss focus areas for inservice training and describe a general framework for preparing teachers to use intervention programs that will be selected for TAPS cases.

Focus Areas of SOPAA Inservice Professional Development

Meta-analyses of professional development studies indicate that student outcomes can be meaningfully influenced by professional development programs, especially when the content is focused on training teachers in specific programs and strategies (e.g., Hattie, 2009; Timperley, Wilson, Barrar, & Fung, 2007; Joyce & Showers, 1995). The core component of the SOPAA is facilitating instructional problem solving through TAPS, and a central feature of TAPS is providing students with evidence-based intervention programs that target their individual academic deficits. To effectively facilitate TAPS cases, teachers must be able to implement the selected intervention program.

Considering these facts, the first priority for teachers' inservice training should be preparing them to use intervention programs that will be used during TAPS cases. Because learning intervention programs is typically the primary professional development activity for teachers during the early years of SOPAA implementation, most discussion about teachers' professional development in this chapter occurs in the context of training them how to use intervention programs. Of course, in order for TAPS to work effectively and efficiently, it is also important that teachers know the process for facilitating TAPS (e.g., how to request support from a TAPS Teacher and what occurs during intervention planning); this topic is covered in Chapter 10 when we discuss how to prepare the SOPAA introductory presentation for teachers.

Secondary Professional Development Focus Areas

Although it is integral for teachers to learn how to implement TAPS intervention programs, teachers must certainly possess other important skills to improve student learning during TAPS cases and in their overall teaching. For example, many teachers will also benefit by improving their knowledge and practice with (1) academic assessment, progress monitoring, and data-based decision-making procedures; (2) general "best-practice" instructional procedures that are common across good core curricula and intervention programs (e.g., explicit instruction procedures, allowing students to practice skills being learned); (3) effective classroom and behavior management practices needed to facilitate instruction; (4) conceptual foundations of teaching in reading, math, and writing (e.g., knowing the key areas that should be targeted in reading instruction); and (5) other topics that can influence teachers' instructional effectiveness (e.g., working with ELLs, communication with families and caregivers, attitudes about one's responsibilities as a teacher). In short, inservice professional development should maximize teachers' effectiveness in the classroom, but to increase the probability of effectively facilitating TAPS cases, preparing teachers to implement intervention programs should be prioritized during the early years of SOPAA implementation. This prioritization should continue until the desired number of teachers can implement the selected TAPS intervention programs with integrity. For this reason we suggest, in Chapter 3, that a SOPAA preparation year would ideally include training some teachers to use one or two of the selected intervention programs.

In the process of teachers learning intervention programs, several other skills are also learned (e.g., academic assessment related to the program, using motivation strategies as part of the program). However, once teachers are comfortable implementing the intervention programs that they will likely use during a TAPS case, professional development might begin to focus more specifically on other areas of learning and assessment (e.g., see the list of five general topics mentioned in the previous paragraph). It is beyond the scope of this book to offer detailed information about facilitating professional development with teachers across the range of topics that would help to improve teachers' classroom instruction, but to assist SOPAA facilitators with determining which areas to focus for continued inservice professional development (i.e., after teachers learn the necessary intervention programs), a teacher "needs survey" is available on the companion website *www.sopaaforschools.org*. This sample needs survey and the related information were developed based on several existing teacher surveys that have

been used to identify teachers' strengths, weaknesses, and training needs (e.g., Begeny & Martens, 2006a; Coalition for Psychology in Schools and Education, 2006; Hasbrouck & Denton, 2005).

A Framework for Training Teachers to Use Intervention Programs

In general (i.e., in schools not using the SOPAA model), when teachers learn how to implement an intervention program (or set of strategies) that target specific academic skills, they must also learn the rationale for using the intervention, how the intervention aligns with the school's curricular goals, how to evaluate the effectiveness of the intervention, as well as when and how (if needed) to modify the intervention to maximize its effectiveness. In our view, this level of knowledge about intervention implementation is quite complex, and when combined with training teachers to accurately *use* the intervention procedures, it is often very difficult, within one or two workshops, to ensure that teachers have learned the wide range of skills associated with successfully using an intervention. This difficulty is especially true if the intervention does not come with a detailed manual that teachers can easily reference for implementation and decision-making information, and relates to one of our reasons for recommending the use of manualized intervention programs (also discussed in Chapter 3).

The complex set of skills teachers need to successfully use an intervention is also why we developed the TAPS process. Specifically, through TAPS, teachers are assisted with the additional decision making that goes along with intervention implementation. In addition, the decision making is well documented in the student's IPF, and through the systematic TAPS process teachers are likely to strengthen the decision-making skills associated with the particular intervention and possibly the overall intervention process. Therefore, because the TAPS process supports teachers with the instructional decision making that is necessary for successful intervention delivery, the focus of inservice training for teachers to use intervention programs can be directed toward (1) program implementation, and (2) the rationale for using the program and how it aligns with a student's core curriculum.

With respect to intervention–curriculum alignment and providing teachers with a rationale for using an intervention program, the workshop presenter will likely obtain a great deal of information from the program's manual, as well as from her overall knowledge of what skill(s) the intervention targets and the importance of that skill. A rationale for using the program might also be derived from research supporting the program and other possible benefits of it (e.g., it is easy to implement, can be used to monitor students' progress, and can be used by assistive school personnel and school volunteers). With respect to training teachers in program implementation, we now describe a workshop model we have successfully used to train teachers in intervention programs and strategies. This model may be familiar to others who have conducted or attended inservice professional development workshops throughout the United States and should serve as an example for helping SOPAA facilitators design their own workshops.

Modeling, Demonstrating, and Providing Practice Opportunities

After specifying the workshop goals and outcomes, as well as offering a rationale (approximately 10–20 minutes) for using the intervention program, workshop presenters should model (i.e., demonstrate) the program procedures for teachers. Depending on the complexity and length of implementing the entire intervention program within a session, we recommend that presenters plan a logical sequence for how they will introduce the intervention procedures and when they will offer teachers practice opportunities. For example, long intervention procedures or protocols might be segmented into more teachable units and then

sequenced according to prerequisite skills teachers must have for implementing the program in its entirety. On the companion website *www.sopaaforschools.org* we offer a general outline for how workshop presenters might train teachers to implement one specific reading intervention, which should serve as an example for developing workshops for other intervention programs.

Modeling intervention programs can be done live (e.g., one workshop presenter implements the procedures while another acts as the student) or with available video clips. We generally recommend that presenters demonstrate (sometimes multiple times) how to implement all key *procedures* of the intervention program (e.g., strategies for having the student segment or blend sounds, having the student read aloud, asking the student vocabulary questions). As needed, presenters might provide a running commentary about what is occurring while the specific procedure is being demonstrated. During this modeling activity, teachers should have access to all forms and checklists that are needed for implementation so that they can follow along with the demonstration. In short, while specific procedures are being modeled, teachers should know which instructional procedure is being used, learn how to implement the procedure, and ultimately understand why the procedure is integrated as part of the intervention program. When time permits, it may also be useful for teachers to watch the intervention being implemented properly from start to finish (without running commentary), thereby allowing teachers to get a comprehensive "picture" of how the program is used.

After teachers have previewed each intervention procedure, in isolation and/or in the complete sequence dictated by the intervention program, they should then practice using each specific procedure or a small sequence of procedures with each other (one teacher plays the role of implementer, one teacher plays the role of student). After teachers have had practice and feedback implementing each of the intervention procedures, they should then integrate all procedures and practice implementation in the way the program should actually be implemented with a student. Of course, workshops will be particularly effective if there are multiple facilitators (i.e., those who are experienced with implementing the intervention) available to answer questions while teachers are practicing implementation. These role-playing/practice opportunities thereby provide the first opportunity for "coaching" from the workshop facilitator(s), a topic that is discussed in more detail later in this chapter.

When time permits, teachers' initial experience with learning the program can be strengthened by watching purposely flawed demonstrations of procedures and being asked to identify the errors. For example, teachers can be asked to say what is wrong, why it is wrong, and what should have happened instead. For an illustration of these types of "identifying the errors" activities, the reader can refer to the Teacher's Manual and training procedures that are discussed for the HELPS reading program. The HELPS manual and the associated training video can be accessed for free at *www.helpsprogram.org.*

Although in-workshop practice opportunities are an integral part of training, continued training requires the teacher to practice implementing the intervention in a more authentic setting (e.g., in a classroom with students).

Practicing with other adults in a workshop is usually not enough to learn an intervention program and be able to implement it with integrity. Role playing provides important and good first opportunities for practice, but it fails as a complete approach. For example, it is difficult to replicate the pace of an intervention session during role playing, and it is unlikely teachers will leave even a full-day workshop (or two) having fully mastered all intervention procedures within the program they are learning. For these reasons, the workshop should end by asking teachers to continue practicing the intervention program with any student from their classroom. The student need not be a student who actually needs the specific intervention program (i.e., the student could be an average or above-average learner in that intervention target area), but practicing with a student will increase the teacher's practice opportunities and allow for a more realistic context in which she will actually implement the intervention program. During this classroom-based practice opportunity, teachers should be encouraged to regularly consult the intervention program manual and all other resources provided to them during the workshop. Only by practicing and reviewing the program materials will teachers get closer to being able to implement the program with integrity.

After the teacher practices implementing the program with a student at least two to five times (across 1–2 weeks from the date of the initial workshop), an "expert" teacher who has experience implementing the program (e.g., a workshop facilitator or possibly another teacher in the school who has experience successfully using the program) should observe the teacher implementing the program and offer her needed feedback. This "expert" teacher will, in many cases, be a SOPAA facilitator (e.g., a TAPS Teacher); but to maximize resources, other teachers who have documented strong implementation integrity with the program could observe and provide feedback to the teacher. Having other teachers available to help in this capacity is another reason for incremental implementation of the SOPAA and for gradually training teachers in intervention programs that will be used with TAPS cases. For example, as discussed in Chapter 3, SOPAA implementation may start with only kindergarten through second-grade teachers in the area of reading, and once those teachers learn and use one to three selected intervention programs, some of them could assist with training teachers in grades 3–6.

Henceforth we refer to the observation and feedback activities for newly trained teachers as coaching. By *coaching*, we mean exchanges between educators that facilitate the trainee's learning, particularly of intervention programs, but at some point may also include learning instruction practices for core curricula, assessment procedures, and even classroom management. In all cases, coaching is *not* synonymous with teacher evaluation, because coaching is intended to improve a teacher's instructional practice rather than to simply evaluate it. What follows are suggestions for coaching practices that could occur as part of inservice training related to the SOPAA. The recommendations are inspired by school improvement models (e.g., Feinberg-DiNapoli & McKinney, 1990; Johnson & Street, 2004; Joyce & Showers, 1995) as well as by each of our own experiences working with teachers, consulting with schools, and providing coaching. The interested reader can learn about research and benefits of coaching through the available literature (e.g., Bean, Draper, Hall, Vandermolen, & Zigmond, 2010; Biancarosa, Bryk, & Dexter, 2010; Matsumura, Garnier, Correnti, Junker, & Bickel, 2010).

Coaching

Depending on the school's SOPAA implementation plan, the urgency to implement the specific intervention program, and the available number of coaches, coaching sessions can occur by directly observing a teacher implement the intervention program with a student in her classroom, or by having teachers in training return for a follow-up workshop that allows them to be observed by a coach while implementing the intervention. If time and resources are available, coaching a teacher in the context of her classroom would be ideal (the following discussion of coaching uses this specific context). However, the recommendations and information described below could also be facilitated in a follow-up inservice workshop wherein teachers demonstrate their implementation ability and receive feedback from a coach.

A preliminary consideration for coaching is that the coach has spent time getting to know and building rapport with the teacher she is coaching. In most schools, this will have already occurred simply from teachers working together in the same school; but when it has not occurred, rapport building should occur before any coaching sessions. Also, before any coaching session, the coach and teacher should set expectations for the session. For example, they should agree on how long to plan for the coaching session and determine whether the teacher should implement the intervention program in its entirety, implement only some procedures and then get feedback from the coach, implement the program while periodically stopping to ask the coach questions, or any other possible option.

Another important aspect of the precoaching discussion is to agree on when and how the coach will provide positive feedback, correct procedural errors, and prompt more effective or efficient implementation. Immediate feedback from the coach has the advantage of affirming or correcting teacher implementation at the exact moment, but this approach may make some teachers nervous or uncomfortable. Although some teachers may want coaches to hold their feedback until the intervention session has ended, many eventually give consent for immediate feedback, especially if there is good rapport between the teacher and coach and the teacher understands the value of receiving immediate feedback (e.g., this type of feedback prevents the teacher from continuing to use improper or inefficient procedures). Lastly, prior to the coaching session there should be agreement between the teacher and coach about how to explain the role of the coach to the teacher's student(s). For example, the teacher might be encouraged to say to the student, "Just like I'm your teacher, Ms. ____________ is my teacher. She is giving me pointers on a new program I want to try with you."

During the coaching sessions, teachers implement the agreed-upon program or procedure and coaches observe and record data on the corresponding coaching feedback form and/or implementation protocols that are developed for the specific intervention program. During this time, coaches should carefully monitor their own body language and maintain a positive attitude throughout the session. Examples of coaching feedback forms are available on the companion website *www.sopaaforschools.org*. Although the forms may not be appropriate for all intervention programs and coaching sessions, they can be modified to fit each coach's specific purpose.

When the teacher's performance matches the intervention protocol, or she demonstrates good judgment about a deviation, the coach should provide positive but relatively unobtrusive feedback. This feedback lets the teacher know that she is on the right track without interrupting her flow. When the teacher's performance falls outside of the acceptable range, the coach should analyze the errors to determine their source. Seven common errors include a mix of generic and program-specific problems:

1. The teacher applies a procedure incorrectly.
2. The teacher applies a procedure correctly but in the wrong circumstance or sequence.
3. The teacher's praise rate or enthusiasm with the student(s) is too low.
4. When a student makes an error, the teacher fails to provide an immediate correction, provides a poor correction, or otherwise does not correct the student's error as she should.
5. The teacher's pacing is too slow or fast.
6. The teacher's organization of program materials is poor or not the most efficient.
7. The teacher does not fully attend to student behaviors that may hinder the student's responsiveness to the intervention.

After identifying an error in the teacher's implementation, the coach should intervene according to what she and the teacher agreed prior to the coaching session. As noted previously, there are varying levels of intrusiveness in providing feedback to the teacher when a mistake occurs, and the appropriate time and method of providing feedback will depend on the teacher, the context of implementation, the intervention, and other factors. As a general rule of thumb, the coach and teacher might agree on a rubric for what represents a "major" versus "minor" implementation error; the coach may then advocate for immediate correction and interruption of implementation when a major error occurs, but will discuss minor implementation errors with the teacher after the intervention session ends and the student is no longer present. An example of one intervention program's determination of major versus minor errors is available on the companion website *www.sopaaforschools.org*.

Regardless of when and how the coach provides corrective feedback to the teacher, the coach should plan to spend at least some time reviewing the teacher's implementation strengths and weaknesses, as well as determining whether an additional coaching session is needed before the teacher begins implementing the intervention in the absence of a coach. If an additional coaching session is needed, specific areas/procedures for improvement should be discussed, and the teacher might be encouraged to practice the intervention (with another adult or a student not specifically in need of intervention) once or twice more before the next coaching session. The coach should also provide the teacher with a written summary of her feedback as soon as possible, and the feedback should contain honest praise for specific strengths, objective criticism for specific skills that need improvement, and suggested resources to help the teacher improve (e.g., pages within the teacher's manual of the intervention program, vignettes of the program's training video). The coach should also maintain a copy of all written feedback for her own records, which will likely help in the continued training with that particular teacher and in planning for training with other teachers. In many schools it will be unrealistic to ask teachers to videotape or audiotape their implementation of the intervention and then review it to assess their own strengths and weaknesses, but in situations when this is possible or needed, this added element of training can be very effective (e.g., Fukkink & Tavecchio, 2010).

The number of coaching sessions per teacher will vary depending on the teacher, her prior background knowledge and experience with the procedures in the intervention program, and the overall complexity of the intervention program. With some intervention programs, one coaching session that follows an inservice workshop and some classroom practice opportunities are sufficient to ensure that teachers can implement the intervention with integrity. Other scenarios will require additional coaching sessions. As a general rule of thumb, the coach—given her knowledge of the program and the teacher's ability to implement it—should determine when a teacher can move from being a teacher in training to a teacher who can implement the intervention as part of a TAPS case.

As discussed in Chapter 5, even after the coach determines that a teacher has completed training with an intervention program, the training will be supplemented with continued observations of teacher implementation as part of the TAPS feature that requires ongoing monitoring of implementation integrity. In this chapter we distinguish inservice training from simply monitoring teachers' implementation integrity as part of a TAPS case; however, there are also similarities between training and monitoring because monitoring implementation integrity also includes observation and feedback from an expert implementer (e.g., the TAPS Teacher). Therefore, to clarify the differences as well as similarities between coaching/training and monitoring for implementation integrity, we offer the following: Coaching must occur as part of the training process and ends only when the teacher shows evidence that she can implement each of the intervention procedures accurately and relatively efficiently. Monitoring implementation integrity must occur periodically as part of a student's TAPS intervention plan and decreases only when the teacher shows several consecutive sessions of implementing the program with high (e.g., 90–100%) integrity. Again, Chapter 5 details the TAPS process for monitoring implementers' integrity.

CHARACTERISTICS OF GOOD COACHES

As noted previously, one prerequisite skill for a coach is that she has mastery knowledge of the intervention program that she is coaching another teacher to use. However, there are several additional characteristics of good coaches, including interpersonal skills, content knowledge, knowledge of the intervention, awareness of coaching resources, and knowledge of the practice of coaching. In short, we've learned that good teachers who are knowledgeable about the relevant subject matter and intervention are not *necessarily* good coaches. One article about coaching (Feger, Woleck, & Hickman, 2004) begins with a quote from a mathematics coach, in which she says, "When coaching first emerged as a term for on-site staff development, the image that came to mind for many was demonstration lessons. 'I go in and model, and the teacher should do what I model.' But the role is much more complex" (p. 14). We mention this point because SOPAA facilitators who are themselves coaches or recruit other teachers in the school to be coaches should keep in mind that a good coach ultimately ensures that a teacher learns to implement instructional procedures effectively and efficiently, *and* that she feels good, confident, and supported throughout the coaching process.

PROFESSIONAL DEVELOPMENT THAT OCCURS DURING THE TAPS PROCESS

Through interactions between a consultant and consultee in a typical model of triadic consultation, it is expected that the consultee (in our case, the classroom teacher) would build at least some professional skills (Gutkin & Curtis, 1999). This skill building should certainly be true of the TAPS process, as well. For example, the classroom teacher should benefit from strengthening her skills with developing and implementing a comprehensive intervention plan to target a student's specific academic deficit, and she will likely benefit from the systematic nature of this process and having the process repeated over time with each new TAPS case. It should be equally true that the TAPS Teacher will strengthen her consultative skills by continually using the systematic approach to instructional problem solving. However, to make this type of skill building and professional development even more likely, specific steps are embedded within the summative review meeting that occurs within the TAPS process.

This third feature of SOPAA professional development is described only briefly here because it is also discussed in Chapter 5 (as part of the summative review meeting process) and in Chapter 10 (in the subsection, Case-by-Case Reviews, page 193). In short, during the summative review meeting, the teacher involved with the TAPS case ultimately reflects on, documents, and discusses the case (e.g., aspects that were successful, unsuccessful, or improved over time). Professional development occurs during this process because the TAPS Teacher helps the teacher relate the TAPS case to prior experiences (e.g., information obtained during previous TAPS cases or during SOPAA inservice training). An overall goal of this process is to help both the TAPS Teacher and classroom teacher strengthen their applied and conceptual knowledge about topics related to academic instruction, intervention, assessment, and instructional problem solving.

CHAPTER 8

Maximizing Intervention Delivery through Recruiting and Training School Volunteers

This chapter describes how schools can increase their capacity to facilitate TAPS cases by systematically recruiting, training, and coordinating school volunteers to implement appropriate intervention programs (i.e., programs that were designed in a way that can be successfully implemented by volunteers). As such, this chapter is most associated with Component 3 (maximized intervention personnel and resources) and Component 4 (targeted professional development) of the SOPAA.

We begin the chapter by discussing the advantages of including volunteers as part of a school's mission to maximize all students' learning and then discuss important factors to consider before recruiting school volunteers and involving them in the TAPS process. We then discuss specific factors and recommendations for recruiting, training, coordinating, and sustaining school volunteers as part of a systematic approach for maximizing school personnel and resources.

It is important to highlight that throughout the chapter we often refer to this school volunteer feature of the SOPAA as the "SOPAA Volunteer Program." We use this general program title only to be clear and consistent throughout the chapter. Many schools might choose another title for this type of volunteer program, which would perhaps be more fitting to the name and characteristics of their respective schools. Also, we usually reference the TAPS Support Coordinator as the primary coordinator of the volunteer program. Although coordinating the SOPAA Volunteer Program is a key role for the TAPS Support Coordinator, the Lead Coordinator should help to plan and make important decisions about this volunteer program and provide oversight and guidance to ensure its effectiveness. In most cases, TAPS Teachers should also provide input and guidance about the SOPAA Volunteer Program. Chapter 11 describes more specifically how co-facilitators work together to implement the SOPAA (including facilitation of a volunteer program), but for concision and consistency throughout this chapter, we typically refer only to the TAPS Support Coordinator as the decision maker and facilitator of the SOPAA Volunteer Program.

ADVANTAGES OF INCLUDING SCHOOL VOLUNTEERS

At least since the 1970s, U.S. schools have regularly included community volunteers to assist with educating the nation's students. To illustrate, by 1987 it was found that three-fourths of U.S. public elementary schools involved volunteers, with an average of 24 volunteers per school (Michael, 1990). By 1999, largely due to the America Reads Challenge initiated by President Clinton, approximately 1,200 colleges and universities throughout the U.S. committed to placing college students in public schools to serve as tutors (Ritter, Barnett, Denny, & Albin, 2009). The inclusion of volunteer programs for the past several decades has been attributed to a variety of factors, such as schools needing to maximize resources during periods of teacher shortages, public concern that students are not succeeding academically, political initiatives to increase community service in schools, and community members' interest in volunteer service (Rekrut, 1994; Ritter et al., 2009). Today, particularly in an era of school budget cuts and educators being asked to do more with fewer resources, school volunteer programs continue to serve as a beneficial option to help schools maximize their resources and improve student learning outcomes.

Usually referred to as a *tutor* or *mentor*, school volunteers can serve a variety of different roles, and research evidence suggests that volunteers can meaningfully improve students' education. For example, school volunteers can help to improve student behavior (e.g., self-esteem, interpersonal relationships, academic engagement) and academic skills, such as reading, math, and writing (Bernstein, Rappaport, Olsho, Hunt, & Levin, 2009; Dappen & Isernhagen, 2005; Ritter et al., 2009; Wasik, 1998). A recent meta-analysis of volunteer tutoring programs showed that, compared to students who were not tutored, tutored students showed significantly better outcomes when assessed on tasks of letter naming, word reading, oral reading of text, and writing (Ritter et al., 2009). There is also evidence that volunteer tutoring programs targeting reading are particularly successful when (1) the programs are structured, (2) there is a designated volunteer coordinator knowledgeable about reading instruction, (3) the volunteer tutors are well trained, (4) there is coordination between the tutoring activities and the student's classroom instruction, and (5) tutors' instructional activities are observed and tutors show they can implement the instructional activities with integrity (Elbaum, Vaughn, Hughes, & Moody, 2000; Senesac & Burns, 2008; Wasik, 1998).

Research also suggests that there are many benefits of volunteering for the school volunteers, such as having positive feelings that come with helping others and building positive relationships, gaining experiences that will help them better understand others and themselves, improving their teaching and training skills, improving other forms of professional development, and expanding their social networks (Caldarella, Gomm, Shatzer, & Wall, 2010; Clary & Snyder, 1999; Ellis & Granville, 1999; Karcher, 2009). In summary, including school volunteers can be beneficial for (1) a school that is trying to maximize its instructional resources, (2) a student who is receiving assistance from a school volunteer, and (3) a volunteer who is working with a student in the school. We therefore advocate that schools carefully consider including volunteers to benefit students' instruction. For the many schools that already include volunteers for this purpose, we encourage those schools to consider whether their system for including volunteers is resource-efficient and maximizes its potential effectiveness. We now describe an approach to including school volunteers that aligns with the SOPAA model and aims to maximize the overall benefits of including volunteers.

A well-developed plan and system for including school volunteers represent another feature of the SOPAA that is absent from most existing models of instructional problem solving.

PRELIMINARY CONSIDERATIONS FOR DEVELOPING A SOPAA VOLUNTEER PROGRAM

Before recruiting, training, and coordinating volunteers as part of a structured volunteer program, there are several factors the TAPS Support Coordinator must consider. This section highlights those preliminary considerations and offers guidance and suggestions when applicable.

What Is the SOPAA Volunteer's Primary Function?

As instructional tutors, school volunteers might (1) assist classroom teachers with an assortment of in-class activities during the teacher's day-to-day instruction, (2) work one on one or with small groups of students to assist them with homework or in-class assignments, and/or (3) implement structured intervention programs that are appropriate for school volunteers to use (Caldarella et al., 2010; Ritter et al., 2009; Wasik, 1998). Of course, a school's decision about how to best involve volunteers depends on each volunteer's availability, skills, and experiences, as well as the school's needs and characteristics.

Although a school volunteer might benefit a school in a variety of ways, this chapter mainly discusses how to involve volunteers as implementers of structured, evidence-based intervention programs that are selected as part of a student's TAPS intervention plan (for examples of such programs, see Chapter 12 for programs that can be successfully implemented by volunteers). In other words, this chapter describes how to integrate a systematic SOPAA Volunteer Program that allows volunteers to assist with TAPS cases by implementing one or more intervention programs with students. Our recommendations are guided by both research (e.g., Caldarella et al., 2010; Elbaum et al., 2000; Senesac & Burns, 2008; Wasik, 1998) and practice that suggests how to best coordinate and maximize a school volunteer program designed to improve students' academic skills. It is important to note, however, that the TAPS Support Coordinator may determine that some volunteers are not suitable for this type of program, or that volunteers should be involved with both the SOPAA Volunteer Program *and* other volunteer activities. This topic of possibly utilizing multiple roles for volunteers is discussed in greater detail later in this chapter.

For volunteers who *will* implement intervention programs as part of the specific SOPAA Volunteer Program, it is also important to highlight that these volunteers should serve in a *support* role during the TAPS process, not as the *only* person to implement the student's intervention program. Put simply, a volunteer can meaningfully support the student's intervention plan, but should not function as the student's only (or even primary) "intervention teacher." Although many volunteers will have experiences and insights that will allow them to assist the student academically, compared to the student's classroom teacher, they usually will not have sufficient instructional interactions with the student throughout the school day to best understand the effectiveness of the intervention. Likewise, most volunteers will not have sufficient training in a field of education to make the most effective instructional decisions about the student and his or her intervention plan—such decisions are often based on a complex set of interactions between student, classroom teacher, instructional, and assessment variables. Therefore, the classroom teacher should always maintain primary responsibility for overseeing the student's intervention plan and should be regularly involved with implementing the selected intervention program. The TAPS Teacher will support the teacher with this responsibility, and a school volunteer might assist the TAPS process by serving as one of at least two implementers of the intervention program.

Overall then, the primary goal of the SOPAA Volunteer Program is to train volunteers to use one or more intervention programs that will be implemented as part a student's TAPS intervention plan. The following steps outline the basic approach to facilitating a SOPAA Volunteer Program:

1. Select evidence-based intervention programs that school volunteers should be able to implement.
2. Through recruitment and/or considering current school volunteers, ensure that there is an adequate number of volunteers to implement each of the selected intervention programs.
3. Train each applicable volunteer in one or more of the selected intervention programs.
4. Develop a schedule of volunteers' availability that corresponds with their training in the selected intervention programs and use that schedule to help the TAPS Teacher coordinate volunteers who can assist with specific TAPS cases.
5. Ensure volunteer quality, satisfaction, and sustainability to improve and/or maintain the effectiveness of the SOPAA Volunteer Program.

Throughout this chapter we describe how to facilitate these five primary steps.

Is a Volunteer Program Appropriate for Your School?

A structured volunteer program like the one described in this chapter may not be possible or advantageous for all schools. For example, as it relates specifically to the SOPAA, the feasibility of a SOPAA Volunteer Program depends on whether the TAPS Support Coordinator (given her availability and obligations) can recruit and train volunteers in addition to training and coordinating assistive school personnel (see Chapters 7 and 11 for information about training and coordinating assistive personnel). Similarly, the TAPS Support Coordinator may have other reasons for not being able to recruit and train school volunteers as part of a systematic program. As described in Chapter 3, it is also possible that a SOPAA Volunteer Program would be best started after the initial year of SOPAA implementation, or after multiple years of implementation.

Another reason a SOPAA Volunteer Program may not be appropriate is because some schools will have sufficient support from assistive school personnel in implementing intervention programs. Thus, developing and maintaining a SOPAA Volunteer Program might create unnecessary work. Conversely, a school may benefit from volunteers who can help to support the TAPS process, but not all communities will have the capacity to sustain an effective school volunteer program. For example, if there is lack of interest or feasibility for community members to volunteer frequently enough or consistently enough throughout the school year, starting or sustaining a SOPAA Volunteer Program may not be viable.

Information within the recruitment section of this chapter should help the TAPS Support Coordinator better understand whether a SOPAA Volunteer Program is appropriate for her school. Here, we simply highlight the point that during the SOPAA implementation planning stages there are several factors SOPAA facilitators should consider when determining whether a structured volunteer program is feasible, and if so, when and how such a program should begin.

Which Intervention Programs Should Volunteers Implement?

As described in Chapter 3, before initiating SOPAA implementation, the facilitators should determine which intervention programs will be used to target each of the academic subskills associated with each academic area. For example, if the initial year of SOPAA implementation will target only students with reading difficulties, SOPAA facilitators should select intervention programs designed to address phonemic awareness, phonics, fluency, vocabulary, and comprehension. In considering which intervention programs to use, facilitators should also consider which intervention programs school volunteers could reasonably implement after sufficient training, and for each program, what "sufficient training" would entail (e.g., 3 hours, 9 hours). Of course, the extent to which the intervention programs can be used by both classroom teachers and school volunteers might influence the selection of particular programs. As noted previously, Chapter 12 lists a number of learner-verified and/or evidence-based intervention programs for the various subskills of each academic area, and the tables in that chapter specify whether school volunteers could reasonably learn the given program.

When selecting intervention programs to use during the TAPS process, we want to make clear that the SOPAA facilitators should develop only one list of intervention programs they plan to use for TAPS cases; they should *not* select programs that will be used only by educators within the school and then a different set of programs that will be used only by volunteers. In Chapter 3, Table 3.1 (p. 32), we illustrate one school's selection of intervention programs for early reading skills and whether school volunteers will be trained to use those programs.

When Should the SOPAA Volunteer Program Planning and Implementation Begin?

Put simply, the SOPAA facilitators, particularly the TAPS Support Coordinator, must have a clear plan, timeline, and set of goals for recruiting, training, and sustaining a SOPAA Volunteer Program, and this planning should ideally be done during the school year prior to initiating the volunteer program. If possible, planning the volunteer program might also include the school principal and/or a small number of teachers who will be involved with SOPAA, as their involvement with planning may positively influence their support of the program.

A predetermined infrastructure for the volunteer program in place, at least for the first 2 years of the program's implementation, will help to dictate the TAPS Support Coordinator's primary actions in developing, strengthening, and sustaining the program. If, for example, a volunteer program will begin during the initial year of SOPAA implementation, planning for a volunteer program should occur during the initial SOPAA planning stages. If the SOPAA Volunteer Program will not begin until Year 3 of the overall implementation plan, the volunteer program plan should be completed by the end of Year 2. If possible, volunteer recruitment might also occur toward the end of Year 2, assuming that potential volunteers will know that they can commit during the fall of the upcoming academic year (even if they do not know specific days and times of availability). Also important, the volunteer program plan and timeline should be approved by all SOPAA facilitators and the school principal. If district or school board approval is also needed, this plan should also be approved by those individuals.

To assist the TAPS Support Coordinator with developing a SOPAA Volunteer Program plan, Figure 8.1 shows a sample 2-year timeline and plan. Information about the number of volunteers needed in this school, the recruitment options, and the training procedures are hypothetical, but they reflect a logical plan that might occur in a school. Content in Figure 8.1 reflects information we describe later in this chapter (e.g., approaches to recruitment and program evaluation); thus, Figure 8.1 should be reviewed again after reading this entire chapter.

Figure 8.1 also corresponds with Example 1 of Table 3.3 (pp. 35–37), which illustrates a SOPAA implementation timeline in which the SOPAA Volunteer Program does not begin until Year 3 (academic year 2014–2015) of the overall SOPAA implementation plan. Example 1 of Table 3.3 also shows that in Year 3, the SOPAA model will target both reading and writing for students in grades K–5. Figure 8.1 shows a sample plan and timeline for starting a volunteer program in academic year 2014–2015. The figure also shows that there are two SOPAA co-facilitators: the Lead Coordinator (who also serves as the TAPS Reading Teacher) and the school psychologist (who serves as the TAPS Writing Teacher and TAPS Support Coordinator). As shown in the figure, after the plan is developed by the TAPS Support Coordinator, the Lead Coordinator and the school

Plan created by: *Ana Paez*

Date that plan was developed: *December 10, 2013*

Primary and Long-term Goals of the SOPAA Volunteer Program

1. By June 1, 2014, recruit 5–8 school volunteers who can assist in the school at least 2 days per week for 1.5–2 hours per day.
2. By October 2014, train 2–3 school volunteers to implement Sound Partners for TAPS cases targeting students' phonics.
3. By October 2014, train 2–3 school volunteer to implement the HELPS Program for TAPS cases targeting students' reading fluency.
4. Each year, evaluate the SOPAA Volunteer Program and determine methods to improve the program during the subsequent year. Use recommendations from Chapter 8 of the SOPAA book to evaluate and sustain the volunteer program.
5. By fall 2016, increase the total number of school volunteers to 8–12 so that more volunteers can implement Sound Partners and the HELPS Program and also assist with TAPS cases targeting writing and math.

Plan and Timeline for Developing the SOPAA Volunteer Program

1. In academic year 2013–2014 (i.e., 2nd year of the overall SOPAA implementation), prepare to implement the SOPAA Volunteer Program. Preparation will include:
   a. Developing a plan (and materials needed) for evaluating the SOPAA Volunteer Program. **Developing an evaluation plan and materials will occur January 1, 2014, through May 15, 2014.**
   b. Recruiting volunteers, facilitated through assessing whether current volunteers in the school are suitable for the SOPAA Volunteer Program, displaying informational flyers, sending mass e-mails to parents of children in the school and local community college students, making announcements at the PTA meetings, hosting an information/registration booth at the community farmer's market. **Recruitment activities will occur January 1, 2014, through May 15, 2014.**
   c. Reviewing volunteer applications, selecting applicants who are likely to benefit the volunteer program, and holding a small-group information session with those selected applicants. **Review of applications will occur as they are submitted, and the small-group information sessions will occur April 1, 2014, and June 1, 2014.**
   d. Selecting 5–8 applicants who can volunteer during the 2014–2015 academic year and confirming volunteers' commitment. **Selecting applicants and confirming their commitment will occur within 2 weeks following the small-group information sessions.**
   e. Preparing volunteer training materials (for small-group training) to train them in Sound Partners and the HELPS Program. **Preparing training materials will occur January 1, 2014, through May 15, 2014.**
   f. Developing ideas for volunteer awards and a Volunteer Appreciation Day. **Developing these ideas will occur January 1, 2014, through May 15, 2014.**
2. Begin implementing the SOPAA Volunteer Program in academic year 2014–2015. First-year implementation should include:
   a. Orienting volunteers to the school and their role in the SOPAA Volunteer Program through a group meeting. **Orientation activities will occur during the evening of September 10, 2014.**
   b. Training half of the volunteers to implement Sound Partners. **Training will occur September 17, 2014, with follow-up training planned for September 24, 2014.**
   c. Training half of the volunteers to implement the HELPS Program. **Training will occur September 25, 2014, with follow-up training planned for October 2, 2014.**
   d. Monitoring volunteers' implementation of Sound Partners and the HELPS Program. **Monitoring will occur periodically throughout the school year, and this responsibility will be shared by classroom teachers, the TAPS Teacher, and the TAPS Support Coordinator.**
   e. Recruiting additional volunteers (as needed) during the beginning and middle of the school year. **As needed, recruitment activities will occur October 1, 2014, through February 15, 2015.**
   f. Holding a Volunteer Appreciation Day. **This day will occur February 20, 2015.**
   g. Collecting information that will eventually be integrated into a Volunteer Handbook. **Information will be gathered throughout the academic year.**
   h. Collecting information that will eventually be integrated into a Coordinator's Manual. **Information will be gathered throughout the academic year.**

(cont.)

FIGURE 8.1. Sample 2-year plan and timeline for developing a SOPAA volunteer program.

i. Evaluating the SOPAA Volunteer Program. **Teacher and volunteer survey will be administered April 1, 2015, and a final report of the volunteer program will be completed May 25, 2015.**
j. Presenting volunteer awards for the two volunteers who committed the most hours per year. **Award presentations will occur at the May 2015 PTA meeting.**

3. Continue SOPAA Volunteer Program implementation from 2015 on, and improve the program with each successive year. Continued implementation and improvements may include:
   a. Increasing the number of SOPAA volunteers and training them to implement intervention programs in math and writing
   b. Completing a Volunteer's Handbook
   c. Completing a Coordinator's Manual
   d. Increasing the amount of data generated for program evaluation
   e. Writing local grants to generate additional funding for the program

Plan Developed by:

Ana Paez

Signature: ______________________________

Approval of Plan (signatures specify approval)

SOPAA Lead Coordinator and TAPS Reading Teacher: ______________________________

School Principal: ______________________________

FIGURE 8.1. Sample 2-year plan and timeline for developing a SOPAA volunteer program.

principal must sign the plan before it is approved. Although there are several unknown factors (e.g., budget cuts, redistricting of students) that can influence a school's plan to develop and maintain a program such as a volunteer program, having an organized plan and timeline from which to work should better ensure that the program is developed effectively and sustained.

Is Financial Support Needed to Begin the Volunteer Program?

Developing an effective volunteer program can usually be achieved without specific funding for it, as long as the TAPS Support Coordinator is allotted the time to coordinate the program, has access to intervention materials that volunteers can use, has access to training materials and space within the school, and has an adequate budget for printing and photocopying. This time allotment and resource allocation are established prior to implementing the SOPAA and are discussed when the Lead Coordinator communicates with the school principal (see Chapter 9).

However, initiating a SOPAA Volunteer Program may be a great way for lead educators within the school to secure some additional funding for the program, which in turn should benefit overall SOPAA implementation. For example, local or state grants from nonprofit organizations, national grants, or funding allocated by the associated school board may assist the TAPS Support Coordinator in developing and maintaining an effective volunteer program. It is beyond the scope of this book to describe how to prepare such grants, but several communities (e.g., community colleges) offer basic courses to help individuals find and write grants appropriate to their needs. Grants written to facilitate a school volunteer program should be customized to each school's specific needs and rationale for the program, but if SOPAA facilitators apply for funding to support a volunteer program, it may be useful for them to describe in the grant application how the volunteer program fulfills a key component for facilitating the SOPAA model and ultimately increasing the school's capacity to assist struggling learners.

For further support and information, the companion website *www.sopaaforschools.org* book lists examples of some community-based grants that might fund a type of SOPAA Volunteer Program. This information is intended to help SOPAA facilitators generate additional ideas regarding where to look for related grants in their community or state.

What Type of Volunteer Screening Is Required?

The majority of schools throughout the United States have involved school volunteers in some way (Ritter et al., 2009). As such, most schools are familiar with the process of screening individuals who want to volunteer in the school, and many schools have a specific system for screening. For example, many schools have a fairly basic screening procedure for volunteers who will work with children only within sight of an employed educator in the school. In this case, screening may simply require getting the volunteer's name, contact information, reason for volunteering, personal references, and related information. However, for volunteers who may work with students in a setting where they cannot be easily observed by a school employee, screening procedures are often more detailed and may include a criminal background check. With respect to the SOPAA Volunteer Program, it is possible that volunteers will work one on one with students to implement an intervention program, and this may sometimes occur in a location out of sight from a school employee because interventions are often best implemented in locations free of noise and possible distractions.

It is beyond the scope of this book to describe all possible actions a school should take to screen and monitor school volunteers, but it is important to highlight that the TAPS Support Coordinator and Lead Coordinator should be aware of the school's policies for screening and monitoring volunteers, and they should follow those policies when facilitating the SOPAA Volunteer Program. Related to this point, the TAPS Support Coordinator should know whether agencies outside of the school (e.g., the school board, school district administration, and occasionally local police departments) sometimes have guidelines and policies about involving school volunteers.

Overall, although a goal of the SOPAA Volunteer Program is to help improve students' academic skills, a child's safety is of even greater importance; no child should be put at risk of physical or emotional harm when working with a volunteer. This is likely a point that should be obvious but we state it explicitly given its importance. If policies for volunteer screening do not exist within the school, we highly encourage the school leaders to establish appropriate procedures to best ensure that students are safe and to protect the school from liability in a worst-case scenario.

What Will Be the Name of the Volunteer Program?

As stated earlier, the type of volunteer program we describe in this chapter is specified by using the generic title of "SOPAA Volunteer Program" so the reader can distinguish it from other volunteer programs that have different purposes (e.g., volunteers to improve students' interpersonal skills or to assist students with homework). Each school should designate the most appropriate name for their SOPAA Volunteer Program.

There are at least a few possible advantages of developing a name for the volunteer program. With respect to volunteer recruitment, for example, potential volunteers may better perceive the program as an established, organized system for involving volunteers, and this perception may increase their interest. Likewise, having a program name should help with overall communication involved in volunteer recruitment and may help current volunteers communicate with one another or recruit interested members from the community. Thus, prior to recruitment, we encourage each school to develop a specific name for their volunteer program, though it is also appropriate, if desired, to call the program the "SOPAA Volunteer Program."

RECRUITING VOLUNTEERS

There are several factors to consider when determining a plan to recruit volunteers for the SOPAA Volunteer Program. First and foremost, the SOPAA facilitators should determine the ideal and minimum number of volunteers needed to ensure a successful and resource-efficient program. Determining this number should take into consideration, among related factors, the (1) number of intervention programs volunteers will be trained to use as part of the TAPS process, (2) anticipated number of TAPS cases per month, (3) frequency in which school volunteers would be needed to implement intervention programs (e.g., 2 days per week for at least 75% of TAPS cases), and (4) anticipated and realistic level of volunteer availability (e.g., 1 day per week, for 1–2 hours per day). After determining approximately how many volunteers are needed to fully support that year's SOPAA implementation plan, the TAPS Support Coordinator needs to consider the following issues related to recruitment.

Type of Recruitment Needed

Before taking action in recruiting new volunteers to support the SOPAA Volunteer Program, the TAPS Support Coordinator should consider the following questions:

1. Is there some form of a volunteer program (perhaps with a slightly different purpose) already in place within the school (or within the school district)?
2. Is there already a group of reliable school volunteers that can be included in the SOPAA Volunteer Program?
3. Are there current school volunteers who already know how to implement specific intervention programs that will be used for TAPS cases?
4. Is there already a recruitment system in place for identifying and selecting volunteers, and is that system sufficient for meeting the goals of the SOPAA Volunteer Program?

After answering these questions, it should be clearer for the TAPS Support Coordinator what level of recruitment is needed, if any.

For example, if there is a volunteer program already in place within the school or district, the TAPS Support Coordinator can determine how that program aligns with the goals of the SOPAA Volunteer Program and decide what modifications, if any, are needed with the current program so that volunteers can assist more specifically with the goals of the SOPAA Volunteer Program. If it is determined that the existing volunteer program has goals that are too different from the SOPAA Volunteer Program, this may indicate a need for two (or more) separate volunteer programs within the school.

If a specific volunteer program does not already exist within the school, but the school does involve some consistent school volunteers, the TAPS Support Coordinator can determine the extent to which those volunteers (some of them or all of them) could be involved with the SOPAA Volunteer Program. In many cases, there will be a need to recruit additional volunteers specifically for the SOPAA Volunteer Program. The following sections

In some schools, a SOPAA volunteer program may exist independently from another type of volunteer program that has a different structure or set of goals.

provide some guidance in recruiting volunteers. The guidance can be used as supplemental information for schools that already have a volunteer recruitment system in place, or as a means of developing a recruitment system to support the SOPAA Volunteer Program.

Individuals to Target for Recruitment

Information available from schools with structured volunteer programs as well as the research literature on school volunteers (e.g., Wasik, 1998; Ritter et al., 2009) indicate that the following categories represent individuals most likely to volunteer in schools: (1) parents who have a child attending the school, (2) retirees (including but not limited to former educators), (3) college/university undergraduate and graduate students, (4) volunteers of other community organizations (e.g., the YMCA, Boys and Girls Clubs), (5) high school students attending the same school district, and (6) community members not otherwise specified. For the TAPS Support Coordinator, this list may outline the groups to consider when recruiting for the SOPAA Volunteer Program.

Recruitment Strategies

There are numerous strategies for recruiting school volunteers. For example, recruitment can be facilitated by displaying informational flyers, posting information on the school website, sending mass e-mails to potentially interested community members, placing advertisements in local media, making public service announcements on local radio stations, and making in-person announcements or appearances (e.g., announcing the need for volunteers at the school's PTA meeting or setting up a volunteer information and registration booth at appropriate community events or festivals). Table 8.1 lists several examples of recruitment methods and specifies the categories of individuals most likely targeted through each method.

The sample of recruitment methods listed in Table 8.1 could certainly be extended. The purpose of the table is to identify multiple approaches to recruitment so that the TAPS Support Coordinator can identify the best methods for her school. In general, multiple methods for recruitment should be used, since no one method will reach all potential volunteers.

There are a few additional factors to consider about recruitment. First, the demographic and racial background of school volunteers will ideally be comparable to the demographic and racial background of the students attending the school. As an example in a hypothetical school, if the school consisted of students who are 35% white, 30% black, 20% Hispanic, 10% Asian American, and 5% Native American, the racial background of school volunteers should be as similar as possible to the racial background of the student body. Recruitment strategies would probably need to be changed if the racial background of the school volunteers was 95% white. In this example, recruiting volunteers who are more racially diverse might require targeting university and community organizations that have racially and ethnically diverse populations.

Second, we know that not all schools are located near a college or university, and in such circumstances, recruiting college student volunteers may not be possible. However, many communities throughout the United States are located near at least one college, university, or community college; and as noted by Ritter and colleagues (2009), thousands of colleges and universities are committed to having their students volunteer in schools. For these reasons, we highlight this group of volunteers as a good target for recruitment. There are many routes by which the TAPS Support Coordinator could recruit college-age students; a particularly time-efficient route would be to establish an ongoing partnership with a specific university faculty member or department, such that a steady number of college student volunteers could commit each year to a specific schedule and number of hours. Although there are several departments and programs within a

TABLE 8.1. Sample Methods for Recruiting School Volunteers and the Individuals Most Likely Targeted per Method

Method for recruitment	Individuals most likely targeted with method
Display informational flyers in the school	Parents who have children attending the school
Display informational flyers in the general community (e.g., grocery stores, department stores, restaurants, libraries), senior centers, and/or on a college campus	Community members (general); retirees; university undergraduate and graduate students
Post information on homepage of the school website or of the district high school website	Parents who have children attending the school; high school students attending the same school district
Post information on community organization websites, if appropriate (e.g., university clubs, local restaurants, literacy-focused nonprofit organizations)	University undergraduate and graduate students; community members (general)
Send mass e-mail to parents of children in the school, to university clubs or organizations, to other community organizations that involve volunteers (e.g., YMCAs), and/or to retired teachers from the school district	Parents who have children attending the school; university undergraduate and graduate students; volunteers of other community organizations; retired educators
Place advertisement in local newspapers or magazines, possibly with specific readership for college students, retirees, parents, etc.	Community members (general), including university students and retirees
Make public service announcement on local radio stations, possibly with specific listening audience of targeted groups	Community members (general)
Make in-person announcements during meetings of PTA, community-based organizations (e.g., Rotary Club, veterans associations), or university clubs, groups, and/or departmental meetings	Community members (general), including parents who have children attending the school, retirees, and university students
Create an information and registration booth to place at local events or festivals, possibly with specific attraction of targeted groups	Community members (general)
Ask current school volunteers to share information and ask others they know to consider volunteering	Community members (general), including all designated categories

university that would be a natural fit for developing an ongoing commitment of student volunteers (e.g., departments in regular education, special education, social work, school psychology, educational psychology, general psychology, extension and engagement offices, and specific university–community volunteer programs), universities on the whole provide a large pool of capable students who could assist schools and derive benefit themselves from volunteering.

Third, although we listed possible recruitment of high school students in Table 8.1, many of the intervention programs described in Chapter 12 cannot be implemented successfully by the typical high school student, or at least there is no research evidence to suggest otherwise. As such, the TAPS Support Coordinator should carefully consider whether a high school student could be trained to participate in the SOPAA Volunteer Program. With this said, it may be possible to train highly motivated and academically capable 11th- or 12th-grade students to use some of the evidence-based intervention programs that exist. For example, one of us (J.C.B.) has worked with a small number of 11th- and 12th-grade high school students with strong motivation and above-average grades who learned to successfully implement the HELPS reading fluency program. However, training with these students required approximately 2 hours more than what is required when training most college-age students.

Describing the SOPAA Volunteer Program and Identifying Suitable Volunteers

Recruiting volunteers obviously includes describing the program to those potentially interested in volunteering. In general, all recruitment information should explain to potential volunteers (1) how to become a volunteer (e.g., how to register a volunteer application and the application screening that is involved); (2) what the volunteer experience will involve, including training experiences; and (3) the likely benefits of the experience (for volunteers and for children in the school). Depending on the method used to stimulate initial interest in volunteering, descriptions of these three primary pieces of information will vary in length. For example, information on a school website may be able to provide greater detail (and perhaps supplemental forms) compared to information presented in a newspaper or via a radio announcement.

Depending on the school's history and policy with recruiting volunteers and whether there will be school volunteer opportunities outside of the SOPAA Volunteer Program, there are multiple options for providing additional information to potential volunteers and identifying individuals who would benefit from the SOPAA Volunteer Program. Described next is one possible approach for continuing the recruitment process.

Assuming the school has a history of involving volunteers in multiple ways, a reasonable next step in the SOPAA Volunteer Program recruitment process is to have interested volunteers complete a general volunteer application form that requests the individual's contact information, demographic information, employment information (past or present), history of illegal activity (e.g., *yes* or *no* questions about involvement with illegal activity), volunteer status (e.g., student, parent of child at the school, retiree), volunteer interests and skills, and availability (the companion website *www.sopaaforschools.org* shows a good example of an application form that requests this information). After receiving an individual's volunteer application, the TAPS Support Coordinator should review it to determine whether the individual could meaningfully contribute to the SOPAA Volunteer Program. In most cases, a volunteer would meaningfully contribute to the program as long as he or she is not a high school student, has regular availability that corresponds with TAPS intervention schedules, and has interest in working with students in any of the academic areas targeted with TAPS.

After identifying a potentially capable SOPAA volunteer through the person's written application, we recommend having the TAPS Support Coordinator provide a more detailed description of the SOPAA Volunteer Program to the applicant for his or her consideration. The more detailed description should let applicants know that (1) they will be trained to implement a research-based, structured intervention program; (2) they will implement that program as part of the school's system for assisting struggling learners; and (3) they will likely experience these benefits (specify) from volunteering as part of the SOPAA Volunteer Program. Also, if there are clear and specific expectations in order to become part of the SOPAA Volunteer Program (e.g., the person must attend a training session on a specific date and show up on time each day scheduled to volunteer), this information might also be conveyed so that the applicant knows the primary activities, benefits, and expectations associated with the program. Aligned with good overall recruitment, all of the above information should be presented to the applicant in a positive and enticing manner; being clear and accurate about the SOPAA Volunteer Program roles and expectations should minimize potential problems during the school year.

In some cases, the TAPS Support Coordinator may want to schedule a 10- to 15-minute meeting with potential volunteers, which could be done with groups of applicants or one on one. In either case, this meeting would occur before registering a volunteer to the SOPAA Volunteer Program. This meeting would not only allow the TAPS Support Coordinator to provide more specific information about the activities, goals, benefits, and expectations of the SOPAA Volunteer Program, but it might also help in determining whether there are any factors that would not make the applicant suitable for the program. In-person meetings also allow the TAPS Support Coordinator to learn more about what the applicant wants to get from the volunteer experience and his or her strengths and experiences.

Time Frame for Recruiting

The aforementioned recruitment process describes one approach to identifying appropriate volunteers for the SOPAA Volunteer Program. However, the efficiency and effectiveness of the process will depend on whether the TAPS Support Coordinator uses an ongoing recruitment process (i.e., volunteer applications are accepted at all times throughout the school year) or a periodic process (e.g., volunteer applications are accepted two to four specific times per year). In our view, the process for reviewing volunteer applications, providing additional information about the SOPAA Volunteer Program (ideally one to one or in small-group meetings), and then selecting SOPAA volunteers will be most efficient if it is done only at key times of the school year. For example, this review and selection process might occur once in the summer to select volunteers for the upcoming school year, once at the beginning of the school year (if the summer recruitment did not generate the needed level of support), and once again (if needed) in the middle of the school year. However, this template represents only one approach to recruiting and selecting volunteers. In many schools, a different approach, including having an ongoing recruitment process, will best meet recruitment goals.

TRAINING VOLUNTEERS

Once individuals are successfully recruited for the SOPAA Volunteer Program, they must be trained to implement the selected evidence-based intervention program (or programs) that is appropriate for implementation by school volunteers. The amount of training required of the volunteers will depend on their prior experiences, the specific intervention program(s) they will be trained to use, and the overall approach to training designed by the TAPS Support Coordinator. For volunteers who will ultimately learn more than one intervention program, we recommend that they first learn only one program, get experience using that program as part of the TAPS process, and then learn any additional programs that are suitable.

In a meta-analysis of interventions for students with reading difficulties, the authors reported: "College students and trained, reliable community volunteers were able to provide significant help to struggling readers" (Elbaum et al., 2000, p. 616).

Volunteer Orientation

Before a formal training experience with an intervention program, the TAPS Support Coordinator should consider holding a general volunteer orientation session. The session would serve as an introductory meeting to cover the type of information that would be appropriate in a volunteer handbook (described later). As part of this orientation, the TAPS Support Coordinator should describe the basic structure of the TAPS process so that volunteers have a good understanding of how they fit within, and meaningfully contribute to, the overall process.

General Training Options

When ready to train the volunteers in an intervention program, the TAPS Support Coordinator will probably have several options for training, and facilitating training may be done in collaboration with other SOPAA facilitators (as described in Chapter 11). The general training options and their relative advantages and possible disadvantages are described in Table 8.2. If the recruitment approach has attracted a group of volunteers at once, group-based training would likely be most time- and resource-efficient. However, because recruitment will differ depending on the school, so will the approach to training volunteers (hence the multiple options in Table 8.2). Elsewhere in this book (e.g., Chapter 7), additional information is presented about what to include in professional development workshops, and much of that information is also applicable for conducting workshops that include volunteers.

The options for training volunteers listed in Table 8.2 might also be combined in some fashion, depending on the needs of the school and which training options are available. For example, Options 1 and 6 might be combined, such that volunteers first learn the intervention program during a workshop that includes educators, and then the volunteers work together to improve their knowledge of the implementation procedures and practice them with each other. Overall, the goal of training is to effectively train the needed number of volunteers in the most time-efficient way.

It is also important to highlight that the disadvantages listed in Table 8.2 are only *possible* disadvantages. As such, there are several ways those disadvantages can be eliminated or reduced. For example, with Option 1, after holding the group workshop, the facilitator might (1) add Option 6 to the training sequence, (2) hold a follow-up training session only for volunteers, and/or (3) schedule volunteers to observe an expert teacher implement the program. Each of these follow-up training activities should better ensure that volunteers understand how to implement the intervention program. As another example, with Option 6, in many cases it may not be feasible for an experienced volunteer to effectively train new volunteers, but this option might be more feasible if the volunteer also gets experience assisting the educator who normally conducts the training (e.g., the TAPS Support Coordinator) and possibly holds a training session while the educator observes and provides feedback. As noted previously, the decisions about training and finding the most effective and time-efficient approach ultimately relate to the school's most feasible options and the specific intervention program the volunteers are being taught to implement.

In short, the TAPS Support Coordinator should consider each of the options and comments presented in this section and think creatively about how to maximize the effectiveness and efficiency of volunteer training. Also, the TAPS Support Coordinator must recognize that training is not complete after using any (or a combination) of the aforementioned training approaches. That is, to ensure training effectiveness (i.e., the volunteer consistently implements the respective intervention program with appropriate integrity), the volunteer's implementation integrity must be observed and feedback about his or her implementation should be provided by an expert implementer.

TABLE 8.2. Options for Training School Volunteers to Use an Intervention Program

General description of training approach	Primary Advantages	Possible Disadvantages
Option 1: Train volunteers as a group during the same workshop(s) developed for educators in the school.	1. Time efficiency, because all educators and volunteers can learn the intervention program in the same workshop or series of workshops.	1. Some volunteers may need more attention from the workshop facilitator to learn the intervention program, and thus may decrease the effectiveness of the workshop for the educators attending. 2. Scheduling group training may be complicated due to incompatible availability of those who need to attend the training.
Option 2: Train volunteers as a group during a separate workshop (or series of workshops) from educators in the school.	1. Can maintain at least some time efficiency because multiple volunteers are trained at once, and pacing of the training can be adjusted specifically for volunteers.	1. This option may be less time-efficient than including educators and volunteers in the same workshop(s).
Option 3: Individual volunteers or small groups of three or four volunteers observe an expert implementer of the program (e.g., classroom teacher, TAPS teacher) while it is used with a student during an actual TAPS case.	1. Assuming the volunteer has the time and the teacher can take the opportunity to explain implementation procedures, this option allows the volunteer to directly observe the program being used in context and could help the volunteer learn more idiosyncratic aspects of the intervention program (e.g., tips, suggestions) that may not be emphasized in a group-based training session. 2. This training option is useful when it is urgent to train one or a small number of volunteers to use the intervention program.	1. The approach is much more time consuming compared to training larger groups of volunteers. 2. The teacher may not be able to successfully train one or a small group of volunteers while also effectively implementing the intervention with the student. 3. The option would likely require multiple observations of the teacher's implementation of the program and thus may take as long as holding a group training session where volunteers learn through a presentation, modeling of the intervention, role-play and practice activities, etc.
Option 4: Have experienced volunteers (those who implement the program with 100% integrity) train a new group of volunteers to use the program.	1. Highly time-efficient for school staff because they would not need to facilitate the training workshop(s). 2. Increased level of responsibility and new role for the volunteer(s) facilitating the training, which may increase volunteer satisfaction with the experience.	1. Approach may not be practical given volunteers' experiences with training others. 2. If new volunteers are not trained by an educator, the effectiveness of the training may be compromised.
Option 5: Have each volunteer train him- or herself using materials associated with the intervention program.	1. Highly time-efficient for school staff because they would not need to facilitate the training workshop(s). 2. Volunteers could train themselves on their own time, and thus there would be no complications with scheduling and availability.	1. Approach may be ineffective because materials alone are not often sufficient for noneducators to learn an intervention program. 2. Many intervention programs do not have sufficient materials and/or independent training exercises to help individuals learn the program with integrity.

(cont.)

TABLE 8.2. *(cont.)*

General description of training approach	Primary Advantages	Possible Disadvantages
Option 6: Using materials associated with the intervention program, have a small group of volunteers work together to learn and practice the program.	1. Highly time-efficient for school staff because they would not need to facilitate the training workshop(s). 2. Learning the program with a group of new volunteers may, overall, be more effective than each one learning the program independently.	1. The two disadvantages listed directly above also apply here. 2. Scheduling conflicts among the group may lengthen the time needed for the volunteers to learn the program. 3. Without a designated "trainer," individual personalities could have a negative influence on group interactions and long-term cohesion of the volunteer group.

Monitoring Implementation Integrity after General Training

After general training procedures are complete, the TAPS Support Coordinator cannot assume that volunteers are ready and able to implement the program with perfect integrity. For this reason, the TAPS process is structured in a way to ensure that all implementers are implementing the program with integrity. Chapter 5 discusses the topic of monitoring implementation integrity in the greatest detail, and it relates to all implementers' integrity (e.g., volunteers, classroom teachers, teacher assistants).

Here we simply reiterate that consistent and highly accurate implementation integrity (e.g., 90–100%) should be the key criterion by which the trainer can be sure that the training process was effective. With respect to training volunteers, it may be particularly important to evaluate each volunteer's implementation integrity more often during the initial weeks of implementation, as it is likely that the volunteer will have the most questions and need feedback regarding his or her implementation during this period. Observations of implementation and immediate feedback therefore constitute the second major part of training a volunteer to use an intervention program, and this second part should continue regularly until the volunteer meets an acceptable level of implementation integrity (e.g., 100% implementation integrity during two consecutive observations).

COORDINATING VOLUNTEERS AND FACILITATING INTERVENTION SUPPORT

This section of the chapter is relatively brief because the TAPS Support Coordinator's role of coordinating volunteers and assistive school personnel is detailed in Chapter 11. In Chapter 11 we highlight how the TAPS Support Coordinator manages schedules of those who can assist with intervention program implementation (e.g., volunteers, teacher assistants, other educators in the school) and communicates with the TAPS Teacher to identify individuals in the school who can support a TAPS case though intervention program implementation.

In this section of the chapter we merely point out that coordinating volunteers as part of a SOPAA Volunteer Program might be more efficient and effective if the TAPS Support Coordinator develops a brief handbook of information that can be easily shared with applicants when they apply to become a volunteer. The handbook might include, for example, important contact information, answers to frequently asked questions (e.g., How do I apply to become a volunteer? What activities arc involved with volunteering? What type of training will I receive? What is the school dress code?), building maps, how to address inappropriate student behavior, how to address emergency situations, lists of teacher names and classrooms, and various other bits of information that will maximize the TAPS Support Coordinator's time when orienting and working with SOPAA volunteers.

Also to maximize efficiency, the TAPS Support Coordinator might develop a Coordinator's Manual specific to her school, which she can use to recruit, train, coordinate, and sustain the volunteers. A Coordinator's Manual should ultimately be useful for maximizing time and effectiveness when coordinating volunteers each year and would also be valuable if a new TAPS Support Coordinator later takes on that role in the school. Neither the Volunteer Handbook or Coordinator's Manual are needed to start the SOPAA Volunteer Program, but we mention them so the TAPS Support Coordinator can consider developing these resources and determine early on what would be the best time and most efficient process for doing so.

SUSTAINING THE SOPAA VOLUNTEER PROGRAM

Like any structured program, its sustainability is as important as its development. With the SOPAA Volunteer Program, we believe that there are two primary components related to its sustainability: (1) teacher and administrative support for the program, and (2) volunteers' satisfaction with the program. As illustrated in Figure 8.2, for each of these components, there are also two subcomponents. As shown in the figure, *teacher and administrative support for the program* requires (1) data collection and evaluation of the program, and (2) teachers' knowledge of the program and volunteers' training. *Volunteers satisfaction with the program* requires (1) a rewarding experience for the volunteer, and (2) the TAPS Support Coordinator having ongoing and clear communication with the volunteer. The dual-pointing arrows shown connecting the primary components and the subcomponents indicate that each of the four subcomponents is inter-related and influences the other. To maximize sustainability for the SOPAA Volunteer Program, the TAPS Support Coordinator must attend to each of the four subcomponents. In this section, we discuss each subcomponent and provide some suggestions for ensuring that it is addressed as part of the volunteer program.

Data Collection and Program Evaluation

To document the importance of, and services provided by, the SOPAA Volunteer Program, the TAPS Support Coordinator should collect, summarize, and evaluate data related to it. These data can then be communicated to others to maintain or increase administrative (e.g., the school principal's and/or the school board's) support for the volunteer program, and they can also be shared with teachers to strengthen their knowledge and support of the program. Further, having the SOPAA leaders evaluate all data collected should help to facilitate stronger recruitment, training, and communication with the volunteers as well as a beneficial experience for them. For example, summarized data that detail the amount of hours contributed and how the school has benefited may increase school volunteers' perception of the value of their role and, in turn, improve the overall sustainability of the program. Data collection and evaluation may also help with writing grants and securing additional funding for the SOPAA Volunteer Program, a topic we described earlier in this chapter.

The type of data to collect on the SOPAA Volunteer Program will vary depending on the school and the specific ways the program is facilitated. Table 8.3 offers some suggestions for the kinds of data that might be collected, summarized, and evaluated. As shown in Table 8.3, there are

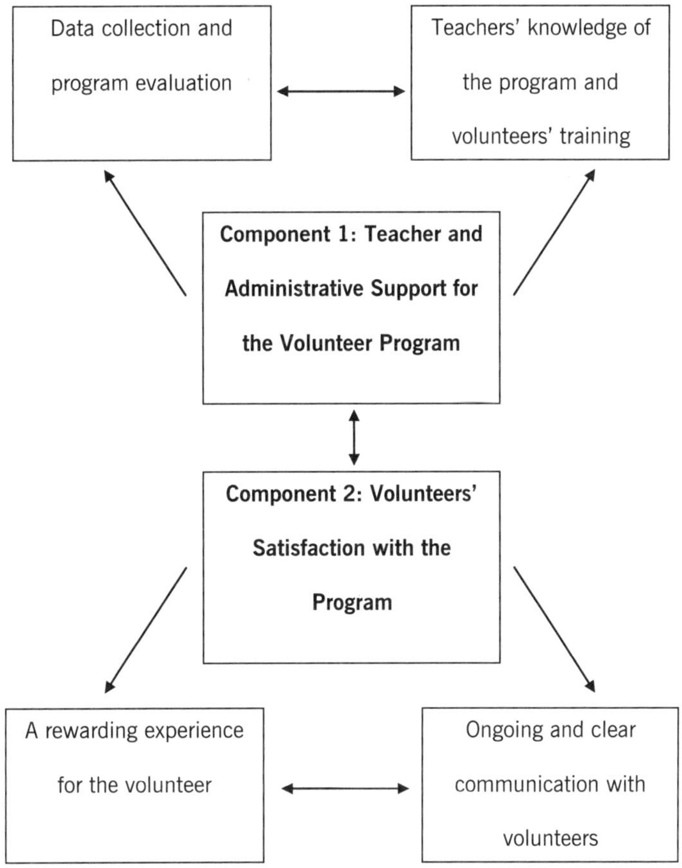

FIGURE 8.2. The key components and subcomponents for sustaining the SOPAA volunteer program.

multiple domains the TAPS Support Coordinator may want to consider when collecting data. We recommend collecting data in as many domains as possible and summarizing them accordingly. This approach should help with interpreting the data and identifying successes and weaknesses of the program, as well as determining areas to improve during the subsequent school year.

Ideally, SOPAA Volunteer Program data would be collected in a way that maximizes comprehensiveness (e.g., by ensuring that all volunteers complete an evaluation at the end of the school year or before a volunteer ends his or her volunteer role). Also, most schools have a specified "check-in/check-out" system for nonemployees, and such a system could be used to generate important data (e.g., number of hours volunteers committed, number of volunteers). Volunteer registration/application forms and the TAPS Intervention Planning Form will also serve as reliable ways to gather useful data.

The reader might notice that the impact of volunteers on students' learning is not listed in Table 8.3. It would be ideal to evaluate this type of outcome, but doing so is complicated for many reasons. Namely, student improvements in learning are going to be influenced by several factors (e.g., classroom instruction, others using interventions with the student, home-based factors, and more). Thus, to fully evaluate the impact of *only* the volunteer on the student's academic outcomes, a relatively sophisticated experimental design would be needed, and this option for program evaluation is usually unrealistic without a team of researchers devoted to the evaluation. In fact, even

TABLE 8.3. Possible Domains and Areas in Which to Collect and Summarize Annual Data for the SOPAA Volunteer Program

General domain	Sample areas to collect data
Volunteer characteristics	1. Total number of volunteers, including new volunteers for the school year and returning volunteers 2. Identifying characteristics of volunteers, such as "status" (e.g., university student, parent of child in the school, retiree), race, gender, etc. 3. Volunteer attendance record (e.g., percentage of no-shows, percentage of time volunteers showed up on time, percentage of time volunteers fulfilled entire time period as scheduled) 4. Percentage of volunteers who committed more than 3 hours per week 5. Percentage of volunteers who committed 1, 2, 3, 4, or 5 days per week 6. Percentage of volunteers who were regularly involved more than 10, 20, 30, or 40 weeks during the school year
Recruitment	1. List all types of recruitment strategies and when the recruitment strategies were implemented. 2. If known, report the success of each recruitment strategy (e.g., how many registered volunteers indicated that they learned of the experience because of the recruitment strategy).
Activities (general)	1. Summary of activities performed by the volunteers (e.g., received training in intervention programs, implemented intervention programs, trained new volunteers to use intervention programs, observed other implementers to provide feedback and record implementation integrity) 2. Total number of hours volunteers committed to SOPAA Volunteer Program activities. This number might also be converted to a monetary value of volunteer contributions, which can be determined by multiplying the total number of hours by an hourly dollar rate one might be given for volunteer activities (e.g., in 2009 the U.S. Bureau of Labor Statistics placed a dollar value of $20.85 on each hour of volunteer service).
Activities related to TAPS Process	1. Total number of TAPS cases with which volunteers assisted 2. Total number of teachers who benefited from involving a volunteer during a TAPS case 3. Names of all intervention programs that volunteers used 4. Total number of hours that volunteers implemented each specific intervention program 5. Names of all intervention programs that volunteers were trained to use during that school year 6. Number of volunteers who learned a new intervention program 7. Number of volunteers who can successfully implement one, two, three, or more intervention programs 8. Averaged implementation integrity data for all volunteers and with each specific intervention program
Teacher evaluations	1. Summary data from classroom teacher evaluations that rate each volunteer using a 5-point Likert scale (e.g., Strongly Disagree to Strongly Agree) and state items such as (a) My interpersonal interactions with the volunteer were positive, (b) The volunteer regularly showed up on time, (c) The volunteer regularly made the student(s) feel comfortable, (d) The volunteer regularly showed important qualities, such as enthusiasm, sensitivity, kindness, competence, and professionalism, and (e) Overall, the volunteer was an asset to facilitating the TAPS process. 2. Summary data from TAPS Teacher evaluations that use a similar rating format and set of questions as those listed above.

(cont.)

TABLE 8.3. *(cont.)*

General domain	Sample areas to collect data
Volunteer evaluations	1. Summary data from volunteer evaluations that use a 5-point Likert scale (e.g., Strongly Disagree to Strongly Agree) and address issues and experiences in areas such as training, communication with the TAPS Intervention Support Coordination, interactions with classroom teachers and TAPS teachers, enjoyment of working with students, enjoyment in implementing the intervention program, access to needed materials, access to an adequate work space, comfort with being observed for implementation integrity checks, whether he or she would recommend the experience to others who want to volunteer in the community, perceived effectiveness in the role, perceived interest from the student(s) to work with the volunteer, overall enjoyment of the experience.
Awards and appreciation	1. Summary of volunteer awards given 2. Summary of appreciation-related activities for volunteers

the research evaluating the effects of school volunteers has been limited because very few research studies can adequately account for specific effects of volunteers compared to factors such as those mentioned above (Ritter et al., 2009; Wasik, 1998).

After acquiring all relevant data, a report should be developed that summarizes the main outcomes of the SOPAA Volunteer Program. If shared with others (either in full or partially), the report should adhere to requirements for confidentiality and should therefore exclude teacher, student, and volunteer names, unless there is good reason and permission given to include names. For example, a report might include names of volunteers who were recognized with a volunteer award. Data in the report (both midyear and end-of-year) might also be evaluated in comparison with the previous year. The report could conclude with statements of how to improve program weaknesses during the following year. We show a sample report that has been used to summarize one school district's volunteer program on the companion website *www.sopaaforschools.org*.

Teachers' Knowledge of the Program and Volunteers' Training

Depending on the approach used for recruiting and training volunteers, classroom teachers may not know how volunteers are trained or that volunteers should be well prepared to assist the teacher in carrying out a student's TAPS intervention plan. Likewise, teachers may not know about the structured SOPAA Volunteer Program and how that program is designed to support the SOPAA in general and the TAPS feature specifically. As shown in Table 8.3, teacher knowledge and support for the SOPAA Volunteer Program is one important piece of the data collection and evaluation plan.

Overall, teachers' knowledge of how volunteers are trained and how they can meaningfully assist is important because such knowledge should increase the likelihood that teachers will support and appreciate school volunteers and recognize how they can meaningfully benefit the overall TAPS process. Lack of support for volunteers from teachers or their lack of awareness about volunteers' roles and capabilities may significantly decrease volunteers' experiences and the likelihood that they will continue assisting in the school. Chapter 10 describes how and when the SOPAA Lead Coordinator might discuss the SOPAA Volunteer Program with teachers, but we emphasize here how teachers' knowledge of the volunteer program may influence its sustainability.

A Rewarding Experience for the Volunteer

As noted earlier, to sustain a useful volunteer program, teachers and administrators need to support the program, and the volunteers themselves need to enjoy the program. Evaluating volunteers' perceptions of the experience in the ways shown in Table 8.3 will help identify whether volunteers find the experience rewarding. There are also several actions the TAPS Support Coordinator can take (in addition to generating teacher and administrative support) to better ensure that volunteers enjoy the experience. The following list provides some ways the TAPS Support Coordinator can promote a rewarding experience for volunteers.

1. Hold a structured School Volunteer Appreciation Day (or week), in which all volunteers are recognized (e.g., through posters, announcements, access to food/snacks) for their hard work.
2. Create specific awards (e.g., one to three per school year) for volunteers who should be recognized for their unique effort (e.g., committing a certain number of hours or weeks per school year, committing for a number of consecutive years, engaging in activities that are beyond typical volunteer roles).
3. Increase awareness of the SOPAA Volunteer Program by showcasing volunteers' efforts in local newspapers, school newsletters, the school website, through posting and announcements in the school, or through other mediums.
4. Encourage classroom teachers and TAPS Teachers to thank volunteers for their assistance, using specific and genuine praise for the ways volunteers assist in the school.
5. Create specific awards for teachers who work particularly well with volunteers, help with training, assist with recruiting, or do some other unique activity related to the volunteer experience. Recognizing teachers who support the SOPAA Volunteer Program may increase teacher support of the program.
6. Communicate regularly with volunteers to see if they are enjoying the experience or if they have questions or concerns (this topic is discussed in greater detail in the next section).
7. Allow volunteers flexibility and options in their roles, if possible.

With respect to this last point of allowing volunteers flexibility and options in their roles, it may be that some SOPAA volunteers do not *only* want to work with students in the context of TAPS and implementing student intervention programs. The TAPS Support Coordinator should identify early on (e.g., during the brief interview or information session) whether the volunteer would like to be involved with the primary roles of the SOPAA Volunteer Program *and* something else (e.g., general homework tutoring, supervising games or activities, doing miscellaneous tasks requested by teachers). For example, some volunteers may have a particular interest in working with students and building relationships with them. Although this can certainly be done through implementing a structured intervention program, working with students in other ways may further allow volunteers to assist students while building relationships. In addition, some volunteers might prefer to have varied tasks during their time in the school, especially if they volunteer several hours per week. As reported by Caldarella and colleagues (2010), school volunteers tended to be more satisfied when their experience was consistent with their initial motivations for volunteering and their perceived benefits.

In conclusion, although the TAPS Support Coordinator needs to ensure a successful SOPAA Volunteer Program (according to the goals of that program), allowing interested volunteers to get experiences outside of the activities associated with the SOPAA Program may ultimately improve the volunteers' overall experiences.

Ongoing and Clear Communication with the Volunteers

The TAPS Support Coordinator's regular and clear communication with volunteers should help to promote a rewarding experience for them. However, this activity is also related to gathering data from volunteers (such as through satisfaction surveys) and bridging communication with teachers who may not be supportive of volunteers or fully aware of their roles. We therefore devote specific attention to this aspect of promoting volunteer satisfaction.

Overall, the TAPS Support Coordinator wants to make sure that volunteers have a voice in their experience and that their questions and concerns can be addressed quickly and fairly. The following list provides general suggestions for the TAPS Support Coordinator to structure an ongoing and effective mode of communication with volunteers.

1. To generate more "informal" communication and input, maintain periodic check-ins with volunteers to make sure that their concerns and questions are addressed, and that they are enjoying their experience. This might be done by checking in with volunteers in person, by phone, or e-mail. Ultimately, in addition to feeling that their work is valued, the volunteers should feel that someone is overseeing the volunteer program and checking with them to ensure that their questions and concerns get addressed.

2. Make sure that volunteers know they can seek you out when questions or concerns arise, and tell them where you will likely be in the school (if possible). If they cannot find you when they have a question, develop a system that allows them to state their question or concern immediately. For example, they might be referred to a specific teacher to talk with, asked to leave a message in your school mailbox, or encouraged to e-mail you.

3. Let volunteers know that they can submit anonymous feedback, suggestions, or concerns, and that you will respond to their comments as soon as possible. As a method for receiving anonymous comments, a "drop box" system for messages might be placed in the main office.

4. To generate more formal feedback, use volunteer satisfaction evaluations with items addressing topics like those presented in Table 8.3.

5. Provide both formal (e.g., newsletter, written notes) and informal updates about things such as (a) students who seem to be benefiting from volunteers' assistance, (b) changes that might be made to the SOPAA Volunteer Program, (c) updates about training opportunities, and (d) how volunteers' suggestions and comments have been addressed.

6. Ensure that volunteers are clear about their role and the expectations associated with being a volunteer. This information is communicated before the volunteer begins the experience (such as during the information session or volunteer orientation), but as needed, volunteers should be reminded about roles and expectations.

7. Provide feedback about how the volunteer is doing (either formally and/or informally), such as how well he or she is implementing a particular intervention program. Of course, emphasize strengths and improvements in the volunteer's performance but do not hesitate to provide constructive criticisms that align with the goals and expectations of the SOPAA Volunteer Program. One way to facilitate formal feedback about volunteers' implementation integrity is through the data collected during the standard TAPS documentation process. Relatedly, soliciting informal information from classroom teachers and TAPS teachers about volunteers' performance will also assist with providing feedback to volunteers.

CHAPTER 9

Obtaining Support for the SOPAA through Effective Communication with School Leaders

As we highlighted in Chapter 2, a systems-level approach to addressing students' learning needs requires effective communication about the SOPAA components and procedures, as this communication is critical to ensuring and sustaining proper implementation (McIntosh et al., 2009; Sindelar et al., 2006). Likewise, one must effectively communicate a rationale for using the SOPAA, as well as anticipated outcomes resulting from implementation, to generate and maintain support from school leaders (e.g., the school principal) and the educators involved with implementation (Adelman & Taylor, 2003; Cherniss, 2006). For these reasons, Component 5 of the SOPAA (methods for communication and generating support) is integrated within the model as a means to generate schoolwide support for SOPAA implementation, ensure that implementation occurs as planned, and sustain implementation over time. Chapters 9 and 10 of this book are dedicated to Component 5.

In this chapter, we first describe how one educator within a school can begin to generate support for the SOPAA by communicating with a small number of school leaders and potentially recruiting those educators as SOPAA co-facilitators. When co-facilitators do not include the school principal, gaining support from the principal is also essential to successfully implementing and sustaining the SOPAA. Therefore, this chapter also provides recommendations and resources that one or more SOPAA facilitators can use when discussing implementation with the principal. In short, the recommendations and resources provided in this chapter are intended to generate adequate time, materials, and principal support for SOPAA implementation.

COMMUNICATION WITH POSSIBLE CO-FACILITATORS OF THE SOPAA

As was listed at the end of Chapter 3 in the step-by-step recommendations for implementing the SOPAA (pp. 48–49), the Lead Coordinator begins the SOPAA implementation process by familiarizing herself with the core principles, procedures, and resources described in this book, and then eventually (see Step 3) completing the Intervention Planning Summary Checklist as a means of thinking about options for an immediate and long-term implementation plan. As part of these preliminary considerations for SOPAA implementation, the Lead Coordinator should also determine whether other educators within the school (e.g., a special education teacher, reading specialist, and/or school psychologist) could help to implement and facilitate SOPAA components, and if so, how facilitation could be shared effectively. Depending on the characteristics of the Lead Coordinator's school (e.g., number of students, shared philosophies among teachers about addressing the needs of struggling learners), SOPAA implementation will sometimes work best if the Lead Coordinator shares implementation responsibilities. Chapter 11 describes in detail how multiple educators might facilitate the key components of the SOPAA and who within the school would likely serve as a good facilitator. In this section we simply present information about initial communication with possible SOPAA co-facilitators.

What and When to Communicate with a Possible Co-Facilitator

If the Lead Coordinator decides that the SOPAA would be best facilitated by multiple educators, she should communicate with the possible co-facilitators to describe the overall components of the SOPAA (e.g., using Figure 2.1, p. 26, Appendices A and M, as well as Tables 3.3–3.6 pp. 35–45) and how she believes the co-facilitator would make a meaningful contribution to SOPAA implementation. For example, a co-facilitator may serve in one or more of the SOPAA-designated roles described in Chapter 2 (e.g., TAPS Math Teacher, TAPS Support Coordinator).

In terms of when to approach one or more possible co-facilitators, the Lead Coordinator must carefully decide whether communication should occur before or after communication with the school principal. For example, communicating with a potential co-facilitator about the SOPAA before discussing its possible implementation with a principal may be advantageous because the Lead Coordinator and co-facilitators could (1) collectively generate a more effective implementation plan and proposal for the principal, (2) better problem-solve possible implementation barriers or reservations the principal may raise about the proposal, and (3) orchestrate their efforts in communicating the proposal to the principal. Also, a principal may have even greater support for the SOPAA plan if he or she knows that two or more educators within the school (i.e., the co-facilitators) agree that the plan would benefit the school and seems feasible to implement.

Principals with a shared leadership style may be quite comfortable with the aforementioned approach and timing for communication. However, the Lead Coordinator may encounter weak support from the school principal if, for example, the school has a history of initiating change only after schoolwide proposals are first discussed with the principal. In other words, the Lead Coordinator must be aware that some principals may feel uncomfortable if small groups of educators discuss possible schoolwide changes prior to approaching administration, seeing it as a usurpation of the administrative role. Similarly, some schools have a formal shared leadership structure, such as a site-based management team that influences schoolwide change, with specific goals and plans that must be approved by the team. If a school has this type of a shared leadership structure, SOPAA planning should probably include the leadership team.

COMMUNICATION WITH THE SCHOOL PRINCIPAL

As stated previously, without the principal's support, SOPAA implementation will not be successfully initiated or sustained. In fact, a central goal of communicating with the principal should be not only to generate support, but to help the principal view SOPAA implementation as a high priority and be willing to convey that priority to teachers throughout the school (McIntosh et al., 2009). Therefore, assuming that the Lead Coordinator is not the school principal or did not learn of the SOPAA from the principal, and assuming it is appropriate for the Lead Coordinator to approach the principal with the types of schoolwide change ideas embedded within the SOPAA model, the Lead Coordinator should seek the principal's support for (1) each component of the SOPAA she hopes to implement during the introductory SOPAA school year, and (2) an incremental implementation proposal of the SOPAA that could occur across multiple years. Although generating support from the principal may actually include all SOPAA co-facilitators (as discussed in Chapter 11), for consistency throughout this chapter we discuss SOPAA communication only between the Lead Coordinator and principal. Depending on the school and who is involved with initiating the SOPAA, communication with the principal may actually include all SOPAA co-facilitators. What follows are key topics related to communication with the principal about the SOPAA.

Effective communication is critical not only to developing and initiating the SOPAA, but also for sustaining it.

When to Communicate with the Principal

Because a fair amount of preparation is needed prior to successfully initiating SOPAA implementation, communication with the principal should probably occur no later than the end of the academic year preceding the year in which the Lead Coordinator hopes to either begin SOPAA implementation or begin the SOPAA planning year (as discussed in Chapter 3). For example, if the Lead Coordinator hopes to begin a planning year during academic year 2013–2014, initial communication with the principal about the SOPAA should occur no later than spring 2013. However, this is a general suggestion, and there will likely be good and bad times during a school year to arrange the initial SOPAA meeting with the principal. Forthcoming information in this chapter will help the Lead Coordinator determine the best time to approach the principal about implementing the SOPAA.

Preparing for the Meeting with the School Principal

To help the principal recognize how the school could benefit from the SOPAA, the Lead Coordinator should thoroughly prepare before arranging this initial meeting. We provide six recommendations below that should help the Lead Coordinator prepare for this meeting. Recommendations 2–5 are elaborated on within this chapter.

1. Develop a strong understanding of the SOPAA and each of its six components.
2. Prepare a clear overview of the SOPAA, including a description of its primary components.
3. Prepare a summary for how the SOPAA aligns with the school's existing system for addressing students' learning needs, and how the SOPAA would improve the existing system.
4. Prepare a well-conceived plan and proposed timeline for how to implement the SOPAA components within the school. Assuming that all SOPAA components will not be implemented in the same school year, the Lead Coordinator would also want to develop a general timeline for how to integrate more SOPAA components systematically during subsequent school years.

5. Prepare a list of ideal and necessary resources (e.g., time for SOPAA facilitators, materials) needed to successfully implement the SOPAA.
6. Anticipate implementation-related questions and barriers the principal may pose and prepare meaningful responses to address those questions. Preparing for this aspect of the meeting with the principal will occur, in essence, when the Lead Coordinator completes the schoolwide capacity assessment described in Chapter 3.

When requesting a meeting to discuss the SOPAA, the principal should know that the discussion will probably last at least 45–60 minutes and center on ways to improve the needs of struggling learners in the school. If the Lead Coordinator is unclear about the SOPAA components, her proposal for implementation, her rationale for implementation, and/or does not obtain sufficient time to discuss the proposed plan with the principal, one or more of these factors may meaningfully weaken the principal's potential support for SOPAA implementation.

Presenting an Overview of the SOPAA

In presenting an overview of the SOPAA to the principal, we recommend that the Lead Coordinator first state what the SOPAA is (generally) and then specify its primary components. For example, depending on the school's needs and characteristics, any of the following descriptions (also presented in Chapter 1), or a combination of them, may be a useful way of generally defining the SOPAA and its goals:

1. A step-by-step model for moving toward a schoolwide system of instructional support for low-performing students.
2. A pragmatic path for an educator or small group of educators to use well-aligned procedures that can improve how the school responds to struggling learners in the general education classroom.
3. A comprehensive yet time- and resource-efficient approach to improving students' learning outcomes that also documents how struggling learners are assisted.

Figure 2.1 and Appendix A could be used to describe the primary components and features of the SOPAA and to discuss how they are interrelated. In describing the SOPAA components and features, however, the Lead Coordinator may decide that a complete description of all features could seem overwhelming to the principal if the school's existing procedures are notably different from what the SOPAA model looks like when implemented at full-scale. Accordingly, a description of the components and features should simply be enough to generate the principal's interest in possible implementation without making the model appear impossible to implement. Considering this balance, Component 6 (adaptable and incremental implementation) should be emphasized to help the principal understand that most schools can systematically integrate the various components and features across multiple school years. Just as one example, the Lead Coordinator may focus the initial meeting on how the SOPAA and its components could first be used to improve academic outcomes for struggling readers in grades K–2.

Presenting a Rationale for the SOPAA

A primary goal of meeting with the school principal is to generate support for implementing the SOPAA. To generate this support, the rationale for implementation must be clear and should justify the time and resources needed to facilitate effective implementation. The overall rationale for using the SOPAA will differ depending on each school's needs and characteristics. The Lead Coordinator should therefore determine the strongest rationale and clearly present it to the principal. For guidance, the Lead Coordinator may use some of the information described within the following sections as a means for developing a sound rationale for using the SOPAA. We organize possible reasons for implementing the SOPAA according to two primary categories: (1) the need to improve a school's existing practices for addressing the needs of struggling learners, and (2) the need to improve a school's existing practices for documenting and evaluating academic interventions. The Lead Coordinator may find relevant reasons to use the SOPAA in one or both of these categories.

Improving Practices for Addressing the Needs of Struggling Learners

In most cases the Lead Coordinator will be more likely to generate support for the SOPAA if it is described as an approach that fits with and can improve upon the school's existing practices for assisting struggling learners, rather than describing the model as a completely new approach to assisting students (Adelman & Taylor, 2003; Vaughn, Klingner, & Hughes, 2000). Of course, the ways in which the SOPAA aligns with a school's existing procedures will depend on each school's specific method and resources for assisting teachers with struggling learners. As such, this aspect of the rationale should be developed according to the specific characteristics of the Lead Coordinator's school.

Although each school is unique, the examples provided in Table 9.1 may serve as a helpful resource for determining how the SOPAA may align with and improve a school's existing practices. As shown, the left-hand column of the table specifies a variety of practices and resources that are found within many schools (although not all practices listed in the table would be found in any one school). The column of existing school practices is followed by columns describing how the SOPAA aligns with the given practice or resource, and how the SOPAA should enhance the practice or resource. In addition to the information shown in Table 9.1, if the SOPAA is being suggested for a school using RTI as a model of problem solving, the Lead Coordinator should develop a rationale that illustrates for the principal how the SOPAA can be used and aligns with RTI and how using both RTI and the SOPAA should improve how the school supports struggling learners. Chapter 3 offers specific information the Lead Coordinator can use to develop this rationale.

Discussing how the SOPAA aligns with and can enhance existing school practices should help in developing a rationale for its implementation, but additional reasons for using the SOPAA might be supported by reviewing schoolwide data with the principal. For example, if the Lead Coordinator can access and summarize data suggesting that large percentages of students perform below expected levels in key academic areas such as reading and/or math, these data should further encourage the principal to support schoolwide efforts to improve the school's system of instructional problem solving. Likewise, the principal may show increased support for the SOPAA if schoolwide data suggest that many teachers have limited access to (or knowledge about implementing) evidence-based academic interventions.

Accessing and summarizing schoolwide data will require additional work for the Lead Coordinator in preparation for the meeting with the principal, but presenting such data may be particularly compelling in getting the principal's support for SOPAA implementation. Of course, before possible data collection and summarization, the Lead Coordinator should ensure that collecting such data would not be viewed by the principal or other administrators as a threat or as outside of her perceived role or qualifications.

TABLE 9.1. Possible Existing School Practices and Resources Used to Address Student Learning Difficulties and Their Alignment with the SOPAA Model

Existing school practice or resource	How the SOPAA aligns with or offers something very similar to the existing practice or resource	Why the SOPAA should enhance the practice or resource
1. Student is referred to a prereferral intervention team and the team makes a decision about how to plan for intervention and monitor intervention effectiveness.	Teachers continue to receive high levels of assistance for academic concerns by working with a skilled academic consultant (i.e., a TAPS Support Teacher).[a] If the academic problem is not solved through the TAPS process, a multidisciplinary team might then meet to discuss additional options for student support.	A. *Teachers should receive more immediate assistance* because there is no need to schedule around team meeting times and multiple teachers' availability. B. *The consultant's[a] support may be faster and more time-efficient* because of the systematic TAPS process. C. *The consultant is ensured to have high levels of expertise* (e.g., knowledge about the academic problem and evidence-based interventions that can target the problem). Thus, *problem solving between the teacher and consultant should still result in meaningful solutions* to the teacher's concern. D. The consultant will continually serve as the case "manager," which should result in *a more centralized and time-efficient process for managing academic interventions and overseeing proper implementation and documentation of interventions.* As such, this role should eliminate problems with "diffusion of responsibility" that can sometimes result in poor case management (e.g., ineffective or absent monitoring of intervention effectiveness, implementation integrity, follow-up problem solving). E. *When needed, multi-disciplinary input can be facilitated by the consultant,* but this would not always require the time needed for all members of a team to be present for a meeting.
2. Student is discussed during weekly grade-level team meetings and the grade-level team makes a decision about how to plan for intervention and monitor intervention effectiveness.	Teachers continue to receive the same level of assistance and collaborative problem solving, but this comes from an expert consultant rather than from the grade-level team. However, if desired by the teacher needing assistance, the TAPS intervention plan could still be discussed with members of the grade-level team.	In addition to points A–D above: F. Designating time with the consultant should *ensure adequate time to develop a comprehensive intervention plan.* Sometimes weekly grade-level team meetings do not allow adequate time to develop a full intervention plan. G. *The consultant may be better able to facilitate implementation support* from assistive school personnel or volunteers.

(cont.)

TABLE 9.1. ***(cont.)***

Existing school practice or resource	How the SOPAA aligns with or offers something very similar to the existing practice or resource	Why the SOPAA should enhance the practice or resource
3. When requested, the teacher can formally consult with an educator (e.g., school psychologist, reading specialist) in the school about a student's academic difficulties.	Teachers continue to consult with an educator in the school, which is a central aspect of the SOPAA model and TAPS. In fact, the educator serving as a consultant with the current school practice may now be a TAPS Teacher (i.e., consultant), so consultation services may still be provided by the same educator.	In addition to points C and D above: H. *The TAPS process should add continuity and ensure comprehensiveness and follow-up* throughout the process, particularly because the TAPS Teacher will be designated for that consulting purpose.
4. When a student experiences academic difficulties, the teacher informally gets consultative support from an educator (e.g., special education teacher, reading specialist) in the school.	Teachers continue to consult with a school staff member about a student's academic difficulties, but the consultation process becomes more structured to better ensure successful intervention development and implementation. Also, the educator serving as a consultant with the current school practice may now be a TAPS Teacher (i.e., consultant), so consultation services may still be provided by the same educator.	See points C, D, G, and H above.
5. Teacher attempts to address academic concerns without seeking support from other school staff.	Teachers might continue to address students' academic difficulties on their own, but the SOPAA model will allow teachers an added level of support.	See points C–H above.
6. Evidence-based academic interventions are used to address the needs of struggling learners.	Evidence-based interventions will continue to be used to address the needs of struggling learners.	I. *The SOPAA model ensures that the consultant is highly familiar with several evidence-based intervention programs* in each of the key academic areas, which will likely add to the school's options for implementing evidence-based interventions.
7. Teachers receive periodic staff development workshops to improve their knowledge and implementation of interventions designed to address student learning difficulties.	Teachers continue to receive periodic staff development workshops to improve their knowledge and implementation of interventions designed to address student learning difficulties.	J. *The SOPAA facilitators organize a systematic sequence of staff development workshops* that align with teachers' stated needs and the areas of staff development that will most likely improve the effectiveness of the SOPAA and student learning outcomes. K. *The SOPAA model of professional development ensures that teachers receive training only in evidence-based or learner-verified interventions.*

(cont.)

TABLE 9.1. *(cont.)*

Existing school practice or resource	How the SOPAA aligns with or offers something very similar to the existing practice or resource	Why the SOPAA should enhance the practice or resource
8. Teachers receive support from school volunteers and/ or assistive school personnel when implementing interventions for students with learning difficulties.	Teachers will continue to receive support from school volunteers and/ or assistive school personnel to implement interventions for students with learning difficulties.	L. *The SOPAA facilitators will work to recruit and train additional school volunteers* to implement evidence-based interventions, which will increase support services for teachers. M. *The SOPAA facilitators will coordinate support services across assistive school personnel*, which should increase efficient use of resources throughout the school. N. *The SOPAA facilitators will help to train assistive school personnel in evidence-based interventions* that teachers will likely adopt. This training should increase the implementation effectiveness of assistive school personnel. O. *The SOPAA facilitators will help to monitor the implementation integrity of assistive school personnel*, which should increase their implementation effectiveness. P. *TAPS Teachers will assist with intervention implementation*, which will increase the number of intervention implementers and better facilitate the TAPS Teacher's knowledge base and consultation effectiveness.
9. Teachers use periodic and systematic assessment procedures (e.g., quarterly assessments of students' reading) as a means of identifying students with learning difficulties.	The school will continue to support and administer systematic assessment procedures to identify low-performing students.	Q. *The TAPS Teacher may help in identifying new assessments that will improve the effectiveness and efficiency of identifying low-performing students.* R. *The TAPS Teacher will help to organize a system of administering assessments that may be less time-consuming for teachers* (e.g., training and coordinating for other assistive school personnel to assist with administering assessments). S. *The TAPS Teacher will help to ensure that all teachers are using and responding to assessment data* as best as possible.

[a] The terms *consultant* and *TAPS Teacher* can be considered synonymous. We generally use *consultant* to describe this role for an existing school practice, and use *TAPS Teacher* in reference to activities specific to the SOPAA.

To avoid a potential conflict with school administration, the Lead Coordinator may want to first seek permission from the principal before collecting and/or summarizing school data and, as needed, explain her qualifications and motives for gathering and summarizing such data. For example, the Lead Coordinator might explain that she wants to collect schoolwide data to better understand students' academic achievement on a schoolwide level and/or to understand teachers' resources and perceptions related to academic interventions. Of course, a desire to develop new ideas for assisting struggling learners would justify the Lead Coordinator wanting to better understand these school characteristics. To further avoid a potential conflict, the Lead Coordinator could work as part of a small team of educators within the school to collect schoolwide data.

Table 9.2 offers examples of data the Lead Coordinator might collect and summarize in preparation for the meeting with the principal. The Lead Coordinator should *not* attempt to acquire data for each of the examples shown in the table—this would likely be a very burdensome task. Rather, generating the most important data for at least two or three categories may be useful in presenting a data-based rationale for the SOPAA to the principal.

By reviewing Tables 9.1 and 9.2 and considering the characteristics of her own school, the Lead Coordinator should be able to develop several ideas for justifying why the SOPAA should be implemented. For additional ideas and illustrations of how the SOPAA may benefit schools with varying characteristics, the case examples described in Chapter 13 may be useful.

Improving Practices for Documenting and Evaluating Academic Interventions

Two strong bases for justifying SOPAA implementation to a principal include (1) how implementation will align with and improve existing practices, and (2) how schoolwide data suggest that the school is not yet meeting the needs of all its learners. A third rationale the principal may attend closely to is that the TAPS process will improve the school's ability to document the implementation of academic interventions for struggling students and that each student's response to the specialized instruction will be evaluated. This feature of the TAPS process is important because it aligns with the 2004 IDEIA requirement that the academic progress of children who are referred for learning disabilities has been monitored prior to identification and placement.

Discussing Needed Time and Resources for SOPAA Implementation

Assuming that the school principal agrees with the Lead Coordinator's rationale for implementing the SOPAA and believes that the model has potential to improve learning outcomes for students in the school, the discussion should then turn to the time and resources needed for SOPAA implementation. Indeed, without adequate time and resources devoted to implementation, even the most well-supported and potentially effective school-improvement plan will unlikely to be implemented (Latham, 1988).

In an initial meeting it may not be possible (or appropriate) to discuss all details related to needed time and resources, but the Lead Coordinator should demonstrate how the time and resources needed for SOPAA implementation can ultimately improve student outcomes and eventually save the school time and resources. Part of this justification will come from the overall rationale for using the SOPAA; but to discuss implementation time and resource needs, the Lead Coordinator should rely heavily upon the information and tables presented in Chapter 3 (e.g., Table 3.3, pp. 35–37). When using this information, the Lead Coordinator will want to again highlight the incremental nature of SOPAA implementation and perhaps develop her own table of

TABLE 9.2. Possible Data to Collect and Summarize during the Initial SOPAA Meeting with the Principal

Broad category of data	Type of data	Likely method for obtaining the data	How to summarize the data	Why the data may be important
Academic achievement	Annual assessments of academic achievement[a]	Obtain scores from a school database.	Categorize students by percentile rank or a category determined by the specific measure (e.g., Below Basic, Basic, Proficient, Advanced).	Data may show that there are a substantial number of students who are, for example, in a low-performing category or achieving below grade-level standards.
Academic achievement	Benchmark assessments of academic achievement that are used more than once per school year (e.g., during the fall, winter, and spring)[b]	Obtain scores from a school database or possibly from each teacher's records of student scores.	Categorize students by percentile or a category determined by the specific measure (e.g., At Risk, Some Risk, or Low Risk).	Data may show that there are a substantial number of students performing below benchmark levels or who are not making progress across the year.
Current system of instructional problem solving	Summary characteristics of the school's current problem-solving system (e.g., number of students referred for academic assistance, general outcomes associated with system of academic intervention plans)	Conduct brief teacher interviews with a sample of teachers, hold a focus group of three to six teachers, examine school records related to the school's problem-solving model, and/or report personal knowledge about the problem-solving model.	Provide descriptions of the current problem-solving model.	Data may show that there are important limitations or barriers associated with the current instructional problem-solving model.
Current system of instructional problem solving	Survey of teachers' satisfaction with the current problem-solving model (and their input about strengths and weaknesses)	Administer anonymous survey of teachers.[c]	Present descriptive statistics for each survey item.	Data may show that teachers are dissatisfied with some aspects of the current problem-solving model.
Evidence-based intervention programs[d]	The number and names of evidence-based intervention programs that are used in the school	Review teachers' instructional resources within the school.	List evidence-based intervention programs in the key academic areas.	Data may show that teachers have little access to evidence-based intervention programs in one or more of the key academic areas.

(cont.)

TABLE 9.2. *(cont.)*

Broad category of data	Type of data	Likely method for obtaining the data	How to summarize the data	Why the data may be important
Evidence-based intervention programs[d]	Percentage of teachers who use evidence-based intervention programs and how frequently teachers use the programs	After identifying each of the intervention programs teachers use in the school, survey teachers about which ones they use and how often they use them.	Present descriptive statistics for each survey item.	Data may show that many teachers rarely use evidence-based intervention programs in one or more of the key academic areas.
Evidence-based intervention programs[d]	The types of staff development training teachers receive to learn evidence-based intervention programs or strategies over the past 3 years and (possibly) teachers' satisfaction with those workshops	Review school records about teachers' opportunities for staff development in evidence-based interventions (and possibly survey them regarding their satisfaction with previous staff development).	List and summarize descriptive statistics of staff development opportunities (and, if applicable, teacher satisfaction).	Data may show that teachers have minimal opportunities to learn intervention programs and/or have been dissatisfied with previous staff development opportunities.
Personnel resources	Number of teacher assistants (TAs) in the school and a description of the type of work TAs do	Review school records to determine the number of TAs and how they are assigned to classrooms (e.g., each classrooms has a TA 8–10 hours per week; each classroom has a TA 2 hours per day); survey TAs or classroom teachers to determine the type of work TAs typically do.	Report summary statistics such as the amount of time a TA is designated per classroom or per grade level; summarize the types of instructional activities with which each TA is involved.	Data may show, for example, that TAs are not designated per classroom and/or assisting in ways that would be most beneficial for classroom teachers (e.g., they are not implementing evidence-based instructional strategies they could otherwise implement with struggling learners).
Personnel resources	Number of volunteers in the school and a description of the type of work volunteers do	Review school records to determine number of school volunteers per school year and the frequency with which each volunteer assists in the school (e.g., 2 hours per week); survey some school volunteers to determine the type of work they do, or meet with a school staff member who knows volunteers' activities.	Report summary statistics such as average number of school volunteers per month and the average number of hours each volunteer assists in the school; summarize the types of activities with which each volunteer is involved while at the school.	Data may show, for example, that there are very few school volunteers assisting in the school and/or that school volunteers are not assisting in ways that would be most beneficial (e.g., they are not implementing evidence-based instructional strategies they could otherwise implement).

(cont.)

TABLE 9.2. *(cont.)*

Broad category of data	Type of data	Likely method for obtaining the data	How to summarize the data	Why the data may be important
Effectiveness of academic interventions and special education characteristics	Number of students for whom teachers request academic support and outcomes of those requests	Review school records (e.g., records of school assistance teams, records of how many students tested and placed in special education) or survey teachers to determine for how many students they requested support in the previous academic year and the outcome of their request.	Summarize school records by describing, for example, the number of students for whom teachers requested some form of academic support and the ultimate outcome of the request (e.g., student was assessed and now obtains special education services; student does not receive additional services; student receives support services from a teaching assistant; student has not improved in the related skill).	Data may help to show that teachers' requests for academic support lead to outcomes that exhaust school resources (e.g., too much student assessment and minimal intervention; students routinely designated to receive special education services) and/or that requests do not lead to desired changes in the student's academic performance.
Effectiveness of academic interventions and special education characteristics	Number of students getting primary instruction in general education classroom, but also receive academic support services from special education teachers	Review school records or survey special education teachers.	Summarize descriptive statistics about number of students getting services from special education teachers and how much service (e.g., in hours per week) students receive.	Data may reveal that special education teachers have an overwhelming caseload and that too many students are eligible for special education services, which may suggest the need for a more systematic approach to targeted and early intervention before eligibility for special education services.

[a] Examples of annual academic assessments include end-of-grade statewide assessments and other measures of academic achievement, such as the Iowa Tests of Basic Skills (ITBS) or the Terra Nova.

[b] Examples of benchmark assessments include fluency-based assessments of reading (e.g., the Dynamic Indicators of Basic Early Literacy Skills [DIBELS], EasyCBM) or math (e.g., AIMSweb), or other relatively brief measures of academic skills (e.g., the Developmental Reading Assessment, DRA, or the Qualitative Reading Inventory, QRI).

[c] Sample survey items that the Lead Coordinator may consider are available on the companion website *www.sopaaforschools.org*. When a survey is recommended in this table, sample survey items are available on the website.

[d] *Evidence-based intervention programs* refer to instructional programs that (1) are designed for use with struggling learners, (2) include a systematic set of instructional strategies that are research-based, and (3) offer teachers guidance for how to implement the program, such as through a teacher's manual. For example, to improve students' reading fluency, the method of "repeated reading" represents an evidence-based *strategy*, but Helping Early Literacy with Practice Strategies (HELPS) represents an evidence-based intervention *program*.

time and resource needs in alignment with her proposal of an appropriate first-year implementation plan—a plan that would likely be adapted from full-scale implementation. Using information from Chapters 3 and 11, the Lead Coordinator will also want to emphasize that the time needed for implementation should be feasible, and that (if applicable) co-facilitation will minimize the time needed from any one educator.

Developing an Implementation Plan

Assuming that the school principal has expressed interest in SOPAA implementation, the discussion should then turn to co-developing an implementation plan and confirming the time and material resources that will be needed to make implementation successful. Depending on the time needed to introduce the SOPAA to the principal and explain why it should be useful in the school, the discussion to develop an intervention plan would ideally occur in a separate meeting, likely after the principal has had the opportunity to more fully consider the possible benefits of SOPAA implementation. We note this recommendation only to caution the Lead Coordinator from trying to introduce the SOPAA *and* develop an intervention plan all in one meeting, as developing and confirming an intervention plan could take more than an hour.

In most cases, meeting with the school principal to develop a plan for SOPAA implementation should occur sometime after the meeting that allows the Lead Coordinator to introduce the SOPAA.

To prepare for the meeting to develop an intervention plan, the Lead Coordinator should again rely heavily on the preliminary considerations for SOPAA implementation that were detailed in Chapter 3 and may also keep in mind the responses to the Schoolwide Capacity Assessment (Appendix B). For example, prior to meeting with the principal, the Lead Coordinator would likely benefit by preparing a tentative multiyear proposal for how the SOPAA might be implemented in the school, with a focus on what Year 1 of implementation would entail. This proposal should be based on the topics related to incremental implementation and the potential need for a SOPAA preparation year that were discussed in Chapter 3. Of course, this proposal should be presented to the principal as possible ideas for implementation, and during the discussion the Lead Coordinator and principal should reach an agreement about how to best implement the SOPAA in the first year. Ideally, a tentative but realistic plan for implementing the SOPAA across subsequent school years should also be agreed upon so that the Lead Coordinator and principal can envision and plan for SOPAA implementation and sustainability over time—assuming each year's SOPAA evaluation shows evidence of improved school and/or student performance. Related to improved student and school performance, the implementation planning meeting should also be used to discuss plans and ideas for how to evaluate the SOPAA each year (a topic we describe in detail in Chapter 10).

Summary of the SOPAA Meetings with the Principal and Planning for Next Steps

Overall, the primary goals of meeting with the principal are to ensure that (1) he or she clearly understands and supports SOPAA implementation; (2) he or she understands and supports the time and resources needed to ensure successful implementation; (3) there is unambiguous agreement about the Year 1 plan for implementation; and (4) the agreed-upon plan for implementation conforms to the recommendations discussed throughout Chapter 3 (e.g., Table 3.1, p. 32). Furthermore, the Lead Coordinator should confirm with the principal that she may proceed with the more immediate "next steps" for implementation (e.g., introducing the SOPAA and TAPS procedures to teachers) and show the principal the timeline for those immediate next steps.

To assist the Lead Coordinator with concluding the SOPAA introduction and planning meetings with the principal, we suggest that she consider the following set of questions and, as needed, discuss any disagreements or ambiguous plans related to implementation. We do not necessarily suggest that the Lead Coordinator pose the following questions to the principal as they are written below, but simply consider whether the meetings established answers to these questions.

1. Is there agreement about the Year 1 SOPAA implementation plan?
2. Will a preparation year increase the likelihood of successful implementation in Year 1?
3. Is more discussion needed between the principal and Lead Coordinator to finalize implementation plans and a confirmed timeline for Year 1 of implementation?
4. Have there been proposed changes to the implementation plan that could potentially compromise the effectiveness of the SOPAA? For example, have there been proposed modifications by the principal that fall outside of the parameters discussed in Chapter 3 (e.g., Table 3.1), or is the principal unsupportive of any requested time and/or material resources? If so, how can the proposed changes be negotiated so that Year 1 of implementation will have the highest chance for success?
5. If a Year 1 timeline for implementation has been established, has a detailed timeline of week-by-week steps for early implementation been established? For example:
   a. When can the Lead Coordinator hold an introductory presentation with all classroom teachers who will be involved with the SOPAA (discussed in Chapter 10), and will each of those teachers be required to attend the presentation?
   b. Who will communicate with the classroom teachers to tell them about attending the introductory presentation (e.g., the principal, the Lead Coordinator)?
   c. Should the Lead Coordinator communicate with other well-respected educators in the school (i.e., other school leaders) before seeking input and support from the classroom teachers? If so, which school leaders would likely endorse SOPAA implementation? (This topic is discussed later in this chapter).
   d. Will any of the SOPAA co-facilitators and/or the principal present information about the SOPAA during the introductory presentation with the classroom teachers?
   e. When can the Lead Coordinator obtain the necessary materials (e.g., intervention programs) needed to begin SOPAA planning and implementation?
6. Have the Lead Coordinator and principal agreed on a general plan for evaluating the SOPAA during Year 1 (discussed in Chapter 10), and if a final evaluation plan has not yet been established, when will the plan be finalized and who will need to finalize it?
7. Assuming Year 1 of implementation is beneficial for students and teachers in the school, is there agreement about a general implementation plan after Year 1? If agreement has not been established, will this compromise the possible effectiveness of Year 1 implementation?

Last, if possible, encouraging or assisting the principal to incorporate the SOPAA implementation plan into a more formal written policy (e.g., a school improvement plan) might further establish the SOPAA as a priority for the principal and the school (Vaughn et al., 2000).

GENERATING ADDITIONAL SUPPORT FOR THE SOPAA

In preparation for Year 1 of SOPAA implementation, in addition to acquiring support from the school principal and possibly SOPAA co-facilitators, another approach to generating schoolwide support for the model is to identify other well-respected educators in the school (i.e., school leaders) who may not co-facilitate the SOPAA, but may influence teachers' support for the model if they approve it. This final section of the chapter therefore discusses how to garner support from other leaders within the school. We then conclude with a brief discussion about the potential need (or aspiration) to gain support for the SOPAA from educational leaders outside of the school (e.g., the district superintendent or school board members).

Generating Support from Other Leaders within the School

As described throughout this chapter, the Lead Coordinator will need support from the school principal to increase the likelihood of successful SOPAA implementation and sustainability. One reason for obtaining the principal's support is because his or her support may also help in generating support from the classroom teachers who will be most involved with the SOPAA (i.e., the teachers who will request support via the TAPS process). For example, if the classroom teachers respect the school principal and value his or her overall approach to improving students' learning, they may be more likely to support the SOPAA if they know the principal also endorses it. Likewise, classroom teachers may have even greater initial support for the SOPAA if they know that other respected educators in the school see strong value in implementing the model (Adelman & Taylor, 2003). As such, before the Lead Coordinator introduces the SOPAA to classroom teachers, she should consider describing the model to a small number of educators in the school who are respected professionally by most of teachers in the school (i.e., school leaders other than the principal).

Planning for and acquiring support from multiple school leaders should make it more likely to get classroom teachers' support.

During the initial SOPAA meeting with the principal, the Lead Coordinator and principal should discuss and identify potential school leaders who would likely endorse SOPAA implementation. Also, if the Lead Coordinator has not already identified other educators in the school who may co-facilitate implementation, and believes co-facilitation would be useful, a discussion with the principal about other school leaders who would support the SOPAA may help to identify possible co-facilitators. The first section of this chapter describes how the Lead Coordinator might introduce the SOPAA to possible co-facilitators. What follows is how the Lead Coordinator might discuss the SOPAA with school leaders who will not co-facilitate implementation.

Once she has identified the school leader(s) for whom she will seek a verbal endorsement, the Lead Coordinator should introduce the SOPAA to those educators. The amount of information to share with these school leaders will vary, but the goals in discussing the SOPAA with these school leaders are to (1) clearly explain the SOPAA, (2) describe the rationale for using it in the school, and (3) determine whether each school leader seems supportive of implementation. If a school leader endorses implementation (and assuming the leader is not going to co-facilitate implementation or take part in the introductory presentation with classroom teachers), the Lead Coordinator should ask the school leader if she can discuss his or her endorsement with other teachers. The reason for discussing this endorsement should be straightforward: because that school leader is widely respected by teachers in the school, the endorsement might also generate stronger support from other teachers in the school. Of course, discussing the SOPAA with other school leaders should also involve getting input and possible suggestions about implementation and, to the extent possible, such suggestions should be shared with the principal and integrated into the implementation plan.

Generating Support and Resources from Leaders beyond the School Level

We recognize that effective systems-level change in schools must sometimes include support from leadership "above" the school principal in a school district's hierarchy of administration (e.g., school board members or the superintendent), as this level is sometimes integral for sustainable change within a given school (Adelman & Taylor, 2003). However, our focus in this chapter, and throughout the book, is with schoolwide change that can take place within a school without material support from district-level leaders. Indeed, others highlight the necessity of a principal's support for creating schoolwide change, which can produce meaningful schoolwide improvements even in the absence of systems-level support or changes at the district level (e.g., Furney et al., 2003; Simmons et al., 2002).

With this said, if the school principal feels that SOPAA implementation would benefit from support beyond the school (e.g., the district's superintendent or school board), the SOPAA facilitators and principal should be able to use the resources provided in this book and determine the most beneficial approach for generating district-level support (and potential resources) for implementation within the school. With time, one school's success with the SOPAA may even influence other schools in the district to adopt this model for assisting low-performing students, and wider-scale adoption throughout a district could strengthen sustainability within each school.

CHAPTER 10

Obtaining and Sustaining Support for the SOPAA through Effective Communication with Teachers

Having classroom teachers view SOPAA implementation as a priority is as important for effective and sustainable implementation as it is to ensure support from school leaders (McIntosh et al., 2009). Therefore, after the Lead Coordinator obtains support for SOPAA implementation from the school principal and, as applicable, from other school leaders and possible co-facilitators of the SOPAA (all described in Chapter 9), she should then communicate the purpose, procedures, and goals of the SOPAA to all teachers who will be involved with implementation. More specifically, based on the Year 1 implementation plan developed with the principal, the Lead Coordinator will host an introductory SOPAA presentation to the teachers in the school who will take part in the TAPS process (e.g., selected classroom teachers and assistive school personnel). This chapter describes in detail what information the Lead Coordinator should present to these teachers. Additionally, this chapter describes methods for sustaining and possibly improving teacher and principal support after SOPAA implementation has begun. The topics discussed in this chapter primarily relate to Component 5 of the SOPAA: methods for communication and generating support.

Similar to our discussion of meeting with the school principal to generate support for the SOPAA (Chapter 9), for consistency throughout this chapter we discuss communication as coming from or being directed only by the Lead Coordinator. As pointed out in Chapter 9, however, if the SOPAA implementation plan includes co-facilitators, the communication activities described in this chapter should probably include (and would benefit from) the co-facilitators. For example, co-facilitators should take part in the introductory presentation to the teachers, and this presentation may also include the school principal.

COMMUNICATION WITH TEACHERS WHO WILL REQUEST ACADEMIC SUPPORT THROUGH THE SOPAA

During a 1- to 2-hour presentation, occurring no later than 4 weeks into the beginning of the school year, the Lead Coordinator should introduce the SOPAA to all teachers who plan to participate in the TAPS process (i.e., those who can request support through TAPS and those who will support TAPS intervention plans through implementing interventions). If deemed appropriate, educators in the school who are not directly involved with the SOPAA might also attend the introductory presentation to understand how and why this model will be used to assist teachers in their efforts to address the need of struggling learners. However, the Lead Coordinator and principal should determine exactly who should attend this presentation. For example, if the SOPAA will be implemented only with first- and second-grade teachers during the initial year of implementation, it may be better to formally inform other educators in the school about the SOPAA during a subsequent implementation year.

The introductory presentation for teachers is a critical step in SOPAA implementation because it is important to both initiating and sustaining the SOPAA model.

During the introductory presentation, the Lead Coordinator must provide a clear and accurate description of the SOPAA components and rationale so that teachers fully understand (1) the purpose of the model, (2) their role as part of the SOPAA and TAPS process, and (3) the procedures they must follow as part of the TAPS process. We recommend that the Lead Coordinator practice using TAPS with at least a couple cases prior to the introductory presentation so that the TAPS process can be presented with examples of actual students (and possibly outcomes) from her school. For example, these cases might be facilitated during a SOPAA preparation year (described in Chapter 3) or during the preceding academic year when the Lead Coordinator is becoming familiar with the TAPS process and communicating with the principal about using the SOPAA. Using actual examples in describing TAPS may decrease teachers' skepticism of what may appear to them as simply a theoretical process.

A clear description of the SOPAA goals and components also allows teachers to generate an initial impression of the model. Teachers' perceptions of the model and its value are important because they may influence the level of support and adherence to the model, which in turn will influence the overall success of implementation (Adelman & Taylor, 2003; McIntosh et al., 2009). As such, toward the end of the introductory presentation, the Lead Coordinator should systematically evaluate teachers' initial support for, and concerns regarding, SOPAA implementation.

In summary, the introductory presentation for teachers is a critical component of SOPAA implementation and consists of two core activities: (1) presenting a clear and accurate description of the SOPAA procedures and rationale, particularly as it related to the TAPS process; and (2) systematically evaluating teachers' support of the SOPAA. We first turn our attention to the specific content the Lead Coordinator should present to teachers as part of the SOPAA description and rationale. In most cases we recommend that the Lead Coordinator discuss the content described in each of the following subsections because doing so should help to provide teachers with a comprehensive understanding of the SOPAA procedures and rationale. However, in some cases the Lead Coordinator may benefit by modifying some aspects of the presentation content so it more specifically aligns with her school (e.g., the characteristics of the school's instructional problem-solving approach). To assist the Lead Coordinator with determining content she may wish to modify, we offer suggestions when applicable.

Introduction to Instructional Problem Solving

We recommend that the Lead Coordinator begin the introductory presentation with first stating the overall topic of the presentation: how the school can best address the needs of struggling learners through a systematic approach to instructional problem solving. To this end, the Lead Coordinator may start the presentation by asking teachers some simple questions that will get them thinking about this topic. For example, the Lead Coordinator might ask:

- In a typical school year, approximately how many students in your class would benefit from additional academic support in an academic area (e.g., 0, 1–2, 3–4, 4–5, 6 or more)?
- During what month in the school year do you typically begin to recognize struggling learners in your classroom (e.g., August, September, October)?
- During what month in the school year do you feel that you should start implementing an intervention to address the academic challenges faced by a student?

The Lead Coordinator may obtain teacher responses to questions such as these via a brief (and anonymous) paper survey or simply by asking for a show of hands when the questions are posed. Following these questions, the Lead Coordinator should define instructional problem solving and summarize its key components in the ways described in Chapter 2. A definition and rationale for prescriptive instructional problem solving could follow.

Teachers should also know that the instructional problem-solving process should occur *each time* a teacher first identifies that a student is not making (or likely to make) adequate progress in reading, math, and/or writing. The Lead Coordinator can then highlight the five primary components of instructional problem solving:

It is important to highlight for teachers exactly what instructional problem solving means in terms of the SOPAA model.

1. Pinpoint the primary academic weakness(es) the student is experiencing (e.g., phonics, reading comprehension, spelling).
2. Determine an intervention strategy that has evidence of successfully improving students' skills in the area of difficulty (e.g., reading comprehension).
3. Ensure that the intervention is implemented as planned and with sufficient intensity to address the student's academic difficulty.
4. Evaluate the effects of the intervention *during* its implementation process *and* at a predetermined endpoint.
5. Determine what should be done to further address the academic difficulty (if anything) after evaluating the intervention at the specified endpoint.

The Lead Coordinator should then acknowledge that this process of instructional problem solving often presents both conceptual and practical challenges. For example, from a conceptual point of view teachers may struggle with this question: "When there is a particular skill deficit (e.g., reading comprehension), how do I know whether that skill should be targeted for intervention or whether I should target a related skill (e.g., reading fluency or phonemic awareness)? Also, teachers face pragmatic challenges such as not having training or access to evidence-based intervention programs, or not having the time or support to implement an appropriate intervention.

Overall, it is important to start the SOPAA introductory presentation in the context of instructional problem solving so that teachers know the discussion has to do with (1) *their* process of developing, implementing, and evaluating interventions for students with learning difficulties; and with (2) identifying ways that teachers can be supported in this challenging process. As needed, it may also be helpful to emphasize the overall importance of instructional problem solving as it relates to a school's obligation to serve *all* students in a way that promotes academic success for every student.

Following an overview of instructional problem solving, the Lead Coordinator should be ready to introduce the SOPAA as a systematic process for instructional problem solving—a process that is intended to (1) fit within the school's existing instructional problem-solving practices and resources, (2) increase the efficiency and effectiveness of the school's current instructional problem-solving practices, and (3) increase learning outcomes for students in the school who experience academic difficulties. Following this segment, the Lead Coordinator can provide an overview of the topics related to SOPAA implementation that will be discussed during the remainder of the introductory presentation.

Definition and Overview of the SOPAA Components

Similar to the Lead Coordinator's meeting with the school principal, we recommend that the Lead Coordinator begin describing the SOPAA by first stating what the SOPAA is (generally) and then specifying its primary components and features. The content we provide in Chapter 9 about the SOPAA definition and its components should assist the Lead Coordinator in providing an overview for teachers. In some cases the SOPAA description will be the same as it was for the principal, but focusing particularly on the TAPS and professional development components will be important because these are the component teachers with which will be most involved during SOPAA implementation.

Rationale for the SOPAA and How It Aligns with Existing School Procedures

After presenting teachers with a basic overview of the SOPAA, the Lead Coordinator should tell teachers how the SOPAA aligns with some of the school's existing procedures for assisting low-performing students and the primary rationale for implementing the SOPAA and using the TAPS process. Providing a clear rationale is as important as describing the details of the TAPS process. That is, unless teachers understand the value of using the SOPAA and TAPS, they (1) may not follow the TAPS procedures as designed; (2) may not use the TAPS procedures at all; and/or (3) may convey negative attitudes about TAPS (or the overall SOPAA model) to other teachers, thereby negatively influencing those teachers' use of the TAPS process.

Similar to discussing reasons for using the SOPAA with school principals, the Lead Coordinator will likely benefit by describing for teachers (1) how key components of the SOPAA (particularly TAPS) already align with existing practices within the school, and (2) how SOPAA procedures should enhance existing school practices and resources. Doing so should help teachers understand that the TAPS procedures are not entirely new and should help to improve the efficiency and effectiveness of existing school practices, and consequently, improve the school's overall effectiveness of addressing all students' learning needs.

As stated in Chapter 9, the ways in which the SOPAA aligns with a school's characteristics and existing procedures will depend on each school's specific methods and resources for assisting teachers with struggling learners. This part of the introductory presentation should therefore be developed according to the characteristics of the Lead Coordinator's school. Again, the Lead Coordinator may wish to use information provided in Chapter 9 (e.g., the rationale developed from Tables 9.1 and 9.2 that was shared with the principal) as an approach to discussing the SOPAA rationale with teachers, and the rationale for teachers might focus particularly on the need for TAPS and a well-aligned professional development system.

Sharing both practical (e.g., teachers need more support to implement evidence-based interventions) and data-based (e.g., too many students in the school continue to perform below grade level) reasons for using the SOPAA should be a succinct way of generating teachers' support, but the Lead Coordinator will likely benefit by also presenting an overall (summarized) rationale for why teachers should use and benefit from the SOPAA. This summary should include direct statements about why the Lead Coordinator *and* other school leaders (e.g., the principal, well-respected teachers) believe that the SOPAA will be beneficial. As noted in Chapter 9, the Lead Coordinator may be more likely to obtain widespread teacher support for the SOPAA if she clearly articulates personal support and support from key leaders in the school. Examples of supportive summary statements the Lead Coordinator may use are as follows:

- The TAPS process should help to streamline the school's and teachers' existing approach to instructional problem solving.
- The TAPS process helps to ensure comprehensive intervention development and documentation, as well as the necessary procedures for intervention monitoring and evaluation.
- The SOPAA model is multidisciplinary and involves input from numerous educators, and TAPS is more efficient in supporting teachers than other forms of instructional problem solving.
- Schoolwide data suggest that the school is not yet meeting the needs of all struggling learners, so current practices must be enhanced in order to improve students' learning outcomes.

In addition, sharing information about other advantages of the SOPAA (see Chapter 1) may also help the Lead Coordinator summarize a rationale for the SOPAA and generate teachers' support. Likewise, teachers may pose the types of questions we discussed in Chapter 1, so the Lead Coordinator may wish to address those same questions during the introductory presentation.

When and How Teachers Request Academic Support

We recommend that the aforementioned information be presented to teachers in no more than 15–30 minutes. Following the overview and rationale for the SOPAA and TAPS process, teachers then need to know what the TAPS process involves, starting with when and how to request support through the process, so teachers can follow the procedures as designed.

As described in Chapter 4, a teacher requests academic support when she (1) has a concern that a specific student is not performing at grade level in an academic area; (2) has at least some evidence (e.g., classroom assessment data, schoolwide assessment data, student work samples) that the student is performing below grade level; and (3) would likely benefit from intervention planning assistance (from the TAPS Teacher) and/or assistance with intervention implementation (e.g., the TAPS Teacher may assist with finding others in the school to help implement the intervention, monitoring the student's progress during intervention, and monitoring implementers' implementation integrity).

Also described in Chapter 4, a teacher requests academic support by completing the Request for TAPS Form (Appendix E). During the introductory presentation with teachers, we recommend that the Lead Coordinator provide teachers with a blank copy of the Request for TAPS Form and a sample copy of a completed Request for TAPS Form (e.g., see Figure 4.1 in Chapter 4, pp. 54–55). The Lead Coordinator should then illustrate for teachers (item by item) how to complete this form, ideally using an example of an actual TAPS case that was completed in her school. In doing so, the Lead Coordinator should specify the type of information a teacher should include in each item, the amount of detail expected for each item, the total time it will likely take teachers to complete the form (typically 15–20 minutes), and the process and expectations involved when a teacher submits evidence (when possible) related to the primary concern. For example, Items 3 and 5 of the Request for TAPS Form ask teachers to submit evidence of the primary concern, and teachers might be told that "evidence" includes student work samples, academic assessment reports, and/or other types of information deemed reasonable by the SOPAA facilitators. Overall, if teachers do not receive detailed instructions about how to use the Request for TAPS Form, they are unlikely to provide the information that TAPS Teachers will need to effectively prepare for the intervention planning meeting. This point should be highlighted for teachers while also briefly summarizing how the TAPS Teacher will prepare for the intervention planning meeting after receiving the teacher's request form (see Chapter 4 for the list of preparation steps).

The Lead Coordinator should also specify how she prefers teachers to submit the Request for TAPS Form and associated "evidence" documents related to Items 3 and 5 of the request form. Electronic submissions (e.g., via e-mail), hard-copy submissions (e.g., via a school mailbox), or a combination of the two (e.g., Request for TAPS Form by e-mail, associated evidence as a hard copy) are likely the most effective ways of receiving the teacher's information and request for support. Because the Lead Coordinator wants to ensure that the request for assistance process is completed accurately but is also convenient for teachers, she may want to solicit teacher comments and suggestions during the introductory presentation to determine the best way for teachers to complete and submit the information on the Request for TAPS Form. The Lead Coordinator should also emphasize that the teacher (rather than a regularly assigned teacher assistant) should be responsible for completing the request form, but that teachers may benefit by getting the teacher assistant's input about information requested on the form.

Last, because a teacher's primary concern should specify the subskill(s) the student struggles with most, the Lead Coordinator should decide whether it would be appropriate to describe the primary subskills of each main academic area during the introductory presentation. Chapter 12 lists and describes the subskills for each academic area. If the Lead Coordinator decides that presenting this information would be appropriate to include in the introductory presentation, then she should present it to further ensure that teachers complete the Request for TAPS Form accurately. If presenting the information about subskills is too much to cover during this presentation, the Lead Coordinator would probably be better off helping teachers understand core subskills of each academic area during the intervention planning meeting and/or during other aspects of the TAPS process. Alternatively, this information might be best presented during a specific SOPAA-related professional development workshop offered for teachers later in the school year.

The Intervention Planning Meeting

Similar to how she described the item-by-item process for teachers to complete the Request for TAPS Form, the Lead Coordinator should explain what will occur before and during the intervention planning meeting and how the intervention plan (and record) will develop as a result of that meeting. Chapter 5 details the process for the intervention planning meeting, and Appendix G and Figure 5.1 (pp. 68–69) show a blank and a sample filled-in TAPS Intervention Planning Form (IPF), respectively.

Just as she did for the Request for TAPS Form, the Lead Coordinator should provide teachers with sample copies of the IPF so that they can follow along during the Lead Coordinator's description of the form and the general process for completing it during the planning meeting. Because teachers will learn the IPF and planning meeting process best by actually experiencing it during a TAPS case, the level of detail needed to describe the IPF and planning meeting can be minimized, as long as the following points are highlighted:

1. The intervention planning meeting should take 20–30 minutes, depending on the complexity of the teacher's concern and the amount of information provided on the Request for TAPS Form.

2. The TAPS Teacher will likely need at least 5–10 school days from the time of receiving the teacher's request for support before actually meeting with the teacher for the intervention planning meeting. During this time the TAPS Teacher will prepare for the planning meeting, as mentioned in the previous section.

3. Within 3–7 days of receiving the Request for TAPS Form, the TAPS Teacher will plan to provide the teacher with a list of the most suitable intervention options, and the teacher can review those options if she chooses. The options will be discussed during the intervention planning meeting, where the teacher is also encouraged to suggest alternative intervention options.

4. A goal of the intervention planning meeting is to ensure that the classroom teacher has support from the TAPS Teacher (reflected by the entire TAPS process) and from one or more educators in the school who will sometimes assist the teacher by implementing the student's intervention program.

5. Unless a parent refers a child for a psychoeducational evaluation or there are other unique circumstances about the teacher's concern (e.g., a targeted skills observation suggests that the student would not likely benefit from a TAPS intervention plan), all academic concerns should result in an intervention program, implemented with integrity for a minimum number of weeks and sessions. This requirement for the intervention plan represents a minimal standard that must be followed before a student can be referred for psychoeducational assessment and possible classification with a disability. (As noted in Appendix I, Item 12, SOPAA facilitators and the school principal should ultimately determine the minimum amount of intervention implementation. In that appendix we recommend at least 6–7 weeks of intervention before having the summative review meeting).

When introducing these five points about intervention planning, the Lead Coordinator should emphasize that the goal of the planning meeting (and TAPS, more generally) is to select, implement, and evaluate an evidence-based intervention plan that should improve the student's learning in a way that should preclude classifying the student with a disability. That is, it must be clear for teachers that the TAPS process should be viewed as a means to improve student learning, not as a necessary process that ultimately leads to psychoeducational assessment and classification of a disability.

Intervention Follow-Up Meetings

The Lead Coordinator should also explain to teachers that there will be two main types of follow-up meetings after the IPF is developed during the planning meeting. Both types of follow-up meetings are detailed in Chapter 5, but we summarize the information here so that the Lead Coordinator can use this information when introducing the SOPAA to teachers.

The first type of follow-up meeting is brief (5–15 minutes) and allows the teacher and TAPS Teacher to (1) ensure that intervention implementation has started; (2) review the intervention plan and address any possible problems or concerns from all implementers; (3) determine whether the student's parent(s) provided any input or suggestions that should influence the originally designed intervention plan; and (4) obtain signatures on the original IPF from the teacher and TAPS Teacher, after they agree upon all parts of the intervention plan and make any necessary modifications. Assuming that the the intervention planning meeting results in a well-designed intervention plan that the teacher and TAPS Teacher support, the brief follow-up meeting should simply confirm that the plan is appropriate and allow the teacher and TAPS Teacher to make minor changes if needed.

The second type of follow-up meeting that teachers should know about is the periodic follow-up meeting. This type of meeting should occur once every 1–3 weeks and should usually last no more than 2–5 minutes. The purpose of these meetings are for the TAPS Teacher and implementer (e.g., classroom teacher, teacher assistant) to (1) ensure that all parts of the intervention plan are being implemented as intended, (2) quickly review intervention data and progress, (3) address any concerns or questions, and (4) determine whether to make any minor changes to the intervention plan (e.g., change the times of the intervention sessions, change the implementers' schedule to better facilitate the intervention plan).

Intervention Implementation Support and Monitoring

Teachers should know that the TAPS Teacher and all assistive school personnel who implement an intervention as part of the TAPS process will be observed periodically while implementing the intervention. This means that teachers, the TAPS Teacher, assistive school personnel, and school volunteers (when applicable) will be observed occasionally while implementing the intervention with a student. Observations will be conducted by those who know the intervention well, including the TAPS Teacher and possibly the classroom teacher. For convenience, the observations will probably occur immediately before or after some of the periodic follow-up meetings.

One primary goal in explaining the TAPS process to teachers is to convey that the process is designed to support their efforts toward assisting all struggling learners in the classroom.

Teachers should know that the purpose of the observations are to (1) ensure that the implementer follows the intervention procedures accurately (i.e., has strong *implementation integrity*), and (2) support the implementer if he or she has questions, concerns, or difficulties with implementing the intervention procedures. The importance of implementation integrity and providing feedback to implementers is well documented in the research, which further shows that implementation integrity and feedback are likely to improve intervention outcomes (e.g., Roach & Elliott, 2008). Also, if implementation integrity is poor and students do not show improvement at the end of the intervention process, educators cannot be sure whether lack of progress is due to poor alignment of the intervention procedures with the student's academic deficit, an otherwise ineffective intervention, failure to implement the intervention as it is designed, or a combination of these factors.

In this way, teachers should be aware that failure to implement an intervention with integrity substantially decreases their ability to interpret the effectiveness of the intervention plan, thereby decreasing the effectiveness of subsequent instructional problem solving. Given the importance of implementation support and monitoring, teachers must know that this process will be coordinated and discussed during the intervention planning meeting, and implementation integrity data will be included in the formal review of intervention effectiveness. Documenting implementation integrity data for a student receiving intervention helps educators support their educational decisions about that student.

Summative Review of Intervention Effectiveness

Similar to the review of the Request for TAPS Form and IPF, the Lead Coordinator will also want to present teachers with a blank version and a sample filled-in version of the Summative Review Form (SRF; Appendix L and Figure 5.3, respectively) and state that the SRF will be completed during a meeting with (at minimum) the teacher and TAPS Teacher. However, to avoid overwhelming teachers with too much information during the SOPAA introductory presentation, the description of the SRF and related procedures can be less detailed than the descriptions of the other two forms. Another reason for providing relatively less detail about this step of the TAPS process is that the TAPS Teacher will ultimately facilitate completion of the SRF (with the teacher present). Thus, during that time the teacher will have increased opportunity to understand the process for reviewing and documenting the effectiveness of the intervention plan. With this said, during the introductory presentation, there are some key points the Lead Coordinator should communicate to teachers about the review of intervention effectiveness. Specifically, the Lead Coordinator should list the following goals of the formal intervention review process:

1. Determine the extent to which the intervention was effective.
2. Determine the extent to which the intervention plan was carried out as planned, and (if applicable) how weaknesses in implementation of the plan possibly compromised intervention effectiveness.
3. Determine what should occur next (e.g., monitor the student to ensure that he maintains desired progress, continue with the same intervention plan for a specified number of additional weeks).
4. Determine the overall strengths and weaknesses of the intervention plan and determine whether a similar plan may (in the future) be a feasible option for students with the same academic deficit.

Last, teachers should know that the review of intervention effectiveness meeting can (and in most cases, should) include the student's parent(s).

Other Components Designed to Improve Student Learning through the SOPAA

During this part of the presentation the Lead Coordinator should briefly point out additional components of the SOPAA. Like the previously described components, these additional components should increase the school's capacity to implement the SOPAA and better assist struggling learners. Some of the following components may have been discussed in sufficient detail earlier in the Lead Coordinator's presentation, or may not be applicable for the Lead Coordinator's school at the time of the introductory presentation (given the school's incremental implementation plan), so the Lead Coordinator should choose which of the additional components to underscore.

1. Periodic staff development opportunities for teachers that focus specifically on instructional problem solving and evidence-based interventions for addressing academic difficulties.
2. Ongoing professional development activities the TAPS Teacher will complete to enhance her expertise in academic assessment and intervention.
3. Recruiting school volunteers, training them to use select intervention programs, and coordinating them to assist teachers with implementing students' intervention plans.

4. Using academic progress monitoring during TAPS to enhance instructional decision making for the student.
5. Conducting an end-of-year evaluation of the SOPAA and of the interventions used as part of the TAPS process (e.g., how was the SOPAA successful and unsuccessful, how was each academic intervention successful and unsuccessful?) so that the SOPAA and TAPS process can continue to improve in supporting teachers and students.

Last, based on the school's Year 1 implementation plan, in some cases it will be beneficial for the Lead Coordinator to mention to teachers that the full-scale SOPAA model will be implemented incrementally and therefore across multiple school years. Specifically, the Lead Coordinator may reiterate some of the key components and features of the SOPAA that will be implemented in the current school year and (if those show effectiveness within the school) the components that will be implemented in subsequent school years.

Summary of the Responsibilities for SOPAA Implementation

To conclude the presentation about the SOPAA and the TAPS process that occurs as part of the SOPAA, the Lead Coordinator should summarize the teacher's role and the role of each SOPAA facilitator. Each SOPAA facilitator should be designated by name so that all teachers know who in the school is facilitating the SOPAA and what each person will be doing, specifically. The role of each SOPAA facilitator can be summarized using the information about SOPAA roles in Chapter 2. Of course, depending on the overall SOPAA implementation plan for the current school year, some SOPAA components or features will not be implemented and some facilitators will have multiple roles (e.g., one person may function as the Lead Coordinator, the TAPS Math Teacher, and the TAPS Support Coordinator). SOPAA facilitators' roles should therefore be summarized accordingly.

A summary of the teacher's responsibilities should include the following, and is most directly connected to the TAPS process that occurs within the broader SOPAA implementation plan:

1. Identify students in the class who are struggling in an academic area and try to identify the key academic subskill(s) with which the students struggles most.
2. Attempt to gather evidence (e.g., assessment data, student work samples) that demonstrates the primary concern about the student.
3. Complete the Request for TAPS Form and submit it to the appropriate TAPS Teacher.
4. Meet with the TAPS Teacher to discuss the primary concern, develop an intervention plan, and meet again briefly to finalize the intervention plan.
5. Implement the intervention according to the intervention plan, ensuring good implementation integrity.
6. Meet with the TAPS Teacher periodically to discuss the effectiveness of the intervention plan.
7. Meet with the TAPS Teacher at the specified endpoint of the intervention plan in order to evaluate intervention effectiveness and discuss what to do next.

Of course, providing a handout summary of the TAPS process, the relevant SOPAA components, and teachers' expected role should help them understand the process while it is being presented and serve as a reference if they have questions about the SOPAA, TAPS, or their role.

Evaluating Teachers' Support of the SOPAA

Following the Lead Coordinator's presentation of the SOPAA core procedures, components, and rationale, she will then solicit teachers' initial feedback. The Lead Coordinator can choose to obtain initial teacher input about the SOPAA in multiple ways; Appendix S illustrates one type of brief survey that can be used.

Regardless of the method the Lead Coordinator uses to obtain teachers' initial input about the SOPAA, interpretation of their feedback should help the Lead Coordinator answer the following main questions:

1. What percentage of teachers appears supportive of the SOPAA (e.g., those who rate items as Agree or Strongly Agree in a survey such as the one shown in Appendix S)?
2. What percentage of teachers is supportive versus unsupportive of the overall SOPAA?
3. What aspects of the SOPAA and TAPS process do teachers perceive as most beneficial?
4. What aspects of the SOPAA and TAPS process do teachers perceive as least beneficial?

Once she knows the percentage of teachers who are unsupportive of the SOPAA and teachers' perceptions of the least beneficial aspects, the Lead Coordinator should consider how to address their concerns and potentially increase their support for the SOPAA. Ideally, if addressing teachers' concerns and strengthening their support is needed (e.g., if more than 20–25% of teachers appear unsupportive of the model), it should occur in collaboration with school principal, SOPAA co-facilitators, and perhaps key teachers in the school (including those who may have some concerns about implementation).

Some suggest that it is important to have at least 80% of educators show commitment to schoolwide change efforts (McIntosh et al., 2009), but this only reflects a good estimate.

Initiating Follow-Up with Teachers after the SOPAA Introductory Presentation

Approximately 2 weeks after the SOPAA introductory presentation, we recommend that the Lead Coordinator make brief contact with teachers (by e-mail or with a letter in the teacher's mailbox) to remind them that they should use the TAPS process to obtain support for students experiencing academic difficulties. The timing for this follow-up should be particularly appropriate because it is usually around this time (approximately 4–6 weeks into the school year) that teachers recognize or confirm that a student in the class may need some additional academic assistance. The follow-up contact should also reiterate the specific process teachers should use to request academic support. Finally, the Lead Coordinator may wish to summarize the initial feedback about the SOPAA that was obtained from teachers at the end of the introductory presentation, and if applicable, highlight any possible modifications that were made to the original plan based on teachers' feedback. Appendix T shows a follow-up letter that can be used.

OBTAINING AND SUSTAINING SUPPORT FOR THE SOPAA AND THE TAPS PROCESS

Teacher and principal support of the SOPAA is critical to its success and sustainability over multiple school years (McIntosh et al., 2009; Simmons et al., 2002). By following the recommendations described earlier in this chapter and those in Chapter 9, the Lead Coordinator will likely generate support from key leaders within the school and most classroom teachers. The recommendations below are designed to increase the support of those teachers who initially had little or no support for the SOPAA. The following suggestions should also help to sustain and perhaps increase the support of teachers and school leaders who initially supported the SOPAA.

Case-by-Case Reviews

One way to strengthen a teacher's support of the SOPAA is by specifically highlighting successes that occurred during a TAPS case. One indicator of success is the student's skill improvement in the academic area targeted during the TAPS process. For example, if the teacher requested academic support to improve a student's addition facts, the teacher and TAPS Math Teacher should have developed a measurement system to monitor the student's improvement in that academic area. Thus, by the end of the TAPS process, the teacher and TAPS Math Teacher would have obtained evidence showing whether the student improved in addition facts. If meaningful improvements occurred, the TAPS Math Teacher should highlight this for the teacher and discuss how the process helped to facilitate the academic improvements. Equally important, the TAPS Math Teacher should ask the classroom teacher what aspects of the process seemed most beneficial in improving the student's addition facts. Of course, if the TAPS Math Teacher is not also the Lead Coordinator, the Lead Coordinator should ensure that all TAPS Teachers are using these strategies of highlighting and discussing student successes as part of the process.

If the student in the above example did not demonstrate the level of academic improvement the classroom teacher hoped for, the TAPS Math Teacher might be able to highlight (if true) that although the student has not yet mastered his addition facts, his improvements during the TAPS process suggest that he will master this skill soon. If this is not true of the situation, the TAPS Math Teacher can still emphasize other possible successes achieved during the process. For instance, teachers (e.g., the classroom teacher, a teacher assistant) involved with the case may have learned how to implement a new evidence-based intervention for math facts and ultimately implemented it with implementation integrity above 90%. Other success stories might include effective coordination of multiple implementers to help address the teacher's academic concern about the student, a relatively quick but well-planned start to the implementation process (e.g., within 2–3 weeks of the teacher's request for academic support), and/or the knowledge that was obtained from using the TAPS process. For example, the classroom teacher and TAPS Teacher may have learned—and generated important documentation—that relatively intense intervention with the student did not address the academic deficit, which provides necessary evidence that the student may need more intensive academic support in this area. Of course, the teacher's effort throughout the process should also be emphasized and appreciated.

We are not suggesting that the TAPS Teacher should make false claims about success in the TAPS process, but if the process is implemented as designed, she should be able to identify many notable successes throughout the process. Pinpointing and discussing those successes should help the classroom teacher understand that using TAPS for instructional problem solving likely improves upon previous approaches commonly used in the school—a depiction that should increase the teacher's support and use of the process for assisting future struggling learners.

In addition to identifying successes in the TAPS process, however, it is also important for the TAPS Support Teacher and classroom teacher to identify and discuss aspects of the process that did not work and the possible reasons those aspects were unsuccessful. This discussion should ultimately lead to valuable feedback the TAPS Teacher can use to avoid similar unsuccessful situations in the future and should help the classroom teacher understand that the process will continually improve by discussing and acting upon its strengths and weaknesses. The SRF is designed to help TAPS Teachers facilitate conversation about successes and weaknesses in the process, but we also encourage the TAPS Teacher to discuss aspects of the process beyond what is written on the SRF, such as the topics just mentioned.

Summary Review of Multiple Students

Another way to increase and/or sustain teachers' support in the SOPAA and TAPS process is to summarize meaningful data related to the process and share those data with teachers two to four times per school year. For example, the Lead Coordinator may benefit by providing descriptive statistics regarding the average number of TAPS cases started each month, the amount of coordinated intervention services provided for students per month, and the percentage of students who showed improvement during the TAPS process. There are numerous sources of data that might be shared with teachers, and the Lead Coordinator should ultimately decide which data would be most meaningful to teachers in a particular school. For guidance, consider the list below, which, though not exhaustive, highlights several examples of data the Lead Coordinator may consider in a periodic report for teachers and the school principal. Depending on the specific type of data and the Lead Coordinator's decision regarding how often to provide a report, the sources of data noted below may be summarized quarterly, in the middle of the school year, or a similar equal-interval time frame.

1. The total number of TAPS cases started and completed. This might also be categorized according to grade level, severity of teacher's concern, number of requests for TAPS support per month, or similar types of dimensions.
2. The number (and perhaps type) of evidence-based intervention programs implemented to specifically address reading, math, and writing deficits.
3. The total number (and/or percentage) of students who received a rating of "Agree" or "Strongly Agree" on key items of the SRF, such as Item 1 (the intervention successfully addressed the concern) and Item 6 (intervention program procedures were implemented with integrity). Likewise, summarizing the frequency of other response options for these items (e.g., Neither Agree nor Disagree, Strongly Disagree) may also be valuable.
4. The average level of implementation integrity (see Item 5 of the SRF), which may be summarized according to (a) academic area (reading, math, and writing), (b) type of teacher (e.g., classroom teacher, teacher assistant, school volunteer), (c) specific intervention program; and/or (d) other relevant dimensions.
5. The total number (and/or percentage) of students who were supported with TAPS and eventually "moved up" in the categorization rubric of a commonly used assessment (e.g., moving from Some Risk to Low Risk or moving from Below Basic to Basic).
6. The total number (and/or percentage) of students who were supported with TAPS and later received a comprehensive assessment due to continued academic difficulties.
7. The total number (and/or percentage) of students who were supported with TAPS and were later classified with a learning disability.
8. The total (and/or average) amount of time each type of TAPS Teacher (i.e., reading, math, and writing) spent working on TAPS cases with classroom teachers. When meaningful, time could be categorized for any of the main functions of the TAPS Teacher (e.g., preparing for the intervention planning meeting, meeting with the teacher to develop an intervention plan, implementing interventions with students, conducting periodic follow-ups).

9. The total number of school volunteers and/or assistive school personnel who provided intervention services for students as part of the TAPS process.
10. The total (and/or average) number of hours (estimated or real time) that school volunteers and assistive school personnel implemented interventions for students as part of the TAPS process.
11. The total number of SOPAA or TAPS-related staff development workshops provided for classroom teachers, assistive personnel, and/or school volunteers (i.e., workshops developed or initiated because of the SOPAA).

We also note that the aforementioned data sources may be particularly and/or differentially important to different educators in the school (e.g., the principal, classroom teachers, special education teachers). For example, school principals may be particularly interested in how much time TAPS Teachers spend in their various activities, whereas such data may be less important for classroom teachers. Similarly, the Lead Coordinator should select sources of data that may demonstrate a trend of improvements that supports SOPAA implementation and continued use of TAPS. For instance, if the Lead Coordinator knows that the start of the school year will likely result in recruiting only a small number of school volunteers, but recruitment efforts will increase later in the school year, reporting such data early and later in the school year may help educators see progress as a result of implementing the SOPAA. Likewise, anticipating changes in the data across multiple school years may be equally important to consider, and when possible, reporting data from school years prior to SOPAA implementation may be useful in showing how the school's system of instructional problem solving is improving.

Overall, before SOPAA implementation begins, the Lead Coordinator should consider each of these factors when determining the types of data that will be most important to collect and later share with other educators in the school. Consulting with the principal, school leaders, and SOPAA co-facilitators should help the Lead Coordinator determine the best sources of data to reliably collect and later report as an ongoing evaluation of the SOPAA.

End-of-Year Summary of Teachers' Perceptions

Another way to potentially demonstrate and strengthen support of the SOPAA is to ask teachers to provide their impressions of the model and TAPS process at the end of the school year. Two general approaches to obtaining teachers' impressions are through the use of an anonymous survey of teachers who are involved with the TAPS process or focus group sessions with a small number of (e.g., four to eight) willing teachers involved with TAPS. This final section of the chapter focuses on using surveys, but much of the information that follows can also be applied to generating teacher input through focus group sessions.

An ongoing understanding of teachers' perspectives regarding the SOPAA model should help make the model more effective and sustainable.

Appendix U provides a sample survey the Lead Coordinator may use to gather input from teachers. As shown, the survey asks teachers to provide feedback across a range of SOPAA features and components, particularly TAPS, because teachers will be the most directly involved with this component. Note also, Appendix U is designed to evaluate TAPS and the SOPAA with regard to only one academic area per survey (see Item D at the beginning of the survey). This is done so that the Lead Coordinator can evaluate teachers' perceptions separately across different academic areas (reading, math, and writing), because the TAPS process in one academic area may be perceived as stronger or weaker than another, and if this is so, the information is useful to have. If the

Lead Coordinator uses Appendix U, she should write the respective academic area on the line in Item D before distributing the survey(s) to teachers.

The Lead Coordinator will likely obtain the most honest responses from teachers if their surveys are kept anonymous. As such, the Lead Coordinator should use procedures to protect teachers' anonymity and tell teachers that survey data will be viewed only by the principal and other SOPAA facilitators after all teachers' responses have been aggregated. Also, teachers might be asked to complete the survey and deliver it to someone unaffiliated with SOPAA implementation (e.g., an office assistant), and then that person can enter the survey data in a spreadsheet and send the spreadsheet to the Lead Coordinator.

After obtaining end-of-year data on teachers' perceptions, these data should be summarized and shared with educators in the school and perhaps with relevant school volunteers. To summarize the survey data, the Lead Coordinator may report average ratings per survey item and their associated ranges and standard deviations. These data can also be categorized according to teachers' grade level or some other dimension that may be meaningful to those interpreting the information. The Lead Coordinator should also provide a brief narrative description of the data to help educators interpret the average ratings across items, and she may even indicate how she and the school will "act" on the data. That is, the Lead Coordinator will ensure that those characteristics of the SOPAA remain if the ratings are high; the Lead Coordinator might specify how she and other school leaders hope to address those problem areas if the ratings are low.

Ultimately, input from an end-of-year teacher survey will help to facilitate additional communication with educators that allows them to (1) participate in the analysis and possible modification of the SOPAA, and (2) help them see (via a summary of the survey) how other educators in the school perceive the SOPAA and the TAPS process. Of course, teachers' survey data should also help the Lead Coordinator identify perceived strengths and weaknesses of the SOPAA and stimulate ideas for possible modifications to the short- or long-term implementation plan. Survey data may also highlight the need for additional resources that would make implementation more effective and/or feasible (e.g., the need for more intervention programs and/or trained personnel in an academic area). Finally, if teachers report liking many aspects of the SOPAA at the end of the school year, these data should help generate support from those teachers to integrate additional components of the SOPAA the following school year (depending on the school's incremental implementation plan) and/or generate support from new teachers who will become involved with the TAPS process.

CHAPTER 11

Using the SOPAA with Multidisciplinary Co-Facilitators

Adaptable and incremental implementation is Component 6 of the SOPAA. Whereas features of incremental implementation are described elsewhere throughout this book, this chapter focuses on how the SOPAA allows for adaptable implementation by multidisciplinary co-facilitators. Although the SOPAA can be successfully facilitated by only one educator within a school, this chapter describes several advantages of including two to four co-facilitators. Before discussing those advantages, we start the chapter by reviewing the six SOPAA components, reviewing the primary roles needed for SOPAA implementation, and then offering some suggestions for identifying co-facilitators. Next, we discuss how SOPAA co-facilitators would likely interact throughout implementation and how co-facilitation relates to the six SOPAA components.

Most of the content in this chapter is not described elsewhere in the book, but the reader will likely find some information that overlaps with content from another chapter. This occasional overlap in information is purposeful, and this chapter should help to clarify and consolidate how the SOPAA can be implemented successfully by more than one educator. Further, it is important to highlight that the descriptions and options for co-facilitation throughout this chapter are not exhaustive. That is, the Lead Coordinator or other SOPAA facilitators may find advantageous ways to co-facilitate SOPAA implementation beyond what is illustrated in this chapter. Of course, varied approaches to co-implementation are expected because different schools have unique characteristics, and the option for implementation flexibility represents a core feature of the SOPAA. Nonetheless, this chapter offers detailed descriptions of how to systematically implement the SOPAA with a multidisciplinary team of two to four educators.

REVIEW OF SOPAA COMPONENTS AND ROLES

Because this chapter frequently refers to the six SOPAA components and the five key roles needed for SOPAA implementation, the components and roles are listed below as a quick reference. Detailed information about the components and roles is available in Chapter 2. The six SOPAA components are as follows:

1. Targeted Assistance Program for Students (TAPS)
2. Assessment for instruction
3. Maximized intervention personnel and resources
4. Targeted professional development
5. Methods for communication and generating support
6. Adaptable and incremental implementation

The five roles needed for SOPAA implementation are as follows:

1. The SOPAA Lead Coordinator (i.e., the Lead Coordinator)
2. The TAPS Support Teacher in Reading (i.e., the TAPS Reading Teacher)
3. The TAPS Support Teacher in Math (i.e., the TAPS Math Teacher)
4. The TAPS Support Teacher in Writing (i.e., the TAPS Writing Teacher)
5. The TAPS Intervention Support Coordinator (i.e., the TAPS Support Coordinator)

As described elsewhere in the book (e.g., Chapter 3, Table 3.2, p. 34), some SOPAA roles and/or components may not be relevant in the early years of implementation if the model is implemented incrementally. For the purposes of describing SOPAA co-facilitation in this chapter, discussion and recommendations are based on a school's full-scale SOPAA implementation (i.e., all components and all roles are included in implementation). When a school's implementation is not at full-scale, the information from this chapter can be easily interpreted according to the school's specific implementation plan.

IDENTIFYING SOPAA CO-FACILITATORS

A primary goal of this book is to provide educators with a systems-level framework for addressing the needs of struggling learners, and in doing so, to offer detailed recommendations and resources that will allow educators to successfully use that framework (i.e., to successfully implement the SOPAA). As such, there are a variety of educators who could use this book, making use of existing knowledge and resources, to successfully fulfill any of the five SOPAA roles. Special education teachers, school psychologists, reading specialists, RTI coordinators, and interventionists, curriculum specialists, and speech–language pathologists are just some of the educators who might facilitate one or more SOPAA roles. Indeed, there are many others (e.g., social workers, ELL teachers, principals, assistant principals) who might also serve as a SOPAA co-facilitator. Therefore, given the framework, resources, and recommendations described throughout this book, as well as the unique roles and characteristics of educators in any particular school, there is no one type of educator that must fulfill any SOPAA role. However, to provide some guidance in identifying possible SOPAA co-facilitators, we offer some general considerations.

Of the five roles, the Lead Coordinator role and any of the three TAPS Teacher roles would be best facilitated by an educator who has at least some background experience (1) working with classroom teachers to address students' learning difficulties (e.g., facilitating school-based consultation), and (2) using and/or identifying evidence-based academic interventions and assessment methods. From our experience, a school psychologist or special education teacher, for example, often has these types of ongoing professional experiences.

An educator with particular experience using and/or identifying interventions in a particular academic area (e.g., math) would obviously be a good fit for the respective TAPS Teacher role (in this example, the TAPS Math Teacher). For instance, a school's reading specialist or Title I teacher may be a good candidate as the TAPS Reading Teacher. However, given the SOPAA professional development activities that occur for all TAPS Teachers and the resources provided throughout this book, a TAPS Teacher does not necessarily need to take on that role with extensive background knowledge or experience to be effective. To illustrate, the TAPS Writing Teacher may not begin this role with a strong background using and identifying writing interventions. Rather, someone who has background with reading interventions and assessment could likely become an effective TAPS Writing Teacher through the ongoing professional development activities and resources described in Chapter 7.

This role of TAPS Support Coordinator would be best facilitated by an educator who has at least some background experience (1) using and/or identifying evidence-based academic interventions, and (2) training other educators to use educational programs or procedures. In addition, having knowledge about recruiting, training, and/or managing schedules for school volunteers would also be advantageous for the person in this role. For each of the SOPAA roles, given the structured nature of the model, including facilitators who have strong organizational skills, time management, and attention to detail will also be beneficial.

Within a school, regardless of who fulfills each SOPAA role, we recommend that the SOPAA be facilitated by no more than four educators, and it is probably best facilitated by two or three educators. Table 11.1 provides some examples for how the full SOPAA model might be implemented by two, three, or four educators. The examples do not illustrate exactly how each educator *must* be assigned (e.g., with three facilitators, Educator 2, rather than Educator 3, could serve as the TAPS Support Coordinator), but the examples show a reasonable illustration of how to assign SOPAA roles depending on co-facilitation with two, three, or four educators. Note, however, it is necessary for the Lead Coordinator to also serve as a TAPS Teacher, as was discussed in Chapter 2.

HOW CO-FACILITATORS INTERACT DURING IMPLEMENTATION OF THE SOPAA

This section describes how the three basic types of SOPAA facilitators (i.e., the Lead Coordinator, TAPS Teachers, and the TAPS Support Coordinator) interact to successfully implement all components of the SOPAA. In describing the interactions, the relevant SOPAA component is also highlighted to strengthen the reader's understanding of how the SOPAA roles and components correspond to accomplish a comprehensive approach to instructional problem solving.

TABLE 11.1. Role Designation Examples for Co-Facilitating the SOPAA

	SOPAA role				
No. of facilitators	Lead Coordinator	TAPS Reading Teacher	TAPS Math Teacher	TAPS Writing Teacher	TAPS Support Coordinator
2	Educator 1	Educator 1	Educator 2	Educator 1	Educator 2
3	Educator 1	Educator 2	Educator 3	Educator 1	Educator 3
4	Educator 1	Educator 2	Educator 1	Educator 3	Educator 4

Note. The Lead Coordinator must always serve in that role and as at least one type of TAPS Teacher (i.e., a TAPS Reading, Math, and/or Writing Teacher).

Co-Facilitation Activities That Include All SOPAA Roles

In most collaborative interactions among the SOPAA co-facilitators, the Lead Coordinator serves as the person who oversees and coordinates each of the SOPAA roles and components. By having one person oversee all aspects of implementation, there is better assurance that roles and activities are aligned, systematic, and most resource efficient. With this said, the Lead Coordinator should function as a democratic leader, in which she solicits, respects, uses, and benefits from input from all other co-facilitators. Indeed, co-facilitation should work best when all facilitators co-learn and co-generate knowledge, but there is one person who helps ensure an integrated and consistent process for learning and implementation. There are seven primary ways that all SOPAA co-facilitators interact to strengthen implementation of the system; each is described below.

Although the Lead Coordinator oversees SOPAA implementation and aligns all of its components, co-facilitation of this model should embrace and benefit from the knowledge, experiences, and input of all co-facilitators.

Prepare for Initial SOPAA Meeting with the Principal

If the principal is not a SOPAA co-facilitator, communication with co-facilitators about the SOPAA (before discussing its possible implementation with the principal) may be advantageous because the Lead Coordinator and co-facilitator(s) can (1) collectively generate a more effective implementation plan and proposal for the principal (e.g., timelines and procedures for implementation); (2) better problem-solve possible implementation barriers or reservations the principal may raise about the proposal; and (3) orchestrate their efforts in communicating the proposal to the principal. As deemed appropriate by the SOPAA co-facilitators, the actual meeting with the principal might also be best achieved with all co-facilitators attending.

However, as described in Chapter 9, co-hosting and/or preparing for a meeting about the SOPAA before meeting with the principal should be done only if the co-facilitators are certain the principal would not view this as overstepping administrative hierarchies or co-facilitators' perceived professional roles. In most cases, however, co-planning for a meeting with the principal should be advantageous. Co-preparation for the initial SOPAA meeting with the principal is most related to Component 5 of the SOPAA.

Prepare and Host Introductory SOPAA Presentation with Teachers

Similar to working together to prepare for meeting with the principal to introduce the SOPAA, co-facilitators should also benefit from planning for and hosting the introductory presentation for teachers (described in Chapter 10). Beyond developing an integrated and consistent message for the teachers about SOPAA plans and procedures, co-presenting this information should also help teachers recognize that SOPAA implementation is supported by multiple educators within the school. Co-preparation and hosting the introductory presentation for teachers is most related to SOPAA Component 5.

Obtain and Sustain Teacher Support for the SOPAA

As described in Chapter 10, one job of the Lead Coordinator is to obtain and sustain teachers' support for the SOPAA and TAPS process, and one general approach to achieving this is by getting input from teachers about the SOPAA (including the TAPS process) and sharing relevant data with them. Chapter 10 describes three primary ways to accomplish this: facilitating case-by-case reviews with teachers, summarizing key data and sharing those data with teachers, and soliciting end-of-year teacher perceptions of the SOPAA.

Although supervised and managed by the Lead Coordinator, co-facilitation can occur with any of these three tasks. For example, TAPS Teachers will be involved with case-by-case reviews and should share the information obtained from those reviews with all SOPAA facilitators. Also, SOPAA facilitators can assist the Lead Coordinator with interpreting and summarizing SOPAA and TAPS data, collecting end-of-year teacher perceptions of the SOPAA, and preparing reports to share with teachers. Co-generation and co-interpreting this knowledge about the SOPAA and TAPS process should ultimately facilitate continued communication about, and improvements with, the process. Collectively, these activities are also most related to Component 5 of the SOPAA.

Meet Each Month to Plan, Review, and Organize

Related to communicating, obtaining input from teachers, and using input to improve the SOPAA and TAPS process (all relevant to Component 5), it is equally important that co-facilitators solicit and share input about their SOPAA and TAPS experiences with one another. As shown toward the bottom of Table 3.4 (the monthly time needed to facilitate the SOPAA; p. 41), the method for communication among all SOPAA facilitators should occur through a monthly meeting that lasts at least 1 hour and might include the school principal. Out of convenience, this monthly meeting might be scheduled to take place immediately before or after any monthly discussions among TAPS Teachers about their professional development activities (as described in Chapter 7).

During the monthly meeting to plan, review, and organize, the Lead Coordinator should guide and help to summarize the discussion, but each SOPAA facilitator should contribute what she views as strengths, weaknesses, and needs related to the SOPAA and TAPS process. Based on these collaborative meetings, the SOPAA should continually improve in a direction that is understood and endorsed by all facilitators. Because there may be minor or even major changes that evolve from these monthly meetings, as well as discussions about what is working well with the process, involving the principal in each meeting may further facilitate effective communication and reinforce the principal's support for the SOPAA.

Facilitate TAPS Cases to Address Student Learning Difficulties

Because we have described this process throughout this book, the reader should recognize how multiple educators can work collaboratively in their respective SOPAA roles to facilitate TAPS cases (Component 1 of the SOPAA). Later in this chapter we summarize these collaborative efforts among specific SOPAA roles. Here we want to highlight that TAPS cases are primarily facilitated through the SOPAA roles but almost always involve other educators in the school. For example, other educators will typically implement intervention programs selected for TAPS cases and may assist the TAPS Teacher with monitoring student progress and/or monitoring implementation integrity. The degree to which other educators are involved with these tasks is primarily discussed in Chapters 4 and 5.

Prepare and Deliver Workshops for Educators

Component 4 of the SOPAA involves a process for targeted professional development that helps educators improve their skills in addressing student learning difficulties. The professional development workshops that should occur with classroom teachers, assistive school personnel, and/or school volunteers are relevant here. Chapter 7 describes this aspect of professional development in depth (and Chapter 8 adds to the discussion as it relates to school volunteers), but here we highlight that all SOPAA facilitators can and should be involved with other educators' professional development activities. For example, multiple SOPAA facilitators can prepare and host one or more of the workshops that target SOPAA professional development areas for teachers or volunteers. Furthermore, although the Lead Coordinator should ultimately ensure a systematic plan for professional development workshops and continuity between them, other SOPAA facilitators should assist the Lead Coordinator with her planning and decision making. Much of this collaborative planning and decision making will occur during the initial planning stages of SOPAA implementation, as well as during some of the monthly planning meetings.

Acquire Needed Resources for SOPAA Implementation

Starting with the initial planning stages for SOPAA implementation and continuing throughout the incremental implementation process, all SOPAA facilitators should discuss the resources that are needed most to strengthen implementation. Although it may be the Lead Coordinator who ultimately determines which resources are needed at any given time, and communicates that information to the principal, the resources identified as needed should always reflect input from all SOPAA facilitators. For example, if any one facilitator cannot fulfill her SOPAA role because resources are unavailable, this shortcoming will likely have a negative impact on the entire SOPAA implementation process. Because each SOPAA component requires at least some material and/or time resources, acquiring resources for implementation is related to all SOPAA components.

Co-Facilitation between the Lead Coordinator and TAPS Teachers

As noted elsewhere, the Lead Coordinator must always serve as a TAPS Teacher for at least one academic area. This dual role thereby allows the Lead Coordinator appropriate knowledge and experience to work with other TAPS Teachers, with the primary goal of ensuring that all TAPS cases are handled as well as possible and are procedurally consistent for all TAPS Teachers. That is, although each TAPS Teacher will mange her cases independently from the Lead Coordinator, the Lead Coordinator essentially serves as the "lead" TAPS Teacher and should be available to other TAPS Teachers to assist them with problem solving and procedural questions that may arise. In addition, the Lead Coordinator helps to ensure quality and consistency across assessment and professional development activities that involve TAPS Teachers. This section highlights the three key areas in which the Lead Coordinator and TAPS Teachers work together.

Ensure That TAPS Cases Are Being Managed as Well as Possible

As we just noted, the Lead Coordinator works to ensure that all TAPS cases are managed well by each TAPS Teacher. For example, the Lead Coordinator aims to ensure that all TAPS Teachers are selecting the most appropriate intervention programs, monitoring student progress regularly and with valid measures, evaluating implementation integrity, and following all of the correct procedures for each case.

Typically, discussion of TAPS cases and questions or problems that arise should occur during the monthly planning meeting described previously. But when more immediate concerns or questions arise, the Lead Coordinator should communicate her willingness to assist the other TAPS Teachers before the monthly meeting, if necessary. Of course, the monthly meeting should also allow for group discussion among all TAPS Teachers about case problems, questions, or procedural issues. In this way, the TAPS team should work collaboratively to address problems or questions that arise about a particular case, but the Lead Coordinator should offer the final recommendation if group discussion does not lead to consensus. The collaboration between the Lead Coordinator and TAPS Teachers in this way is most related to Component 1 of the SOPAA.

Discuss Professional Development Activities

As a TAPS Teacher, the Lead Coordinator completes professional development activities in the same way that the other TAPS Teachers do. As such, the Lead Coordinator and TAPS Teachers collaborate by discussing their professional development, and the Lead Coordinator helps to ensure meaningful and (when appropriate) congruent professional development activities for all TAPS Teachers. Chapter 7 offers additional information about TAPS Teachers' and the Lead Coordinator's collaboration regarding professional development. As noted earlier, discussion about professional development activities may be best scheduled immediately before or after the monthly planning, review, and organization meeting. Collaboration between the Lead Coordinator and TAPS Teachers regarding professional development is related to Component 4 of the SOPAA.

Select, Plan, and Facilitate Schoolwide Benchmark Assessments

As described thoroughly in Chapter 6, an important component of the SOPAA (Component 2) is eventually having a schoolwide system of assessing all students—usually three times per year as part of a "benchmark" assessment (i.e., universal screening)—to help teachers determine whether students in their classrooms are having learning difficulties. Because the TAPS Teachers need to be knowledgeable about assessment (e.g., progress monitoring during TAPS cases), they should assist the Lead Coordinator with selecting, planning, and facilitating schoolwide benchmark assessments in reading and math.

In most schools, conducting schoolwide benchmark assessments requires a substantial amount of time. The Lead Coordinator and TAPS Teachers' facilitation of benchmark assessments does not mean that they are the *only* educators in the school who can administer the assessments and summarize the data. That is, many other educators in the school can assist with this process, including (but not limited to) the TAPS Support Coordinator and special education teachers. For example, other educators can assist with administering benchmark assessments with students, inputting student scores into data management software (e.g., Microsoft Excel), and preparing reports for teachers. Depending on educators' knowledge of the assessment, some may also be able to assist the Lead Coordinator and TAPS Teachers with interpreting students' assessment scores (e.g., identifying struggling learners). As long as the Lead Coordinator and TAPS Teachers oversee and manage the benchmark assessment process, having assistance from other educators is appropriate and usually very helpful.

Co-Facilitation between the Lead Coordinator and TAPS Support Coordinator

A primary set of responsibilities for the TAPS Support Coordinator is to recruit and train others (e.g., school volunteers, teacher assistants, and other assistive school personnel) to implement intervention programs for TAPS cases, as well as to summarize and communicate those individuals' availability to assist with these cases. Information about these responsibilities is also discussed in Chapters 5 and 8. Here we simply point out that the Lead Coordinator should ensure that the TAPS Support Coordinator is successfully fulfilling her responsibilities, and when possible, should help the TAPS Support Coordinator with these tasks. Given the relatively complex nature of these tasks and their importance in facilitating the SOPAA and TAPS systems, assistance and ongoing communication between the Lead Coordinator and the TAPS Support Coordinator should ensure maximizing of intervention personnel and resources (i.e., Component 3 of the SOPAA).

Co-Facilitation between TAPS Teachers and the TAPS Support Coordinator

To facilitate a TAPS case effectively, the TAPS Teacher will usually work with the TAPS Support Coordinator in multiple ways. In this section we describe how the two roles can effectively interact during a case and how the TAPS Teacher and TAPS Support Coordinator should utilize Appendices J and K, first mentioned in Chapter 5.

Monitor Implementation Integrity

As described in multiple chapters throughout this book, an important aspect of the TAPS process (Component 1 of the SOPAA) is monitoring and documenting the implementation integrity of the intervention program selected for students' intervention plans. Chapter 5 explains the importance of this task and also describes how the TAPS Teacher and TAPS Support Coordinator can each contribute to the task of monitoring implementation integrity. To facilitate the process, the TAPS Teacher and TAPS Support Coordinator can use Appendix J (Request for Information from the TAPS Support Coordinator). Details for using Appendix J appear later in this chapter.

Identify Educators Who Can Assist with Implementing an Intervention Program

As discussed in Chapter 5, the TAPS Teacher and TAPS Support Coordinator work together during a TAPS case to identify educators in the school who, in addition to the classroom teacher, can assist with implementing the selected intervention program. This process of identifying educators for intervention support is initiated by the TAPS Teacher using a form such as Appendix J and is later facilitated by the TAPS Support Coordinator using a form such as Appendix K. Through this process, the TAPS Support Coordinator ultimately works with the TAPS Teacher to maximize the performance of intervention personnel (Component 3 of the SOPAA) by identifying school volunteers (explained further in Chapter 8) and/or other educators in the school (e.g., teacher assistants) who can support a TAPS case.

In addition to using Appendices J and K to facilitate intervention support during a TAPS case, the TAPS Support Coordinator might also use a scheduling guide like the example shown in Figure 11.1. To maximize the benefit of this type of scheduling guide, the TAPS Support Coordinator should start entering teacher names and their availability on this table at the start of the school year and continue updating it when applicable (e.g., after more assistive personnel become available, after assistive personnel receive training in a new intervention program, when assistive personnel lose or reduce availability, when assistive personnel are assigned to a TAPS case). To determine the list of educators who could potentially provide intervention support, the TAPS Support Coordinator would likely work with the Lead Coordinator, the TAPS Teachers, the principal, and communicate directly with educators who could potentially offer support.

Because Figure 11.1 is only a sample scheduling tool the TAPS Support Coordinator might use, it is important to highlight that the teacher roles and intervention programs referenced below the table are only illustrative and certainly not exhaustive. Depending on the characteristics within

Academic Area: Reading

Teacher (and role)	Availability	Intervention Programs		Current TAPS cases (student name, times, location)	Notes
		Trained to use	Could probably learn quickly		
C. Charles (TA)	M–F 8:00–10:30	SPart; HELPS	HSprout	R. Jones; T, Th 9:00–9:30; Rm 206	Wants to assist 1-2 more TAPS cases
M. Dudley (RS)	M, W, F 2:00–3:30	SPart; L-Lrng; HSprout	HELPS		Has some difficulty implementing SPart
J. Ho (SL)	M 10:00–11:00 W 9:00–10:00	SPart; L-Lrng;	HELPS; HSprout	V. Ross; M 10:00–10:35; Rm 420	
J. Marr (SpEd)	T, Th 10:00–12:00 F 8:00–9:00	HELPS; L-Lrng	SPart; HSprout		Very experienced with HELPS
A. Ponte (SV)	W, F 8:00–10:30	HELPS		J. Martinez; W, F 8:15–8:30; Rm 317	Can increase hours on W if needed
S. Stevens (AT)	M 9:00–10:00 T 1:00–3:30	HSprout			

Abbreviation key. **Teacher roles:** AT, Art Teacher; GC, Guidance Counselor; PE, Physical Education Teacher; RS, Reading Specialist; SL, Speech–Language Pathologist; SP, School Psychologist; SpEd, Special Education Teacher; SV, School Volunteer; SW, Social Worker; TA, Teacher Assistant. **Intervention programs:** SPart, Sound Partners; HELPS, HELPS program; L-Lrng, Language for Learning; HSprout, Headsprout Reading Comprehension.

FIGURE 11.1. Sample scheduling guide for TAPS Support Coordinator to facilitate intervention support.

a given school, the intervention programs selected for use and the availability of different types of educators for intervention support will differ. Also, in this example we show a specific table for only one academic area (reading); the TAPS Support Coordinator may organize this information best by creating separate tables for each academic area. Also, this example shows six available assistive personnel. In some schools, fewer or more than six teachers may needed to best facilitate intervention support for TAPS cases.

The sample guide in Figure 11.1 also allows us to highlight four additional points about organizing and facilitating intervention support. First, educators listed in this organization guide should not include TAPS Teachers because they must *identify* intervention support for each case, not provide a high level of intervention implementation support for the case. Chapter 5 describes in detail how the TAPS Teacher will facilitate intervention support and only implement the intervention program on occasion. Second, using a guide like Figure 11.1 should also help the TAPS Support Coordinator and other SOPAA facilitators recognize possible gaps in the training and availability of support teachers. Recognizing such gaps may then result in targeted plans for professional development workshops and/or efforts to recruit additional educators for intervention support.

Third, all educators listed in the guide should know that the TAPS Support Coordinator will confirm each educator's availability and willingness to implement an intervention program before his or her name is given to the TAPS Teacher. This process should ultimately make the intervention support educator feel more comfortable about being listed on the scheduling guide and help ensure that the TAPS Teacher has a clear sense of who can actually provide intervention support. Fourth, when the TAPS Support Coordinator works to identify intervention support, she should first try to identify educators who are available and already trained to use the relevant intervention program(s). Only when no educators meet these criteria should the TAPS Support Coordinator identify educators who can probably learn the program quickly.

Collectively, Figure 11.1 and the associated recommendations should help the TAPS Support Coordinator develop an organized system for quickly identifying educators who can offer intervention support during a TAPS case. Although Figure 11.1 represents a sample form, the same or a similar form could be developed using standard word processing software.

Recruit and Train Others to Provide Implementation Support

In addition to the planned professional development workshops that should occur as part of SOPAA implementation, maximizing intervention personnel and resources (Component 3 of the SOPAA) sometimes requires case-by-case training of an intervention program before beginning a student's intervention plan. Options for case-by-case training are described in Chapter 5, but here we reiterate that such training can (and often should) occur through collaborative efforts between the TAPS Teacher and TAPS Support Coordinator. This is not to suggest that both educators must be involved with the training, but that communication between the two of them will help determine who would best facilitate training, given the circumstances of the TAPS case and each educator's availability. Once again, communication between the TAPS Teacher and TAPS Support Coordinator regarding case-by-case training is facilitated through the forms shown in Appendices J and K.

Communicate Using Appendices J and K

> **Like the other forms and appendices provided in this book, Appendices J and K are designed to assist the SOPAA facilitators with communication, implementation, and documentation.**

As stated above, communication about the three primary collaborative efforts between the TAPS Teacher and TAPS Support Coordinator can be initially (and sometimes fully) facilitated through the forms found in Appendices J and K. To illustrate, we now describe how the TAPS Teacher and TAPS Support Coordinator should use these forms for communication.

The TAPS Teacher initiates communication by completing the Request for Information from the TAPS Support Coordinator form (Appendix J; and see an example of this form when completed by the TAPS Teacher in Figure 5.2, p. 73). Completing this form should be straightforward: Complete the basic information at the top of the form (e.g., student name, academic subskill being targeted); list the intervention programs currently being considered for the TAPS case; and last, specify when the TAPS Support Coordinator should complete and return the request for information. We recommend that the TAPS Teacher submit this request for information form to the TAPS Support Coordinator at least 1 week before the intervention planning meeting, and request a response from the TAPS Support Coordinator at least 2 days before the intervention planning meeting. Important to note, the TAPS Teacher does not do anything with the portion of the form that states, "Questions for TAPS Support Coordinator." This portion is completed by the TAPS Support Coordinator.

Once the TAPS Support Coordinator receives the request for information form from the TAPS Teacher, she should complete the following steps.

1. Review the intervention programs listed, examine the predeveloped scheduling and organization guide (such as the sample guide in Figure 11.1), and identify all possible educators who could potentially provide intervention support based on their training. (Ideally, the TAPS Support Coordinator will identify at least three or four educators who already have training in each of the programs listed, but she may need to resort to identifying those who could probably learn the program quickly if there are not enough educators who have the relevant training.)

2. Communicate with each identified educator and ask if she (a) would be willing to implement the needed intervention program(s) for a TAPS case if needed; and (b) if the response is yes, confirm her availability and ask if she has any comments, questions, or concerns. Note, if approved by the principal, some assistive school personnel could be given specified times that they should maintain availability to support TAPS cases. Scheduling dedicated times to assist with TAPS will minimize the "confirmation check" of availability for assistive personnel.

3. For each educator willing to provide intervention support, complete the information on the Intervention Support Options Identified by the TAPS Support Coordinator (Appendix K). Specifically, indicate the name of each intervention program on the line provided, the educator who can potentially assist with implementation of that program, and the relevant information for each educator (e.g., role within school, experience implementing the program, availability). Ideally, two or three names will be listed for each intervention program.

4. Answer the questions posed on the request for information form given by the TAPS Teacher (Appendix J) by indicating availability and related information about being able to assist with training (if applicable) and monitoring implementation integrity.

5. Staple the completed forms together (i.e., Appendices J and K), write the day's date on the top of Appendix K, and return the stapled set of forms to the TAPS Teacher.

For TAPS Teachers and TAPS Support Coordinators who prefer to use an electronic version of Appendices J and K, the companion website *www.sopaaforschools.org* offers a downloadable electronic version of each form so that educators can type information directly into it.

In terms of identifying educators to implement intervention programs, the TAPS Support Coordinator should comment on Appendix K if the person is particularly good at implementing the program, has had difficulties with implementation, has been trained but may need additional follow-up training, and/or any other comment that may influence the TAPS Teacher's decision to select that educator to assist with the student's intervention plan. Also, when possible, it is most ideal to identify educators who can implement all (or at least more than one) of the intervention programs listed by the TAPS Teacher in Appendix J. Finally, if there are few educators who have experience with the listed intervention programs, the TAPS Support Coordinator may try to identify educators who have experience with intervention programs that are similar (e.g., same structure of implementation, same academic area or subskill). Identifying individuals with similar intervention experience should result in faster case-by-case training when needed.

Concluding Comments

There are numerous ways in which multidisciplinary educators within a school can co-facilitate the SOPAA. Summarized in Table 11.2, each of the aforementioned ways represents a thorough but certainly not exhaustive description of how co-facilitators can collaborate to implement the SOPAA effectively and efficiently. Next, we specify key reasons for co-facilitating the SOPAA.

ADVANTAGES OF CO-FACILITATING THE SOPAA

Co-facilitation is not necessary for SOPAA implementation, but doing so has several advantages. In this section we describe four primary categories of advantages

Most schools should recognize that there are many important advantages to co-facilitating the SOPAA model.

TABLE 11.2. Summary of SOPAA Co-Facilitation Activities According to SOPAA Roles and Components

SOPAA Facilitators according to role	Component 1: Targeted Assistance Program for Students (TAPS)	Component 2: Assessment for instruction	Component 3: Maximized intervention personnel and resources	Component 4: Targeted professional development	Component 5: Methods for communication and generating support
Lead Coordinator, all TAPS Teachers, and the TAPS Support Coordinator (all SOPAA roles)	• Facilitate TAPS cases to address student learning difficulties in reading, math, and writing		• Acquire needed resources for SOPAA implementation (ultimately related to all SOPAA components)	• Prepare and deliver workshops for educators in the school	• Prepare for initial SOPAA meeting with the principal • Prepare and host introductory SOPAA presentation with teachers • Obtain and sustain teacher support for the SOPAA • Meet each month to plan, review, and organize
Lead Coordinator and all TAPS Teachers	• Ensure that TAPS cases are being managed as best as possible	• Plan and facilitate schoolwide benchmark assessments (i.e., universal screenings)		• Discuss and plan professional development activities	
Lead Coordinator and the TAPS Support Coordinator			• Recruit, train, and organize intervention program implementers (e.g., assistive school personnel and school volunteers)		
All TAPS Teachers and the TAPS Support Coordinator	• Monitor implementation integrity during a TAPS case		• Identify educators who can assist with implementing an intervention program • Recruit and train others to provide implementation support		

Note. SOPAA Component 6 (adaptable and incremental implementation) is not listed in this table because the entire focus of Chapter 11 is a key feature of Component 6 (i.e., adaptable implementation using co-facilitators).

for co-facilitation. This list is not exhaustive, as schools will likely find many other advantages to co-facilitation.

Distributed Responsibilities Means Less Time for Each Facilitator

One relatively obvious advantage to co-facilitating the SOPAA is that multiple educators share the time needed for implementation. In Chapter 3 (Table 3.4, p. 41) we provide estimates for the amount of time needed by one SOPAA facilitator to process six TAPS cases per month when using the SOPAA at full scale. As shown, this caseload would require approximately 26–41 hours per month (approximately 6.5–10 hours per week). Devoting 6–10 hours per week to TAPS cases is probably manageable for some educators in a school, but by distributing responsibilities among co-facilitators, one can quickly understand how implementation could become even more feasible within a school.

For example, with an equal distribution of responsibilities and an assumption that requests for TAPS support would be relatively balanced across the academic areas, two SOPAA facilitators would each likely spend approximately 3.5–5 hours per week managing TAPS cases. Of course, these time estimates still reflect full-scale SOPAA implementation, so with incremental implementation occurring from more than one educator, the time needed per week decreases further. Collectively, this information should highlight that SOPAA implementation is manageable, but even more manageable if facilitated by more than one educator.

Multiple Perspectives Should Improve SOPAA Implementation Decisions

Although this book provides relatively detailed guidance for how to implement the SOPAA, it would be impossible to offer specific recommendations for each of the many factors that influence a school's functioning. Therefore, SOPAA facilitators will continually need to balance the recommendations and resources provided in this book with the characteristics and goals of their school. Decisions about SOPAA implementation can be successfully made by one individual, but multiple perspectives from two to four SOPAA facilitators (and possibly including the school principal) will likely result in stronger implementation and greater effectiveness in the school.

There are several decisions related to SOPAA implementation that would likely benefit from multiple (e.g., two to four co-facilitators') perspectives. For example, these include deciding the incremental implementation plan across multiple school years, the areas to target for classroom teachers' and TAPS Teachers' professional development, and the process for conducting schoolwide benchmark assessments. Likewise, complicated TAPS cases may be more successful if all TAPS Teachers have the opportunity to provide input (e.g., Goddard, Goddard, & Tschannen-Moran, 2007).

Note, however, we advocate here for multidisciplinary perspectives from educators who share a common and specific (1) role (i.e., a systems-level intervention facilitator), (2) level of expertise about academic interventions and assessment, and (3) understanding of SOPAA and TAPS implementation processes and components. In this way, a multidisciplinary SOPAA team adds unique perspectives and experiences, but all members work toward a common goal and according to a specific systems-level framework. As such, SOPAA co-facilitators generally differ from other types of instructional and/or intervention teams found in many schools, which may consist of educators with unique and important experiences, but highly varied roles, levels of expertise, and understandings about best practices for addressing student learning needs.

Multiple Facilitators Should Strengthen SOPAA Implementation Sustainability

Implementation sustainability and improvements are integral factors for any successful system (McIntosh et al., 2009; Simmons et al., 2002). One way in which the SOPAA is designed for sustainability and improvement is through adaptable and incremental implementation options (SOPAA Component 6). Incremental implementation ultimately requires early planning to ensure that implementation starts in a way that is feasible and meaningful for a school and gradually increases over subsequent school years to include additional classrooms, grade levels, academic areas, and/or SOPAA components. Chapter 3 describes various ways in which the SOPAA can be implemented incrementally, but here it is important to emphasize that (1) sustaining and strengthening implementation across school years is critical to the success of the SOPAA, and (2) features within the SOPAA system must be well designed and planned to prevent implementation from weakening or terminating.

In addition to having options for incremental implementation, threats to a weakening or failing SOPAA system are reduced through our suggested methods for (1) communication with, and generating support from, the school principal and classroom teachers (Component 5); (2) targeted professional development for classroom teachers and TAPS Teachers (Component 4); and (3) maximizing intervention personnel and resources (Component 3). Furthermore, including multiple facilitators within an integrated infrastructure also reduces the threat of a system failing (Adelman & Taylor, 2008), and is therefore a third advantage of co-facilitation.

For example, it is more likely that a relatively complex system will fail if it is entirely constructed and managed by one person because that one person may, for some reason (e.g., unexpected leave of absence, unexpected requirement to fulfill additional job responsibilities), no longer be able to coordinate and oversee the system with the same degree of effort. Such a situation would most likely result in the weakening and eventually termination of the system. On the other hand, with multiple co-facilitators, if one educator is unexpectedly limited in her time for the SOPAA work, her lost time could be more easily compensated through a shift in roles (e.g., a TAPS Teacher takes responsibility for the now time-compromised member of the team) or by recruiting a new SOPAA facilitator who is trained by the current team.

In addition, a team of co-facilitators should reduce the possible isolation and stress that may occur when only one educator tries to manage a relatively complex system for addressing students' learning difficulties. In other words, implementing a systems-level process will undoubtedly bring challenges and barriers, and having a small team of two to four educators to help work through those challenges should improve implementation decision making and decrease stressors associated with challenging work.

Other Potential Benefits of Collaborative Facilitation

Research and theory related to educators' collaboration within schools suggests a wide range of other potential benefits. For example, through collaboration, educators experience improved self-efficacy (Shachar & Shmuelevitz, 1997), pedagogical knowledge (Brownell, Yeager, Rennells, & Riley, 1997), attitudes toward teaching (Brownell et al.), and even student academic outcomes. For example, Goddard and colleagues (2007) found that teacher collaboration was positively related to academic achievement outcomes for fourth-grade students in both reading and math, confirming their hypothesis that when teachers collaborate, their shared knowledge and experiences can promote student learning. In short, the opportunity for professional discourse about school- and student-based challenges among educators has the potential to strengthen their unique knowledge and experiences, which in turn may positively influence self-efficacy, job satisfaction, and student outcomes.

To conclude this chapter, we offer some statements by Adelman and Taylor (2003) regarding the benefits and importance of collaboration among various stakeholders in producing meaningful and sustainable change. We appreciate these statements because, although "stakeholders" can be interpreted simply as those *leading* SOPAA implementation, the term can also be interpreted as including each of the educators involved with SOPAA implementation. In either case, we feel that the following statements reflect how authentic collaboration, a shared vision, and the motivation to *act* can coalesce and ignite the capacity to influence meaningful change.

> When a broad range of stakeholders are motivated to work together to sustain progress, they come up with more creative and effective strategies than any manual can prescribe. Thus, although concepts and procedures are invaluable guides, building a cadre of stakeholders who are motivationally ready and able to proceed is the first and foremost consideration. The necessary motivation comes from the desire to achieve better outcomes; it comes from hope and optimism about a vision for what is possible; it comes from the realization that working together is essential in accomplishing the vision; it comes from the realization that system changes are essential to working together effectively. And maintaining motivation for working together comes from valuing each partner's assets and contributions. (p. 6)

PART III

ADDITIONAL INFORMATION AND GUIDANCE

CHAPTER 12

Evidence-Based and Learner-Verified Intervention Programs in Reading, Mathematics, and Writing

In this chapter we describe intervention programs for learners who are struggling to master core curriculum objectives in reading, mathematics, and writing. By *intervention program* we mean intensive, supplemental curricula that teach the struggling learner what a good core curriculum fails to teach him or her. All of the intervention programs we recommend are either evidence-based or learner-verified. By *evidence-based* we mean that the program incorporates key ingredients that research has shown to be effective. By *learner-verified* we mean that research demonstrates that the program itself produces significant gains in student achievement compared to a control group of students who receive other interventions. More specifically, we use the term *learner-verified* to mean that at least two experimental or quasi-experimental research studies have been published in peer-reviewed journals and have shown evidence of effectiveness for the respective program. Although most learners will not need an intervention to supplement core curricula, 20% or more of students may need a daily block of time, usually 30 minutes, in addition to their daily core curriculum block, to maintain yearly progress (e.g., see Simmons et al., 2002).

The process of selecting core curricula is crucial to teachers' success with intervention plans. Core curricula inadequate in either (1) content or (2) evidence of effectiveness will necessitate more interventions to help all learners continue to make progress. Thus, large deficiencies in core curricula make it unrealistic to provide the number of necessary interventions. In this chapter we identify a few evidence-based core instructional programs at the beginning of each section on reading, math, and writing. We also provide content analyses of each subject, allowing schools to conduct an in-house evaluation of the core curricula. More general guidelines for evaluating core curricula also exist (e.g., Hughes & Dexter, 2011).

The National Institute for Literacy published a free booklet, *Using Research and Reason in Education* (Stanovich & Stanovich, 2003), to help teachers use scientifically based research to make curricular decisions.

Our content analyses can be used as guidelines for selecting intervention programs to assure that they include all instructional objectives in a given area of student deficiency. Intervention programs also need to be selected according to their empirical effectiveness. The U.S. Department of Education's "What Works Clearinghouse" (WWC; *www.whatworks.ed.gov*), as well as recent research funded by the Institute of Education Sciences (IES; *www.ies.ed.gov*), provide information validating the effectiveness of some intervention curricula. The National Center on Response to Intervention (2010) publishes a research chart validating the effectiveness of intervention curricula (*www.rti4success.org*). Johns Hopkins University School of Education's Center for Data Driven Reform in Education publishes a Best Evidence Encyclopedia (BEE) on its website, *www.bestevidence.org*, listing programs with moderate or strong research evidence. Simmons, Kame'enui, Beck, Brewer, and Fien (2007) have also published a guide to evaluating supplemental and intervention reading programs. However, none of the aforementioned resources is exhaustive. Research reported in the educational and psychological literature also describes evidence-based strategies and programs. In addition, it should be noted that rigorous research evaluating core and intervention programs in reading, math, and writing has only been conducted in earnest in the last decade. Most of the research has evaluated reading curricula. In the past few years, mathematics has become a focus of concern, but writing has barely been addressed. A comprehensive table of the core and intervention programs we review, and the URL of a starting point for further information about each program, is presented in Table 12.1.

We wish to highlight two additional points before beginning an extended discussion of content analyses, core curricula, and effective intervention programs in reading, math, and writing. First, due to space limitations we do not describe evidence-based strategies and procedures that are not components of available intervention programs. As we discussed in Chapter 3 in the section "Selecting Evidence-Based Intervention Programs to Use with TAPS," the research literature is full of excellent examples of nonmanualized instructional and intervention strategies that improve students' learning, but there are several good reasons for teachers to use the types of structured and manualized programs recommended in this chapter.

Second, our lists of recommended programs are not exhaustive. All programs listed are evidence-based, most are learner-verified, and we included several programs listed by the WWC, BEE, and/or the National Center on Response to Intervention guides for effective intervention programs. In addition, we selected programs that one or more of us have used with success, as we did not feel comfortable recommending programs with which we have no (or poor) experience. In short, we aimed to provide a range of suggestions for evidence-based and learner-verified intervention programs, acknowledging that other effective programs exist and that there is currently no list that should be considered "the" exhaustive list of the best intervention programs. Just to list some examples of other intervention programs that may be effective for teachers but we do not discuss in this chapter, teachers may find value in programs such as Ladders to Literacy, Fluency Formula, SpellRead, or Failure Free Reading.

READING

Evaluation of reading programs has received the most emphasis in the past decade. The U.S. Department of Education's National Reading Panel (National Reading Panel, 2000) describes five essential ingredients for reading programs in their Reading First mandate. A U.S. government-funded technical assistance center at the University of Oregon has developed a very practical tool for evaluating core reading programs (Simmons & Kame'enui, 2003). The International Reading Association (Dewitz et al., 2010) has also published a step-by-step workbook for evaluating core reading programs.

We use the five essential areas identified by Reading First as core targets in early reading instruction for our content analysis of reading: (1) phonemic awareness, (2) phonics, (3) fluency, (4)

TABLE 12.1. Core and Intervention Programs with Internet Links

Program listed by academic area	Website
	Reading
Core Programs	
Imagine It!	*www.imagineitreading.com/NA/ENG_US/index.php*
Read Well	*www.voyagerlearning.com/readwell/index.jsp*
Reading Mastery, Signature Edition	*www.mheonline.com/program/view/1/3/21/0076181936*
Scott Foresman Reading Street	*www.pearsonschool.com*
Phonemic awareness plus	
Earobics Connections	*www.earobics.com*
Earobics Foundations	*www.earobics.com*
Fast ForWord	*www.scilearn.com*
Lindamood Phonemic Sequencing Program (LiPS)	*www.ganderpublishing.com/lindamood-bell.html*
PALS Reading	*www.kc.vanderbilt.edu/pals*
Phonological Coding: Phonemic Awareness	*www.haughtonlearningcenter.com*
Rapid Automatic Naming	*www.haughtonlearningcenter.com*
Phonics plus	
Basic Elements	*www.morningsideacademy.org*
Corrective Reading	*www.mheonline.com/program/view/1/3/128/0076181804*
Headsprout Early Reading	*www.headsprout.com*
REWARDS	*www.soprislearning.com/REWARDS*
Sound Partners	*www.wri-edu.org/partners/sound-partners.htm*
Fluency	
Great Leaps	*www.greatleaps.com*
Helping Early Literacy with Practice Strategies (HELPS)	*www.helpsprogram.org*
Read Naturally	*www.readnaturally.com*
Vocabulary	
Language for Learning	*www.mheonline.com/program/view/1/2/194/0076181758/*
Language for Thinking	*www.mheonline.com/program/view/1/2/195/0076020495/*
Comprehension	
Headsprout Reading Comprehension	*www.headsprout.com*
Read to Achieve	*www.mheonline.com/program/view/1/1/139/0076234789*
Reading Success	*www.mheonline.com/program/view/1/2/141/0076185508*
	Mathematics
Core programs	
Math Expressions	*www.eduplace.com/math/mthexp/*
Math In Focus	*www.hmheducation.com/mathinfocus/index.php*
New Elementary Mathematics (Singapore Math)	*www.singaporemath.com*
Primary Mathematics (Singapore Math)	*www.singeaporemath.com*
Saxon Elementary School (Math / Saxon Math), as well as recent research funded	*http://saxonpublishers.hmhco.com/en/sxnm_home.htm*

(cont.)

TABLE 12.1. *(cont.)*

Program listed by academic area	Website
Intervention programs	
Accelerated Math	*www.relearn.com/am*
Hot Math Tutoring	*www.rti4success.org/chart/instructionTools/popups/hot_math_tutoring_info.html*
Morningside Math: Basic Number Skills (2 vols.)	*www.morningsideacademy.org*
Morningside Math: Math Facts (5 vols.)	*www.morningsideacademy.org*
Morningside Math: Teaching Computation Skills: Diagnostic and Prescriptive Instructional Sequences	*www.morningsideacademy.org*
Morningside Math Fluency: Whole Number Computation (4 vols.)	*www.morningsideacademy.org*
Number Rockets	*www.rti4success.org/chart/instructionTools/popups/number_rockets_info.html*
Number Worlds	*www.sranumberworlds.com/*
PALS Math	*www.kc.vanderbilt.edu/pals*
Pirate Math Individual Tutoring	*www.rti4success.org/chart/instructionTools/popups/pirate_math_individual_tutoring_info.html*
Solving Math Word Problems	*www.proedinc.com/customer/ProductView.aspx?ID=4145*
Talk Aloud Problem Solving (Problem Solving & Comprehension)	*www.whimbey.com/Books/books.htm*
Trans Math	*www.voyagerlearning.com/transmath/index.jsp*
	Writing
Intervention programs	
Essentials for Writing	*www.mheonline.com/program/view/1/3/227/0076234797*
Expressive Writing	*www.mheonline.com/program/view/4/2/210/0076020428*
High Performance Writing	*www.mheonline.com/program/view/1/2/199/0076026515*
REWARDS Writing: Sentence Refinement	*www.soprislearning.com*
Spelling Mastery	*www.mheonline.com/program/view/4/2/2215/0076105350*
Spelling Through Morphographs	*www.mheonline.com/program/view/1/2/214/0076021025*
SRSD for Writing Strategies	*www.peabody.vanderbilt.edu/Harris_Karen.xml*
Structured Supplemental Spelling	*www.iris.peabody.vanderbilt.edu/srs/chalcycle.htm*

vocabulary, and (5) comprehension (Armbruster, Lehr, & Osborn, 2006, 2011). However, because we sometimes broaden the five areas to include additional skills, we add the word *plus* to *phonemic awareness* and *phonics* to reflect our additions. Through our content analysis for each of these five essential skill areas of reading (i.e., the subskills), we identify more specific components that are relevant and necessary for a student to learn to become proficient in the respective subskill. We offer a summary list of each essential skill area and its components for reading, math, and writing on the companion website *www.sopaaforschools.org*.

Phonemic awareness is a prereading skill that involves the learner's fluency in manipulating phonemes, the smallest meaningful unit of sound in a language. Phonemic awareness skills include segmenting the sounds in words, blending of sounds into words, and discriminating between one sound and another. Our analysis of prereading behavior also includes three other components: (1) the alphabetic principle, or the understanding that letters represent the sounds in words; (2) rapid automatic naming—the fluent identification of pictures, letters, or numbers in succession; and (3) print conventions—such as identification of book covers, titles, words, pictures, and left-to-right progression from word to word and page to page. In keeping with Reading First terminology, we continue to use the term *phonemic awareness* in our discussion of essential areas for reading instruction but add the word *plus* in our taxonomy to reflect the fact that we subsume a broader set of skills than phonemic awareness under this category.

Phonics refers to a learner's skills in sounding out unfamiliar words by using the basic 44 sounds of the English language. Most words taught in the primary grades are of Anglo-Saxon origin and require only these basic principles of decoding. However, words taught from third grade onward usually require more complex decoding principles in addition to the 44 English sounds. A more accurate term for referring to the full array of decoding principles that students need to master is *word mechanics*, which includes the phonics skills taught in the primary grades and the structural analysis of longer word parts (e.g., prefixes, suffixes, and syllables in multisyllabic words). Multisyllabic word instruction usually begins in the third grade and continues through elementary and middle school. Good word mechanics instruction also includes a word fluency component: to be useful, words that have been initially sounded out need to be quickly remembered as "sight words." In keeping with Reading First terminology, we refer to the conglomerate of phonics, more complex structural analysis of words, and word fluency as *phonics plus*.

Reading fluency refers to a learner's skills in reading connected discourse or prose aloud, with proper pacing, rhythm, and intonation, and without decoding errors, word omissions, and word ending omissions. *Vocabulary* refers to knowledge of word meanings. *Comprehension* refers to learners' skills in demonstrating understanding of what they have read and in adjusting their approach to reading specific text according to their level of understanding.

Reading First's five essential areas are arranged in a loose progression. Often learners who are having difficulty learning the concepts, principles, or facts within a given area no longer have such troubles when the prerequisite components have been mastered. For example, mastery of phonemic awareness skills is a prerequisite for mastery of phonics and other word mechanics skills. Learners who cannot listen to and detect the difference between various spoken sounds have a great deal of difficulty with phonics, which assumes these skills. Likewise, difficulties with phonics make reading fluency improvement unlikely.

Mastery of phonics, fluent reading, and vocabulary all facilitate reading comprehension, as errors in answering reading comprehension questions may occur because the student cannot decode certain words, read the text fluently, and/or understand the meaning of words. As such, comprehension of text, for example, can be facilitated by preteaching relevant vocabulary or ensuring that the student is a fluent reader. Thus, a key point to emphasize here is that the problem that presents is not necessarily the problem to solve! Teachers should keep these relations in mind when determining effective interventions for their students. Simply intensifying instruction at the level of the observed problem is often far less effective than additional instruction and practice in its prerequisites (e.g., phonics, fluency, vocabulary) if they have not been mastered.

Core Reading Programs

Table 12.1 lists four evidence-based core reading programs and their respective web addresses that will allow readers to obtain additional information if needed. These programs were selected because they contain all the essential components we discuss in our content analysis of reading. In our opinion, none of the programs does a perfect job of teaching all of the components, but these four do a good job overall. Very few learner-verified types of empirical evidence exist for core reading programs, but many states have formed committees to conduct a detailed evaluation of these programs (e.g., Alabama Reading Initiative, 2007). Each of the core programs listed in Table 12.1 received one or more favorable reviews in state committees in the United States. Program effectiveness data may also be available from the publishers of these curricula.

Imagine It! (Bereiter et al., 2011), formerly Open Court, provides explicit instruction in each component and is particularly strong in phonemic awareness and phonics in grades K–2 and comprehension in grades 3–6. The scope and sequence are quite elaborate, going well beyond reading into all areas of language arts, thus requiring strong professional development to pick and choose what is most needed in a given classroom.

Read Well (Sprick, Howard, & Fidanque, 2008) offers explicit instructional programs for grades K–3 and is strong in phonemic awareness, phonics, fluency building, and error correction procedures; vocabulary and comprehension are less explicit.

Reading Mastery Signature Edition (Engelmann, 2008b) provides what we believe to be the most explicit instruction of the four programs and is particularly strong in phonemic awareness, phonics, and error correction procedures; vocabulary and comprehension are taught less explicitly in this program. Reading Mastery is currently the only reading program that has been learner-verified in published research (Adams & Engelmann, 1996).

Scott Foresman Reading Street (Afflerbach et al., 2011) provides explicit instruction in each component and a very teacher-friendly skills tracking feature and is particularly strong in comprehension. If–then statements inform teachers about when and how to supplement instruction, based upon student performance. We could find no other core reading programs that were adequate in all five components of reading.

Phonemic Awareness Plus

Phonemic awareness plus refers to four important prereading skills: phonemic awareness, the alphabetic principle, print conventions, and rapid automatic naming. As noted previously, *phonemic awareness* refers to fluency in segmenting the sounds in words, blending of sounds into words, and discriminating between one sound and another. Note that there is no visual component to phonemic awareness; it's all auditory. It is the best predictor of success in learning to read, better than intelligence and listening comprehension (Stanovich, 1993). Reading expert Marilyn Adams calls the discovery of the nature and importance of phonemic awareness to be the single greatest breakthrough in reading pedagogy in the 20th century (Adams, 1990a, 1990b, 1998). The skills associated with phonemic awareness (e.g., blending, segmenting) need to be fluent to prevent disruption of reading (Haughton & Freeman, 1999a, 1999b). Yet, a significant proportion of beginning readers have difficulty acquiring these skills and need explicit instruction in this area (Stanovich, 1986).

Along with phonemic awareness, we include three additional skills in our phonemic awareness plus reading component, primarily because these skills also are important early in the instructional sequence for reading. One of these is the *alphabetic principle*. Some children enter school without an understanding of the alphabetic principle (i.e., that spoken and heard sounds have corresponding letters in print), which then limits these students' ability to pair sounds with symbols. Although some would justifiably categorize the alphabetic principle as a phonics skill, we view this as a prereading skill and categorize it with phonemic awareness plus.

Another early literacy area is *conventions of print*. Many students have learned conventions of print (e.g., that English book pages, words in sentences, and sentences in paragraphs are sequenced from left to right). Other children, who often have not had the benefit of storybook reading at home or preschool, must be explicitly taught this type of knowledge. The final component, rapid automatic naming, is the ability to associate a letter or letter combination (or other graphic symbol, such as a number) with its spoken representation, and later quickly reproduce the spoken representation in response to the corresponding graphic symbol. A telltale sign of the need for explicit instruction in rapid automatic naming is a failure to learn from good instruction in phonics. Research has shown that practice in rapidly identifying pictures, letters, and numbers facilitates reading fluency, but the results are tentative (Kirby, Georgiou, Martinussen, & Parrila, 2010). A good core reading program includes instruction and practice in each of the four skills just described.

Effective Intervention Programs for Phonemic Awareness Plus

An excellent book about phonemic awareness is the classic by Marilyn Jager Adams, *Beginning to Read: Thinking and Learning about Print* (Adams, 1990a). This is a lengthy book (480 pages), but a 148-page summary book is also available (Adams, 1990b). A more recent book for teachers, *Phonemic Awareness in Young Children* (Adams, 1998) is also available. We now describe specific intervention programs designed to improve what we refer to as *phonemic awareness plus*.

Using evidence-based interventions for all skills and content areas is not only emphasized in national legislation, it is also the ethical thing to do.

Elizabeth Haughton has developed two programs for prereading behavior. One teaches phonemic awareness: *Phonological Coding: Phonemic Awareness* (Haughton & Freeman 1999a, 1999b), the other teaches, and is called, *Rapid Automatic Naming* (Haughton, 2002). Each program is contained in a manual that provides a placement test, semiscripted instruction, and finely "sliced" practice materials that lead students through a series of instructional tasks. *Phonological Coding* includes units on segmentation, blending, and auditory discrimination. Over 75 pages of practice materials span the progression of all letters and letter combinations and their positions in words—beginning, middle, and end. The program includes work with nonsense words. *Rapid Automatic Naming* includes many practice sheets with letters, numbers, and pictures of objects, along with tips for teaching students to improve their speed of seeing and naming them. Both programs have been tested with hundreds of learners and revised until they work (Haughton, 2002; Haughton & Freeman, 1999a, 1999b).

Five popular programs are backed with some positive evidence of effectiveness in improving phonemic awareness with severely deficient learners. *Lindamood Phonemic Sequencing* (LiPS) program (Lindamood & Lindamood, 2009), formerly *Auditory Discrimination in Depth*, also teaches students the lip, tongue, and mouth actions needed to produce specific sounds, and has been shown to be very effective (Sadoski & Willson, 2006; Truch, 1994). LiPS is best taught by a speech therapist, but with highly extensive training teachers can also implement the program. *Earobics Foundations* (Earobics, 1995b) is an interactive software program for Pre–K through first-grade learners with data showing its effectiveness (Cognitive Concepts, 2003; Gale, 2006). A similar effective program, *Earobics Connections* (Earobics, 1995a), is designed for second- and third-grade students, but may also be useful for older struggling learners (Cognitive Concepts, 2003). *Fast ForWord* (Scientific Learning, 1997) is another computer software program for K–3 learners with data showing its effectiveness (Merzenich et al., 1996; Schultz Center for Teaching and Leadership, 2009; Tallal et al., 1996).

In *PALS Reading* (Fuchs & Fuchs, 1994) researchers have developed an elaborate set of activities in key component skills of reading, including phonemic awareness, phonics, fluency, and comprehension. Teachers train their students in systematic methods of practicing and coaching each other, using scripted protocols. Reciprocal turn taking provides equal practice in both performing and tutoring. Materials are available for preschoolers through sixth grade. The program shows good evidence of effectiveness (Fuchs, Fuchs, Mathes, & Simmons, 1997).

Detailed information about each of the programs described above is presented in Table 12.2; Table 12.1 provides web addresses that should help readers obtain additional information about the intervention programs and core curricula we discuss throughout this chapter.

Phonics Plus

Phonics, more complex structural analysis of words, and sight word fluency are the gateway to expert reading. Our content analysis of phonics plus includes seven components (again, we insert the *plus* in our taxonomy to reflect the fact that we subsume a broader set of skills than what is typically defined as phonics). The seven components are:

1. Saying letter sounds and letter combination sounds (decoding)
2. Chaining sounds to say a one- to three-syllable word, without pausing between sounds (decoding)
3. Saying a one- to three-syllable word "on sight," without decoding (word fluency)
4. Chunking sounds into larger units by saying the sounds of word parts instead of sounding them out (decoding)
5. Chaining word parts to say a whole multisyllabic word (four or more syllables), without pausing between the units (decoding)
6. Accenting the correct word parts while sounding out multisyllabic words (decoding)
7. Saying multisyllabic words "on sight," without explicit decoding (word fluency)

An examination of state standards for reading indicates that core reading curricula in grades K–2 should include materials for teaching components 1–3. Core reading curricula in grades 4–8 should include materials for teaching components 4–7 (e.g., Alabama Reading Initiative, 2007).

Effective Intervention Programs for Phonics Plus

Several effective programs that focus on phonics plus are commercially available. For example, *Headsprout Early Reading* (Layng et al., 2002) is an Internet-based, cartoon-driven program for preschool and primary grade learners that has been empirically tested with thousands of learners and revised until it works (Huffstetter, King, Onwuegbuzie, Schneider, & Powell-Smith et al., 2010). *Sound Partners* (Vadasy et al., 2000) is a program for below-average K–3 learners that was designed for tutors, teacher aides, parents and guardians, and even older students with minimal training and teaching experience. In addition to its effectiveness in alphabetics, it may also have positive effects on reading fluency and comprehension (Jenkins, Peyton, Sanders, & Vadasy, 2004; Jenkins, Vadasy, Firebaugh, & Profilet, 2000; Vadasy, Jenkins, & Pool, 2000).

Corrective Reading (Engelmann, Johnson, Carnine, & Meyer, 2008) is a program that teaches all aspects of decoding words typically encountered through grade 5 for students with moderate-to-severe decoding problems (Vitale, Medland, Romance, & Weaver, 1993). *REWARDS* (Archer, Gleason, & Vachon, 2005) is a learner-verified program with 25 compact lessons focused on multisyllabic word mechanics (Archer, Gleason, & Vachon, 2003).

The latter two programs employ a technology developed by Engelmann and colleagues that they call *boardwork*. Boardwork is an effective and efficient medium (whether in core or intervention programs) for teaching all students word mechanics and other skills, such as number and computation skills, vocabulary, and punctuation. We mention boardwork for other academic skills throughout this chapter. The website for the Association for Direct Instruction (ADI; *www.adihome.org*) contains several videos that are displayed in a training sequence for mastering boardwork procedures (click on *Support Services > Movie Clips* to view them). The ADI also publishes a program, *Coaches Tool Kit*, which provides checklists for each direct instruction procedure, including boardwork (click on *ADI Store > Books* to access a description of it). The materials on the ADI website will be needed if teachers are to learn how to fully use boardwork procedures, but for added clarity, we provide a general summary of boardwork procedures that would be used to improve skills associated with phonics.

During boardwork for word mechanics, the teacher writes columns of words on a blackboard, white board, overhead projector transparency, or smart board. The words are usually contained within two to four columns, with about 10 words in each column. Efficiency and behavior management are increased when the words are written on the board before the lesson begins. The teacher begins the lesson by demonstrating a specific word mechanics sound, rule, or strategy and then leads students to imitate the process in unison after giving a signal, such as a finger snap, tap on the board, or clap. The teacher facilitates boardwork using the following sequence of procedures:

1. Teacher points to a word.
2. Teacher gives a hint or tip about the sound, rule, or strategy for saying the word.
3. Teacher says, "What word?" and gives a second or two of "think time" for students to consider the correct response.
4. Teacher says, "Get ready," and gives a signal. (Students should respond all together).
5. Teacher gives praise or corrections.
6. Teacher decreases the number of hints over time, requiring correct responses to new words of the same type, without assistance.

Many older learners with poor decoding skills attempt to memorize all the words in the English language as their strategy for coping with the mechanics of words. This coping strategy may initially appear to work, but eventually it fails; it is not realistic to memorize all the words in the English language! We have seen some corrective reading teachers attempt to remediate decoding strategies by using words that the learner has already memorized, allowing the learner to short-circuit instruction and simply say a memorized word instead of applying the strategies being presented. These teachers may think that they are teaching students to use decoding strategies once and for all, but they are not. Using nonsense words instead of real words will require poor decoders to learn and apply word attack rules and procedures instead of relying on memory. *Basic Elements* (Johnson, Casson, Street, Kevo, & Melroe, 2005) is a program that contains four parallel versions of word lists for all types of decoding subskills. All of the words are nonsense words, a strategy of demonstrated effectiveness (Fien et al., 2010). More details about each of the phonics plus programs are presented in Table 12.2.

Reading Fluency

The third component of Reading First is reading fluency: the accurate decoding, rhythm, intonation, and amount of text that, when read aloud, sounds like conversational speech. As such, fluency is a complicated, multifaceted process, often defined as the ability to read text with speed, accuracy, and proper expression (National Institute of Child Health and Human Development [NICHD], 2000).

Oral reading fluency is one of the strongest predictors of elementary students' overall reading ability, including reading comprehension and performance on end-of-grade tests (e.g., Daane,

TABLE 12.2. Intervention Programs for Reading

Name of program	Grade level	Primary content and activities	Possible secondary benefits[a]	Protocols for instruction	Lesson number	Lesson duration	TAs and volunteers can implement?[b]	Forms for monitoring implementation?	Progress monitoring materials?	Learner-verified?[c]
Intervention programs for phonemic awareness plus										
Earobics Connections	2–12	Phonemic awareness, phonics, language		Detailed teacher materials	Software; 6 interactive games, 600 levels	Varies	Yes, with training	Yes	Yes	Yes
Earobics Foundations	K–1	Phonemic awareness, phonics, language		Detailed teacher materials	Software; 5 interactive games, 300 levels	Teacher determines	Yes, with training	Yes	Yes	Yes
Fast ForWord	K–3	Alphabetic principle activities, phonemic awareness, fluency	Comprehension	Detailed teacher materials	Software, 5 days/week	30–100 minutes/day, 4–16 weeks	No	Yes	No	Yes
Lindamood Phonemic Sequencing Program (LiPS)	K–5	Segmenting, blending, tongue and mouth movements	Phonics	Detailed teacher materials	Not applicable	40–50 minutes	No	No	No	Yes
PALS Reading	K–6, 9–12	Phonemic awareness, phonics, fluency, vocabulary, retelling	Comprehension	Scripted lessons, detailed teacher materials	600 lessons, 3 times/week	30–35 minutes	Yes, with training	Yes	Yes	Yes
Phonological Coding: Phonemic Awareness	K–3	Segmenting, blending, auditory discrimination	Phonics	Detailed teacher materials	14 fluency units	20 minutes	No	Placement test and charts	Easily constructed	No

Rapid Automatic Naming	K–3	Rapid automatic naming (pictures, numbers, and letters to build speed)	Reading fluency	Detailed teacher materials	13 lessons	15 minutes	Yes, with training	Placement test and charts	Easily constructed	No
Intervention programs for phonics plus										
Basic Elements	K–8	Phonics, word identification	Reading fluency	Detailed teacher materials	56 practice lessons	30 minutes	No	Easily constructed	Easily constructed	No
Corrective Reading	4–12	Phonics, word mechanics	Reading fluency	Scripted lessons, detailed teacher materials	Up to 320 lessons	45 minutes	Yes, with training	Yes	Yes	Yes
Headsprout Early Reading	K–3	Phonemic awareness, phonics, word mechanics, fluency	Comprehension	Detailed teacher materials	80 Internet lessons	20 minutes	Yes, with training	Yes	Yes	Yes
Reading Boardwork Procedures	K–8	Alphabetic principle activities, phonics, vocabulary		Detailed teacher resources	Not applicable	Varies depending on teacher preference	No	No	No	Yes
REWARDS	5–12	Multisyllabic word mechanics	Reading fluency, spelling	Scripted lessons	25 lessons	30 minutes	No	Yes	No	No
Sound Partners	K–3	Phonemic awareness, phonics, fluency, spelling	Comprehension	Detailed tutoring manual	108 lessons	30 minutes, 4–5 sessions/ week	Yes, with training	Yes	Yes	Yes

(cont.)

TABLE 12.2. *(cont.)*

Name of program	Grade level	Primary content and activities	Possible secondary benefits[a]	Protocols for instruction	Lesson number	Lesson duration	TAs and volunteers can implement?[b]	Forms for monitoring implementation?	Progress monitoring materials?	Learner-verified?[c]
Intervention programs for reading fluency										
Great Leaps	K–5	Fluency (modeling, error correction, feedback with graphing), phonics	Phonics	Semiscripted lessons	100+ sequenced lessons and passages	10–12 minutes, 3–5 times/week	Yes, with training	No	Yes	No
HELPS (Helping Early Literacy with Practice Strategies)	1–8	Fluency (repeated reading, modeling, error correction, feedback with graphing, verbal cuing, goal setting), comprehension retell	Phonics, comprehension	Scripted lessons, detailed teacher materials	100 sequenced lessons and passages	10–12 minutes, 3 times/week	Yes, with training	Yes	Yes	Yes
Read Naturally	1–8	Fluency (modeling, repeated reading, feedback with graphing, goal setting), phonics (for early levels), comprehension questions	Writing, comprehension	Detailed teacher materials and computerized option for student-only learning	100+ sequenced lessons and passages within multiple levels and multiple programs	30–60 minutes, 3–5 times/week	Yes, with training, but may not be able to implement all steps	Yes	Yes	Yes

Intervention programs for vocabulary and comprehension

Headsprout Reading Comprehension	2.5–8	Comprehension skills	Content course performance	Internet lessons, detailed teacher materials	50 lessons	25 minutes	Yes, with training	Yes	Yes	No
Language for Learning, Language For Thinking	K–1	Language of instruction, background knowledge, common information, classification, problem solving	Comprehension	Scripted lessons, detailed teacher materials	150 lessons	30 minutes	Yes, with training	Yes	Yes	Yes
Read to Achieve	5–12	Comprehension skills, social studies, science, literature, vocabulary, study skills	Content course performance	Scripted lessons, detailed teacher materials	250 lessons	50 minutes	No	Yes	No	No
Reading Success	4–12	Comprehension skills	Vocabulary, content course performance	Semiscripted lessons, teacher materials	240 lessons	30 minutes	No	No	Yes	Yes

[a] Although the intervention program does not target the skills specified in this column, improvements in the targeted skills can have the specified secondary benefits.
[b] This column specifies whether school volunteers and/or teacher assistants (TAs) could reasonably implement the intervention program without ongoing support from a classroom teacher.
[c] All programs listed are evidence-based, incorporating key ingredients that research has shown to be effective. *Learner-verified* means that there are at least two experimental or quasi-experimental research studies, published in peer-reviewed journals, showing statistically significant improvement compared to control students or groups.

Campbell, Grigg, Goodman, & Oranje, 2005; McGlinchey & Hixson, 2004). Despite the importance of reading fluency, a study conducted using a large representative sample of U.S. fourth graders shows that approximately 40% of these students were nonfluent readers (Daane, Campbell, Grigg, Goodman, & Oranje, 2005). This finding is consistent with earlier arguments that reading fluency is often neglected in core reading curricula (Allington, 1983; Fuchs, Fuchs, Hosp, & Jenkins, 2001; Rayner, Foorman, Perfetti, Pesetsky, & Seidenberg, 2001). The finding is also consistent with a recent report by Carlisle (2010), who found that a sample of 88- second and third-grade teachers devoted, on average, approximately 4–5 minutes to fluency per language arts period, which was less than any of the other five areas that should be targeted during early reading instruction.

Meta-analyses evaluating research in reading fluency (Chard, Vaughn, & Tyler, 2002; Morgan & Sideridis, 2006; NICHD, 2000; Therrien, 2004) suggest that the following eight instructional components are most associated with beneficial outcomes for students' reading fluency, particularly when combined in a multicomponent instructional program: (1) model reading (i.e., having students listen to a more skilled reader read aloud—ideally an adult), (2) systematic error-correction procedures, (3) goal setting (i.e., practicing text until a predetermined performance criterion is met), (4) performance feedback combined with graphical displays of student progress, (5) use of systematic praise and a structured reward system for student reading behaviors and accomplishments, (6) verbal cues for students to read with fluency, (7) verbal cues for students to read for comprehension, and, most important, (8) repeated reading of ability-appropriate text aloud to an adult at least three times. Using these strategies to improve students' reading fluency has also been shown to improve other reading skills, including comprehension (Begeny & Martens, 2006b; NICHD, 2000; Therrien, 2004).

Effective Intervention Programs for Passage Reading Fluency

Table 12.2 lists three programs that focus upon building students' text (i.e., passage or story) reading fluency, and each program combines one or more of the eight aforementioned instructional strategies. Each program is designed for teacher–student, aide–student, or student–student pairs, though some can be adapted for whole-class or small-group instruction. Each program should be used as a supplement to a student's core reading curriculum.

Great Leaps (Mercer & Campbell, 1998; Mercer, Campbell, Miller, Mercer, & Lane, 2000) includes two primary sets of materials: a K–2 program intended primarily to benefit emerging readers, and a grade 3–5 program intended to improve low-performing students' reading skills. Great Leaps materials include a sequence of reading probes to target letter recognition and phonics, high-frequency words and phrases, and stories/passages. Although Great Leaps includes instructional strategies such as adult modeling of fluent reading and goal setting, it does not integrate repeated reading of text within an instructional session.

The *Helping Early Literacy with Practice Strategies (HELPS) Program* (Begeny, 2009) integrates each of the eight evidence-based instructional strategies shown to improve fluency and has been shown in multiple studies to improve elementary students' reading fluency and comprehension (e.g., Begeny, 2011; Begeny et al., 2010; Begeny, Mitchell, Whitehouse, Harris, & Stage, 2011). Although students generally work one on one with a teacher, teacher assistant, or school volunteer, there is also a small-group version of HELPS. HELPS can be accessed for free from the program website, along with the HELPS curriculum of 100 passages and all needed teacher-training materials.

Read Naturally (Ihnot, Mastoff, Gavin, & Hendrickson, 2001) combines books, audiotapes, and computer software with which students repeatedly read text and listen to an expert model reading fluently. During the program, a student primarily works on an independent basis and progresses through the program at his or her own pace. There is evidence showing positive effects for this program (e.g., Hasbrouck, Ihnot, & Rogers, 1999).

Vocabulary

Good core reading curricula include abundant vocabulary instruction. Vocabulary can be assessed and practiced in many ways. Here are six examples to illustrate the possibilities:

1. Given a word, learner provides a definition in his or her own words.
2. Given a word, learner provides a synonym.
3. Given a word and an example, learner says *correct* or *incorrect (discrimination).*
4. Given a word, learner provides an example.
5. Given a word underlined in a sentence, learner says *used correctly or not used correctly (discrimination).*
6. Given a mundane word underlined in a sentence, learner replaces it with a more specific word learned from his or her vocabulary instruction.

Isabel Beck and her colleagues (Beck, McKeown, & Kucan, 2002, 2008) describe a continuum of vocabulary knowledge that is relevant to vocabulary assessment as well as instruction. A learner may have (1) no knowledge of a word; (2) a general sense of a word, such as knowing it has a negative connotation; (3) narrow, context-bound knowledge, such as knowing the general definition of a word only when it is used in the context of a particular topic (e.g., sports, geography, weather); (4) full but only receptive knowledge of a word (i.e., knowing the word's meaning when seen or heard, but never using it in speech or writing); and (5) rich, receptive, and expressive word use. Good vocabulary instruction brings learners to level 5 mastery. Beck and her colleagues also discuss how to choose words to bring to mastery, describing three tiers of words. Examples are based upon a sixth-grade reading selection, *April's Mud,* by Carolyn Meyer (2002).

- Tier One: Words common to everyday conversation that rarely require explicit instruction (e.g., *concrete, normal, vegetarian*)
- Tier Two: High-frequency words for mature language users, including words found across a variety of domains (e.g., *converted, authentic, hippie, scraggly, philosophy*)
- Tier Three: Low-frequency words from highly specific domains (e.g., *horno, adobe*)

Beck and colleagues recommend that teachers choose words for vocabulary instruction mostly from Tier Two (Beck et al., 2002, 2008).

Effective Intervention Programs for Vocabulary

At the present time we do not know of any specific intervention programs that target vocabulary and are similar in structure to the other intervention programs listed throughout this chapter. As noted earlier, a good core reading curriculum, like the four described in Table 12.1, integrates several opportunities for students to build vocabulary. With this said, there are several supplemental instructional strategies teachers can use to strengthen students' vocabulary when the core curriculum is not effective enough in this area. For example, learners can practice vocabulary with flash card or worksheet definitions that have been generated with Beck's four approaches. A Precision Teaching approach (e.g., Binder, 1996; Johnson, 2008b; Johnson & Layng, 1992, 1994; Johnson &

Street, 2004, in press; Lindsley, 1990) asks students to practice vocabulary tasks (e.g., write or say word definitions, describe examples using target vocabulary words, discriminate between correct and incorrect word definitions) until performance occurs at a specified rate (e.g., Eshelman, 2004).

A strong vocabulary during school-age years also includes an understanding of the words and phrases a teacher uses during instruction. For example, if a teacher says during word mechanics instruction, "Break a word into segments that each contain a vowel sandwiched by consonants," a learner who does not know the meaning of *break*, *vowel*, *consonant*, or *sandwiched* will not learn the rule. Engelmann and colleagues have written two programs, *Language for Learning* (Engelmann & Osborn, 2008) and *Language for Thinking* (Engelmann & Osborn, 2002), to teach the basic vocabulary of instruction to preschoolers and learners in the primary grades. The effectiveness of both programs is substantiated by research (e.g., Benner et al., 2002; Waldron-Soler et al., 2002).

The *decontextualized language* used in books is foreign to many learners whose language background is mostly oral and contextualized, often including ELLs. In *contextualized language*, gestures and voice tones can replace words and clarify pronoun references. By their very nature, books do not use contextualized language. Many learners who live with nonreading adults need interventions in which teachers and peers "play dumb," requiring the speaker to vocalize his or her context. Games in which teachers and peers literally follow only the instructional words a learner speaks can show the speaker these deficiencies. For example, the learner can "teach" others how to make a peanut butter and jelly sandwich. If the learner says, "Use the knife to scoop some peanut butter" without first instructing them to remove the lid on the peanut butter jar, a few jabs of the knife on the jar top can provide very effective feedback. Describing directions to and from destinations within a school (e.g., library, cafeteria, principal's office) or neighborhood also works well (Benson & Cummins, 2000).

Comprehension

The fifth reading subskill in Reading First is reading comprehension, which contains four components:

1. Background knowledge
2. Retelling what was read
3. Comprehension skills
4. Self-monitoring of comprehension

Background Knowledge

Background knowledge is assumed knowledge not explicitly provided in text that is critical to understanding what is being read. There is no way around learning background knowledge. Good core reading programs teach background knowledge in preparation for the selections they provide. Before reading authentic materials such as novels and primary sources, teachers need to preteach relevant background knowledge (Engelmann, 2008a).

Retelling

Retelling what was read is a very good way to assess and practice text recall. Many states have added retelling tasks to their achievement tests. Students read a passage and retell details, in sequence. Benson and Cummins (2000) have written a useful handbook for teaching and assessing retelling, and one of us (K. J.) developed a Precision Teaching approach to retelling (available from the third author) based on their handbook. Good core reading curricula include practice in retelling. Some of our listed intervention programs also integrate retelling tasks. For example, PALS Reading provides peer-assisted practice and coaching opportunities for students to build retelling skills, and HELPS integrates a retelling component as part of its program to target reading fluency.

Comprehension Skills

Good core reading curricula explicitly teach 20–25 comprehension skills that a reader uses when making sense of text. Typical reading comprehension skills inventories include (1) comparing and contrasting; (2) identifying causes and effects; (3) stating the main idea and supporting details; (4) drawing conclusions; (5) making predictions and verifying, revising, or refining them; (6) paraphrasing; (7) summarizing; (8) stating the author's purpose; (9) stating the author's point of view and biases; (10) visualizing the author's descriptions; (11) identifying persuasive devices and propaganda; and (12) identifying inferences. Literary comprehension skills are taught in good core curricula and include, for example, identifying story elements (e.g., plot, setting, character, and theme) and identifying literary devices (e.g., simile, metaphor, mood, personification, foreshadowing, flashback, and exaggeration/hyperbole). Each of the core reading curricula identified earlier explicitly teach all or a subset of these skills.

Self-Monitoring of Comprehension

Good core reading curricula model and ask learners to practice self-monitoring of comprehension during reading, sometimes referred to as *reciprocal reading tactics*. Self-monitoring includes skills related to adjusting one's reading rate or seeking additional information from other sources, depending upon how well text is comprehended. Examples include asking oneself clarifying questions, confirming one's predictions, visualizing difficult descriptions, and periodically summarizing and otherwise checking for understanding. Two of the core curricula described earlier, *Imagine It!* and *Scott Foresman Reading Street*, do a particularly good job teaching self-monitoring of comprehension.

Effective Intervention Programs for Comprehension

A variety of intervention programs has proven effective with learners who struggle with reading comprehension, even though they do not have word mechanics problems that are interfering with comprehension. Two programs mentioned in our earlier discussion of vocabulary, *Language for Learning* (Engelmann & Osborn, 2008) and *Language for Thinking* (Engelmann & Osborn, 2002), teach the basic vocabulary of instruction essential for early reading comprehension. *Headsprout Reading Comprehension* (Layng et al., 2008) is an Internet-based, cartoon-driven program in basic comprehension concepts and skills. Words and passages range from mid-second to fifth grade. These programs and their evidence-based support are described in detail elsewhere (Layng, Sota, & Leon, in press; Leon, Layng, & Sota, in press; Sota, Leon, & Layng, in press). *Reading Success* (Dixon, Boorman, Conrad, Klau, & Muti, 2008) is a program that provides explicit instruction in many of the comprehension skills previously outlined, in a semiscripted, direct instruction format. The program has been learner-verified (Benson, Marchand-Martella, Martella, & Kolts, 2007; Reed, Marchand-Martella, Martella, & Kolts, 2007).

Read to Achieve: Comprehending Content Area Text (Marchand-Martella & Martella, 2010a) is a program that provides direct instruction lessons in comprehending social studies and science textbooks, with instruction in vocabulary, comprehension concepts, and SQ3R (survey, question, read, recite, review) study methods. Authentic two- to four-page text passages are used in each lesson for application (Marchand-Martella, 2010). A related program also provides direct instruction lessons in comprehending authentic literature passages (Marchand-Martella & Martella, 2010b). Further details about these programs are presented in Table 12.2.

MATHEMATICS

Our content analysis of mathematics includes five key areas (or subskills) that provide a math analogue to Reading First for elementary students:

1. Math tool skills, including early numeracy and math facts
2. Computation
3. Standard word problem solving
4. Complex problem solving
5. The language of math, including terminology of all math concepts and principles

In areas 1–4, each lower level facilitates learning and performance of each subsequent level. For example, fluency with math facts facilitates both mastery of computation algorithms and accuracy of computation performance. Mastery of computation skills facilitates accuracy of standard word problem-solving performance, which in turn facilitates competence in complex problem solving. As we noted in the section on reading, often students who are having trouble learning the concepts, principles, and facts within a given subskill no longer have such troubles when the other areas or subskills have been mastered. Again, the problem presented is not necessarily the problem to solve. For instance, errors in solving standard word problems may be eliminated by spending more time mastering computation algorithms or math facts. Finally, component 5, the language of math, facilitates understanding of the first four components. For example, learning the terms and how they are used in sentences, such as "Remember that the numerator goes above the fraction bar," facilitates efficient instructional language, as well as learning and remembering specific conventions and steps.

Our content analysis aligns with the U.S. Department of Education's National Mathematics Advisory Panel study (NMAP; 2008). The NMAP studied the available scientific evidence and concluded that in order to produce mathematically competent adults for the global market, educators must prepare students to be proficient in algebra—the gateway to later mathematical achievement—by the end of seventh grade. The NMAP's route to algebra proficiency includes five principal recommendations that significantly overlap with our Math First analog: (1) automatic recall of math facts; (2) fluency with whole numbers; (3) fluency with fractions, including decimals, percents, and negative fractions; (4) fluency with certain key aspects of geometry and measurement; and (5) simultaneous development of conceptual understanding, computation algorithms, and problem-solving application of those skills.

However, we highlight that our content analysis stands in stark contrast to the plethora of currently popular mathematics programs that concentrate on complex problem solving and do-it-yourself approaches to arithmetic in order for students to demonstrate quantitative thinking. Opposed to our content analysis, many popular mathematics programs also exclude a focus on having students master math tool skills and computation algorithms. Interestingly, a focus on having students master basic math skills and computations was much more evident in math programs produced before approximately 1985.

Core Mathematics Programs

Three core math programs provide a balanced (i.e., computation and problem-solving) approach and demonstrate moderate to substantial evidence for their effectiveness. *Saxon Math* (Larson, Hake, & Wrigley, 2011) advances in small steps from grades 2 to 12, uses a distributed approach to practice rather than a chapter approach, and reviews and assesses each topic frequently.

Available for elementary, middle school, and high school grades, a general approach to teaching known as Singapore Math strips the potpourri of math topics down to the essentials. *Primary Mathematics* (Kho, 2008) and its companion for upper elementary grades, *New Elementary Mathematics* (Sin, 2006), are the most authentic U.S. replications of the original Singapore program (*My Pals Are Here Maths*). The programs provide consistent, child-friendly, carefully guided sequences for each topic, from initially concrete pictorial presentations, to abstract verbal sequences. Also, they teach a model-drawing approach to all problem solving. In three rounds of international math achievement assessment conducted by the Trends in International Mathematics and Science Study (TIMSS; National Center on Education Statistics, 2007), students in Singapore have risen from 26th place to 1st place since they have been taught math from this program (Ministry of Education, Singapore, 1997, 2000, 2004). A much more extensive version, *Math in Focus* (Fong et al., 2011), has recently been published in the United States.

Math Expressions (Fuson, 2009) blends constructivist and teacher-directed approaches to teaching math for grades K–5, with students questioning and discussing math and also learning explicit math algorithms. Students are expected to explain and justify their work. A study sponsored by the Institute of Education Sciences (IES; Agodini et al., 2009) clearly shows the superiority of two programs for first graders, *Saxon Elementary School Math* and *Math Expressions*, as compared to two other programs found to be less effective: *Investigations in Number, Data, and Space* (Murray et al., 2008), and *Scott Foresman/Addison–Wesley Mathematics* (Charles, Crown, & Fennell, 2006).

Table 12.1 lists the recommended core math programs just described. It is worth noting, however, that many schools and districts use these core programs as intervention programs for students who do not learn effectively from the school's core math program. We now describe additional options for math intervention programs.

Effective Math Intervention Programs

We have organized math intervention programs according to the five subskills listed in our Math First analog to Reading First (see beginning of this section on mathematics).

Math Tool Skills

Math "tool skills" are skills that students need to perform fluently in order to be successful with more complex math skills (Johnson & Street, 2004; NMAP, 2008). Math tool skills include skills often referred to as *early numeracy* (Gersten et al., 2008; Griffin, 2005), such as quantity discrimination, rote counting, identifying missing numbers in a number line, one-to-one correspondence when counting objects and events, number reading, and number writing. Tool skills also include skills such as identifying place value and stating math facts. Tool skills taught in grades 5–8 include (1) determining least common denominators; (2) determining greatest common multiples; and (3) three-way conversions of fractions, decimals, and percents.

We believe that tool skills are not the context for teaching mathematical thinking, but rather they are the tools necessary for mathematical thinking. As such, the emphasis on teaching math tool skills is practice, practice, and more practice until automatic. Morningside Academy, a private, not-for-profit school that one of us (K. J.) founded over 30 years ago, has developed math tool skill practice programs that take a Precision Teaching approach (Binder, 1996; Johnson & Street, 2004, in press; Lindsley, 1990). Each tool skill is broken into small chunks and students practice in 1-minute timings until fluent with the skill.

In *Basic Number Skills* (Johnson, 2005) students develop fluency in reading numbers over successive chunks or "slices," beginning with one-digit numbers, then two-digit numbers, then one- and two-digit numbers combined, and so on, until students can read nine-digit numbers quickly and with ease by grade 6. The number of digits practiced in each grade corresponds to place values taught in each successive grade in the core curricula. Fluency in identifying place values is taught simultaneously with number reading. Fluency in writing numbers is most efficiently handled by practicing the 10 digits, 0–9.

Morningside Math Facts Fluency (Johnson, 2008a) adopts a conceptual approach to math facts, teaching number families inherent in complementary operations. By *math facts* we refer to simple solutions that should be memorized, not computed. Math facts are usually presented in tables for each operation. The addition math facts table includes numbers 1–10 added to each other, yielding sums to 20. The subtraction math facts table includes the inverse. The multiplication table includes numbers 1–10 multiplied by each other. Division math facts include the inverse, for a total of 100 math facts across the four operations.

Thus, the addition and subtraction number family 4, 5, 9 contains two addition facts ($4 + 5 = 9$, $5 + 4 = 9$) and two subtraction facts ($9 - 4 = 5$, $9 - 5 = 4$). Multiplication and division families operate the same way (e.g., 7, 9, 63), with two multiplication and two division facts. By learning a number family instead of four isolated facts commonly learned in "fact tables," memorization is reduced by 75%. Students practice math facts until they can identify the missing third number in math fact tasks (e.g., 4__9) at a rate of 80 to 100 missing numbers per minute. Students end with a final exercise in which they practice with worksheets that contain math facts presented in the traditional manner: vertically with symbols. Hundreds of individual graphs of student performance demonstrate that hundreds of students at Morningside Academy have mastered number reading and writing and math facts with these programs.

Published research demonstrates the effectiveness of two other math tool skill programs. The first, called *Number Rockets* (Fuchs et al., 2005), is a small-group tutoring program that uses concrete objects to promote conceptual learning of (1) reading and writing numbers; (2) more, less, and equal quantities; (3) place value; (4) writing number sentences; and (5) addition–subtraction math facts and early computation. Research demonstrates its effectiveness (Fuchs et al., 2005). The second program, an extension of the PALS Reading program described earlier, uses peer practice and reciprocal coaching in key tool skills in math and is called *PALS Math*. It is similarly effective in improving early math skills (Fuchs, Fuchs, Yazdian, & Powell, 2002; Calhoun & Fuchs, 2003).

Engelmann's *boardwork* method (*www.adihome.org*), which we described for teaching phonics and other word mechanics, is another efficient way to teach math tool skills. For example, in teaching number category names, the teacher can present two or three+ columns of whole numbers, proper fractions, improper fractions, and mixed numbers, with about 10 numbers in each column (e.g., 6, $\frac{3}{4}$, $5\frac{1}{2}$, $1\frac{7}{6}$, $2\frac{2}{3}$). The teacher demonstrates rules and how to apply them in identifying number category names, then asks students to repeat and apply the rules on signal, all together. The teacher does this with numbers until the students are 100% accurate. Following instruction, the teacher provides students with independent opportunities to practice these skills to fluency with worksheets.

Number Worlds (see Griffin, 2003, 2004) is an elementary math curriculum that can also be used as an intervention program for struggling students. This program has been in development for almost 20 years and aims to teach students basic math concepts and skills, improve students' number sense, and provide students with opportunities to communicate about math both in writing and orally. Each of the aforementioned programs, as well as the other math intervention programs described below, is detailed in Table 12.3.

Computation Skills

Computation refers to a student's ability to use standard algorithms for adding columns of numbers, subtracting columns of numbers (with regrouping), and computing long multiplication and long division problems. Computation skills also include mastery of these four operations with whole numbers, fractions, decimals, and simple percents, as well as standard algorithms for solving ratios and equations. As with tool skills, we agree with the NMAP (National Mathematics Advisory Panel, 2008) that computation algorithms are the tools, not the context, for teaching mathematical thinking.

Engelmann's *boardwork* method is also an efficient way to teach computation skills for small groups of students. For example, following instruction in adding zeros as placeholders when completing a long multiplication problem, the teacher may write a problem on the board that includes only one zero when multiplying by the hundreds column. The teacher says, "Someone completed a (long) multiplication problem like this. Did they do it correctly?" The job of the students is to find the errors. The teacher provides practice with corrective feedback until students can perform accurately.

We have not located any research or evidence-based intervention programs that focus specifically on instruction of computation algorithms, but all of the effective core math programs described earlier contain well-designed lessons for teaching computation skills. Also, PALS Math for second through sixth grade includes peer-assisted activities for computation.

Like math tool skills, computation proficiency requires practice, practice, and more practice. In a series of six Morningside math computation practice programs (Johnson & Casson, 2005a, 2005b; Johnson & Melroe, 2006a, 2006b, 2009, 2011), students practice more than 200 arithmetic subskills with whole numbers, fractions, and decimals in 5-minute timings. For example, subtraction computation includes 18 subskills, such as two-digit number minus one- or two-digit number, regrouping from 10's to 1's; five-digit number minus four-digit number, regrouping 100's to 10's; three-digit number minus two- or three-digit number, regrouping 10's to 1's, zero in 1's place; multidigit number minus multidigit number with three or four consecutive zeros. The programs also contain diagnostic tests to check for deficient skills in older students.

Standard Word Problem Solving

Problem solving is usually approached as "strategy instruction," which is typically too general for teaching students to learn how to solve word problems. For example, one current math text provides the following general "strategy" for solving word problems:

1. Understand what the question is asking.
2. Find the information given that helps you answer the question.
3. Choose the correct operation.
4. Estimate the answer.
5. Solve the problem.

TABLE 12.3. Intervention Programs for Mathematics

Name of program	Grade level	Primary content and activities	Possible secondary benefits[a]	Protocols for instruction	Lesson number	Lesson duration	TAs and volunteers can implement?[b]	Forms for monitoring implementation?	Progress monitoring materials?	Learner-verified?[c]
Accelerated Math	1–12	Comprehensive standard curriculum		Detailed teacher materials and resources for each grade level	75–300 objectives per grade level	Varies	No	Yes	Yes	Yes
Hot Math Tutoring	3–6	Addition–subtraction word problems		Detailed teacher materials	39 lessons 3 times/week, 13 weeks	30 minutes	Yes, with training	Yes	No	Yes
Math Boardwork Procedures	K–8	Tool skills, computation skills, standard word problem solving		Detailed teacher resources	Not applicable	Varies depending on teacher preference	No	No	No	No
Morningside Math: Basic Number Skills (2 vols.)	K–6	Tool skills: number reading and writing, through nine digits		Teacher materials	10 lessons	20 minutes	Yes, with training	No	Easily constructed	No
Morningside Math: Math Facts (5 vols.)	1–8	Math facts	Computation	Detailed teacher materials	32 lessons	20 minutes	Yes, with training	No	Easily constructed	No

Morningside Math: Teaching Computation Skills: Diagnostic and Prescriptive Instructional Sequences (9 vols.)	4–12	18 addition lessons, 20 subtraction lessons, 16 multiplication lessons, 15 division lessons, 51 fraction lessons, 23 decimal lessons	Problem solving	Teacher materials	143 lessons	40 minutes	Yes, with training	No	Easily constructed	No
Morningside Math Fluency: Whole Number Computation (4 vols.)	4–12	15 addition–subtraction lessons, 18 multiplication–division lessons	Problem solving	Detailed teacher materials	33 lessons	20 minutes	Yes, with training	No	Easily constructed	No
Number Rockets	1–3	Number reading and writing, more–less–equal, place value, math facts, computation	Computation	Detailed teacher materials	17 lessons	40 minutes	Yes, with training	Yes	Yes	Yes
Number Worlds	K–8	Conceptual knowledge, number sense, whole number operations		Detailed teacher materials	Varies by grade	Varies (~15–60 minutes)	Yes, with training	No	Yes	No
PALS Math (Peer Assisted Learning Strategies)	K–6	Standard curriculum		Scripted lessons, detailed teacher materials	14–16 for younger grades, several for older grades	30 minutes	No	No	Yes	Yes

(cont.)

TABLE 12.3. *(cont.)*

Name of program	Grade level	Primary content and activities	Possible secondary benefits[a]	Protocols for instruction	Lesson number	Lesson duration	TAs and volunteers can implement?[b]	Forms for monitoring implementation?	Progress monitoring materials?	Learner-verified?[c]
Pirate Math Individual Tutoring	3–6	Addition–subtraction word problems, computation		Detailed teacher materials	48 lessons 3 times/week, 16 weeks	30 minutes	Yes, with training	Yes	No	Yes
Solving Math Word Problems	3–8 6–8	Vol. 1: Addition and subtraction word problem solving Vol. 2: Multiplication and division word problem solving	Complex problem solving	Scripted lessons, detailed teacher materials	Vol. 1: 5 units, 21 lessons Vol. 2: 3 units, 13 lessons	50–60 minutes	No	No	Yes	Yes
Trans Math	7–12	Whole numbers, factors, fractions, decimals, percents, algebraic expressions, number patterns, computation, and problem solving		Detailed teacher materials	28 units	55 minutes	No	Yes	Yes	Yes

[a] Although the intervention program does not target the skills specified in this column, improvements in the targeted skills can have the specified secondary benefits.
[b] This column specifies whether school volunteers and/or teacher assistants (TAs) could reasonably implement the intervention program without ongoing support from a classroom teacher.
[c] All programs listed are evidence-based, incorporating key ingredients that research has shown to be effective. *Learner-verified* means that there are at least two experimental or quasi-experimental research studies, published in peer-reviewed journals, showing statistically significant improvement compared to control students or groups.

If students can already solve word problems correctly, heuristics such as these may serve as general prompts to be orderly about their work, but they do not help students learn *how to* solve word problems. Research has demonstrated that teaching principle-applying strategies at a procedural level is much more effective than general strategy instruction (Montague & Jitendra, 2006; Prawatt, 1989).

Problem solving can be divided into two types: standard word problems, with identifiable principles or rules that can be learned and applied, and more complex problem solving that requires unique solution sets combining more basic strategies in new ways. Standard word problems are written scenarios, usually 20–80 words in length, that require addition, subtraction, multiplication, and/or division of whole numbers, fractions, decimals, or simple percentages. Morningside Academy has developed rules for writing simple three-term equations with one unknown for nine types of standard word problems. For example, here is a second-grade problem requiring addition and subtraction.

> After Sue found 3 leaves, she had 7 leaves in all. How many leaves did Sue have before she found the 3?

To solve it, students learn that the first position in the equation includes a fact from the "beginning of the story," the second position includes a fact from the "middle of the story," and the final position includes a fact from the "end of the story." Since they don't know how many leaves Ann found in the beginning of the story, the write an x. They know that in the middle of the story she found 3 leaves, so they write a 3. They know that at the end of the story she had 7 leaves in all, so they write a 7 after an equals sign. Students also learn that this is a *joining* problem, not a *separating* problem; so they write an addition sign after the first position, not a subtraction sign. Thus, the final equation is $x + 3 = 7, x = 4$. Standard word problems may also include distracters (i.e., quantitative information that is not relevant to the solution). Students should learn to discriminate critical information from distracters as they learn to solve these problems. Standard word problems may also involve money, pictures, charts, or figures.

Research demonstrates the effectiveness of three standard word problem intervention programs. *Hot Math Tutoring* (Fuchs & Fuchs, 2002b) is a learner-verified program for third graders (Fuchs et al., 2008), but may also be valuable for other elementary school students. It includes a highly specific teacher's manual to teach four addition–subtraction problem types, using algebraic equations for solutions. *Pirate Math Individual Tutoring* (Fuchs et al., 2009) also teaches standard word problem solving, but has a broader scope, including computation concepts and algorithms. It is effective for third graders with learning disabilities (Fuchs et al., 2009; Seethaler, Powell, & Fuchs, n.d.). The third program, *Solving Math Word Problems: Teaching Students with Learning Disabilities Using Schema-Based Instruction* (Jitendra, 2007), is a teacher-directed program that has been used effectively with both elementary and middle school students (Xin, Jitendra, & Deatline-Buchman, 2005).

Complex Problem Solving

Complex problem solving involves thinking and reasoning strategies or routines. Complex problems provide the context for applying new combinations of tool skills, computation algorithms, and standard equation skills. While acknowledging that analytical skills are very important, most schools do not have systematic methods for teaching them. Teachers may encourage analytical thinking and even demonstrate it now and again in their teaching, but such demonstration and encouragement are usually deeply embedded in the context of teaching new objectives in a social or natural science class, or in math or English literature.

One reasoning strategy or routine we found to be effective is the think-aloud problem-solving strategy best described in Whimbey's workbook, *Problem Solving and Comprehension* (Whimbey & Lockhead, 1999). In think-aloud problem solving, teachers model and coach students regarding how to verbalize their thinking (e.g., their observations, thoughts, and decisions) as they solve problems or answer questions. Thinking aloud may involve talking, writing, diagramming, and other activities that support the thinking process. After teachers model good talk-aloud problem solving, students practice with each other in cooperative learning pairs. During their talk-aloud, students often hear themselves more clearly and provide their own self-corrections, in addition to receiving feedback from their teachers and peers. Whimbey's method was developed for college students to use in both verbal and quantitative reasoning and problem solving (Whimbey, 1987). Think-aloud problem solving has also been adapted for elementary and middle school students (Robbins, 1996).

Other cognitive routines besides think-aloud problem solving could be taught. The key point here is that a routine must be taught to all students or only those students who have prior successful experiences in thinking, reasoning, and problem solving will learn mathematical thinking. The routine must also teach the language of mathematics as well as the language of thinking and reasoning. We know of no specific intervention programs specifically designed to help students learn the language of mathematics.

Comprehensive Math Intervention Programs

Transitional Mathematics or *TransMath* (Woodward & Stroh, 2009) is a 1-year program in arithmetic, prealgebra, and pregeometry for middle and high schoolers that promotes mathematical reading skills. Several studies demonstrate its effectiveness (e.g., Woodward & Brown, 2006). *Accelerated Math* (Renaissance Learning, 2009) is a supplementary computer program that provides customized lessons and practice for each learner. Interestingly, in addition to being an effective intervention program (e.g., Ysseldyke & Bolt, 2007; Ysseldyke & Tardrew, 2003), the National Center on Response to Intervention (2011) rates it highly effective as a progress monitoring tool for math.

Riccomini and Witzel (2010) also provide a comprehensive discussion of case studies for explicit instruction in specific math components, such as number sense, whole numbers, fractions, decimals, problem solving, and math vocabulary. They describe key math intervention studies from the educational literature and detail several of the programs we cite in this chapter. The book is also valuable for schools implementing an RTI model for math. Stein, Kinder, Silbert, and Carnine (2006) have written a book describing key mathematical concepts, principles, and procedures taught in grades K–6; they include direct instruction scripts at each level.

WRITING

Far fewer evidence-based programs and published studies on effective instruction exist for writing than for reading and math; thus, this section of the chapter is shorter than the others.

To our knowledge, no evidence-based core writing program exists that includes instruction in each of the three areas of writing described in our content analysis. Our content analysis for writing includes three primary skills:

1. Tool skills (e.g., writing and typing)
2. Mechanics
3. Composition

Based on our content analysis, we now provide information about the three primary areas and some intervention programs that may improve students' skills in these areas.

Writing Tool Skills

The two main tool skills are writing and typing. Many students write or type well below their thinking rate. Under these conditions, thoughts are lost and sentence quality suffers as their thinking rate repeatedly pauses to allow their production rate to catch up. When students are able to write and type at approximately their thinking rate while composing, composition quality and rate greatly improve. Thus, fluency in writing tool skills facilitates mastery of writing mechanics and composition. A Precision Teaching approach is an effective way to practice building legible writing speed (Binder, 1996; Johnson & Street, 2004, in press; Lindsley, 1990). Learners set a timer for 1 minute and transcribe or copy as much text as they can in that timed period, including proper punctuation and capitalization. In addition to transcription, taking dictation from another person who is speaking builds legible writing or typing speed, this time in the context of spoken language. Taking dictation also builds tool skill fluency for learning how to take notes in lecture classes.

Writing Mechanics

The second subskill for writing involves mechanics. Writing mechanics include spelling, parts of speech, grammar, word usage, punctuation, capitalization, and replacing mundane words with richer words. Fluency in writing mechanics facilitates both quality and quantity of composition performance. Two Direct Instruction programs, *Spelling Mastery* (Engelmann, Dixon, Bauer, Steely, & Wells, 2007) and *Spelling through Morphographs* (Dixon & Engelmann, 2007), have been demonstrated numerous times to be effective (e.g., Burnette et al., 1999; Hesse, Robinson, & Rankin, 1983). Both provide systematic instruction in spelling—the first, for grades 1–6, and the second, for grades 4–adult. Ingenious spelling rules are a unique feature of these programs: Learning 10 rules allows the writer to spell over 30,000 words in the English language (Dixon, 1991). Important irregular words (e.g., *kind, they*) and common word parts (e.g., *pre-*, *-tion*) are also taught. Another spelling program, *Structured Supplemental Spelling*, is designed for second graders and learner-verified by Graham, Harris, and Chorzempa (2002). It is an unpublished program but may be available from the first author. These programs and the other writing programs described below are detailed in Table 12.4.

Expressive Writing (Engelmann & Silbert, 2007) is a Direct Instruction program for students in grades 2–5 that teaches basic sentence structure, grammatical conventions, punctuation, capitalization, and editing skills. It also teaches narrative composition of paragraphs based upon pictures and vocabulary that are gradually faded as the program progresses. The program has also been used effectively as an intervention program with middle school, high school, and adult literacy students (Walker, Shippen, Alberto, & Houchins, 2005).

REWARDS Writing: Sentence Refinement (Archer, Gleason, & Isaacson, 2008) is a scripted, supplementary writing program for students in upper elementary, middle school, and high school, with 75 lessons, each 20–30 minutes in length. It is an evidence-based program, with procedures consistent with published research on writing instruction (e.g., De La Paz & Graham, 2002; Graham & Perrin, 2007a; Phillips, 1996). Students are taught to (1) select more precise, sharper words for their sentences; (2) improve the quality, sophistication, and variety of their sentences; (3) combine sentences; and (4) edit sentences and paragraphs by fixing minor errors and eliminating, as well as adding, words and phrases to their work. As with reading and math, *boardwork procedures* are especially effective in teaching writing. For example, poorly written letters, incorrectly spelled words, and sentences with vague word choices or incorrect grammar can be written on the board, in lists that include their correct counterparts, for students to detect and correct.

Composition

The third subskill of writing instruction involves composing. Five different genres of writing are usually taught in elementary school: (1) narrative (fictional, story) writing; (2) descriptive writing, including each of the five senses as relevant to an object or event being described; (3) persuasive writing; (4) expository writing, usually comparing –contrasting and summarizing; and (5) practical writing, such as writing letters, directions to a location, and invitations to an event. The best rubrics we have seen for evaluating each genre of writing and for teaching a *trait* writing approach, are contained in the program *High Performance Writing* (Dodds, 2005). Teachers and students rate compositions according to 20 criteria at increasing levels of writing sophistication (introductory, intermediate, and advanced levels) for each genre. Five criteria at each level and genre are devoted to organization, content, style, and mechanics.

Currently, three studies have examined a writing strategies model for students in grade 2 through high school (e.g., Graham, Harris, & Mason, 2005; Harris, Graham, & Mason, 2006). Six strategies are taught within the model, known as *self-regulated strategy development (SRSD) for writing strategies instruction.* Three books describe in detail how to implement the program, including lesson plans, support materials for instruction, and evaluation instruments (Graham & Harris, 2005; Harris & Graham, 1996; Harris, Graham, Mason, & Friedlander, 2008). Students and teachers collaborate as they develop general and genre-specific writing and editing strategies. Students are also taught the differences between declarative, procedural, and conditional knowledge as they impact different writing genres. After group instruction from a highly specific teacher's manual, students self-pace through successive writing assignments in each genre. Differentiated according to the student's ability level (advanced, average, and at-risk), students also receive individualized feedback until they reach specific criteria. The program has been learner-verified with more than 10 published research articles and chapters (e.g., Graham & Harris, 2009; Graham & Perrin, 2007a, 2007b; Rogers & Graham, 2008). Video examples and an interactive tutorial are also available online (*www.shop.ascd.org/productdisplay.cfm?productid=602084*; *www.iris.peabody.vanderbilt.edu/pow/chalcycle.htm*).

A Comprehensive Corrective Writing Program

Engelmann and Grossen (2010) have written a 1-year, evidence-based writing program (*Essentials for Writing*) for middle school students who are in danger of failing to meet graduation requirements in language arts. The program requires fourth-grade reading skills and minimum grammar and writing skills. It provides a thorough entre into composing, teaching students how to write descriptive essays, narrative essays, and persuasive arguments. A unique feature of the program is the teaching of logic, argument rules, and debating methods. The program also teaches sentence coherence, punctuation, proper noun and verb usage, as well as letter writing.

Reading and Writing, or Language Arts?

Beginning in grade 4 or 5, most U.S. schools schedule a language arts block instead of separate reading and writing blocks. Language arts blocks are usually shorter than the amount of daily time that had been devoted to reading and writing in the primary grades. By grade 6, basic reading and writing skills generally receive even less instruction, with literature or even a content area becoming the primary focus for applying reading and writing skills. Many teachers ask us which is better: separate blocks or an integrated block? Our answer is compatible with our first-things-first approach to teaching and learning. If students can still make good progress mastering each subject in a shortened, application-oriented, and integrated approach, then language arts provides a good context for more naturally integrating reading and writing. Those students who do not continue to make progress in reading and writing in a language arts format will need separate interventions more focused upon direct teaching of reading and/or writing skills. Progress monitoring data (see Chapter 6) should help reveal whether some students may benefit more or less from an integrated language arts block, compared to separate reading and writing blocks.

TABLE 12.4. Intervention Programs for Writing

Name of program	Grade level	Primary content and activities	Possible secondary benefits[a]	Protocols for instruction	Lesson number	Lesson duration	TAs and volunteers can implement?[b]	Forms for monitoring implementation?	Progress monitoring materials?	Learner-verified?[c]
Essentials for Writing	6–12	Complete sentences, grammar, logic, organizing topics, retelling, writing critically, autobiographical sketches, responding to literature	Composition	Scripted lessons, detailed teacher materials	95 lessons	60 minutes	No	Yes	Yes	No
Expressive Writing	3–12	Writing and editing basic sentences, paragraphs, stories, and mechanics		Scripted lessons, detailed teacher materials	100 lessons, 2 levels	50 minutes	No	Yes	No	Yes
High Performance Writing	3–12	Written composition, genre rubrics for practical, narrative, expository, report, persuasive, and descriptive writing		Teacher materials at beginning, intermediate, and advanced levels	10 lessons each, and rubrics	45 minutes	No	No	Easily constructed	No
REWARDS Writing: Sentence Refinement	5–12	Vocabulary, sentence structure	Composition	Scripted lessons	75 lessons	20–30 minutes each	No	Yes	No	No

Spelling Mastery	1–6	Morpheme and phonics-based spelling curriculum	Composition	Scripted lessons, detailed teacher materials	120 lessons each year	30 minutes	Yes, with training	Yes	Yes	Yes
Spelling through Morphographs	4–12	Word parts, spelling rules		Scripted lessons, detailed teacher materials	140 lessons	30 minutes	Yes, with training	Yes	No	Yes
SRSD for Writing Strategies	2–12	Written composition	Self-regulation	Detailed teacher materials	3 times/week, 6–11 weeks, criteria-based	20–40 minutes	No	Yes	No	Yes
Structured Supplemental Spelling	2–4	Standard second-grade spelling curriculum	Composition	Detailed teacher materials	8 units 3 times/week, 16 weeks	20 minutes	Yes, with training	Yes	No	Yes
Writing Boardwork Procedures	K–8	Handwriting, spelling, grammar, word choice, sentence structure		Detailed teacher resources	Not applicable	Varies depending on teacher preference	No	No	No	No

[a] Although the intervention program does not target the skills specified in this column, improvements in the targeted skills can have the specified secondary benefits.
[b] This column specifies whether school volunteers and/or teacher assistants (TAs) could reasonably implement the intervention program without ongoing support from a classroom teacher.
[c] All programs listed are evidence-based, incorporating key ingredients that research has shown to be effective. *Learner-verified* means that there are at least two experimental or quasi-experimental research studies, published in peer-reviewed journals, showing statistically significant improvement compared to control students or groups.

CHAPTER 13

Case Illustrations of SOPAA Implementation

This chapter describes four examples of how the SOPAA might be initiated and implemented in elementary schools with differing characteristics. It is possible that some schools could use many if not all features of the SOPAA in middle or high schools, but we suspect that this model will be used most in elementary schools (hence the focus of this chapter). Each case example is derived from our work with many different schools throughout the United States. However, none of the examples depicts any one specific school; the illustrations are hypothetical, and all school names are fictitious. For clarity in describing SOPAA timelines and each school's history, the case illustrations are written as if each school begins learning about and considering SOPAA implementation during the 2012–2013 academic year.

The overall goal of this chapter is to show reasonable ways that different types of schools could implement the SOPAA model. As such, the examples do not specify the *only* way a school might plan for and initiate the SOPAA, but the overall approach that is illustrated in each example is logical and fitting with each school's needs and characteristics. In each illustration, we begin by describing the school's characteristics, needs, and strengths. We then describe that school's planning and SOPAA implementation timeline.

CASE ILLUSTRATION 1: KENNEDY ELEMENTARY SCHOOL

Kennedy Elementary School is one of five elementary schools in a relatively small school district. Kennedy includes two classrooms in kindergarten through sixth grade, with approximately 16–18 students per classroom. Based on end-of-year standardized assessments (including state-mandated assessments), approximately 25% of the students in this school have been performing below expectations in reading for several years, and for this reason the school began using a new core reading curriculum during the 2010–2011 academic year. This core reading curriculum included most of the components we discussed in Chapter 12 as strong features of core reading curricula. In math, students at Kennedy perform much better, and only about 10% of the students perform below expectations on end-of-year assessments. In the early grades (K–3), at least 1.5 hours are dedicated to reading and language arts (which includes sound instruction in writing), and in grades 4–6 at least 1–1.5 hours are spent on reading and language arts. Math instruction in each grade lasts at least 1 hour. For many years teachers have used district-developed reading and math assessments, which are administered once in the fall and once in the winter, to evaluate students' progress and overall abilities. However, many teachers administer the assessments in slightly different ways because test administration is not fully standardized, and in general the school has not found a strong correspondence between students identified with difficulties on the district-developed assessment and those who perform poorly on the end-of-year standardized assessments, particularly in reading. Many of the teachers and the school principal recognize that these district-developed assessments are inadequate, but the school has not yet been able to integrate a new system of assessment, primarily because the most recent focus regarding schoolwide changes has been on training teachers to use the new core reading curriculum.

Students with learning difficulties are identified by the classroom teacher. When the teacher deems that the problem is serious enough, he or she refers the student to a student support team (i.e., a prereferral intervention team) that has been in place for approximately 8 years. The student support team consists of the most seasoned special education teacher in the school (henceforth referred to as the *special education teacher* unless otherwise specified), the assistant principal, the classroom teacher, the school counselor, and the teacher who made the referral. Parents and other educators attend the team meeting when deemed appropriate. For example, when deficits are related to reading, the school's reading specialist also attends the team meeting. The reading specialist and the special education teacher are very well-respected educators in the school, and in addition to assisting with student support teams, they regularly provide advice and suggestions to teachers about struggling learners, though this advice and consultation are generally done informally (e.g., during a brief conversation about the teacher's concern after school).

Although the student support team has been in place many years, several school leaders (e.g., the principal, assistant principal, reading specialist, the special education teacher, school psychologist) recognize that the assistance provided to teachers during the team meetings does not usually result in improved student outcomes. The following list summarizes the weaknesses and related characteristics of the school's student support team: (1) the interventions developed often do not align well enough with what are later recognized as "underlying" deficits, primarily because there is little to no assessment of the student's difficulty prior to intervention development; (2) teachers often report insufficient support and training for implementing the developed interventions; (3) there is little to no documentation about intervention implementation (e.g., how many minutes per day and number of times implemented per week); (4) interventions developed during team meetings are designed to be relevant to the teacher's concern, but there is little to no in-school data or research studies available to examine the effectiveness of the interventions (in fact, there are currently no evidence-based intervention programs being used consistently across all teachers who would likely benefit from them); (5) progress monitoring assessment does not occur as part of most intervention plans, and instead teachers are asked to estimate the effectiveness of the intervention after approximately 4–5 weeks from the date of developing the intervention plan during the team meeting; (6) there is no "case manager" to follow up with teachers during intervention implementation periods; and (7) due to team members' schedules, team meetings often do not occur for up to 4 weeks after the teacher expresses concern about the student.

Based on Kennedy Elementary School educators' concerns about how successful they have been with assisting struggling learners through the student support team, the aforementioned weaknesses indicate several school needs. There are, however, important strengths at this school. For example, as noted previously, the special education teacher and the school's reading specialist are well respected by the teachers in the school, possess good consultation skills and experiences, work hard to support as many students as possible, and are always eager to improve their expertise in assisting students with learning difficulties. Also, the assistant principal is highly respected, has worked many years as a classroom teacher, has a strong understanding of the challenges and needed actions associated with assisting students who struggle academically, and is given a great deal of authority by the principal to initiate schoolwide change. It was the assistant principal who initiated the school's change in the core reading curriculum, and the large majority of the teachers in the school are supportive of the new core curriculum. The school also has six dedicated school volunteers, including several retired teachers from the community, and each kindergarten through fourth-grade teacher has a full-time or part-time teaching assistant.

After considering this school's strengths and needs, the reading specialist began considering possible SOPAA implementation during the 2012–2013 academic year. After reading the book about the SOPAA model, she discussed possible implementation with the special education teacher and assistant principal. Both of these educators recognized the possible value of using the SOPAA, and it was determined that the special education teacher and reading specialist should prepare a general proposal and rationale for implementation (e.g., using the guidance described in Chapter 9 and Appendices B–D). After developing a preliminary proposal, they reviewed this information with the assistant principal, and once an even stronger proposal and rationale were developed, the three educators shared the proposal with the school principal. Following meetings with the principal during spring 2013, the implementation plan shown in Table 13.1 was developed.

As shown in the table, SOPAA implementation will be facilitated by the reading specialist (serving first as Lead Coordinator and TAPS Reading Teacher and eventually also as TAPS Writing Teacher) and the special education teacher (serving first as the TAPS Support Coordinator and eventually also as the TAPS Math Teacher). Because implementation will begin only in the area of reading and only with the early grade levels, the special education teacher will complete a similar ongoing professional development plan as the reading specialist, which will allow the special education teacher to (1) become familiar with the intervention programs and assessments that will be used for TAPS cases; (2) assist the reading specialist with training teachers, assistive school personnel, and school volunteers to use the selected reading programs; (3) assist with monitoring implementation integrity during TAPS cases; (4) acclimate to the ongoing professional development process (which will be used later by this teacher more specifically with math); and (5) better participate in monthly SOPAA meetings and discussions related to professional development activities. Furthermore, it was determined that the special education teacher would assist the reading specialist with at least three TAPS cases during Year 1 of implementation to get more accustomed to the TAPS process and eventually manage one or two TAPS cases so that they could be discussed with the reading specialist. The decision to make the reading specialist the Lead Coordinator/TAPS Reading Teacher was made because she had more flexibility in her schedule than the special education teacher, as well as slightly more experience with reading instruction, assessment, and consultation.

It is important to note that although the assistant principal was involved in developing a plan and rationale for the SOPAA, she preferred not to be a co-facilitator due to time constraints and other obligations. However, it was decided that the assistant principal would always attend the hourly SOPAA meetings each month, sometimes sit in on the professional development discussions between the two SOPAA facilitators, and participate in discussion about data collected to evaluate the effectiveness of the SOPAA model (using an evaluation plan based on suggestions and materials described in Chapter 10). In this way, the assistant principal would contribute to overall SOPAA planning and decisions, and would keep the principal informed about SOPAA implementation. The assistant principal would also take a key role in generating classroom teachers' support during the introductory teacher presentation.

TABLE 13.1. Implementation Timeline for Kennedy Elementary School

School year (implementation year)	Description of implementation plan
2013–2014 (Preparation year)	*SOPAA facilitators: The SOPAA model will be facilitated by two individuals: (1) the school's reading specialist (serving as Lead Coordinator and TAPS Reading Teacher and later as the TAPS Writing Teacher) and (2) the special education teacher (serving as TAPS Support Coordinator and later as the TAPS Math Teacher)* Goals of the preparation year: 1. Ensure that the reading specialist and special education teacher have access to, and experience using, the three evidence-based interventions selected for Year 1 implementation. 2. Allow both of these teachers to learn and use CBM progress monitoring strategies in reading. 3. Train all K–6 teachers and K–2 teacher assistants to use two of the three intervention programs that were selected for use during TAPS cases in Year 1. 4. Allow the reading specialist to use the TAPS process and forms during at least three trial cases. 5. Allow both SOPAA facilitators to begin 4–5 hours per month of SOPAA professional development activities.
2014–2015 (Year 1)	General: Implement the SOPAA only with K, 1st-, and 2nd-grade classrooms in reading; include all six teachers from grades K–2 in TAPS process. 1. TAPS: Only target phonics, phonemic awareness, and fluency with TAPS cases. 2. Assessment for instruction: Benchmark assessments in reading will be used with 2nd-grade classrooms and as a pre–post assessment for students supported with TAPS. Intervention progress monitoring will include weekly CBM and monitoring progress through the selected intervention program. 3. Maximized personnel and professional development: Conduct one SOPAA professional development workshop to train all K–6 teachers in the third intervention program selected for TAPS cases. Train all school volunteers, who are available at least 4 hours per week to implement the selected intervention program to target phonics, and train the school counselor and music teacher in this intervention. Begin ongoing professional development 8–10 hours/month for both the SOPAA facilitators in the area of reading. 4. Communication and generating support: Use methods discussed in Chapter 10.
2015–2016 (Year 2)[a]	General: The special education teacher will also become the TAPS Math Teacher in Year 3. Select two evidence-based math interventions and ensure that the special education teacher has access to, and some experience using, the two interventions. Select an intervention program to target comprehension (intervention programs are now available for phonemic awareness, phonics, fluency, and comprehension). 1. TAPS: Begin TAPS in reading with grades 3–6 so that TAPS is now used with all K–6 classrooms in reading. If the TAPS Reading Teacher is supporting too many cases, the special education teacher will serve as another TAPS Reading Teacher. 2. Assessment for instruction: Do benchmark reading assessments in grades K–4 and train four more school personnel to use benchmark assessments. 3. Maximized personnel and professional development: Hold professional development workshops so that all K–6 teachers and teacher assistants learn how to implement the comprehension intervention program. The special education teacher begins ongoing professional development in the area of math, with a particular focus on learning how to use the selected math intervention programs and CBM progress monitoring strategies in math. 4. Communication and generating support: Continue using methods discussed in Chapter 10.

(cont.)

TABLE 13.1. *(cont.)*

School year (implementation year)	Description of implementation plan
2016–2017 (Year 3)	1. TAPS: Begin implementation with 5th and 6th grades so that TAPS is now implemented with all K–6 classrooms in reading. 2. Assessment for instruction: Do benchmark reading assessments in grades K–6 and train two more school personnel to use benchmark assessments. 3. Maximized personnel and professional development: Hold professional development workshops so that all K–6 teachers and teacher assistants know how to implement the two math intervention programs that will be used for TAPS cases in Year 4. Train all school volunteers who are available at least 4 hours per week to implement one of the selected math intervention programs to use with TAPS cases. Also train the school counselor and music teacher in this intervention. 4. Communication and generating support: Continue using methods discussed in Chapter 10.
2017–2018 (Year 4)	1. TAPS: Begin SOPAA implementation with math (with the special education teacher serving as the TAPS Math Teacher) for all grade levels so that TAPS is now being implemented in reading and math for all grades. Based on the prevalence of teacher concerns in the area of writing, determine whether TAPS should be used for writing in Year 5. If so, the reading specialist will serve as the TAPS Writing Teacher and begin professional development and selecting writing programs this year. 2. Assessment for instruction: Use classwide benchmark assessments in math for grades 3–6. 3. Communication and generating support: Continue using methods discussed in Chapter 10.
2018–2019 (Year 5)	1. TAPS: If in Year 4 it is determined that a TAPS Writing Teacher would be useful, begin using TAPS with all grades in the area of writing. 2. Assessment for instruction: Use classwide benchmark assessments in math for grades 1–2. 3. Maximized personnel and professional development: Train three more school personnel to use benchmark assessments in math. 4. Communication and generating support: Continue using methods discussed in Chapter 10.

[a] Unless otherwise specified, the implementation plan from year to year will also include TAPS and assessment for instruction plans that began in a previous school year.

In summary, Kennedy is a school that had many significant challenges with systematically developing, implementing, documenting, and evaluating intervention plans for struggling students. There were also a number of students struggling in reading, and for this reason implementation began with only a few grade levels, and when appropriate, evidence-based small-group interventions were selected for students' intervention plans. As time passed and SOPAA facilitators became more experienced, additional SOPAA features were slowly added to the model, thereby allowing the school to systematically improve its ability to assist struggling learners with evidence-based practices.

CASE ILLUSTRATION 2: PINEVIEW CHARTER SCHOOL

Pineview Charter School began operation in the 2010–2011 school year. In its first year, the school had students in kindergarten through third grade, and in the second year, as their third graders moved up, they added a fourth grade. There are three classrooms per grade in what is now a K–4 school. Pineview's educational model calls for small class size, individualization, and parent involvement. The school has one special education teacher and one part-time speech–language pathologist who both serve the school's special education population. Pineview has limited specialized staff (e.g., no librarian or counselor) because personnel funds go toward assuring the presence of a teaching assistant in each class. However, parent volunteers are a vital part of the school's instructional program and run the library and provide other services at the school.

Pineview has only had 2 years' worth of reading and mathematics achievement scores on the state's standards-based assessments in these subjects. Using test scores to decide where change is needed is difficult because the school's population has been in flux, with some parents moving their children back to the public schools after the first year, and new students entering to replace the departing students. In addition, the state's large-scale assessment program begins in the third grade. With no fourth-grade students at the school in their first year, of operation, Pineview had only third-grade achievement data for 2010–2011. That year, about 40% of third graders scored below grade level in reading on the state assessment, and 20% scored below grade level in mathematics. In the second year of their operation, 45% of third-grade children and 38% of fourth-grade children scored below grade level in reading. As in the first year, only about 20% of students were below grade level in mathematics. The School Improvement Team, composed of elected parent and school staff representatives and the principal, attribute the low reading scores in the first 2 years to the school population, thinking that many parents whose children are having difficulty learning to read transfer to the charter school.

Pineview's core reading curriculum is a guided reading program with leveled books. Students are grouped by reading level and read and discuss books in small groups. They are taught basic letter–sound knowledge and sight words in kindergarten and then move into the leveled book program in first grade, starting with simple picture books. In the lower grades, students rotate through centers when they are not in their reading groups. In the upper grades, students have independent assignments to complete when they are not in guided reading groups with their teachers or teaching assistants. A morning block of 90 minutes is dedicated to reading and writing, with an hour in the afternoon dedicated to mathematics.

At Pineview, reading assessments are done with running records that produce a reading level for each student. The teachers are expected to do four running records each year on each child. Although teachers find the running records quite useful and meaningful, they have difficulty finding the time to complete the four required assessments per student per year. There is a reasonable match between students who are identified as reading below grade level on the running records and those who do not pass the state's reading assessment. In mathematics, the mastery tests at the end of each chapter in their mathematics textbook are used to gauge student progress.

The school has a Student Assistance Team that helps implement the state's mandate for two prereferral interventions before educators refer a student for a special education evaluation. The team is quite busy because the entire school is concerned about the poor reading test scores, and many teachers are referring students who are not benefiting from their reading instruction or are below grade level when they enter Pineview. Because the Student Assistance Team caseload limits the time the team can spend on any one student's intervention plan and because most teachers have already tried to work with the students in their classrooms before referring them (due the focus on individualization at the school), the intervention plans developed in these team meetings tend to be cursory. Many of the plans call for preferential seating and extra attention from the teacher or teaching assistant, with a check-in 6 weeks later when the teacher usually says the interventions did not work. Many students are referred to special education, and almost every one of them is identified.

The special education teacher has been both a general education teacher and a special education teacher. She has a strong background in reading and also came from a school with an RTI model in place. She likes this new school and its energetic staff, but is quickly feeling overwhelmed by the number of students in her caseload. She has broached with some of the teachers the issue of whether the core reading curriculum is appropriate. However, the stress of opening a new school, completing running records four times a year, individualizing work for all students, and planning for adding new grades leaves little energy for reflection by the teachers and administrators. The special education teacher thinks components of the SOPAA would help address some of the reading problems she sees in the school, but she knows that the school isn't ready for any big operational changes because there is too much change going on already. She thinks universal screening in reading and some small-group explicit instruction in phonics might help teachers identify places where their curriculum needs rethinking.

Pineview has some serious issues. They have a core reading curriculum that is only serving a portion of their students. It seems to work well for students who enter with phonics skills or quickly pick them up, but it is leaving behind students who encounter any difficulty with decoding skill or sight word acquisition. The Student Assistance Team is overwhelmed by the number of referrals, and the number of students in special education is rising quickly. But these problems are not as salient as they would be in an established school because Pineview faces so many other issues involved with opening a new school. Each year, a new grade is added and new staff must be recruited. Some teachers change grade assignments with their students, meaning grade level teams change each year. There are new policies to be established for discipline, playground rules, and carpooling. The School Improvement Team members are just getting to know one another and develop goals for the school. Despite these challenges, there are some notable strengths at Pineview. The school staff are willing to try something new, or they would not have volunteered to work at a newly opened charter school. The school's philosophy of individualization means that teachers are prepared to adapt instruction to the needs of individual learners. Parent involvement and commitment to the school is high.

During the 2011–2012 academic year, the special education teacher shared some of her concerns about the reading program with one of the first-grade teachers. The first-grade teacher agreed with the special education teacher that more could be done in first-grade classrooms, but she did not have the time to implement major instructional changes and was not comfortable challenging one of the experienced teachers who felt strongly that comprehension should be the primary (and sometimes only) focus of reading instruction at every grade level. However, the special education teacher saw an opportunity to try something new. The school was preparing to hire another special education teacher for the 2012–2013 academic year because caseloads were increasing yearly. With this plan, the new special education teacher would reduce the current special education teacher's caseload enough to give her a free period, so she asked the principal if she could try two new things the next year. First, she proposed to conduct universal screening with all first-grade students. The first-grade teacher who shared her concerns volunteered to assist her, as did the speech–language pathologist. Second, she wanted to devote one period a day to providing evidence-based small-group instruction (using an alternate core curriculum) to first-grade students who were having difficulty with early literacy skills. She requested to do this in the first-grade teacher's classroom with whom she was partnering, but asked to include in a few students from the other first-grade classrooms for instruction during this period. The principal agreed and during the 2012–2013 year the special education teacher and first-grade teacher implemented universal screening in the first grade and provided small-group instruction—with a focus on phonics—to struggling students.

During the winter of the 2012–2013 school year, the special education teacher presented her fall and winter universal screening results, showing that most of the students identified with reading difficulties in the fall had made significant improvements in their reading skills, especially compared to struggling first-grade students who did not receive the supplemental instruction. She and the first-grade teacher therefore asked the principal to consider a change in the core curriculum. During this same school year, the special education teacher had been introduced to the SOPAA model and was learning how SOPAA components and principles (e.g., using universal screening, evidence-based instruction, and a system for instructional problem solving) aligned well with the changes she was trying to make in the school. The special education teacher also shared information about the SOPAA model with the first-grade teacher, and they introduced the SOPAA to the principal and talked about how TAPS could be a useful model for assisting those first-grade students who did not meet benchmark scores obtained through universal screening.

The principal, concerned with the results of the universal screening and impressed with the first-grade students' improvements, decided to purchase an evidence-based core curriculum (similar to the ones discussed in Chapter 12) and designated some professional development days for the 2013–2014 school year so that a consultant could help train kindergarten, first-, and second-grade teachers in the new core curriculum. The school principal also agreed that the 2013–2014 school year could serve as a preparation year for SOPAA implementation, with implementation of many SOPAA features to begin during the 2014–2015 school year. The end of the 2012–2013 school year also served as the time in which the special education teacher, first-grade teacher, and principal would develop a timeline for SOPAA implementation. Table 13.2 presents the activities to occur during the preparation year and the subsequent timeline for implementing the SOPAA model.

Pineview is the midst of much change. The special education teacher correctly perceives that the prereferral team's heavy caseload and ineffective process is not the first issue to address to help this school tackle its concerns about reading. As stated in Chapter 12, unless core instruction is strong, an individually oriented student assistance program such as TAPS will quickly be overwhelmed with referrals. Here, the special education teacher is initially filling both the Lead Coordinator and TAPS Reading Teacher role as she gathers needs data (in the form of universal screening results) to help her school begin to address some critical instructional issues, and she also pilots a more comprehensive reading curriculum and demonstrates its impact on student outcomes.

In summary, Pineview faced problems with its reading curriculum that were not initially apparent to the teachers and administration. The special education teacher was the first to see the situation because it was affecting her directly. Her data and the accumulating data across years on the state's end-of-year assessments helped to establish the need for a more programmatic approach to reading instruction and for the hiring of a reading coach, who then became integral to the process. Eventually, after several years of developing a better approach to assisting struggling readers, the school was able to start using a similar approach in math. Although change may have been somewhat slow, given the many changes taking place at Pineview during this time period, moving more quickly might have been met with substantial resistance from teachers.

CASE ILLUSTRATION 3: DOBBS ELEMENTARY SCHOOL

Dobbs Elementary School is located in a largely rural school district. However, there are a number of golf retirement communities that increase the tax base and some small towns in the district. A chicken processing plant recently opened in the county and that plant has brought with it a sig-

TABLE 13.2. Implementation Timeline for Pineview Elementary School

School year (implementation year)	Description of implementation plan
2013–2014 (Preparation year)	*SOPAA facilitators: The SOPAA model will be facilitated by the special education teacher (serving as the Lead Coordinator, TAPS Reading Teacher, and Intervention Support Coordinator). One first-grade teacher will be the primary assistant to the special education teacher initially, but the first-grade teacher's role will be limited to helping with universal screening in reading during the fall, winter, and spring.* Goals of the preparation year: 1. Ensure that kindergarten, first-grade, and second-grade teachers are using the new core reading curriculum as designed and provide feedback as needed (with assistance from the principal, first-grade teacher, and special education teacher). 2. Prepare for (e.g., choose instruments and complete needed training) and then implement universal screening in reading measures in all first- and second-grade classrooms. 3. Select an intervention program designed to assist students struggling with reading fluency and allow the special education teacher to use the program with students. 4. Train first- and second-grade teachers (and their teacher assistants) to use the selected reading fluency intervention program. 5. Based on teacher input and fall and winter universal screening results, select a small number of students who are struggling the most and use the phonics-based intervention program (which was selected and piloted during the previous school year) or the reading fluency intervention program to remediate each selected student's particular deficit. For intervention development, implementation, and evaluation, the TAPS Reading Teacher will use the TAPS process. 6. At the end of the school year, report to first- and second-grade teachers, the principal, and School Improvement Team on the successes and challenges of the universal screening and TAPS work that was completed. 7. Allow the TAPS Reading Teacher 6–8 hours per month of SOPAA professional development activities.
2014–2015 (Year 1)	General: Implement the SOPAA with first- and second-grade classrooms in reading. 1. TAPS: Only target phonics, phonemic awareness, and fluency with TAPS cases. 2. Assessment for instruction: Benchmark assessments in reading will be used with K–4 classrooms and as a pre–post assessment for students supported with TAPS. Use running records for reading assessment as an option for teachers if they use benchmark assessments. 3. Maximized personnel and professional development: Conduct one SOPAA professional development workshop to train the remaining teachers (and teacher assistants) in the two intervention program selected for TAPS cases. TAPS Reading Teacher begins ongoing professional development 8–10 hours/month in the area of reading. 4. Communication and generating support: Continue reporting results of universal screening and piloting to school staff, School Improvement Team, and principal. Use methods discussed in Chapter 10.
2015–2016 (Year 2)[a]	General: Assuming successful outcomes from Year 1 and the preparation year, a reading coach is hired to become the TAPS Reading Teacher in Year 2. The special education teacher will focus only on being the Lead Coordinator and TAPS Support Coordinator. 1. TAPS: Expand TAPS in reading to all K–3 classrooms. The TAPS process becomes a required initial step before students are referred to the Student Assistance Team. 2. Select an intervention program for reading comprehension.

(cont.)

TABLE 13.2. *(cont.)*

School year (implementation year)	Description of implementation plan
	3. Maximized personnel and professional development: The reading coach (i.e., new TAPS Reading Teacher) begins ongoing professional development for 8–10 hours/month. Train all teachers to use the comprehension intervention program and how to best use universal screening results to plan instruction. The Lead Coordinator begins professional development in the area of math so that TAPS can be expanded to math in a subsequent school year. Select an intervention program in math that can be used with students in grades 1–4, and allow the Lead Coordinator (now also the TAPS Math Teacher) to practice using this intervention program with a small number of students. 4. Communication and generating support: Continue using methods discussed in Chapter 10.
2016–2017 (Year 3)	1. TAPS: Expand TAPS in reading to all classrooms (K–4). 2. Assessment for instruction: Begin using universal screening in math in first grade. 3. Maximized personnel and professional development: Train all teachers to use universal screening in math by the end of the school year. Train first- and second-grade teachers (and their teacher assistants) to use the selected math intervention program. Select another intervention program in math that can be used with students in grades K–2 and allow the Lead Coordinator (now also the TAPS Math Teacher) to practice using this intervention program with a small number of students. 4. Communication and generating support: Continue using methods discussed in Chapter 10.
2017–2018 (Year 4)	1. TAPS: Begin using TAPS in math in first and second grades. 2. Assessment for instruction: Begin using universal screening in math in grades 1–4. 3. Professional development: Focus teacher training on evidence-based practices and linking assessment with instruction in math. Complete a needs assessment related to the SOPAA to determine one additional professional development workshop for all teachers. 4. Communication and generating support: Continue using methods discussed in Chapter 10.
2018–2019 (Year 5)	1. Maximized personnel and professional development: Train all teachers (and their teacher assistants) to use both of the selected math intervention programs. Repeat needed trainings to deal with staff turnover and new hires. 2. Communication and generating support: Continue using methods discussed in Chapter 10.

[a]Unless otherwise specified, the implementation plan from year to year will also include TAPS and assessment for instruction plans that began in a previous school year.

nificant population of workers who speak Spanish as their first language. About 30% of students at Dobbs Elementary are Hispanic. Many of these students' first exposure to English occurs when they enter kindergarten. Dobbs Elementary has a committed school staff and innovative principal. Although their state test scores are a bit lower than other schools in the district, the lower scores reflect the entry level of their students, not the quality of instruction. If one looks at growth over the years, Dobbs outperforms other schools in the district. Dobbs has four classrooms in kindergarten through fifth grade. Lower grades have teaching assistants, but grades 4 and 5 do not. Two English as a second language (ESL) teachers serve the school's students who have been identified as having limited English proficiency.

Several years ago, Dobbs instituted a professional learning community (PLC) model of professional development. Primarily because of the hands-on leadership style of the principal, the PLC model has been a tremendous success and made Dobbs a better school. Teachers meet by grade level once per week. They plan instruction and collaborate to help students who have difficulty. The focus of these meetings is always the students and the curriculum. The school uses computerized-adaptive testing in reading and mathematics three times per year for universal screening. The instructional technology teacher and vice principal know the system well. There has been extensive professional development on the system, and teachers routinely discuss the data from the universal assessments in their grade-level meetings and use it in making instructional decisions. The school also has set aside a half hour each day for specialized small-group instruction. During this time, teaching assistants, teachers, and support staff all have responsibility to deliver individually tailored intervention activities to a small group of students. Some students get enrichment activities; others get remedial activities. A number of these programs use research-based small-group interventions in reading and mathematics.

The quality of core instruction, the PLCs, and the small-group instruction time have all contributed to the smooth running of the Student Assistance Team. The team, consisting of the principal, the school psychologist, one of the ESL teachers, a fifth-grade teacher, and a first-grade teacher, is confident that the students who are referred to it are truly having difficulty, and there is good documentation of the efforts of the grade-level teams to address these students' needs.

Despite all these strengths, the Student Assistance Team perceives persistent problems in some areas or a need for change. First, a higher-than-expected proportion of the students referred to the team is Hispanic. These students tend to be in the upper grades, and teachers are concerned about their reading comprehension and written language. These students often have exited ESL services. Even if referred for special education services by the team, they frequently don't qualify. Second, the state has recently mandated progress monitoring be used to demonstrate that a student has not benefited from intervention efforts in general education. Although the school can use its universal screening measures in reading and mathematics to document student progress in general education, the state requires progress monitoring in writing if a student is to be identified as having a learning disability that affects her ability in writing. As a result, the school needs to do some kind of progress monitoring in writing, but currently does not have any assessment of writing that is used for universal screening or progress monitoring. Also, the state requires the collection and graphing of 10 data points for progress monitoring for prereferral interventions, and the present system of using the universal screening results as a means of assessing student progress will not meet this requirement.

The Student Assistance Team is intrigued with the SOPAA model and think that it may help them address the needs they have identified. The principal is particularly enthusiastic, as she thinks that the system complements the many supports already in place at the school. The ESL teacher sees the professional development component of SOPAA as a means for helping school staff understand how to accommodate the needs of ELLs and develop more realistic expectations for how long it takes these students to become proficient in reading and writing. Based on continued discussion and planning meetings among the Student Assistance team members during the 2012–2013 school year, they developed the implementation timeline shown in Table 13.3.

As shown in the timeline, Dobbs's SOPAA model will be facilitated by three educators at the start and eventually expand to five. Roles were assigned according to the professionals' interests and expertise. As noted in the figure, there are two TAPS Writing Teachers initially, with the special education teacher having extensive experience teaching writing and consulting with other teachers in this area. The ESL teacher is serving as a second TAPS Writing Teacher because she has expertise in second language learning and wants to learn more about writing instruction because so many of her students struggle in this area. They hope that their teaming together as TAPS Writing Teachers will help them select interventions that fill the needs of all students strug-

TABLE 13.3. Implementation Timeline for Dobbs Elementary School

School year (implementation year)	Description of implementation plan
2013–2014 (preparation year)	*SOPAA facilitators: The SOPAA model will initially be facilitated by three individuals: (1) the school psychologist (serving as Lead Coordinator), (2) one of the ESL teachers (serving as the TAPS Writing Teacher), and (3) a special education teacher (serving as the TAPS Support Coordinator and a secondary TAPS Writing Teacher). The initial focus will be writing.* Goals of the preparation year: 1. Ensure that the SOPAA facilitators have access to, and experience using, the three evidence-based interventions selected for Year 1 implementation. 2. Pilot CBM writing prompts (in grades 1–5) and classroom on-demand writing tasks (grades 2–5) scored with the state's writing rubric as universal screening tools in winter and spring. Compare results with the two tools at each grade level and use results to plan screening for next year. 3. Train all grade 1–5 teachers to use two of the selected intervention programs and train an ESL teacher and volunteer teachers from upper grades to use the selected intervention program that will likely be used the most with older students. 4. Allow the two TAPS Writing Teachers to use the TAPS process and forms during at least three trial cases. 5. Allow both SOPAA facilitators to begin 4–5 hours per month of SOPAA professional developmental activities. 6. At end of school year (instead of at beginning of following year), train all teachers in the TAPS process.
2014–2015 (Year 1)[a]	General: Implement SOPAA and the TAPS process only with grade 3–5 classrooms and only in writing. 1. TAPS: Begin TAPS in grades 3–5. For each intervention implemented, writing products will be targeted on type of writing that is a focus in that grade (e.g., persuasive writing, story writing). 2. Assessment for instruction: Classroom on-demand writing tasks will be used as a universal screening measure in fall and spring in all grade 3–5 classrooms. Writing prompt CBM probes will be used for progress monitoring TAPS cases. TAPS students' fall and spring writing scores on the on-demand writing task scoring rubric will also be used to evaluate TAPS interventions. 3. Maximized personnel and professional development: The TAPS Writing Teachers complete 8–10 hours/month of professional development. The TAPS Support Coordinator trains parent and community volunteers to score CBM writing prompt probes (correct word sequences) and on-demand writing task (state writing rubric). 4. Communication and generating support: Use methods discussed in Chapter 10.
2015–2016 (Year 2)	General: Implement TAPS support and universal screening in writing at all grade levels (except kindergarten). 1. Assessment for instruction: Following training, all teachers begin classwide benchmark assessment procedures in writing during the fall, winter, and spring (with writing prompt CBM probes for grades 1–2, and on-demand classroom tasks in grades 3–5). 2. Maximized personnel and professional development: At beginning of the school year teachers learn benchmark assessment procedures in writing. Writing teachers provide professional development to all teachers in writing and strategies for helping ELLs master writing. 3. Communication and generating support: Use methods discussed in Chapter 10.

(cont.)

TABLE 13.3. *(cont.)*

School year (implementation year)	Description of implementation plan
2016–2017 (Year 3)	General: Reading specialist becomes TAPS Reading Teacher and two new intervention programs for reading are selected. 1. TAPS: Begin TAPS support in reading across all classes and grade levels. 2. Assessment for instruction: Universal screening now available in reading, mathematics, and writing. 3. Maximized personnel and professional development: Parent and community volunteer program is expanded to include two early reading interventions. K–2 teachers are trained in one of the reading programs. A special education teacher is recruited to take on TAPS in mathematics next year and begins 4–6 hours a month of professional development to prepare for the role. 4. Communication and generating support: Use methods discussed in Chapter 10.
2017–2018 (Year 4)	1. TAPS: TAPS support is implemented in mathematics across all grade levels. 2. Maximized personnel and professional development: TAPS Reading Teacher provides schoolwide professional development in enriching oral vocabulary during classroom instruction. All assistants are trained in one of two reading comprehension interventions. Teachers and teacher assistants are trained to use one of the selected math intervention program. 3. Communication and generating support: Use methods discussed in Chapter 10. *Full-scale SOPAA achieved by end of year.*

[a] Unless otherwise specified, the implementation plan from year to year will also include TAPS and assessment for instruction plans that began in a previous school year.

gling in writing, both those who have English as their native language and those for whom English is a second language.

One issue faced at Dobbs that the school psychologist felt well qualified to handle was the choice of appropriate measures for progress monitoring in writing. There is limited research on brief assessments for writing (as noted in Chapter 6), but the state now requires progress monitoring in writing regardless of the state of the research. The school psychologist has read the research on story prompt CBM probes, but she has her doubts that upper elementary teachers will find that a 5-minute writing sample scored for correct word sequences is an acceptable measure for assessing students' writing. This type of assessment does not fit well with the state's rubric for quality writing products. She thinks that if she pilots two types of writing assessments in the first year, she can use those data to help the school decide how to respond to the state's mandate. On-demand writing tasks, one of the options she is considering, consist of typical class writing assignment. Teachers ask students to complete them in class and then use the state's writing rubric to score them. Both types of writing probes take considerable time to score. Therefore, the SOPAA team decides to make use of parent volunteers for scoring. The special education teacher, who has extensive experience in writing, teaches volunteers how to score the on-demand writing samples. They assign student identification numbers to the on-demand samples and CBM writing probes so that parents and other volunteers scoring the samples will not know children's names. The school psychologist's plan is to look at the test–retest correlations and the correlations between the two types of measures at the end of the year and then present that information to all teachers in a professional development session. The classroom teacher will make a decision about which measures will be used for universal screening. The school psychologist plans to lobby for CBM probes for progress monitoring because they are more efficient and sensitive to change. In addition, given that most children referred for writing difficulties to the School Assistance Team have problems simply producing enough writing to score with the state's rubric, she thinks this strategy will be appropriate for most students.

Although the principal was enthusiastic about SOPAA, she did not play a direct role in it because of time limitations. Her role will be to provide the resources to purchase the writing interventions and to make sure that school staff know of her support. Later, she will become actively involved in making sure that SOPAA facilitators have the time and resources they need to move ahead.

To summarize the Dobbs Elementary School case example, Dobbs has strong core instruction in reading and mathematics. Their challenges center on a new school population that requires more intensive instruction and on new state regulations that go beyond what is available in the research literature. The staff of Dobbs has used these challenging situations to advance teachers' knowledge and skills and the effectiveness of assisting struggling learners.

CASE ILLUSTRATION 4: EAST DAVIS ELEMENTARY SCHOOL

East Davis Elementary School is located in a large, urban school district that is well known within the state for its relatively quick adoption of research-based instructional practices and its focus on data-based decision making. Although East Davis is only an average-performing school within its district, more students at East Davis pass proficiency standards in reading compared to demographically comparable schools in other urban districts. East Davis includes two to three classrooms in kindergarten through fifth grade, with approximately 20 students per classroom.

For the past 3 years, East Davis has been using a three-tier RTI model in reading, which at Tier 1 includes an evidence-based core curriculum (one similar to those described in Chapter 12) and schoolwide benchmark assessments during the fall, winter, and spring. Of the approximately 12% of students who do not meet grade-level standards during the fall or winter benchmark assessment, these students move to Tier 2 of the RTI model, where evidence-based interventions are implemented with them for 6–8 weeks while their progress is supposed to be monitored regularly by the teacher throughout this time. Students who do not make sufficient progress with Tier 2 interventions are provided with more intense intervention services and more frequent progress monitoring assessment (which occurs during Tier 3 of the RTI model). Both classroom teachers and special education teachers implement interventions for students in Tier 3, but these students are not specifically eligible for special education while receiving Tier 3 support. Only if Tier 3 supports are deemed ineffective will a student be considered for possible special education services.

Although a relatively structured system is in place at East Davis for assisting struggling readers, teachers within the school have little experience with implementing evidence-based math interventions, monitoring student progress in math, and identifying students with difficulties in math. A relatively good core curriculum in math is used at East Davis Elementary, but at least 15–18% of students perform poorly on end-of-grade math assessments, particularly students in the upper grade levels.

Collectively, East Davis Elementary School has many positive characteristics related to its ability to teach students reading and math skills, including, for example, good core curricula, a systematic problem-solving (i.e., RTI) model for reading, using evidence-based interventions in reading, and using schoolwide benchmark assessment data to identify struggling readers. However, East Davis also experiences important challenges, which are recognized by school and district administrators. Most notably, in reading, the large majority of students receiving Tier 2 interventions are considered nonresponders. A careful analysis of East Davis's RTI model reveals the following weaknesses that may negatively impact their Tier 2 services: (1) progress monitoring is often inadequate (e.g., not carried out regularly enough or not completed by the teacher at all); (2) implementation of selected interventions for students is not well documented, and there is concern from school leaders that teachers do not have the time, training, and/or support to implement the interventions with integrity; (3) selection of reading interventions may sometimes be misguided (e.g., interventions targeting reading fluency are used when the student may benefit more from an intervention targeting phonics and phonemic awareness); and (4) coupled with these challenges, evaluating the effectiveness of each student's Tier 2 intervention plan is complicated and not done in a systematic way, making it unclear what it means when students are deemed *nonresponders*.

Given this school's needs, as well as its relatively progressive and data-based approach to instructional problem solving, the school psychologist, principal, and a well-respected and experienced third-grade teacher began discussing how the SOPAA model may help improve the existing RTI model. Specifically, in addition to using the TAPS process to address the aforementioned challenges, they felt that intervention development and implementation would be strengthened by having a specific TAPS Teacher to assist teachers, and that implementation capacity would benefit from increased professional development of assistive school personnel within the school. Further, they envisioned increased support for intervention implementation by creating more structure in their use of regular volunteers, most of whom are preservice teachers from a neighboring university. Also, the school psychologist, principal, and third-grade teacher agreed that using the SOPAA would eventually help teachers better address students' deficits in writing and math, as well as provide school leaders with a better method for evaluating and systematically modifying instructional problem-solving practices within the school. On the basis of continued discussion and planning meetings among the three educators during the 2012–2013 school year, they developed the implementation timeline shown in Table 13.4.

As shown in the timeline, East Davis's SOPAA model will be facilitated by three educators at the start, and eventually a fourth. The principal, school psychologist, and third-grade teacher ultimately selected the co-facilitators listed in Table 13.4 because each individual was most qualified and preferred to assume that role. For example, the school social worker had coordinated a type of volunteer program with the neighboring university for many years and had experience working with, scheduling, and training school volunteers. The school psychologist was designated as the Lead Coordinator and TAPS Reading Teacher because she had substantial background experience with reading intervention, assessment, and consultation, as well as with data-based decision making. The school psychologist also worked well with the reading specialist, and although the reading specialist also had a strong background with reading instruction, this educator preferred to assume the role as the TAPS Writing Teacher and discuss TAPS reading cases with the school psychologist if needed.

Given the timeline shown in Table 13.4, it is worth pointing out that both the TAPS Reading Teacher and TAPS Writing Teacher practiced using TAPS procedures with at least a few students during the 2012–1013 school year to get accustomed to the procedures and forms. However, because both of these educators were familiar with consultation in general, as well as with interventions and assessment in their respective areas, these factors decreased the need for a preparation year prior to Year 1 of implementation. Recall also that classroom teachers and teacher assistants were familiar with implementing evidence-based reading interventions, which further decreased the potential need for a preparation year.

Although the principal and 3rd-grade teacher were involved with intervention planning, neither of these educators had the availability to co-facilitate the SOPAA. Instead, they planned to maintain involvement with SOPAA implementation by assisting the co-facilitators with generating teachers' support, attending the hourly meeting each month, and helping to evaluate the effects

TABLE 13.4. Implementation Timeline for East Davis Elementary School

School year (implementation year)	Description of implementation plan
2013–2014 (Year 1)	*SOPAA facilitators: The SOPAA model will be facilitated by four individuals: (1) the school psychologist (serving as Lead Coordinator and TAPS Reading Teacher), (2) the reading specialist (serving as the TAPS Writing Teacher), (3) the school social worker (serving as the TAPS Support Coordinator), and (4) starting in Year 2, a special education teacher (serving as the TAPS Math Teacher)* 1. TAPS: Use TAPS to target reading in all grades, using it as part of the RTI Tier 2 intervention process. 2. Assessment for instruction: Continue using universal screenings in reading and use these data in helping to select and prioritize students for TAPS support (with guidance from the TAPS Reading Teacher). 3. Maximized personnel and professional development: Although teachers have been previously trained in (and most are reportedly using) evidence-based interventions in reading, at beginning of the school year do a refresher workshop on two of the intervention programs teachers seem to struggle with implementing. Train all teacher assistants and three additional assistive personnel (the art teacher, librarian, and guidance counselor) to use two of the evidence-based reading interventions. Using a SOPAA volunteer program (with guidance from Chapter 8), train volunteers (mostly university preservice teachers who are "placed" in the school 3 days per week) to implement two of the intervention programs. The TAPS Writing Teacher and TAPS Reading Teacher do 8–10 hours/month of professional development in their respective areas. 4. Communication and generating support: Use methods discussed in Chapter 10.
2014–2015 (Year 2)[a]	General: The TAPS Math Teacher begins involvement with the SOPAA at the start of this school year. 1. TAPS: Begin TAPS support in writing across all classes and grade levels. Continue using TAPS for reading primarily with Tier 2 interventions. 2. Assessment for instruction: Do winter and spring benchmark assessments in math for grades 1–4 (facilitated by the TAPS Math Teacher). 3. Maximized personnel and professional development: The TAPS Math Teacher does 8–10 hours/month of professional development. The TAPS Support Coordinator continues to train preservice teacher volunteers to implement reading programs. All teachers and teacher assistants learn a selected intervention program in math and a selected intervention program in writing. 4 Communication and generating support: Use methods discussed in Chapter 10.
2015–2016 (Year 3)	1. TAPS: Begin TAPS support in math across all classes and grade levels. Begin using TAPS for reading primarily with Tier 3 interventions and allow classroom teachers to select and implement Tier 2 interventions for struggling students (with generally less consultative support from the TAPS Reading Teacher). 2. Assessment for instruction: Following training, all teachers begin classwide benchmark assessment procedures in math during the fall, winter, and spring. 3. Maximized personnel and professional development: At beginning of the school year teachers learn benchmark assessment procedures in math. School volunteers learn to implement one of the selected intervention programs in math. All teachers and teacher assistants learn a second intervention program in math. 4. Communication and generating support: Use methods discussed in Chapter 10. *Full-scale SOPAA achieved by the end of this school year.*

[a] Unless otherwise specified, the implementation plan from year to year will also include TAPS and assessment for instruction plans that began in a previous school year.

of the SOPAA and RTI model in place. Overall, East Davis Elementary School illustrates a school with many strengths and a promising approach to instructional problem solving in place prior to the SOPAA, but a school that would also likely benefit from added structure and implementation support that could be achieved with the SOPAA model.

SUMMARY

In this chapter we described four examples of how and why to develop a SOPAA implementation plan, all of which were derived from our experience working in schools with varying strengths and needs. Each of the examples was intended to be illustrative rather than prescriptive, because there is no "perfect way" to plan for, initiate, and sustain SOPAA implementation. Further, all educators probably recognize that no one school will have the same characteristics as another, so our illustrations were not intended to match any one school's characteristics exactly. In short, as we highlighted at the end of Chapter 11, when educators within a school are motivated to work collaboratively, the concepts, procedures, and recommendations in a book like this should be helpful, but not sufficient, for developing and executing the strategies that will meaningfully improve and sustain students' academic progress.

CHAPTER 14

Using the SOPAA to Support Graduate Students' Training and Applied Experiences in Schools

This chapter describes how trainers of university graduate students can use features of the SOPAA to support those students' training and applied experiences for later work in schools. It is particularly applicable to graduate students (and their university trainers) working in areas such as special education, school psychology, education leadership (for students who may serve as school or district administrators), literacy and language arts (for students training to become reading specialists), speech pathology (for students who plan to work in schools), or any other field that trains students to become specialists or administrators within schools. In some cases, the training activities described in this chapter may also be applicable for regular education preservice teachers.

We begin this chapter by describing a brief rationale for using training activities related to the SOPAA and then describe several specific activities from which trainers can select as opportunities for students to acquire applied, school-based experiences. Although the applied activities are conceptualized in terms of the SOPAA and derived from practice-based recommendations throughout this book, most of the activities should also be relevant for students who work in schools that are not specifically implementing the model. In other words, the training activities are designed to be relevant as school-based experiences that should help students think about, and actually help to address, the needs of struggling learners—even in the absence of a school formally using the SOPAA. In particular, many of the activities described in this chapter should be useful for students learning about approaches to triadic consultation, organizational consultation, and systems-level change that can begin within a particular school, such as evidence-based intervention programs, academic progress monitoring, working with school volunteers, and/or developing professional development activities for oneself or for other educators in the school. Of course, for students who may eventually want to initiate the SOPAA or a similar model of systems-level instructional problem solving, the activities in this chapter should be helpful in increasing their capacity to do so once they complete their graduate training.

BASIC RATIONALE FOR USING SOPAA FEATURES IN GRADUATE STUDENTS' TRAINING

The overall rationale for using the applied experiences described in this chapter is that research suggests that many school practitioners (e.g., school psychologists, special education teachers, regular education teachers) may lack sufficient preservice and inservice training with practices associated with evidence-based interventions, academic progress monitoring, school-based consultation, and other critical practices associated with helping schools meet the needs of all students. For example, although there is evidence that school psychologists are capable of, and would prefer to engage in, professional activities that are aligned with the roles of SOPAA facilitators (e.g., consultation and intervention; Costenbader, Swartz, & Petrix, 1992; Hosp & Reschly, 2002), there is concern that many school psychology graduate programs are not adequately preparing their students for these types of activities (Barnett et al., 2002; Cochrane & Laux, 2008; Costenbader et al., 1992; Kratochwill, 2007; Shernoff, Kratochwill, & Stiober, 2003). For instance, Shernoff et al. (2003) found that most school psychology graduate programs are not adequately preparing their students to understand and/or implement evidence-based intervention and prevention programs, and that applied experiences with evidence-based interventions is particularly low.

There are also notable concerns about the inservice and preservice training for special education and regular education teachers. For example, Begeny and Martens (2006a) found that master's-level regular and special education teachers lacked coursework and applied training in evidence-based academic assessment and intervention practices. Similarly, in a nationally representative survey of practicing teachers, the Coalition for Psychology in Schools and Education (2006) suggested that teachers report being underprepared to teach a variety of basic skills and strategies or to assess student learning. Further, there is evidence to suggest that the effects of teacher education coursework and applied experiences are minimally correlated with student achievement (Hattie, 2009; Levine, 2006; Walsh, 2006).

Collectively, multiple educators within a school must be well versed in practices such as consultation and using evidence-based assessment and intervention. We believe that helping educators and future school leaders obtain these skills should occur during preservice training (e.g., during graduate school) and that the SOPAA model can be used as a platform for helping these future educators better develop their knowledge, skills, and potential for leadership to meet the challenging needs of schools.

TRAINING ACTIVITIES

The list of training activities in this chapter can be assigned by university trainers to graduate students who are receiving applied experiences in a school. The activities can be integrated as part of any graduate-level course associated with key topics discussed in this book, and many are particularly suitable for students taking a semester-long or yearlong practicum course that occurs in an elementary school.

To maximize the learning from these applied training activities, students should also have opportunities to reflect on their experiences, such as through writing assignments and discussion with university supervisors, school-based supervisors, and/or classmates. Furthermore, although the activities are intentionally described as application-based assignments for graduate students, most of the activities also allow for university trainers to supplement the applied experience with didactic lessons that can take place in the university classroom. For illustrative purposes, in this chapter we provide a few specific recommendations for reflection- and didactic-based options that are associated with a particular activity. As desired, university trainers should be able to develop additional reflection and didactic experiences based on the description of each activity and the goals of their particular course.

Our descriptions of suggested training activities are categorized within this section according to primary features of the SOPAA, not by the six SOPAA components. Also, the activity descriptions first state—in relatively broad terms—what the graduate student should do to complete the activity. As needed, the university trainer should provide students with greater specificity regarding his or her expectations and how, specifically, the student should use this book and/or other resources to complete the activity. The trainer may also choose to modify an activity to ensure that the student can complete the activity successfully and best meet the specific goals of the graduate course.

Triadic Consultation

1. Use the TAPS process (or as many features as possible of the TAPS process) with a classroom teacher who needs assistance with improving a student's academic skills. In other words, practice the role of the TAPS Teacher in reading, math, or writing. *As a reflection-oriented supplement to this activity, students should discuss their successes and challenges, as well as the strengths and limitations, associated with using the TAPS process.*

Organizational Consultation and Preparing for Systems-Level Change

2. Use Appendices B and D to consider the strengths, needs, and characteristics of a school that would support or weaken the likelihood of successful SOPAA implementation in that school. (Because the graduate student may be new to a school and unfamiliar with its strengths and weaknesses, this activity might involve having the student interview relevant school leaders).

3. Using the information obtained in Activity 2, identify educators in the school who would be best suited to facilitate the SOPAA and specify why. Then, using information throughout this book (e.g., Table 9.1, pp. 171–173), develop a comprehensive rationale for using the SOPAA in that school, including a description of how the model would align with the school's existing practices for addressing students' learning difficulties.

4. After completing Activities 2 and 3, develop a SOPAA implementation plan for that school, including a realistic implementation timeline. *As a reflection-oriented supplement to this activity (and to Activities 2 and 3), students should regularly discuss their progress and the practical challenges associated with completing the activities. This discussion should help the university trainer evaluate each student's understanding of systems-level change in schools.*

Implementing and/or Facilitating Evidence-Based Intervention Programs

5. Determine which intervention strategies and/or programs teachers are using in the school to address student learning difficulties and summarize the research literature (if any) that has evaluated those strategies and programs. This activity might be focused on one particular academic area (e.g., reading) and/or subskill of that area (e.g., phonics-based interventions in reading). *As a didactic supplement to this activity, students might get instruction on effective teaching practices for one or more of the academic areas, their state's guidelines for instruction in the area, and the key subskills of the area.*

6. Select one or more evidence-based intervention programs, learn how to implement the program, and implement it with one or more students who would likely benefit from the program. The selected intervention program may be one that teachers in the school already use or a program not currently being used but could be useful within the school. *As a reflection-oriented supplement to this activity, students should discuss and critique definitions that have been proposed for terms such as* evidence-based interventions, research-validated, research-based, and learner-verified. *Students should also determine and report the extent to which their selected intervention program is evidence-based.*

7. Using Chapter 8 for guidance, develop a plan for recruiting and training school volunteers to implement an evidence-based intervention program. (This activity would be best completed after the student has had experience implementing the intervention program that is selected to be part of the volunteer training).

Academic Assessment and Progress Monitoring

8. Select one or more psychometrically appropriate assessment tools, learn how to administer the assessment, and use the assessment with one or more students in the school. Ideally, this activity would involve using one or more *progress monitoring* assessment tools and using the assessment with a student in the school who receives intervention in an area targeted by the assessment. *As a didactic supplement to this activity, students might get instruction on contemporary assessment practices for one or more of the academic areas, as well as state or national policies (or best-practices) associated with progress monitoring.*

Professional Development and Communication

9. After completing Activities 2–4, and consistent with the information described in Chapter 9, prepare a plan and all needed materials that would be used to hold an introductory meeting with the school principal.

10. After completing Activities 2–4, and consistent with the information described in Chapter 10, prepare a plan and all needed materials that would be used to hold an introductory presentation of the SOPAA for teachers in the school.

11. Consistent with information provided in Chapter 7, plan one or more professional development workshops (e.g., including presentation slides and handouts) that could be used to support teachers' use of the SOPAA. If possible, actually host the professional development workshop. *As a reflection-oriented supplement to this activity, students should discuss the benefits and challenges associated with facilitating professional development activities with teachers.*

12. Consistent with the information described throughout the book (e.g., Chapter 7), develop a personalized professional development plan that would be used by a TAPS Teacher. If possible, complete activities selected as part of the personalized professional development plan.

Epilogue

As professionals involved on a regular basis with children and schools, we are fully aware of the gap between the idealized visions of how new innovations will transform schools and the reality of educators trying to put these innovations in place. For example, three-tier prevention and intervention models, universal screening, and collaborative problem-solving teams all seem to make so much sense and seem very "doable" in the abstract. However, these visions rarely come with roadmaps and tools that help schools move from where they are to where they want to be. When a school starts to move toward implementation of a new model or innovation, the knowledge needed and the number of decisions that must be made to start and sustain implementation can be overwhelming.

Even small issues or questions about how a new innovation works or blends with existing practices can present roadblocks to change that consume a lot of time and energy to resolve. For instance, educators may ask:

When and how quickly should implementation of the model or innovation occur?
What materials will be needed to facilitate smooth and systematic implementation?
What are the options for screening and assessing academic skills, and how do they differ?
How should all school staff be introduced to the rationale behind implementation, and what is the likelihood that they will resist the changes?
How will teachers be trained to implement research-based interventions, and how will they receive the needed support to ensure that students receive needed interventions?

In short, schools are complex systems where changes in one part of the system ultimately have effects on most or all educators in the school. Failing to anticipate all that is needed for successful implementation, as well as the impact of change on all educators and students in the school, can bring unplanned resistance from the school community and create other barriers that can weaken implementation effectiveness and sustainability.

These complexities, which educators implementing change in their school must address on a daily basis, are part of what accounts for the "research-to-practice" gap in education (Denton, Vaughn, & Fletcher, 2003; Gersten, & Dimino, 2001). In the preceding chapters of this book, we described an integrated, incremental, and adaptable model of instructional support at the student level (i.e., TAPS) and the school level (i.e., the SOPAA). A goal of this model is to address many of the challenges educators encounter when trying to improve students' academic success at a schoolwide level. As a viable way to overcome many of the roadblocks that prevent schools from supporting as many students as possible, we believe in an incremental approach to change that relies on (1) structured and standard strategies to address common learning problems, and (2) a wide range of school staff (and, in some cases, community volunteers) to implement interventions for students experiencing difficulty. We also believe that ongoing professional development and effective communication with teachers and school administrators are critical variables in successfully initiating and sustaining a model for schoolwide instructional problem solving.

By providing specific forms and offering detailed guidance related to assessment tools and research-based interventions, we aim to decrease the substantial amount of time educators often spend on selecting their own interventions or developing their own standardized procedures and forms. We also acknowledge that each school presents a different context for implementing student and school-level learning support models, and we have tried to accommodate this reality by offering a range of choices rather than "an answer" for each complex decision point. Further, we hope educators will use the companion website *www.sopaaforschools.org* to support their implementation of the SOPAA, because the website allows access to additional materials and examples, as well as offers information to help educators address questions that will inevitably arise during implementation.

Despite our best attempts to support educators through this book and the companion website, there is no doubt that implementing change at a school level—or even changing the role of one educator to provide triadic consultation—represents a meaningful commitment of time and energy. However, we are constantly encouraged by the dedicated and successful educators we encounter in schools, who we know *can* create substantial changes within schools for the betterment of their students. We see teachers and administrators who take the challenges and victories of their students personally, working well beyond the school day and school year to meet their students' needs. Our hope is that this book is useful for educators, reflects an understanding of the realities that educators face, and that they and we will continue to learn from each other.

APPENDICES

APPENDIX A

Summary of the SOPAA Components and Roles

The SOPAA Components and Key Features within Each Component

Component 1: Targeted Assistance Program for Students (TAPS)

1. Process for the classroom teacher to request support from the TAPS Support Teacher.
2. Process for pinpointing a student's academic deficit and developing a list of intervention programs that should target and improve the deficit.
3. Process for developing, documenting, and implementing an intervention plan designed to assist the classroom teacher and improve the student's learning difficulty.
4. Process for evaluating and discussing the effectiveness of the student's intervention plan (after it has been implemented a specified number of weeks) and making subsequent decisions that should benefit the student's learning.

Component 2: Assessment for Instruction

1. Targeted skills observation that occurs prior to developing a TAPS intervention plan, to ensure that the intervention plan targets the subskill or subskills with which the student struggles the most.
2. Progress monitoring assessment during implementation of a student's TAPS intervention plan.
3. Schoolwide benchmark assessments in reading and math to help teachers identify students who struggle in these areas and may benefit from a TAPS intervention plan.

Component 3: Maximized Intervention Personnel and Resources

1. System for training and coordinating assistive school personnel (e.g., teacher assistants, librarians, art/music teachers, social workers, school volunteers, counselors, and possibly other types of educators in the school) who can implement targeted intervention programs with students during a TAPS case.
2. System for training and coordinating school volunteers who can implement targeted intervention programs with students during a TAPS case.
3. Identification and selection of evidence-based and/or learner-verified intervention programs that can be used for during the TAPS process to target each subskill for reading, math, and writing.

Component 4: Targeted Professional Development

1. Ongoing professional development for each TAPS Support Teacher that is aligned with the SOPAA.
2. One to three professional development workshops for classroom teachers in areas that are aligned with the SOPAA (e.g., learning how to implement an intervention program or use a type of progress monitoring assessment tool).
   a. As applicable, professional development also occurs for assistive school personnel and/or school volunteers to learn intervention programs that are used with TAPS cases.

(cont.)

3. Embedded within the TAPS process (see Component 1, feature 4), when evaluating the effectiveness of a student's intervention plan, each teacher involved with a TAPS case reflects on, documents, and discusses the case (e.g., aspects that were successful, unsuccessful, or improved over time). The TAPS Support Teacher also helps the classroom teacher relate the TAPS case to prior experiences (e.g., information obtained during previous TAPS cases or during SOPAA professional development workshops).

Component 5: Methods for Communication and Generating Support

1. Steps for communicating with school leaders (e.g., the principal) about key aspects of the SOPAA (e.g., need for using the SOPAA in the school, how the SOPAA aligns with the school's existing practices, time or material resources related to the SOPAA) and ultimately generating leadership's support for SOPAA implementation.
2. Steps for communicating with classroom teachers about key aspects and benefits of the SOPAA, and ultimately generating teachers' support for SOPAA implementation.
3. Process for communicating the TAPS procedures and processes to all educators in the school who will be involved with SOPAA implementation.
4. Steps for evaluating the SOPAA across years and communicating the findings (e.g., strengths, weaknesses, and improvements) to other educators in order to sustain or increase educators' support for implementation.
5. Process for communicating among the SOPAA co-facilitators to ensure effective and efficient SOPAA implementation.

Component 6: Adaptable and Incremental Implementation

1. Multiple options for modifying and adapting SOPAA implementation (particularly in the early years) in a way that is most feasible for a school and that matches the school's needs, strengths, and characteristics. Thus, the model allows for modified but meaningful implementation.
2. Multiple options for incremental implementation so that a school can *start* implementation in a way that is beneficial, but can continually (and systematically) increase the scope of implementation to better meet the needs of all struggling learners.

The Five SOPAA Roles[a]

1. SOPAA Lead Coordinator (or simply, Lead Coordinator) [b]
2. TAPS Reading Teacher
3. TAPS Math Teacher
4. TAPS Writing Teacher
5. TAPS Intervention Support Coordinator (or simply, TAPS Support Coordinator)

[a]Depending on the SOPAA implementation plan, some roles may not be needed. For example, if the SOPAA plan is designed only to target students' reading deficits, there would not be a designated TAPS Math Teacher or TAPS Writing Teacher. Also depending on the SOPAA implementation plan, a SOPAA facilitator may have more than one role.

[b]The Lead Coordinator will always have a TAPS Support Teacher role in addition to the Lead Coordinator role.

APPENDIX B

Preparation for SOPAA Implementation (Part 1): Schoolwide Capacity Assessment of Relevant Characteristics

The purpose of the Schoolwide Capacity Assessment is to help you think specifically about the characteristics of your school that will (or will not) be helpful in starting SOPAA implementation. The questions and topic areas listed below are not intended to be fully comprehensive, nor are they intended to solicit lengthy written responses. Rather, the questions are designed to prompt your thinking about potential school assets and barriers that will be relevant to your SOPAA implementation planning. ***You will likely need 45–60 minutes to complete this assessment.***

To best utilize the Schoolwide Capacity Assessment, write brief notes (or possibly lists) in response to each (or most) of the following questions. As applicable, you might also develop new questions that will be relevant to your SOPAA implementation planning. After reading and responding to the following questions, you should respond to the rating scale items that follow as a way to summarize the characteristics of your school that may strengthen or weaken your implementation of the SOPAA.

1. Does your school use a core curriculum in reading, math, and/or writing? For each of these three academic areas (as applicable), answer the following:
   a. What core curriculum is used and who makes this determination?
   b. How long has the curriculum been used at the school?
   c. To what extent is the core curriculum structured for teachers (e.g., does the curriculum offer scripted or semiscripted lessons or a specific sequence of learning activities)?
   d. Is there research evidence to support the effectiveness of the curriculum?
   e. Is the core curriculum referenced in Chapter 12 of this book, and if not, how well does it align with the content analyses and subskills discussed in Chapter 12?
   f. Do all teachers in the school use the same curriculum?
   g. Do teachers use other instructional activities to supplement the curriculum, and if so, what types of activities are used?
   h. Do students receive the core curriculum based on their general classroom assignment or are they grouped by current skill level?
2. How do teachers in your school identify students with learning difficulties? For each of the three main academic areas (reading, math, and writing), answer the following:
   a. Does the school use universal screening/progress monitoring assessment procedures (e.g., using schoolwide assessments in the fall, winter, and spring)?
   b. Does the school use other standardized assessments to screen for students with learning difficulties (other than those associated with the above question)?
   c. If a standardized assessment is used (including universal screening procedures):
      i. What assessments are used?
      ii. Do all students in the school receive the assessments?
      iii. How regularly are assessments administered?
      iv. Who within the school administers those assessments?
      v. How is assessment data summarized for teachers and when do teachers receive the summarized data?
      vi. How do teachers use the data?

(cont.)

3. If a student is identified with a learning difficulty (and the student is not being evaluated for, nor does he or she currently have, a disability classification), how do teachers assist the student?
   a. At what times during the school year do teachers usually report concerns about student learning difficulties?
   b. To whom does a teacher generally report his or her concerns about a student's learning difficulty (e.g., with key members of the school, with a grade-level team, with an intervention support team)?
   c. Do teachers usually report concerns about student learning difficulties immediately upon recognizing the difficulties or after the difficulties have been present for some period of time?
   d. Is there a schoolwide system in place for teachers to report a student's academic difficulties and seek assistance regarding those difficulties? If so,
      i. How does the system work?
      ii. Do referrals get addressed quickly and efficiently?
      iii. What are the advantages and disadvantages of that system?
      iv. Does the system involve a form of consultation, and if so:
         1. Who within the school provides consultative services?
         2. What are the procedures for facilitating those consultation services?
         3. What are the strengths and weaknesses of those consultative services?
         4. How regularly do teachers rely on those consultative services?
   e. If a team problem-solving approach is used to help teachers address a student's academic difficulties, what are the strengths and weaknesses of that approach? Related questions are as follows:
      i. Which teachers attend the team meetings?
      ii. Do some members of the team contribute more or less to problem solving?
      iii. Is there a person on the team who takes the lead in "managing" the meetings and/or referrals?
      iv. Is the team able to meet and develop an intervention quickly after the teacher's referral for team problem solving?
      v. What is the role of formal assessment with teachers' referrals?
      vi. Are there challenges to scheduling and/or facilitating team meetings?
      vii. Do team meetings efficiently address the academic referral?
   f. Do certain school personnel consult in specific academic areas (e.g., reading, math, and writing) and how successful are they in their consultative roles?
   g. How do teachers within the school select interventions to assist struggling learners? Related to this:
      i. Is there a "menu" of common interventions from which teachers select?
      ii. Are teachers generally able to select interventions that specifically address the primary area of academic concern (e.g., phonemic awareness, addition facts, spelling errors)?
      iii. Do most teachers seek out interventions that have been supported by educational research?
      iv. What resources do teachers commonly use to find academic interventions (e.g., books, journals, websites, colleague recommendations)?
4. After a student is identified as having a learning difficulty (and the student is not being evaluated for, nor does he or she currently have, a disability classification), who provides intervention services once the intervention is selected?
   a. Generally, what proportion of intervention service delivery is provided by regular education teachers, special education teachers, other school personnel (e.g., reading specialists, school psychologists), and school volunteers?
   b. Does your school require that the implementation integrity of an intervention is monitored and/or recorded?
   c. Who within your school has extensive experience implementing evidence-based interventions in reading, math, and/or writing, and what interventions are commonly implemented?

(cont.)

5. What role do school volunteers have in your school?
   a. Who are your school volunteers (e.g., parents of children in your school, university students, high school students, community members)?
   b. Where are school volunteers recruited from and how are they recruited?
   c. Does your school (or district) have a system for recruiting school volunteers, and if so, who manages that system and is it managed successfully?
   d. Are school volunteers sometimes used to implement academic interventions, and if so, what types of interventions do school volunteers provide?
   e. Are school volunteers used in the most helpful ways possible?
   f. Can you think of additional ways that school volunteers could be utilized to support teachers' work in the classroom?
   g. How committed are your school volunteers (e.g., how many days per week do they volunteer, for how long do they volunteer each day, for how many weeks do they maintain involvement)?
   h. Does it appear that school volunteers' work is valued by the teachers and administration in your school?
   i. Does it appear that school volunteers feel satisfied with the work they are providing at your school?
6. In a typical school year, how many staff development workshops are dedicated to helping teachers learn about and address students' academic difficulties?
   a. Do teachers generally seem interested in learning more about and using new academic interventions and/or assessments?
   b. Who within the school and/or district offers workshops on evidence-based academic interventions?
   c. Who within the school and/or district offers workshops on academic assessment?
   d. Have teachers (formally or informally) indicated interest in learning about particular topics that will help them address students' learning difficulties (e.g., a particular academic intervention, general principles related to student learning), and if so, are there teachers in the school who could successfully host a workshop covering those areas of interest?
7. Who are the key leaders in the school that help to influence schoolwide changes?
   a. Are teachers and administrators within your school more likely to be supportive of, or resistant to, schoolwide changes?
   b. What types of schoolwide changes do you believe teachers in your school would be most and least supportive of?
   c. What factors are likely to be most important for influencing the motivation of most teachers to implement new schoolwide procedures and/or policies?
   d. What factors are likely to be most important for influencing the motivation of your administrators to implement new schoolwide procedures and/or policies?
   e. What are the primary assets and barriers associated with school-wide change in your school?
   f. In recent years have there been schoolwide changes in your school that were initiated by someone within your school (as opposed to primarily district, regional, or statewide mandates for change)? If so:
      i. Were those changes implemented successfully?
      ii. How long did it take for all of the changes to be implemented effectively by all teachers?
      iii. Was the entire schoolwide change implemented all at once, or was it implemented incrementally (e.g., starting with only some components, starting with only some grade levels, starting with only some teachers)?
      iv. Did teachers collaborate to support schoolwide change (e.g., did some teachers share management responsibilities for different components)?
      v. How was momentum and support for the change established?

(cont.)

To help you summarize the characteristics of your school that may influence successful SOPAA implementation, respond to the following items.

1. **The core reading curriculum in my school appears effective for at least 80% of our students.**

Strongly Disagree	Disagree	Neither Agree nor Disagree	Agree	Strongly Agree
1	2	3	4	5

2. **The core math curriculum in my school appears effective for at least 80% of our students.**

Strongly Disagree	Disagree	Neither Agree nor Disagree	Agree	Strongly Agree
1	2	3	4	5

3. **Within my school, we have a highly effective and efficient system for immediately identifying students with learning difficulties.**

Strongly Disagree	Disagree	Neither Agree nor Disagree	Agree	Strongly Agree
1	2	3	4	5

4. **Within my school, we have a highly effective and efficient system for remediating students' learning difficulties.**

Strongly Disagree	Disagree	Neither Agree nor Disagree	Agree	Strongly Agree
1	2	3	4	5

5. **The majority of the regular education teachers in my school have the needed skills and resources to effectively address students' learning difficulties.**

Strongly Disagree	Disagree	Neither Agree nor Disagree	Agree	Strongly Agree
1	2	3	4	5

6. **My school has a system for recruiting a desirable number of school volunteers.**

Strongly Disagree	Disagree	Neither Agree nor Disagree	Agree	Strongly Agree
1	2	3	4	5

7. **My school effectively uses our school volunteers.**

Strongly Disagree	Disagree	Neither Agree nor Disagree	Agree	Strongly Agree
1	2	3	4	5

(cont.)

8. **Within my school, staff development workshops are frequent enough and useful enough to help classroom teachers address students' academic difficulties.**

Strongly Disagree	Disagree	Neither Agree nor Disagree	Agree	Strongly Agree
1	2	3	4	5

9. **There are many characteristics of my school that are already aligned with the core components of the SOPAA. (As needed, refer to the Figure 2.2.)**

Strongly Disagree	Disagree	Neither Agree nor Disagree	Agree	Strongly Agree
1	2	3	4	5

10. **Most teachers in my school would probably be in favor of having some of the SOPAA components implemented at this time.**

Strongly Disagree	Disagree	Neither Agree nor Disagree	Agree	Strongly Agree
1	2	3	4	5

11. **Most teachers in my school would probably be in favor of having all components of the SOPAA implemented at this time.**

Strongly Disagree	Disagree	Neither Agree nor Disagree	Agree	Strongly Agree
1	2	3	4	5

12. **I should be able to generate support from teachers and administration in my school in order to implement at least some components of the SOPAA at this time.**

Strongly Disagree	Disagree	Neither Agree nor Disagree	Agree	Strongly Agree
1	2	3	4	5

13. **There are one or more teachers within my school who are likely to co-facilitate SOPAA implementation.**

Strongly Disagree	Disagree	Neither Agree nor Disagree	Agree	Strongly Agree
1	2	3	4	5

APPENDIX C

Preparation for SOPAA Implementation (Part 2): TAPS Support Teacher Self-Assessment of Relevant Characteristics and Experiences

The purpose of this self-assessment is to help you think more specifically about your characteristics and experiences that will (or will not) be conducive to facilitating the TAPS process. For the purposes of completing this self-assessment, items about "consultation" refer to the descriptions of the triadic consultative process that is described in Chapter 2.

The questions and topic areas listed below are not intended to be fully comprehensive, nor are they intended to solicit lengthy written responses. Rather, the questions are designed to prompt your thinking about potential assets and barriers that will be relevant to your role as a TAPS Teacher. ***You will likely need 20–40 minutes to complete this self-assessment.***

To best utilize this self-assessment, write brief notes (or possibly lists) in response to each item. As applicable, you might also develop new questions that will be relevant to your planning as a TAPS Teacher. After considering each of the questions, you should respond to the rating scale items that follow as a way to summarize your academic consultation characteristics and experiences.

1. What training experiences have you had with school-based consultation? For example,
   a. Have you learned about specific models of consultation (e.g., behavioral consultation, team-based problem solving, instructional consultation), and if so, to what extent?
   b. Did you have opportunities during your professional training to implement one or more models of consultation, and if so, to what extent?
   c. Did you receive direct supervision when you implemented those models of consultation?
   d. What specific training experiences have you had with using consultation to improve students' academic skills?
2. During your professional work, have you used consultation skills to improve students' reading, math, and/or writing abilities? For example,
   a. What was the nature of that consultation (e.g., one-on-one consultation with teachers, team problem solving, "hallway troubleshooting" with teachers)?
   b. How many years have you been using consultation to address students' academic difficulties?
   c. In a given month of a school year, how often do you use consultation to address students' academic difficulties, and have you consulted more or less often to address reading, math, and/or writing problems?
   d. What specific types of academic difficulties have you addressed during your consultation experiences? For example, with reading-related referrals, have you addressed student difficulties in decoding/phonics, fluency, vocabulary, comprehension, etc.?
   e. What methods of academic progress monitoring have you used to evaluate the effectiveness of interventions that were developed through your consultation activities?
3. What were the primary successes and challenges you experienced during your academic consultation experiences?
   a. Did the teacher/consultee seem to benefit from the consultative process? For example,
      i. Was there usually evidence that your consultation services addressed the teacher's primary concern and improved the student's learning?
      ii. Was there usually evidence that your consultation services helped teachers to strengthen their instructional decision making and intervention development skills?

(cont.)

  b. Did teachers appear to learn new instructional/intervention skills as a result of receiving your consultation services?
  c. What were the most significant challenges you faced when consulting with teachers (e.g., assuring sufficient knowledge of available interventions, ensuring implementation of the intervention, monitoring implementation integrity, helping teachers to generalize skills learned during the consultation process, finding time to follow up with teachers afterward, developing structure for the consultative process, generating support from the principal to afford the time for consultation)?

4. How knowledgeable are you about evidence-based interventions for the primary academic area(s) (i.e., reading, math, and writing) for which you are the designated TAPS Support Teacher?
  a. Have you received formal instruction in evidence-based academic interventions (e.g., university coursework, professional development workshops)?
  b. To what extent have you implemented interventions (within your designated academic area) with students experiencing learning difficulties?
  c. What challenges and successes have you had with implementing those academic interventions?
  d. Are there particular intervention programs that you are very comfortable implementing?
  e. Of the intervention programs you know well, how effective are those programs for students with academic difficulties (e.g., what does the research report about those programs, what evidence have you observed regarding the program's effectiveness)?
  f. What resources do you use to find potentially useful academic interventions (e.g., books, journals, websites)?

To help you summarize your academic consultation characteristics and experiences, respond to the following items.

1. My professional training (e.g., university coursework, professional development workshops) in academic consultation has been extensive.

Strongly Disagree	Disagree	Neither Agree nor Disagree	Agree	Strongly Agree
1	2	3	4	5

2. I have had extensive professional experience consulting with teachers to address students' reading difficulties.

Strongly Disagree	Disagree	Neither Agree nor Disagree	Agree	Strongly Agree
1	2	3	4	5

3. I have had extensive professional experience consulting with teachers to address students' math difficulties.

Strongly Disagree	Disagree	Neither Agree nor Disagree	Agree	Strongly Agree
1	2	3	4	5

4. I have had extensive professional experience consulting with teachers to address students' writing difficulties.

Strongly Disagree	Disagree	Neither Agree nor Disagree	Agree	Strongly Agree
1	2	3	4	5

(cont.)

5. Overall, my consultation services have helped teachers to meaningfully improve the target student's learning difficulty.

Strongly Disagree	Disagree	Neither Agree nor Disagree	Agree	Strongly Agree
1	2	3	4	5

6. Overall, my consultation services have helped teachers to strengthen their knowledge of, and ability to use, effective academic interventions.

Strongly Disagree	Disagree	Neither Agree nor Disagree	Agree	Strongly Agree
1	2	3	4	5

7. I feel knowledgeable about evidence-based interventions in the area of reading.

Strongly Disagree	Disagree	Neither Agree nor Disagree	Agree	Strongly Agree
1	2	3	4	5

8. I feel knowledgeable about evidence-based interventions in the area of math.

Strongly Disagree	Disagree	Neither Agree nor Disagree	Agree	Strongly Agree
1	2	3	4	5

9. I feel knowledgeable about evidence-based interventions in the area of writing.

Strongly Disagree	Disagree	Neither Agree nor Disagree	Agree	Strongly Agree
1	2	3	4	5

10. Overall, I feel confident delivering professional development workshops that will help other educators address students' academic deficits.

Strongly Disagree	Disagree	Neither Agree nor Disagree	Agree	Strongly Agree
1	2	3	4	5

APPENDIX D

SOPAA Implementation Planning Summary Checklist

Based on the information gathered from the questions in the TAPS Support Teacher Self-Assessment and the Schoolwide Capacity Assessment, specify (with a checkmark) the likelihood that the following SOPAA components or features can be implemented successfully during the upcoming academic school year. If it is clear that SOPAA implementation will begin with only some grades or classrooms, respond to the checklist according to only those grades or classrooms. As needed, write notes that reflect your response and specify features that should be prioritized over others. Refer to Appendix A for an overview of the SOPAA, if needed.

	Likelihood of Successful Implementation during Upcoming School Year					
SOPAA Component or Feature	Very Unlikely	Unlikely	Unsure	Likely	Very Likely	Notes
1. TAPS process for reading, including progress monitoring						
2. Selecting and using evidence-based intervention programs in reading						
3. Universal screening in reading						
4. TAPS process for math, including progress monitoring						
5. Selecting and using evidence-based intervention programs in math						
6. Universal screening in math						
7. TAPS process for writing, including progress monitoring						

(cont.)

SOPAA Implementation Planning Summary Checklist *(page 2 of 2)*

	Likelihood of Successful Implementation during Upcoming School Year					
SOPAA Component or Feature	Very Unlikely	Unlikely	Unsure	Likely	Very Likely	Notes
8. Selecting and using evidence-based intervention programs in writing						
9. Ongoing professional development for TAPS Teacher(s)						
10. SOPAA professional development workshops for classroom teachers						
11. Professional development workshops for assistive personnel						
12. SOPAA volunteer program						
13. Generating support from school leaders (e.g., the principal)						
14. Generating support from teachers						
15. Evaluating the effectiveness of the SOPAA						

Request for TAPS (Targeted Assistance Program for Students) Form

Teacher's Name: ______________________________ Date: ______________

Student's Name: ______________________________ Student's Grade: __________

1. Describe your primary concern as specifically as possible. For example, if you have concerns about reading, specify the reading skill(s) (e.g., phonics, fluency, comprehension) with which the student struggles the most. ______________________________

____

____

2. How long have you had the primary concern? ______________________________

____

3. Briefly describe and/or attach evidence that supports your primary concern. For example, you may want to write down classroom observations, student grades/progress reports, scores from relevant assessments, and/or attach relevant documents such as assessment forms or student work samples.

____

____

____

____

4. If applicable, briefly describe strategies that have been used to address your primary concern.

____

____

____

____

5. If you responded to item 4, how successful were those strategies (e.g., what were strengths and/or weaknesses of the strategies used)? If applicable, attach relevant documents such as assessment forms or student work samples that help to show the effects of the strategies used.

____

____

____

____

Note: If you are submitting this referral electronically, please check one of the boxes below:

☐ I am also submitting hard copies of evidence (e.g., assessment forms, work samples) to support Items 3 and/or 5.

☐ I am NOT submitting hard copies of evidence (e.g., assessment forms, work samples) to support Items 3 and/or 5.

(cont.)

6. Describe any secondary concerns that may be related to your primary concern (e.g., student behavior, motivation, related academic skill deficits).

7. Provide any additional information that may be relevant to your concerns. For example, are there factors that may complicate intervention development or implementation (e.g., English language learner, scheduling logistics, behavioral concerns, presence of a medical condition, frequent student absences)?

8. Specify the student's strengths (academic and/or other).

9. Based on the information described in Item 1, are there other students in your class who exhibit the same types of academic difficulties at approximately the same level of severity? If so, write the name(s) of the student(s) and provide any additional information about the other student(s) if you would like.

10. Indicate days and times you are generally available and can meet for a 20- to 30-minute intervention planning meeting. This meeting will likely be scheduled 1–3 weeks from today's date.

11. Indicate days and times during the next 2 weeks that the TAPS Teacher can meet briefly (5–20 minutes) with the student. When possible, the TAPS Teacher will conduct a brief observation and/or assessment of the student before meeting with you for the intervention planning meeting.

APPENDIX F

TAPS Case Tracking Form

Student's Name: ______________________________

Teacher who requested TAPS support: ______________________________

Date the request for TAPS Form was received: ______________________________

Specify the date when each activity is completed. Write notes about activities as needed.

Activity	Date Completed	Important Notes If Not Specified Elsewhere
Conduct targeted skills observation		
Develop a list of intervention options and share list with teacher		
Prepare clarification questions and consider responses for IPF items		
Communicate with TAPS Support Coordinator to recruit intervention assistance		
Conduct intervention planning meeting		
Contact student's parent(s) about intervention plan		
Begin intervention plan		
Conduct summative review meeting		

APPENDIX G

TAPS Intervention Planning Form (IPF) and Record

Teacher's Name: ______________________________

Student's Name: ______________________________ Student's Grade: ____________

TAPS Support Teacher's Name: _________________ Date of planning meeting: __________

Goal 1: Share results from skills observation, ask follow-up questions to specify the teacher's primary concern, and get ratings on the TAPS Case Rating Scale.

Write primary concern here: ______________________________

Write additional notes that may be relevant to intervention implementation and success: __________

____

☐ *Check this box to indicate that the TAPS Case Rating Scale has been completed.*

Goal 2: Discuss the list of feasible, evidence-based intervention programs and select the most suitable program that will directly address the primary concern.

Write the selected intervention program here: ______________________________

Goal 3: Develop the Intervention Plan.

1. Who will implement the intervention program? ______________________________

   ____

2. Will a predeveloped intervention protocol be modified in any way, and if so, how and why? ________

   ____

3. How will intervention implementers get trained (if applicable)? ______________________

   ____

4. Where will the intervention be implemented and at what times of day? __________________

   ____

5. How many minutes of intervention (and/or lessons) will occur each day, and how many days per week will intervention occur? ______________________________

6. On what date will implementation begin and what days per week will the intervention occur? ______

   ____

7. How will implementation integrity be evaluated, by whom, and when? __________________

   ____

8. How will student progress be monitored (e.g., with what form of assessment, how often, by whom)?

   ____

9. Who will contact the student's parent(s) to inform him or her about the intervention plan, seek parent input, and seek possible support? ______________________________

(cont.)

10. When will the parent(s) be contacted: ______________ *(If a parent offers objections, input, or support that prompts a change in the intervention plan, this should be communicated between the classroom teacher and TAPS teacher immediately; if applicable, changes should be made to the intervention plan.)*
11. Date for initial review of intervention plan and signatures *(this meeting must occur no more than 1–2 weeks after the date specified in Item 6)*: ______________
12. How many weeks of intervention will occur before the TAPS Formal Review of Intervention Effectiveness? ______________
13. Specify an objective goal the student should meet, resulting from the intervention: ______________
14. By approximately what date will the intervention period (specified in Item 12) be completed? ______________
15. Specify the date for the Summative Review of Intervention Effectiveness meeting (*must be within 2 weeks of the date specified in Item 14*): ______________
16. How will periodic "follow-ups" of intervention success occur (e.g., who will initiate them, approximately how often)? ______________

Signatures below specify agreement on the intervention plan and that both parties agree to fulfill their roles unless extenuating circumstances arise. Signatures also specify that the student's parent(s)/guardian(s) was contacted to obtain verbal consent for this intervention plan. Signatures should occur during the meeting date specified in Item 11.

Classroom Teacher: ______________ Date: ______________

TAPS Teacher: ______________ Date: ______________

Student's parent/guardian gave verbal consent for plan (check one): ☐ **Yes** ☐ **No** ☐ **No reply**
(List all dates parent[s] was called: ______________)

Intervention Follow-Up Information

Date of follow-up:	Notes from follow-up (e.g., implementation difficulties/successes, minor changes to intervention plan, need for extended meeting):
1. ______	
2. ______	
3. ______	
4. ______	
5. ______	
6. ______	
7. ______	
8. ______	
9. ______	
10. ______	
11. ______	
12. ______	
13. ______	

APPENDIX H

TAPS Case Rating Scale

Student's name: ______________________________ Date: ______________

Classroom Teacher's name: ______________________________

TAPS Teacher's name: ______________________________

The following ratings were completed by the student's classroom teacher during the (check one):

☐ **Intervention planning meeting** ☐ **Summative review meeting**

1. **At the present time, where is this student functioning in the specific skill area(s) that represents your primary concern?**

Far Below Grade Level		Exactly at Grade Level*		Well Above Grade Level
1	2	3	4	5

* *Performing exactly where he or she is expected to be according to grade level and month of the school year.*

2. **At the present time, where is this student functioning in the broad academic area that represents your primary concern (i.e., overall reading, mathematics, or written expression achievement)?**

Far Below Grade Level		Exactly at Grade Level*		Well Above Grade Level
1	2	3	4	5

* *Performing exactly where he or she is expected to be according to grade level and month of the school year.*

3. **At the present time, how likely is it that your concerns about this student can be addressed through typical instruction in your classroom?**

Very Unlikely		Neither Likely nor Unlikely		Very Likely
1	2	3	4	5

4. **How concerned are you about this student's academic progress at the present time?**

Very Concerned		Neither Concerned nor Unconcerned		Not at All Concerned
1	2	3	4	5

5. **At the present time, how severe would you consider this student's academic problems?**

Very Severe		Typical for Grade		Not Severe at All
1	2	3	4	5

APPENDIX I

Comments and Suggestions Related to Completing the TAPS Intervention Planning Form (IPF)

Item and Brief Description	Comments for TAPS Teacher	Suggestions for TAPS Teacher
1. Who will implement the intervention program?	• Implementers should include the classroom teacher and, on at least some occasion, the TAPS Teacher. • Other implementers might include trained teachers within the school (e.g., teacher assistants or other assistive school personnel) and/or school volunteers. Chapters 7 and 8 discuss aspects related to training intervention implementers. • The TAPS Support Coordinator will assist the TAPS Teacher with understanding who within the school may be available to support the teacher with intervention implementation. • Also see extended comments in Chapter 5.	• Ensure that the teacher feels supported with implementing the intervention. • Know whether the intervention can be implemented successfully across multiple implementers (e.g., the teacher and teacher assistant). • Avoid assigning too many (e.g., more than three) implementers, and know which intervention programs work best if always implemented by the same person. • Also see extended comments in Chapter 5.
2. Will the program be modified?	• In general, intervention programs should not be modified; they should be implemented as described in the intervention manual. • The TAPS Teacher's expertise and knowledge of the intervention program and the specific student should dictate whether modifications to the program can or should be made. • Some broad modifications to intervention programs that may be acceptable include, for example, use of a reward/motivation system, having a parent practice related skills in the home, and/or increasing the student's practice with the skill in multiple settings (e.g., small-group and one-on-one instruction).	• Ensure that the teacher understands that modifying the intervention program should only be done under specific circumstances and that any modifications must be collectively agreed on as part of the intervention plan. • If modifications are made, ensure that the teacher understands that the planned modification should occur consistently throughout implementation unless otherwise determined by the teacher and TAPS Teacher.

(cont.)

Item and Brief Description	Comments for TAPS Teacher	Suggestions for TAPS Teacher
3. How will implementers be trained?	• Ideally, as discussed in Chapter 7, teachers and assistive personnel will be trained in the selected intervention program. However, sometimes the TAPS Teacher, on a case-by-case basis, may need to provide or facilitate training so that all implementers are capable of implementing the selected intervention. • The extended comments in Chapter 5 discuss two primary approaches to case-by-case training, as well as important considerations. • As the TAPS Teacher decides the most effective, feasible, and time-efficient approach for case-by-case training, it is important to remember the overall goal of this training: to ensure that all implementers are able to implement the intervention procedures accurately and consistently. • Chapter 7 discusses aspects related to training intervention implementers.	• If needed, the training required to implement interventions may come from any individual in the school who can implement the interventions successfully and train others to do so, including the TAPS Support Coordinator, other teachers, or assistive school personnel. Thus, consider others in the school that may be able to train teachers in the interventions. • Also see extended comments in Chapter 5.
4. Where and when will the intervention occur?	• The setting for the intervention should be one that best allows the student to be on-task and motivated (e.g., settings that are free from noise and distractions) and that minimizes transition times between the student's classroom and the intervention setting. • Intervention can occur in numerous types of school locations (e.g., the student's classroom, in the hall outside the student's classroom, in a media center). Prior to the intervention planning meeting the TAPS Teacher should know all the possible places the intervention could be implemented.	• When specifying when the intervention will occur, list the implementer for that session in parentheses. For example, information might be written as, "Tuesdays, 9:00–9:30 (NAME OF TEACHER); Wednesdays, 10:00–10:30 (NAME OF TEACHER ASSISTANT), Fridays, 9:00–9:30 (NAME OF TEACHER)." • The teacher will likely be the person who manages the student's daily instructional schedule, so ensure that the teacher fully agrees with the intervention setting and times. • When possible, select intervention times that do not interfere with other important instructional times. • Consider whether the setting or times for intervention will negatively or positively impact the student's self-esteem.

(cont.)

Item and Brief Description	Comments for TAPS Teacher	Suggestions for TAPS Teacher
		• Ensure that the times and setting for intervention implementation are unlikely to be interrupted with other school- or classroom-related events.
5. How many minutes of intervention per day and how many days per week?	• The number of minutes per day scheduled for intervention implementation should be consistent with any recommendations found in the intervention program manual. Not all intervention programs recommend implementation for a specific number of minutes, but many do. If a specified number of minutes is not stated in the program manual, the TAPS Teacher should determine the number of lessons that should be implemented per day and the approximate amount of time to complete the daily lesson(s). • In general, intervention should occur no less than 2-3 days per week. Ideally, intervention should occur as many days as possible, as long as the schedule is consistent with the recommendations in the intervention program.	• The teacher's manual of the intervention program, as well the TAPS Teacher's experience with the intervention program, should help to dictate the number of minutes per day and days per week needed to increase the likelihood that the program will be effective with the student.
6. What date will the intervention start and on what days will it occur?	• Specifying a start date and actual days (e.g., M, W, F) for intervention implementation supports the "contract-related" aspect of the IPF and should increase the likelihood that the intervention will start and occur as specified. • The start date for the intervention should occur as soon as possible. One reason to delay the date 1–2.5 weeks would be if the TAPS Teacher needs to train one or more implementers for the intervention.	• Ensure that the specified start date and days planned for intervention are carefully considered by the teacher and considered feasible. It is better to know of possible scheduling conflicts before starting the intervention plan, compared to learning about them later.
7. Implementation integrity details (how, who, when)?	• The TAPS Teacher and/or the TAPS Support Coordinator will likely take primary responsibility for monitoring implementers' integrity, but when possible, other educators can share this responsibility.	• Ensure that all implementers understand the purpose and importance of evaluating implementation integrity. Address any possible concerns about this during the intervention planning meeting.

(cont.)

Item and Brief Description	Comments for TAPS Teacher	Suggestions for TAPS Teacher
	• The time for the TAPS Teacher to monitor for implementation integrity may be best scheduled immediately before or after designated follow-up meetings (as discussed in Chapter 5). • Also see extended comments in Chapter 5.	• At the beginning of the intervention plan (e.g., weeks 1–4), an implementation integrity check (of all implementers) should occur at least once every 1–2 weeks to ensure that all implementers are adhering to the intervention procedures. • Once confident that all implementers are implementing the program with integrity, implementation integrity can occur less frequently (e.g., once every 3–4 weeks). • Also see extended comments in Chapter 5.
8. How will student progress be monitored?	• The TAPS Teacher should take responsibility for ensuring that progress monitoring data are collected for the target student in a timely and meaningful way. • Progress monitoring may be "built in" within the selected intervention program, but in most cases, a separate type of progress monitoring assessment should occur once every 1–2 weeks. • Chapter 6 describes appropriate assessment activities and options in detail, and should be reviewed to ensure appropriate progress monitoring for each TAPS case.	• If the classroom teacher has the time and skills to use the designated progress monitoring assessment tools, have the teacher do (or assist with) the progress monitoring assessments. • If the classroom teacher assists with collecting progress monitoring data, ensure that the data are organized and easily accessible by the teacher and TAPS Teacher.
9. Who will contact the student's parent(s)?	• The target student's parent(s) (or legal guardian) should always be notified that the teacher wants to implement an academic intervention to help the student. • The person who contacts the student's parent(s) should explain the teacher's primary concern, describe the core features of the student's intervention plan (e.g., the type of intervention and who will work with the student), and attempt to get input and/or suggestions from the parent(s). When possible, parent input should be integrated into the student's intervention plan and the parent(s)	• Typically, encourage the classroom teacher to contact the parent(s) because the teacher is more likely to know the parent(s) better and to communicate more frequently about the student. Of course, there are circumstances when the TAPS Teacher should instead or additionally contact the student's parent(s). • Determine with the teacher whether a face-to-face meeting with the parent(s) should occur before starting the intervention plan. Depending on the specific TAPS case, there may be important advantages (e.g., parent suggestions or home-based support)

(cont.)

Item and Brief Description	Comments for TAPS Teacher	Suggestions for TAPS Teacher
	should be encouraged to contact the school with any subsequent questions, concerns, or comments. • Under most circumstances, the student's intervention plan should not begin until the parent(s) provides verbal consent. If, however, the parent(s) does not reply to multiple attempts (e.g., four or five) for communication across a 2-week period, the teacher, TAPS Teacher, and the school principal should use their judgment about whether to start the intervention plan.	and/or disadvantages (e.g., delays with starting intervention) to meeting with the parent(s) before starting the intervention plan. • If a face-to-face meeting with the parent(s) does not occur before starting the intervention plan, encourage the teacher to discuss the plan with the parent(s) during the next possible face-to-face meeting and attend the meeting if possible or requested.
10. When will the parent(s) be contacted?	• Once the parent(s) is contacted, told about the intervention plan, and offered the opportunity to provide input or suggestions, verbal consent (Yes or No) should be specified on the IPF. • As stated above, the intervention plan might begin after 2 unsuccessful weeks of trying to reach the student's parent(s). The person trying to contact the parent(s) should keep accurate records of when and how the parent(s) was contacted. This information should be recorded on the IPF if the intervention plan begins without a parent reply regarding consent.	• Ensure that the parent(s) will be contacted using the most appropriate method (e.g., phone, letter, e-mail) within 1–3 days of the intervention planning meeting. If the parent(s) does not reply to the initial contact, someone should continue trying to make contact every 3–4 days until the communication occurs.
11. Date for review of intervention plan?	• Within 1–2 weeks of the start date specified in Item 5, the TAPS Teacher and classroom teacher will meet briefly to (1) discuss any possible problems or concerns since starting the intervention plan, (2) make any needed modifications to the intervention plan, and (3) sign the IPF to indicate agreement of the plan. • This initial review-of-plan meeting is also described in greater detail in Chapter 5.	• If the intervention plan is not being implemented as originally intended, determine the likely reasons and modify the plan if needed. However, ensure that any modifications help to strengthen rather than weaken the plan. • This initial review-of-plan meeting is also described in greater detail in Chapter 5.

(cont.)

Item and Brief Description	Comments for TAPS Teacher	Suggestions for TAPS Teacher
12. How many weeks of intervention will occur?	• The number of intervention weeks should be sufficient to allow for reasonable student progress and to be able to detect it through progress monitoring assessments (see Chapter 6), but should not be so many that too much time passes before a more formal review of the intervention effectiveness. • The number of intervention weeks may be determined by school policy or the recommended implementation time listed in the intervention program's manual. If no such policy or guidance exists, all TAPS Teachers within the school should develop appropriate guidelines for determining this number and attempt to get support for these guidelines from the school principal. • As a very general recommendation, we believe that at least 6–7 weeks of an evidence-based intervention should occur before evaluating the overall effectiveness of the intervention, assuming that there are periodic follow-up meetings in which minor changes to the intervention can be made if needed.	• Ensure that the teacher understands the importance of implementing an appropriate number of interventions sessions. • Ensure that the teacher understands that the goal of the intervention plan is to help the student improve academically and ultimately reach his or her full potential; the goal of the plan is not to do something for an extended period of time just so eligibility for more comprehensive services (or assessment) can be determined later.
13. What is the objective student goal?	• Based on the progress monitoring assessment system determined as part of Item 7, the TAPS Teacher should suggest a reasonable goal that will move the student toward grade-level achievement standards. • Chapter 6 describes appropriate goal-setting standards and options and should be reviewed to ensure an appropriate goal level is set for the target student.	• Ensure that the teacher understands how the student's goal was determined, what it means, and how it corresponds to helping the student meet grade-level standards in the targeted area of deficit.

(cont.)

Completing the TAPS Intervention Planning Form (IPF) *(page 7 of 7)*

Item and Brief Description	Comments for TAPS Teacher	Suggestions for TAPS Teacher
14. By what date will all intervention sessions be implemented?	• Similar to determining the number of intervention sessions that should occur, the monthly time frame to implement the intervention plan should be long enough that student progress could reasonably occur, but should not be so long that too much time passes before a more formal review of intervention effectiveness. • The time frame for implementing the intervention plan may be determined by school policy. If no such policy exists, all TAPS Teachers within the school may develop appropriate guidelines for determining this time and attempt to get support for these guidelines from the school principal. • The time frame for implementing the intervention plan should correspond with the school calendar and the number of intervention sessions determined in Item 12.	• Ensure that the teacher understands the importance of implementing the intervention across a specified and predetermined period of time.
15. What is the date for the summative review of intervention effectiveness?	• Specifying this date should help the TAPS Teacher and classroom teacher with scheduling and ensuring that the intervention plan occurs as intended until the formal review of the plan. The date must occur within 2 weeks of the date specified in Item 14.	
16. How will follow-ups occur?	• Details regarding this item are described in Chapter 5, within the section "Follow-up Meetings throughout Intervention Plan Implementation."	• Ensure that the teacher understands the purpose, schedule, and expected value of the planned follow-up meetings.

APPENDIX J

Request for Information from the TAPS Support Coordinator

Dear TAPS Support Coordinator:

Please see the information below to determine whether there is one or more educators within the school who can assist with implementing an intervention program as part of this TAPS case.

Name of student: ______________________ Student's grade: ______

TAPS Teacher: ______________________ Classroom teacher: ______________________

Academic subskill we plan to target during the TAPS case:

____

Date of intervention planning meeting: __________

Date this request was submitted to TAPS Support Coordinator: __________

Intervention programs that are currently being considered for this TAPS case:

1. ____
2. ____
3. ____
4. ____

Questions for TAPS Support Coordinator (*Please respond to the questions below and attach this form to your Intervention Support Options Form.*)

- If needed, are you available within the next 2 weeks to train one or more educators to implement any of the above intervention programs (check one)? ☐ **Yes** ☐ **No**
- If you can assist with training, please specify any of the above intervention programs you **do not** feel comfortable training others to use, and make any additional comments as needed.

____

____

____

____

- If needed, are you available to monitor implementation integrity with the selected intervention program (check one)? ☐ **Yes** ☐ **No**
- If you can assist with monitoring implementation integrity, please specify any of the listed intervention programs you **do not** feel comfortable monitoring, and make any additional comments as needed.

____

____

____

____

(cont.)

Request for Information from the TAPS Support Coordinator *(page 2 of 2)*

If you can assist with monitoring implementation integrity, please specify days and times you are likely available: ____

____

____

____

It would be greatly appreciated if you can reply to this request by ____________________.

Please remember to reply by submitting your responses to this form along with your completed Intervention Support Options Form.

APPENDIX K

Intervention Support Options Identified by the TAPS Support Coordinator

This form was submitted to the requesting TAPS Teacher on the following date ___________, and specifies individuals within the school who should be available and competent to assist with implementing the below named intervention programs.

Name of Intervention Program: ______________________________

Name of Educator	Role within School	Experience Implementing Program?	Trained to Implement Program?	Availability (specify days and times)	Comments (if applicable)
		Yes No	Yes No		
		Yes No	Yes No		
		Yes No	Yes No		

Please see the following pages for additional information. The Request for Information from the TAPS Support Coordinator Form is also attached to this packet.

(cont.)

Intervention Support Options Identified by the TAPS Support Coordinator *(page 2 of 3)*

Name of Intervention Program: ______________________

Name of Educator	Role within School	Experience Implementing Program?	Trained to Implement Program?	Availability (specify days and times)	Comments (if applicable)
		Yes No	Yes No		
		Yes No	Yes No		
		Yes No	Yes No		

Name of Intervention Program: ______________________

Name of Educator	Role within School	Experience Implementing Program?	Trained to Implement Program?	Availability (specify days and times)	Comments (if applicable)
		Yes No	Yes No		
		Yes No	Yes No		
		Yes No	Yes No		

(cont.)

Intervention Support Options Identified by the TAPS Support Coordinator *(page 3 of 3)*

Name of Intervention Program: ______________________________

Name of Educator	Role within School	Experience Implementing Program?	Trained to Implement Program?	Availability (specify days and times)	Comments (if applicable)
		Yes No	Yes No		
		Yes No	Yes No		
		Yes No	Yes No		

Name of Intervention Program: ______________________________

Name of Educator	Role within School	Experience Implementing Program?	Trained to Implement Program?	Availability (specify days and times)	Comments (if applicable)
		Yes No	Yes No		
		Yes No	Yes No		
		Yes No	Yes No		

APPENDIX L

TAPS Summative Review of Intervention Effectiveness Form (SRF)

Student name: ______________________ Date of meeting: ______________

Individuals present during the meeting: ______________________

Is date of meeting within 2 weeks of the date specified on Item 14 of Goal 3 on the TAPS IPF? (check one): ☐ **Yes** ☐ **No**

If the response above is "No," state why: ______________________

Academic area targeted for intervention (check one): ☐ **Reading** ☐ **Writing** ☐ **Math**

Primary skill(s) targeted during intervention (and name of intervention program, if applicable): ________

____

Number of intervention sessions implemented up to this date: __________

Number of weeks student was in school since intervention start date: __________

Indicate the student's goal (specified in Item 13 of the IPF) and student's current academic performance related to that goal: ______________________

____

Intervention Effectiveness Summary

1. The intervention successfully addressed the primary concern (check one and then describe details and relevant assessment data to support your response):

☐ 1–Strongly Disagree ☐ 2–Disagree ☐ 3–Neither Agree nor Disagree ☐ 4–Agree ☐ 5–Strongly Agree

____

____

____

2. The student should receive additional services in the same academic area subskill(s) targeted for intervention (check one and then describe your rationale):

☐ 1–Strongly Disagree ☐ 2–Disagree ☐ 3–Neither Agree nor Disagree ☐ 4–Agree ☐ 5–Strongly Agree

____

____

____

3. The student should receive additional intervention services in the same academic area, but different subskill(s) (check one and then describe your rationale):

☐ 1–Strongly Disagree ☐ 2–Disagree ☐ 3–Neither Agree nor Disagree ☐ 4–Agree ☐ 5–Strongly Agree

____

____

____

(cont.)

4. Students with the same skill-area deficit would likely benefit from the same intervention program (check one and then describe your rationale):

☐ 1–Strongly Disagree ☐ 2–Disagree ☐ 3–Neither Agree nor Disagree ☐ 4–Agree ☐ 5–Strongly Agree

____

____

____

☐ ***Check this box to indicate that the TAPS Case Rating Scale has been completed.***

Intervention Implementation Summary

5. Average implementation integrity of the intervention program across all sessions and implementers: ________% *(Write "NA" if not applicable.)*

For Items 6–12, rate the degree to which the component of the overall intervention plan was implemented according to the student's TAPS IPF. If your rating is not "Agree" or "Strongly Agree," indicate the reason(s) for this using the following list, "Reasons for deviating from the intended intervention plan," and write comments as needed.

Reasons for deviating from the intended intervention plan, as specified in the student's TAPS IPF:

a) Plan described in the TAPS IPF was unclear to one or more individuals implementing the component.
b) Due to school and/or classroom scheduling challenges, there was insufficient time to always complete the component.
c) Student needed academic or behavioral support beyond expected levels, which minimized opportunities to always complete the component.
d) Implementer had insufficient training or knowledge to always complete the component.
e) High level of student or implementer absences—specify number of absences and who (implementer or student) had the high level of absences.
f) Inadequate space and/or resources within the school to always complete the component.
g) Other reasons—explain the reason(s) on the respective lines.

6. Intervention program procedures were implemented with integrity (if rating = 3 or less, write corresponding number[s] for reason[s]: ___)

☐ 1–Strongly Disagree ☐ 2–Disagree ☐ 3–Neither Agree nor Disagree ☐ 4–Agree ☐ 5–Strongly Agree

Explain reason if needed: ____

____

7. All Implementers were well trained, as intended (if rating = 3 or less, write corresponding number[s] for reason[s]: _)

☐ 1–Strongly Disagree ☐ 2–Disagree ☐ 3–Neither Agree nor Disagree ☐ 4–Agree ☐ 5–Strongly Agree

Explain reason if needed: ____

____

(cont.)

8. Intervention program was implemented the minimum number of weeks stated (if rating = 3 or less, write corresponding number[s] for reason[s]: ____)

☐ 1–Strongly Disagree ☐ 2–Disagree ☐ 3–Neither Agree nor Disagree ☐ 4–Agree ☐ 5–Strongly Agree

Explain reason if needed: ______________________________

____

9. Per day, the intervention program was implemented the minimum number of minutes stated (if rating = 3 or less, write number[s] for reason[s]: _____)

☐ 1–Strongly Disagree ☐ 2–Disagree ☐ 3–Neither Agree nor Disagree ☐ 4–Agree ☐ 5–Strongly Agree

Explain reason if needed: ______________________________

____

10. Implementation integrity of intervention program was evaluated as intended (if rating = 3 or less, write corresponding number[s] for reason[s]: ____)

☐ 1–Strongly Disagree ☐ 2–Disagree ☐ 3–Neither Agree nor Disagree ☐ 4–Agree ☐ 5–Strongly Agree

Explain reason if needed: ______________________________

____

11. Progress monitoring assessments occurred as intended (if rating = 3 or less, write corresponding number[s] for reason[s]: ____)

☐ 1–Strongly Disagree ☐ 2–Disagree ☐ 3–Neither Agree nor Disagree ☐ 4–Agree ☐ 5–Strongly Agree

Explain reason if needed: ______________________________

____

12. Periodic follow-up meetings occurred as intended (if rating = 3 or less, write corresponding number[s] for reason[s]: ____)

☐ 1–Strongly Disagree ☐ 2–Disagree ☐ 3–Neither Agree nor Disagree ☐ 4–Agree ☐ 5–Strongly Agree

Explain reason if needed: ______________________________

____

13. Deviations of the intervention plan (such as deviations possibly noted above) weakened the success of the plan (check one and describe, if needed):

☐ 1–Strongly Disagree ☐ 2–Disagree ☐ 3–Neither Agree nor Disagree ☐ 4–Agree ☐ 5–Strongly Agree

Explain reason if needed: ______________________________

____

14. Describe successes related to implementing the intervention plan: ______________________________

____

____

(cont.)

Summary of Next Steps

What steps should now be taken? Check all that apply and write additional information that describes how the classroom teacher, the TAPS Teacher, and/or other school professionals will proceed to ensure positive learning outcomes for the student.

☐ 1. Discontinue all intervention program(s) described in TAPS IPF.

☐ 2. Monitor student's academic performance every ____________ week(s) with assessment (specify frequency on the given line).

☐ 3. Continue implementing the intervention program(s) described in the current TAPS IPF; on lines below, specify frequency, duration, etc.

☐ 4. Modify the intervention program(s) described in the TAPS IPF; on lines below, specify how the program will be modified.

☐ 5. Begin a new intervention program that addresses the same skill; on lines below, specify the new intervention program and rationale for new intervention.

☐ 6. Modify the intervention plan (other than the specified intervention program); on lines below, specify how the plan will be modified.

☐ 7. Develop and implement an intervention that specifically addresses student behavior/motivation; on lines below, describe basic aspects of the intervention.

☐ 8. Seek additional problem-solving support from other school staff; on lines below, specify who, how, why, and related details.

☐ 9. Conduct a thorough student assessment to improve instructional problem solving; on lines below, describe details (when, what assessments, why, etc.).

☐ 10. Have classroom teacher request assistance regarding a different academic area or subskill; on lines below, describe the teacher's new concerns.

☐ 11. Other; describe on lines below.

APPENDIX M

Summary of TAPS Activities and Estimated Time Needed for the TAPS Support Teacher to Complete Each Activity for a TAPS Case

1. Process Request for TAPS Form
   a. Conduct targeted skills observation = 5–20 min
   b. Develop intervention options and share list with teacher = 10–15 min
   c. Prepare clarification questions and consider responses for IPF items = 10–20 min
   d. Communicate with TAPS Support Coordinator = 10–15 min
2. Conduct intervention planning meeting = 20–30 min
3. Hold initial review meeting = 5–15 min
4. Hold periodic meetings = 2–5 min every 1–3 weeks
5. Implement intervention program with student = 15–30 min every 2–3 weeks
6. Monitor implementation integrity = ~10–30 minutes every 2 weeks, but this varies
   a. For first 4 weeks, do every 1–2 weeks; then do every 3–4 weeks.
   b. The above suggestion would differ for teachers with evidence of implementation accuracy.
7. Progress monitoring assessment = ~5 min each week
8. Summative review meeting = 20–45 min per case (time will vary depending on case)

Miscellaneous activity (duration highly variable): As needed, train teachers to implement intervention program on case-by-case basis.

APPENDIX N

Recommended Professional Development Topics for the TAPS Reading Teacher

Broad Topic	Subtopic	General Importance of Topic	Suggested Resources and/or Guidance
Evidence-Based Instruction and Intervention	Implementing evidence-based intervention programs in reading	TAPS Teachers must know how to implement the intervention programs that are selected for use with TAPS cases.	1. After reviewing Chapter 12 (particularly Table 12.2), the TAPS Teacher should use the teacher's manuals of selected and acquired intervention programs to learn how to implement the respective programs.
	Identifying and evaluating core reading curricula	The TAPS process will be more effective and efficient if teachers in the school are using a good core curriculum.	1. Chapter 12 of this book provides an introduction to this topic. 2. Dewitz, Leahy, Jones, & Sullivan (2010)[a] 3. Simmons & Kame'enui (2003)[a] 4. Florida Center for Reading Research, reviews of core curricula (*www.fcrr.org/FCRRreports/CReports.aspx?rep=core*)[a]
	Using research to select and evaluate instruction and interventions	When selecting new intervention programs and evaluating existing programs, TAPS Teachers should understand how research is used in this process.	1. Stanovich & Stanovich (2003)[a] 2. Rathvon (2008)
	The state's standards for core reading curricula	TAPS Teachers should be familiar with their state's standards for reading instruction.	1. The TAPS Teacher must identify his or her state's standards for reading instruction. For guidance, one can review common standards adopted by many states (see *www.corestandards.org*), and the following link is an example of one state's standards: *www.ncpublicschools.org/curriculum*.
	Implementing intervention programs with integrity	The TAPS Teacher must understand the importance of, and issues associated with, implementing interventions as they are designed.	1. Roach & Elliott (2008) 2. Lane, Bocian, MacMillan, & Gresham (2004)

(cont.)

Broad Topic	Subtopic	General Importance of Topic	Suggested Resources and/or Guidance
Academic Assessment and Data-Based Decision Making	Progress monitoring in reading	To facilitate an effective intervention program, TAPS Teachers must know procedures, strengths, and limitations associated with academic progress monitoring.	1. Chapter 6 of this book provides an introduction to this topic. 2. Resources provided by the National Center on Student Progress Monitoring (*www.studentprogress.org*)[a] 3. Hosp, Hosp, & Howell (2007)
	Schoolwide screening (sometimes referred to as *universal screening*)	Using schoolwide screening may be useful in identifying students who should receive intervention through the TAPS process.	1. Chapter 6 of this book provides an introduction to this topic. 2. Johnson, Mellard, Fuchs, & McKnight (2006)[a] 3. Ikeda, Neesen, & Witt (2008)
	Direct academic assessment and curriculum-based measurement (CBM)	As part of the TAPS process for progress monitoring and targeted skills observations, direct assessment (including CBM) will likely occur.	1. Chapter 6 of this book provides an introduction to this topic. 2. Shapiro (2011a, 2011b) 3. Howell, Hosp, & Kurns (2008) 4. Christ (2008)
	Response to intervention (RTI)	As discussed in Chapters 1 and 2, the SOPAA can be used in schools that adopted RTI or in schools that have not yet adopted RTI but may want to in future years. For schools in the latter scenario, TAPS Teachers will benefit by understanding topics related to RTI.	1. National Center on Response to Intervention (*www.rti4success.org/*)[a] 2. Gersten et al. (2008)[a] 3. Brown-Chidsey & Steege (2010) 4. Burns & Gibbons (2008)
Academic Subskills and Conceptual Foundations	Key subskills of reading	To better develop and evaluate core reading instruction and TAPS intervention plans, the TAPS Teacher must have a sound understanding of the key subskills in reading.	1. Chapter 12 of this book. Content learned from the professional development topic, "Evidence-Based Instruction and Intervention," is also relevant for learning key subskills. 2. Armbruster, Lehr, & Osborn (2006)[a] 3. Resources available from the National Institute for Literacy[a] (*http://lincs.ed.gov/publications/publications.html*) 4. Moats (1999)[a]

[a] At the time of publishing this book, this suggested resource can be accessed electronically for free.

APPENDIX O

Recommended Professional Development Topics for the TAPS Math Teacher

Broad Topic	Subtopic	General Importance of Topic	Suggested Resources and/or Guidance
Evidence-Based Instruction and Intervention	Implementing evidence-based intervention programs in math	TAPS Teachers must know how to implement the intervention programs that are selected for use with TAPS cases.	1. After reviewing Chapter 12 (particularly Table 12.3), the TAPS Teacher should use the teacher's manual of selected and acquired intervention programs to learn how to implement them.
	Identifying and evaluating core math curricula	The TAPS process will be more effective and efficient if teachers in the school are using a good core curriculum.	1. Chapter 12 of this book provides an introduction to this topic. 2. Resources related to mathematics core curricula at What Works Clearinghouse (*http://ies.ed.gov/ncee/wwc*)[a]
	Using research to select and evaluate instruction and intervention	When selecting new intervention programs and evaluating existing programs, TAPS Teachers should understand how research is used in this process.	1. Stanovich & Stanovich (2003)[a] 2. Rathvon (2008)
	The state's standards for core math curricula	TAPS Teachers should be familiar with their state's standards for math instruction.	1. The TAPS Teacher must identify his or her state's standards for math instruction. For guidance, one can review common standards adopted by many states (see *www.corestandards.org*), and the following link is an example of one state's standards: *www.ncpublicschools.org/curriculum.*
	Implementing intervention programs with integrity	TAPS Teachers must understand the importance of, and issues associated with, implementing interventions as they are designed.	1. Roach & Elliott (2008) 2. Lane, Bocian, MacMillan, & Gresham (2004)

(cont.)

Recommended Professional Development Topics for the TAPS Math Teacher *(page 2 of 2)*

Broad Topic	Subtopic	General Importance of Topic	Suggested Resources and/or Guidance
Academic Assessment and Data-Based Decision Making	Progress monitoring in math	To facilitate an effective intervention program, TAPS Teachers must know procedures, strengths, and limitations associated with academic progress monitoring.	1. Chapter 6 of this book provides an introduction to this topic. 2. Resources provided by the National Center on Student Progress Monitoring (*www.studentprogress.org*)[a]
	Direct academic assessment and curriculum-based measurement (CBM)	As part of the TAPS process for progress monitoring and targeted skills observations, direct assessment (including CBM) will likely occur.	1. Chapter 6 of this book provides an introduction to this topic. 2. Hosp, Hosp, & Howell (2007) 3. Shapiro (2011a, 2011b) 4. Kelley (2008)
	Schoolwide screening (sometimes referred to as *universal screening*)	Using schoolwide screening may be useful in identifying students who should receive intervention through the TAPS process.	1. Chapter 6 of this book and the citations provided in that chapter. 2. Johnson, Mellard, Fuchs, & McKnight (2006)[a] 3. Ikeda, Neesen, & Witt (2008)
	Response to intervention (RTI)	As discussed in Chapters 1 and 2, the SOPAA can be used in schools that adopted RTI or in schools that have not yet adopted RTI but may want to in future years. For schools in the latter scenario, TAPS Teachers will benefit by understanding topics related to RTI.	1. National Center on Response to Intervention (*www.rti4success.org*)[a] 2. Gersten et al. (2009)[a] 3. Brown-Chidsey & Steege (2010)
Academic Subskills and Conceptual Foundations	Key subskills of math	To better develop and evaluate core math instruction and TAPS intervention plans, TAPS Teachers must have a sound understanding of the key subskills in math.	1. Chapter 12 of this book provides an introduction to this topic. Content learned from the professional development topic, "Evidence-Based Instruction and Intervention," is also relevant for learning key subskills. 2. National Mathematics Advisory Panel (2008)[a] 3. Resources on mathematics instruction available from the Center on Instruction at *www.centeroninstruction.org/math-summit-providing-evidence-based-practices-and-implications-of-nctm-focal-points.*[a] 4. Donovan & Bransford (2005)

[a] At the time of publishing this book, this suggested resource can be accessed electronically for free.

APPENDIX P

Recommended Professional Development Topics for the TAPS Writing Teacher

Broad Topic	Subtopic	General Importance of Topic	Suggested Resources and/or Guidance
Evidence-Based Instruction and Intervention	Implementing evidence-based intervention programs in writing	TAPS Teachers must know how to implement the intervention programs that are selected for use with TAPS cases.	1. After reviewing Chapter 12 (particularly Table 12.4) the TAPS Teacher should use the teacher's manual of selected and acquired intervention programs to learn how to implement them.
	Using research to select and evaluate instruction and intervention	When selecting new intervention programs and evaluating existing programs, TAPS Teachers should understand how research is used in this process.	1. Stanovich & Stanovich (2003)[a] 2. Rathvon (2008)
	Implementing intervention programs with integrity	The TAPS Teacher must understand the importance of, and issues associated with, implementing interventions as they are designed.	1. Roach & Elliott (2008) 2. Lane, Bocian, MacMillan, & Gresham (2004)
Academic Assessment and Data-Based Decision Making[b]	Progress monitoring in writing	To facilitate an effective intervention program, TAPS Teachers must know procedures, strengths, and limitations associated with academic progress monitoring.	1. Chapter 6 of this book and the citations provided in that chapter. 2. Malecki (2008) 3. McMaster & Espin (2007)
	Direct academic assessment and curriculum-based measurement (CBM)	As part of the TAPS process for progress monitoring and targeted skills observations, direct assessment (including CBM) will likely occur.	1. Chapter 6 of this book and the references provided in that chapter. 2. Hosp, Hosp, & Howell (2007) 3. Shapiro (2011a, 2011b)
Academic Subskills and Conceptual Foundations	Key subskills of writing	To better develop and evaluate core writing instruction and TAPS intervention plans, TAPS Teachers must have a sound understanding of the key subskills in writing.	1. Chapter 12 of this book provides an introduction to this topic 2. Resources available from Education Northwest (*http://educationnorthwest.org/traits*)[a] 3. Graham & Harris (2005)

[a] At the time of publishing this book, this suggested resource can be accessed electronically for free.

[b] As noted in Chapters 6 and 12, at the time of publishing this book there is generally less research and fewer resources available in the area of writing. For example, progress monitoring and schoolwide screening in writing have not been well developed, compared to reading and math. Our suggested resources provide some guidance, but the TAPS Writing Teacher will probably recognize that we have fewer recommendations for resources compared to reading and math.

APPENDIX Q

Yearly Professional Development Planning Guide

TAPS Teacher's Name: ______________________ School year and (SOPAA Implementation Year): ____________

TAPS Teacher's Target Area (circle one): Reading Math Writing

Topic(s) to Cover	Type of Activity	Resources Needed	Reasons to Cover the Topic	Dates and Times to Cover Topic	Topic Covered as Planned?
					Yes No
					Yes No
					Yes No

(cont.)

Yearly Professional Development Planning Guide *(page 2 of 3)*

Topic(s) to Cover	Type of Activity	Resources Needed	Reasons to Cover the Topic	Dates and Times to Cover Topic	Topic Covered as Planned?
					Yes No
*					Yes No
					Yes No
					Yes No

*With the Lead Coordinator, remember to review your professional development plan during the middle of the school year.

(cont.)

Yearly Professional Development Planning Guide *(page 3 of 3)*

Topic(s) to Cover	Type of Activity	Resources Needed	Reasons to Cover the Topic	Dates and Times to Cover Topic	Topic Covered as Planned?
					Yes No
					Yes No
					Yes No
					Yes No
					Yes No

APPENDIX R

Professional Development Documentation Form

Specify the following information for each day you complete professional development activities.

Name: ______________________________ Date of Activity: ____________

Topic(s) Covered during Activity: ______________________________

____

Type of Activity: ______________________________

____

Resources Used and/or Sponsor of Activity: ______________________________

____

____

Description of What You Did and Learned and How You Might Use the Information:

____

____

____

____

____

____

____

____

____

____

____

____

____

____

____

Attach additional pages of description if needed.

Exact Clock Hours Engaged in Activity: ____________

Provide your signature below to attest that the activities reported on this form reflect actual activities you completed.

Signature: ______________________________ Date: ____________

APPENDIX S

Teacher Survey about the Potential Value and Feasibility of the SOPAA and TAPS

A. Are you a regular education teacher (circle one)? **Yes** **No**

B. If **Yes**, what grade level(s) do you currently teach? ________________

C. If **No**, specify your current teaching role in the school: ____

Please complete this brief survey regarding your initial impressions of the SOPAA model. As a facilitator of the SOPAA in our school, it is important for me to understand teachers' initial feelings about this approach to addressing the needs of struggling learners.

Please rate the following items on a scale from 1 to 5, where:

1 = Strongly Disagree (SD)
2 = Disagree (D)
3 = Neither Agree nor Disagree (N)
4 = Agree (A)
5 = Strongly Agree (SA)

Item	SD	D	N	A	SA
1. During a typical school year I would like to have more support with assisting struggling learners whom I teach.	1	2	3	4	5
2. I understand the primary steps in the TAPS process.	1	2	3	4	5
3. I believe that the TAPS process will be an effective way to assist struggling learners.	1	2	3	4	5
4. I believe that the TAPS process will be a feasible way to assist struggling learners.	1	2	3	4	5
5. I plan to use the TAPS process when I need assistance with a struggling learner.	1	2	3	4	5
6. I believe that the SOPAA professional development workshops will be helpful in learning about academic interventions and assessment strategies.	1	2	3	4	5
7. Overall, the SOPAA model (including the TAPS process) should be an effective way to assist struggling learners.	1	2	3	4	5

Based on what you learned today, please share your comments about the SOPAA and/or TAPS process (use the backside of this page to write your comments). For example:

Q1. What aspects of the SOPAA and/or TAPS appear **most beneficial** to you with respect to meeting the needs of struggling learners?

Q2. What aspects of the SOPAA and/or TAPS appear **least beneficial** to you with respect to meeting the needs of struggling learners?

Q3. Write any additional comments you have about our school's use of the SOPAA or TAPS.

APPENDIX T

Follow-Up Letter to Distribute to Teachers after the SOPAA Introductory Presentation

Date: ________________

Dear Teacher:

This letter is to remind you about the SOPAA model we described a couple weeks ago, and we again encourage you to use the TAPS process to obtain support for struggling learners in your class. **As a reminder, a brief summary of the TAPS process is as follows:**

1. You request academic support for your student using the Request for TAPS Form.
2. You meet with the TAPS Teacher to co-develop an intervention plan for the student.
3. You implement the intervention plan, receiving planned support from the TAPS Teacher and possibly other educators in the school.
4. You evaluate the effectiveness of the intervention plan, with support from the TAPS Teacher.

Also remember, you can access the Request for TAPS Form as an electronic version or as a hard-copy version I provided for you during the SOPAA introductory presentation. You can submit your request form and associated materials to me electronically and/or by placing materials in my mailbox. **Once the TAPS Teacher receives your request form, s/he will then:**

1. Observe the student you identified in your Request for TAPS Form (if needed).
2. Schedule a time to meet with you for the intervention planning meeting.
3. Provide you with a short list of relevant intervention programs that will be discussed during the intervention planning meeting. (Before the intervention planning meeting, if at all possible, I encourage you to review the list of intervention programs and, if desired, let the TAPS Teacher know if you would like to also discuss other intervention options).

Last, we want to share with you some of the feedback we received from teachers at the end of the SOPAA introductory presentation.

1. 84% of the teachers reported that they Agree or Strongly Agree that they would like to have more support with assisting struggling learners whom they teach.
2. 92% of the teachers reported that they Agree or Strongly Agree that TAPS should be an effective way to assist struggling learners.
3. 98% of the teachers reported that they Agree or Strongly Agree that they plan to use the TAPS process when they need assistance with a struggling learner.

Overall, it appears that teachers who attended the introductory presentation perceive the TAPS process and SOPAA model favorably, and most look forward to using the process to support their students with academic difficulties. As part of the team of SOPAA co-facilitators, we look forward to working with you as part of the SOPAA and TAPS process, and we encourage you to ask us questions or pose comments that you have at any time.

Sincerely,

Name, SOPAA Lead Coordinator

E-mail address

Phone number and extension

APPENDIX U

Teacher End-of-Year Survey about the SOPAA and TAPS Process

A. Are you a regular education teacher (circle one)? **Yes** **No**

B. If **Yes**, what grade level(s) do you currently teach? ____________

C. If **No**, specify your current teaching role in the school: ____________

D. ***Please respond to this survey only in terms of TAPS cases in the area of:*** ____________

E. How many TAPS cases were you involved with this year in this academic area? ____________

Please rate the following items on a scale from 1 to 5, where:

1 = Never or Almost Never (N)
2 = Rarely (R)
3 = Approximately Half of the Time (H)
4 = Usually (U)
5 = Always or Almost Always (A)

Item	N	R	H	U	A
1. The intervention planning meeting was useful in developing a strong intervention for my student.	1	2	3	4	5
2. The TAPS Teacher and I were able to develop an comprehensive intervention plan with which I agreed.	1	2	3	4	5
3. The intervention plan I developed with the TAPS Teacher was started within 3 weeks of my TAPS request.	1	2	3	4	5
4. I learned important teaching and/or assessment skills by being involved with TAPS cases.	1	2	3	4	5
5. The TAPS Teacher communicated well with me.	1	2	3	4	5
6. Based on the established intervention plan, I was able to provide the time I agreed to for the plan.	1	2	3	4	5
7. Based on the established intervention plan, the TAPS Teacher appeared to provide the time he/she agreed to.	1	2	3	4	5
8. I was satisfied with how assistive school personnel helped with my student's intervention plan.	1	2	3	4	5
9. The TAPS process was effective in making sure my student received a high-quality intervention plan.	1	2	3	4	5
10. Overall, the TAPS process improved the academic skill we targeted for my student.	1	2	3	4	5

Please continue this survey on the following page.

(cont.)

Teacher End-of-Year Survey about the SOPAA and TAPS Process *(page 2 of 2)*

Please rate the following items on a scale from 1 to 5, where:

1 = **Strongly Disagree (SD)**
2 = **Disagree (D)**
3 = **Neither Agree or Disagree (N)**
4 = **Agree (A)**
5 = **Strongly Agree (SA)**

Item	SD	D	N	A	SA
11. I felt supported by the TAPS Teacher during the TAPS process.	1	2	3	4	5
12. The TAPS process for monitoring student progress throughout the intervention plan is beneficial.	1	2	3	4	5
13. The TAPS process for evaluating student progress at the end of the intervention plan is beneficial.	1	2	3	4	5
14. There is a suitable number of evidence-based intervention programs available in the school.	1	2	3	4	5
15. I feel well trained to implement evidence-based interventions in this specific academic area.	1	2	3	4	5
16. SOPAA and TAPS-related professional development activities and workshops were beneficial.	1	2	3	4	5
17. I plan to continue using the TAPS process when I need assistance with a struggling learner.	1	2	3	4	5
18. I feel we should broaden the scope of the SOPAA to include more teachers in the school.	1	2	3	4	5
19. There was good communication from the SOPAA Lead Coordinator about things related to the SOPAA.	1	2	3	4	5
20. Overall, the SOPAA model (including the TAPS process) is an effective way to assist struggling learners.	1	2	3	4	5

Based on your experiences this year, please share your comments about the SOPAA and/or TAPS process (use the backside of this page to write your comments). For example:

Q1. What aspects of the SOPAA and/or TAPS were **most beneficial** to you with respect to meeting the needs of struggling learners?

Q2. What aspects about the SOPAA and/or TAPS were **least beneficial** to you with respect to meeting the needs of struggling learners?

Q3. Write any additional comments you have about our school's use of the SOPAA or TAPS.

References

Adams, G., & Engelmann, S. (1996). *Research on direct instruction: 25 years beyond DISTAR*. Seattle, WA: Educational Achievement Systems. Available from the Association for Direct Instruction, *www.adihome.org*.

Adams, M. (1990a). *Beginning to read: Thinking and learning about print*. Cambridge, MA: MIT Press.

Adams, M. (1990b). *Beginning to read: Thinking and learning about print. A summary*. Urbana–Champaign, IL: Center for the Study of Reading, University of Illinois at Urbana–Champaign.

Adams, M. (1998). *Phonemic awareness in young children*. Baltimore, MD: Brookes.

Adelman, H. S., & Taylor, L. (2003). On sustainability of project innovations as systemic change. *Journal of Educational and Psychological Consultation, 14*, 1–25.

Adelman, H. S., & Taylor, L. (2008). Best practices in the use of resource teams to enhance learning supports. In A. Thomas & J. Grimes (Eds.), *Best practices in school psychology (5th ed.)* (pp. 1689–1706). Bethesda, MD: National Association of School Psychologists.

Afflerbach, P., Blachowicz, C., Dawson, C., Boyd, A. E., Juel, C., Kame'enui, E., et al. (2011). *Scott Foresman Reading Street* [Curriculum program]. Glenview, IL: Pearson Education.

Agodini, R., Harris, B., Atkins-Burnett, S., Heaviside, S., Novak, T., & Murphy, R. (2009). *Achievement effects of four early elementary school math curricula: Findings from first graders in 39 schools* (NCEE 2009-4052). Washington, DC: National Center for Education Evaluation and Regional Assistance, Institute of Education Sciences, U.S. Department of Education.

Alabama Reading Initiative. (2007). *Expert review of core reading programs*. Retrieved from *www.alsde.edu/general/Expert_Review_of_Core_Reading_Programs.pdf*.

Alberto, P. A., & Troutman, A. C. (2009). *Applied behavior analysis for teachers* (8th ed). Upper Saddle River, NJ: Pearson/Merrill Prentice Hall.

Algozzine, B., Ysseldyke, J. E., & Christensen, S. (1983). An analysis of the incidence of special education placement: The masses are burgeoning. *Journal of Special Education, 17*, 141–147.

Allington, R. L. (1983). Fluency: The neglected reading goal. *Reading Teacher, 36*, 556–561.

Archer, A., Gleason, M., & Isaacson, S. (2008). *REWARDS writing: Sentence refinement*. Longmont, CO: Sopris West.

Archer, A., Gleason, M., & Vachon, V. (2003). Decoding and fluency: Foundation skills for struggling older readers. *Learning Disability Quarterly, 26*, 89–101.

Archer, A., Gleason, M., & Vachon, V. (2005). *REWARDS: Multisyllabic word reading strategies*. Longmont, CO: Sopris West.

Armbruster, B., Lehr, F., & Osborn, J. (2006). *Put reading first: Kindergarten through grade 3*. Washington, DC: National Institute for Literacy. Retrieved from *http://lincs.ed.gov/publications/pdf/PRFbooklet.pdf*.

Arter, J. A., & Jenkins, J. R. (1979). Differential diagnosis. Prescriptive teaching: A critical appraisal. *Review of Educational Research, 49*, 517–555.

Association for Direct Instruction. (2011). *Boardwork procedures and videos* [Online video clips]. Eugene, OR: Association for Direct Instruction. Available at *www.adihome.org*.

Barnett, D. W., Hamler, K., Conway-Hensley, L., Maples, K., Murdoch, A., Nelson, K., et al. (2002). Preparing school psychologists for early intervention settings. In M. R. Shinn, H. M. Walker, & G. Stoner (Eds.), *Interventions for academic and behavior problems II: Preventive and remedial approaches* (pp. 1021–1045). Washington, DC: National Association of School Psychologists.

Batsche, G., Elliot, J., Graden, J., Grimes, J., Kovalski, J., Prasse, D., et al. (2005). *Response to intervention: Policy considerations and implementation.* Alexandria, VA: National Association of State Directors of Special Education.

Bean, R., Draper, J., Hall, V., Vandermolen, J., & Zigmond, N. (2010). Coaches and coaching in Reading First schools: A reality check. *Elementary School Journal, 111,* 87–114.

Beck, I. L., McKeown, M. G., & Kucan, L. (2002). *Bringing words to life: Robust vocabulary instruction.* New York: Guilford Press.

Beck, I. L., McKeown, M. G., & Kucan, L. (2008). *Creating robust vocabulary: Frequently asked questions and extended examples.* New York: Guilford Press.

Begeny, J. C. (2009). *Helping Early Literacy with Practice Strategies (HELPS): A one-on-one program designed to improve students' reading fluency.* Raleigh, NC: Helps Education Fund. Retrieved from *www.helpsprogram.org.*

Begeny, J. C. (2011). Effects of the Helping Early Literacy with Practice Strategies (HELPS) reading fluency program when implemented at different frequencies. *School Psychology Review, 40,* 149–157.

Begeny, J. C., Laugle, K. M., Krouse, H. E., Lynn, A. E., Tayrose, M. P., & Stage, S. A. (2010). A control-group comparison of two reading fluency programs: The Helping Early Literacy with Practice Strategies (HELPS) program and the Great Leaps K–2 reading program. *School Psychology Review, 39,* 137–155.

Begeny, J. C., & Martens, B. K. (2006a). Assessing pre-service teachers' training in empirically validated behavioral instruction practices. *School Psychology Quarterly, 21,* 262–285.

Begeny, J. C., & Martens, B. K. (2006b). Assisting low-performing readers with a group-based reading fluency intervention. *School Psychology Review, 35,* 91–107.

Begeny, J. C., Mitchell, R. C., Whitehouse, M. H., Harris, C. F., & Stage, S. A. (2011). Effects of the HELPS reading fluency program when implemented by classroom teachers with low-performing second-grade students. *Learning Disabilities Research and Practice, 26,* 122–133.

Benner, G., Trout, A., Nordess, P., Nelson, J., Epstein, M., Knobel, M., et al. (2002). The effects of the Language for Learning program on the receptive language skills of kindergarten children. *Journal of Direct Instruction, 2,* 67–74.

Benson, K., Marchand-Martella, N., Martella, R., & Kolts, R. (2007). Assessing the effects of the Reading Success Level B program with fifth grade students at a Title I elementary school. *Journal of Direct Instruction, 7,* 29–44.

Benson, V., & Cummins, C. (2000). *The power of retelling: Developmental steps for building comprehension.* Bothell, WA: Wright Group/McGraw-Hill.

Bereiter, C., Biemiller, A., Campione, J., Carruthers, I., Fuchs, D., Fuchs, L., et al. (2011). *Imagine It!* [Curriculum program]. Columbus, OH: SRA/Macmillan McGraw-Hill.

Bergan, J. R. (1977). *Behavioral consultation.* Columbus, OH: Merrill.

Bergen, J. R., & Kratochwill, T. R. (1990). *Behavioral consultation and therapy.* New York: Plenum.

Berninger, V., Yates, C., Cartwright, A., Remy, E., & Abbott , R. (1992). Lower-level developmental skills in beginning writing. *Reading and Writing: An Interdisciplinary Journal, 4,* 257–280.

Bernstein, L., Rappaport, C., Olsho, L., Hunt, D., & Levin, M. (2009). *Impact evaluation of the US Department of Education's student mentoring program.* Final report. NCEE 2009-4047. Washington, DC: National Center for Education Evaluation and Regional Assistance.

Biancarosa, G., Bryk, A., & Dexter, E. (2010). Assessing the value-added effects of literacy collaborative professional development on student learning. *Elementary School Journal, 111,* 7–34.

Binder, C. (1996). Behavioral fluency: Evolution of a new paradigm. *The Behavior Analyst, 19,* 163–197.

Brown-Chidsey, R., & Steege, M. W. (2010). *Response to intervention: Principles and strategies for effective practice* (2nd ed.). New York: Guilford Press.

Brownell, M. T., Yeager, E., Rennells, M. S., & Riley, T. (1997). Teachers working together: What teacher educators and researchers should know. *Teacher Education and Special Education, 20,* 340–359.

Buck, G. H., Polloway, E. A., Smith-Thomas, A., & Cook, K. W. (2003). Prereferral intervention processes: A survey of state practices. *Exceptional Children, 69,* 349–360.

Burnette, A., Bettis, D., Marchand-Martella, N., Martella, R., Tso, M., Ebey, T., et al. (1999). A comparison of Spelling Mastery and a whole-word approach across elementary grades in a Title I school. *Effective School Practices, 18,* 8–15.

Burns, M. K., Appleton, J. J., & Stehouwer, J. D. (2005). Meta-analytic review of responsiveness-to-intervention research: Examining field-based and research-implemented models. *Journal of Psychoeducational Assessment, 23,* 381–394.

Burns, M. K., & Gibbons, K. A. (2008). *Implementing response-to-intervention in elementary and second-*

ary schools: Procedures to assure scientific-based practices. New York: Routledge.

Burns, M. K., & Symington, T. (2002). A meta-analysis of prereferral intervention teams: Student and systemic outcomes. *Journal of School Psychology, 40*, 437–447.

Caldarella, P., Gomm, R., Shatzer, R., & Wall, G. (2010). School-based mentoring: A study of volunteer motivations and benefits. *International Electronic Journal of Elementary Education, 2*, 199–216.

Calhoun, M., & Fuchs, L. (2003). The effects of peer-assisted learning strategies and curriculum-based measurement on mathematics performance of secondary students with disabilities. *Remedial and Special Education, 24*, 235–245.

Caplan, G. (1964). *Principles of preventive psychiatry*. New York: Basic Books.

Caplan, G. (1970). *The theory and practice of mental health consultation*. New York: Basic Books.

Carlisle, J. F. (2010, February). *Providing (necessary?) instruction in vocabulary in high poverty schools*. Paper presented at the Pacific Coast Research Conference, Coronado, CA.

Catts, H. W., Adolph, S. M., & Weismer, S. E. (2006). Language deficits in poor comprehenders: A case for the simple view of reading. *Journal of Speech, Language, and Hearing Research, 49*, 278–293.

Chard, D. J., Vaughn, S., & Tyler, B. (2002). A synthesis of research on effective interventions for building reading fluency with elementary students with learning disabilities. *Journal of Learning Disabilities, 35*, 386–406.

Charles, R., Crown, W., & Fennell, F. (2006). *Scott Foresman/Addison–Wesley mathematics* [Curriculum program]. Upper Saddle River, NJ: Pearson Education.

Cherniss, C. (2006). *School change and the MicroSociety program*. Thousand Oaks, CA: Corwin Press.

Christ, T. J. (2007). Estimates of the standard error of measurement for curriculum-based measures of oral reading fluency. *School Psychology Review, 36*, 130–146.

Christ, T. J. (2008). Problem analysis. In A. Thomas & J. Grimes (Eds.), *Best practices in school psychology (5th ed.)* (pp. 159–176). Bethesda, MD: National Association of School Psychologists.

Christ, T. J., & Silberglitt, B. (2007). Estimates of the standard error of measurement for curriculum-based measures of oral reading fluency. *School Psychology Review, 36*, 130–146.

Clarke, B., & Shinn, M. R. (2004). A preliminary investigation into the identification and development of early mathematics curriculum-based measurement. *School Psychology Review, 33*, 234–248.

Clary, E. G., & Snyder, M. (1999). The motivations to volunteer: Theoretical and practical considerations. *Current Directions in Psychological Science, 8*, 156–159.

Coalition for Psychology in Schools and Education. (2006). *Report on the Teacher Needs Survey*. Washington, DC: American Psychological Association, Center for Psychology in Schools and Education.

Cochrane, W. S., & Laux, J. M. (2008). A survey investigating school psychologists' measurement of treatment integrity in school-based interventions and their beliefs about its importance. *Psychology in the Schools, 45*, 499–507.

Codding, R. S., Shiyoko, M., Russo, M., Birch, S., Fanning, E., & Jaspen, D. (2007). Comparing mathematics interventions: Does initial level of fluency predict intervention effectiveness? *Journal of School Psychology, 45*, 603–617.

Cognitive Concepts (2003). *Outcomes report: Los Angeles Unified School District, California*. Retrieved from *www. earobics.com/results/la.php*.

Coplon, J. (2010, April 25). The patron saint (and scourge) of lost schools. *New York Times Magazine*, Retrieved from *http://nymag.com/news/features/65614*.

Costenbader, V., Swartz, J., Petrix, L., (1992). Consultation in the schools: The relationship between preservice training, perception of consultative skills, and actual time spent in consultation. *School Psychology Review, 21*, 95–108.

Daane, M. C., Campbell, J. R., Grigg, W. S., Goodman, M. J., & Oranje, A. (2005). *Fourth-grade students reading aloud: NAEP 2002 special study of oral reading*. Washington, DC: U.S. Department of Education, National Center for Education Statistics.

Dappen, L. D., & Isernhagen, J. C. (2005). Developing a student mentoring program: Building connections for at-risk students. *Preventing School Failure, 49*, 21–25.

David, J. L., & Cuban, L. (2010). *Cutting through the hype: The essential guide to school reform*. Cambridge, MA: Harvard University Press.

De La Paz, S., & Graham, S. (2002). Explicitly teaching strategies, skills, and knowledge: Writing instruction in middle school classrooms. *Journal of Educational Psychology, 94*, 687–698.

Deno, S. L. (1985). Curriculum-based measurement: The emerging alternative. *Exceptional Children, 52*, 219–232.

Deno, S. L., & Mirkin, P. K. (1977). *Data-based program modification: A manual*. Reston, VA: Council for Exceptional Children.

Denton, C. A., Vaughn, S., & Fletcher, J. M. (2003). Bringing research-based practice in reading intervention to scale. *Learning Disabilities Research and Practice, 18*, 201–211.

Dewitz, P., Leahy, S. B., Jones, J., & Sullivan, P. M. (2010). *The essential guide to selecting and using core reading programs*. Newark, DE: International Reading Association.

Diamond, L., & Thorsnes, B. J. (2008). *Assessing read-*

ing: Multiple measures for kindergarten through eighth grade (2nd ed). Berkeley, CA: Consortium on Reading Excellence.

Dixon, R. (1991). The application of sameness analysis to spelling. *Journal of Learning Disabilities, 24,* 285–291.

Dixon, R., Boorman, L., Conrad, L., Klau, K., & Muti, K. (2008). *Reading Success* [Curriculum program]. Columbus, OH: McGraw-Hill Education.

Dixon, R., & Engelmann, S. (2007). *Spelling through morphographs.* Columbus, OH: McGraw-Hill Education.

Dodds, T. (2005). *High Performance Writing* [Curriculum program]. Columbus, OH: McGraw-Hill Education.

Doll, B., Haack, K., Kosse, S., Osterloh, M., Siemers, E., & Pray, B. (2005). The dilemma of pragmatics: Why schools don't use quality team consultation practices. *Journal of Educational and Psychological Consultation, 16,* 127–155.

Donovan, M. S., & Bransford, J. D. (Eds.). (2005). *How students learn: Mathematics in the classroom.* Washington, DC: National Research Council.

DuFour, R., Eaker, R., Karhanek, G., & DuFour, R. (2004). *Whatever it takes: How professional learning communities respond when kids don't learn.* Bloomington, IN: Solution Tree.

Durlak, J. A., & DuPre, E. P. (2008). Implementation matters: A review of research on the influence of implementation on program outcomes and the factors affecting implementation. *American Journal of Community Psychology, 41,* 327–350.

Earobics. (1995a). *Earobics Connections* [Curriculum program]. Boston, MA: Houghton Mifflin Harcourt Learning Technology.

Earobics. (1995b). *Earobics Foundations* [Curriculum program]. Boston, MA: Houghton Mifflin Harcourt Learning Technology.

Education for All Handicapped Children Act of 1975, 20 USC § 1401 *et seq.*

Elbaum, B., Vaughn, S., Hughes, M. T., & Moody, S. W. (2000). How effective are one-to-one tutoring programs in reading for elementary students at risk for reading failure?: A meta-analysis of the intervention research. *Journal of Educational Psychology,* 92, 605–619.

Elias, M. J., Zins, J. E., Graczyk, P. A., & Weissburg, R. P. (2003). Implementation, sustainability, and scaling up of social–emotional and academic innovations in public schools. *School Psychology Review, 32,* 303–319.

Ellis, S. W., & Granville, G. (1999). Intergenerational solidarity: Bridging the gap through mentoring programmes. *Mentoring and Tutoring: Partnership in Learning, 7,* 181.

Engelmann, S. (2008a). *Reading Mastery series guide.* Columbus, OH: McGraw-Hill Education.

Engelmann, S. (2008b). *Reading Mastery signature edition.* Columbus, OH: McGraw-Hill Education.

Engelmann, S., Dixon, R., Bauer, M., Steely, D., & Wells, T. (2007). *Spelling Mastery* [Curriculum program]. Columbus, OH: McGraw-Hill Education.

Engelmann, S., & Grossen, B. (2010). *Essentials for Writing* [Curriculum program]. Columbus, OH: McGraw-Hill Education.

Engelmann, S., Johnson, G., Carnine, L., & Meyer, L. (2008). *Corrective Reading: Decoding* [Curriculum program]. Columbus, OH: McGraw-Hill Education.

Engelmann, S., & Osborn, J. (2002). *Language for Thinking* [Curriculum program]. Columbus, OH: McGraw-Hill Education.

Engelmann, S., & Osborn, J. (2008). *Language for Learning* [Curriculum program]. Columbus, OH: McGraw-Hill Education.

Engelmann, S., & Silbert, J. (2007). *Expressive Writing* [Curriculum program]. Columbus, OH: McGraw-Hill Education.

Erchul, W. P., & Martens, B. K. (2010). *School consultation: Conceptual and empirical bases of practice* (3rd ed.). New York: Springer.

Eshelman, J. W. (2004). *SAFMEDS on the web: Guidelines and considerations for SAFMEDS.* Retrieved from *www.standardcelerationcharttopics.pbworks.com/w/page/15573489/SAFMEDS-on-the-Web.*

Feger, S., Woleck, K., & Hickman, P. (2004). How to develop a coaching eye. *Journal of Staff Development, 25,* 14–18.

Feinberg-DiNapoli, J., & McKinney, P. (1990). *Direct instruction and accelerated cognitive growth implementation: Guidelines handbook.* Baldwinsville, NY: J/P Associates.

Fien, H., Park, Y., Baker, S. K., Mercier Smith, J. L., Stoolmiller, M., & Kame'enui, E. J. (2010). An examination of the relation of nonsense word fluency initial status and gains to reading outcomes for beginning readers. *School Psychology Review, 49,* 631–653. Retrieved from *www.nasponline.org/publications/spr/39-4/spr394fien.pdf.*

Flugum, K. R., & Reschly, D. J. (1994). Prereferral interventions: Quality indices and outcomes. *Journal of School Psychology, 32,* 1–14.

Foegen, A., Jiban, C., & Deno, S. (2007). Progress monitoring measures in mathematics: A review of the literature. *Journal of Special Education, 41,* 121–139.

Fong, H. K., Sharpe, P., Gan, K. S., Ramakrishnan, C., Lau, B., & Choo, M. (2011). *Math in Focus* [Curriculum program]. Boston, MA: Houghton Mifflin Harcourt.

Freeman, R., Lohrman, S., Irvin, L. K., Kincaid, D., Vossler, V., & Ferro. (2009). Systems change and the contemporary roles of in-service and preservice training in schoolwide positive behavior support.

In W. Sailor, G. Sugai, R. H. Horner, & G. Dunlap (Eds.), *Handbook of positive behavior support* (pp. 603–629). New York: Springer.

Fuchs, D., & Fuchs, L. S. (1989). Exploring effective and efficient prereferral interventions: A component analysis of behavioral consultation. *School Psychology Review, 18*, 260–283.

Fuchs, D., & Fuchs, L. (1994). *PALS Reading* [Curriculum program]. Available at *www.kc.vanderbilt.edu/pals*.

Fuchs, D., Fuchs, L., Bahr, M. W., Fernstrom, P., & Stecker, P. M. (1990). Prereferral intervention: A prescriptive approach. *Exceptional Children, 56*, 493–513.

Fuchs, D., Fuchs, L., Harris, A. H., & Roberts, P. H. (1996). Bridging the research-to-practice gap with mainstream assistance teams: A cautionary tale. *School Psychology Quarterly, 14*, 244–266.

Fuchs, D., Fuchs, L., Mathes, P., & Simmons, D. (1997). Peer-assisted learning strategies: Making classrooms more responsive to student diversity. *American Educational Research Journal, 34*, 174–206.

Fuchs, D., Fuchs, L., & Stecker, P. M. (2010). The "blurring" of special education in a new continuum of general education placements and services. *Exceptional Children, 76*, 301–323.

Fuchs, L., Compton, D., Fuchs, D., Paulsen, K., Bryant, J., & Hamlett, C. (2005). The prevention, identification, and cognitive determinants of math difficulty. *Journal of Educational Psychology, 97*, 493–513.

Fuchs, L., Deno, S. L., & Mirkin, P. K. (1984). The effects of frequent curriculum-based measurement and evaluation on pedagogy, student achievement, and student awareness of learning. *American Educational Research Journal, 21*, 449–460.

Fuchs, L., & Fuchs, D. (1986). Effects of systematic formative evaluation: A meta-analysis. *Exceptional Children, 53*, 199–208.

Fuchs, L., & Fuchs, D. (2002a). Curriculum-based measurement: Describing competence, enhancing outcomes, evaluating treatment effects, and identifying treatment nonresponders. *Peabody Journal of Education, 77*, 64–84.

Fuchs, L., & Fuchs, D. (2002b). Hot Math: Promoting mathematical problem solving among children with disabilities. *CASL News: Promoting Success in Grades K–3, 7*, 1–4.

Fuchs, L., Fuchs, D., & Compton, D. L. (2004). Monitoring early reading development in first grade: Word identification fluency versus nonsense word fluency. *Exceptional Children, 71*, 7–21.

Fuchs, L., Fuchs, D., Craddock, C., Hollenbeck, K., Hamlett, C., & Schatschneider, C. (2008). Effects of small-group tutoring with and without validated classroom instruction on at-risk students' math problem solving: Are two tiers of prevention better than one? *Journal of Educational Psychology, 100*, 491–509.

Fuchs, L., Fuchs, D., Hamlett, C. L., & Allinder, R. M. (1991). The contribution of skills analysis to curriculum-based measurement in spelling. *Exceptional Children, 57*, 443–452.

Fuchs, L., Fuchs, D., Hamlett, C. L., & Stecker, P. M. (1991). Effects of curriculum-based measurement and consultation on teacher planning and student achievement in mathematics operations. *American Educational Research Journal, 28*, 617–641.

Fuchs, L., Fuchs, D., Hosp, M. K., & Jenkins, J. R. (2001). Oral reading fluency as an indicator of reading competence: A theoretical, empirical, and historical analysis. *Scientific Studies of Reading, 5*, 239–256.

Fuchs, L., Fuchs, D., Yazdian, L., & Powell, S. (2002). Enhancing first grade children's mathematical development with peer-assisted learning strategies. *School Psychology Review, 31*, 569–584.

Fuchs, L., Powell, S., Seethaler, P., Cirino, P., Fletcher, J., Fuchs, D., et al. (2009). Remediating number combination and word problem deficits among students with mathematical difficulties: A randomized control trial. *Journal of Educational Psychology, 101*, 561–576.

Fukkink, R. G., & Tavecchio, L. W. (2010). Effects of video interaction guidance on early childhood teachers. *Teaching and Teacher Education, 26*, 1652–1659.

Furney, K. S., Hasazi, S. B., Clark-Keefe, K., & Hartnett, J. (2003). A longitudinal analysis of shifting policy landscapes in special and general education reform. *Exceptional Children, 70*, 81–94.

Fuson, K. (2009). *Math Expressions* [Curriculum program]. Boston, MA: Houghton Mifflin Harcourt.

Gale, D. (2006). *The effect of computer-delivered phonological awareness training on the early literacy skills of students identified as at-risk for reading failure.* Retrieved from the University of South Florida website: *purl.fcla.edu/usf/dc/ et/SFE0001531.*

Gersten, R., Beckmann, S., Clarke, B., Foegen, A., Marsh, L., Star, J., et al. (2009). *Assisting students struggling with mathematics: Response to intervention (RtI) for elementary and middle schools.* Washington, DC. Institute of Education Sciences. Retrieved from *http://ies.ed.gov/ncee/wwc/pdf/practiceguides/rti_math_pg_042109.pdf.*

Gersten, R., Chard, D. J., & Baker, S. K. (2000). Factors enhancing sustained use of research-based instructional practices. *Journal of Learning Disabilities, 33*, 445–456.

Gersten, R., Compton, D., Connor, C.M., Dimino, J., Santoro, L., Linan-Thompson, S., et al. (2008). *Assisting students struggling with reading: Response to intervention and multi-tier intervention for reading in the primary grades. A practice guide* (NCEE

2009-4045). Washington, DC: National Center for Education Evaluation and Regional Assistance, Institute of Education Sciences, U.S. Department of Education. Retrieved from *http://ies.ed.gov/ncee/wwc/ publications/practiceguides.*

Gersten, R., & Dimino, J. (2001). The realities of translating research into classroom practice. *Learning Disabilities Research and Practice, 16,* 120–130.

Gersten, R., Jordan, N. C., & Flojo, J. R. (2005). Early identification and interventions for students with mathematics difficulties. *Journal of Learning Disabilities, 38,* 293–304.

Goddard, Y. L., Goddard, R. D., & Tschannen-Moran, M. (2007). A theoretical and empirical investigation of teacher collaboration for school improvement and student achievement in public elementary schools. *Teachers College Record, 109,* 877–896.

Good, R. H., & Kaminski, R. A. (2011). *DIBELS Next assessment manual.* Eugene, OR: Dynamic Measurement Group. Retrieved from *http://www.dibels.org.*

Gough, P. B., & Tunmer, W.E. (1986). Decoding, reading, and reading disability. *Remedial and Special Education, 7,* 6–10.

Graden, J. L., (1989). Redefining "prereferral" intervention as intervention assistance: Collaboration between general and special education. *Exceptional Children, 56,* 227–231.

Graham, S., & Harris, K. R. (2005). *Writing better: Teaching writing processes and self-regulation to students with learning problems.* Baltimore, MD: Brookes.

Graham, S., & Harris, K. (2009). Almost 30 years of writing research: Making sense of it all with *The Wrath of Khan. Learning Disabilities Research and Practice, 24,* 58–68.

Graham, S., Harris, K., & Chorzempa, B. (2002). Contribution of spelling instruction to the spelling, writing, and reading of poor spellers. *Journal of Educational Psychology, 94,* 669–686.

Graham, S., Harris, K., & Mason, L. (2005). Improving the writing performance, knowledge, and self-efficacy of struggling young writers: The effects of self-regulated strategy development. *Contemporary Educational Psychology, 30,* 207–241.

Graham, S., & Perrin, D. (2007a). A meta-analysis of writing instruction for adolescent students. *Journal of Educational Psychology, 99,* 445–476.

Graham, S., & Perrin, D. (2007b). *Writing Next: Effective strategies to improve writing of adolescents in middle and high school—A report to Carnegie Corporation of New York.* Washington, DC: Alliance for Excellence in Education. Retrieved from *www.all4ed.org/publications/WritingNext/WritingNext.pdf.*

Graves, D. H. (1983). *Writing: Teachers and children at work.* Exeter, NH: Heinemann.

Griffin, S. (2003). Number Worlds: A research-based mathematical program for young children. In D. H. Clements and A. DiBiase (Eds.), *Engaging young children in mathematics: Standards for early childhood mathematics education* (pp. 325–342). Mahwah, NJ: Erlbaum.

Griffin, S. (2004). Building number sense with Number Worlds. *Early Childhood Research Quarterly, 19,* 173–180.

Griffin, S. (2005). Fostering the development of whole-number sense: Teaching mathematics in the primary grades. In M. S. Donovan & J. D. Bransford (Eds.), *How students learn: Mathematics in the classroom* (pp. 257–308). Washington, DC: National Research Council.

Grimes, J., & Kurns, S. (2003, December). *An intervention-based system for addressing NCLB and IDEA expectations: Multiple tiered model to ensure every child learns.* Paper presented at the National Research Center on Learning Disabilities Responsiveness-to-Intervention Symposium, Kansas City, MO. Retrieved from *www.nrcld.org/symposium2003/grimes/grimes11.html.*

Grimes, J., Kurns, S., Tilly, W. D., III. (2006). Sustainability: An enduring commitment to success. *School Psychology Review, 35,* 224–244.

Gutkin, T. B., & Curtis, M. J. (1999). School-based consultation theory and practice: The art and science of indirect service delivery. In C. R. Reynolds & T. B. Gutkin (Eds.), *Handbook of school psychology* (3rd ed., pp. 598–637). New York: Wiley.

Haring, N. G., Lovitt, T. C., Eaton, M. D., & Hansen, C. L. (1978). *The fourth R: Research in the classroom* Columbus, OH: Merrill.

Hansen, C. L., & Eaton, M. D. (1978). Reading. In N.G. Haring, T. C. Lovitt, M. D. Eaton, & C. L. Hansen (Eds.), *The fourth R: Research in the classroom* (pp. 41–92). Columbus, OH: Merrill.

Harris, K., & Graham, S. (1996). *Making the writing process work: Strategies for composition and self-regulation* (2nd ed.). Cambridge, MA: Brookline Books.

Harris, K., Graham, S., & Mason, L. (2006). Improving the writing performance, knowledge, and motivation of struggling writers in second grade: The effects of self-regulated strategy development. *American Educational Research Journal, 42,* 295–340.

Harris, K., Graham, S., Mason, L. H., & Friedlander, B. (2008). *Powerful writing strategies for all students.* Baltimore, MD: Brookes.

Hasbrouck, J. E., & Denton, C. (2005). *The reading coach: A how-to manual for success.* Longmont, CO: Sopris West.

Hasbrouck, J. E., Ihnot, C., & Rogers, G. H. (1999). "Read Naturally": A strategy to increase oral reading fluency. *Reading Research and Instruction, 39,* 27–38.

Hasbrouck, J. E., & Tindal, G. A. (2006). Oral reading fluency norms: A valuable assessment tool for reading teachers. *The Reading Teacher, 59*, 636–644.

Hattie, J. (2009). *Visible learning: A synthesis of over 800 meta-analyses relating to achievement.* London: Routledge.

Haughton, E. (2002). *Rapid automatic naming: RAN.* Jackson, CA: Haughton Learning Center.

Haughton, E., & Freeman, G. (1999a). *Phonological coding: Phonemic awareness.* Jackson, CA: Haughton Learning Center.

Haughton, E., & Freeman, G. (1999b). *Phonological coding: Word and syllable awareness.* Jackson, CA: Haughton Learning Center.

Hausman, C. S., & Goldring, E. B. (2001). Sustaining teacher commitment: The role of professional communities. *Peabody Journal of Education, 76*, 30–51.

Hesse, K., Robinson, J., & Rankin, R. (1983). Retention and transfer from a morphemically based direct instruction spelling program in junior high. *Journal of Educational Research, 76*, 276–279.

Hintze, J. M., Christ, T. J., & Keller, L. A. (2002). The generalizability of CBM survey-level mathematics assessments: Just how many samples do we need? *School Psychology Review, 31*, 514–528.

Hirsch, E., & Church, K. (2009). *North Carolina teacher working conditions research brief: Summary of findings.* Retrieved from *www.ncteachingconditions.org.*

Hosp, M. K., Hosp, J. L., & Howell, K. W. (2007). *The ABC's of CBM: A practical guide to curriculum-based measurement.* New York: Guilford Press.

Hosp, J. L., & Reschly, D. J. (2002). Regional differences in school psychology practice. *School Psychology Review, 31*, 11–29.

Howell, K. W. (2000). *Resources for implementing Howell and Nolet's curriculum-based evaulation* (3rd ed). Belmont, CA: Wadsworth.

Howell, K. W., Hosp, J. L., & Kurns, S. (2008). Best practices in curriculum-based evaluation. In A. Thomas & J. Grimes (Eds.), *Best practices in school psychology (5th ed.)* (pp. 349–362). Bethesda, MA: National Association of School Psychologists.

Howell, K. W., & Morehead, M. K. (1987). *Curriculum-based evaluation for special and remedial education: A handbook for deciding what to teach.* Columbus, OH: Merrill.

Howell, K. W., & Nolet, V. (2000). *Curriculum-based evaluation for special and remedial education* (3rd ed.) Belmont, CA: Wadsworth.

Huffstetter, M., King, J., Onwuegbuzie, A., Schneider, J., & Powell-Smith, K. (2010). Effects of a computer-based early reading program on the early reading and oral language skills of at-risk preschool children. *Journal of Education for Students Placed at Risk, 15*, 279–298.

Hughes, C., & Dexter, D. D. (2011). *Selecting a scientifically based core curriculum for Tier 1.* RTI Action Network. Retrieved from *www.rtinetwork.org/learn/research/selectingcorecurriculum-tier1.*

Ihnot, C., Mastoff, J., Gavin, J., & Hendrickson, L. (2001). *Read Naturally* [Curriculum program]. St. Paul, MN: Read Naturally.

Ikeda, M. J., Neesen, E., & Witt, J. C. (2008). Best practices in universal screening. In A. Thomas & J. Grimes (Eds.), *Best practices in school psychology (5th ed.)* (pp. 103–114). Bethesda, MD: National Association of School Psychologists.

Individuals with Disabilities Education Improvement Act of 2004, 34 CFR § 300.309 (2006).

Jenkins, J. R., Peyton, J. A., Sanders, E. A., & Vadasy, P. F. (2004). Effects of reading decodable texts in supplemental first-grade tutoring. *Scientific Studies of Reading, 8*, 53–86.

Jenkins, J. R., Vadasy, P., Firebaugh, M., & Profilet, C. (2000). Tutoring first-grade struggling readers in phonological reading skills. *Learning Disabilities Research and Practice, 15*, 75–84.

Jenson, W. R., Rhode, G., & Reavis, H. K. (1994). *The tough kid tool box.* Longmont, CO: Sopris West.

Jitendra, A. (2007). *Solving math word problems: Teaching students with learning disabilities using schema-based instruction.* Austin, TX: Pro-Ed.

Johnson, E., Mellard, D. F., Fuchs, D., & McKnight, M. A. (2006). *School-wide screening: Section 1 of responsiveness to intervention (RTI): How to do it.* Lawrence, KS: National Research Center on Learning Disabilities. Retrieved from *www.rti4success.org/images/stories/pdfs/rtimanualsection1.pdf.*

Johnson, K. (2005). *Morningside mathematics fluency: Basic number skills* (Vols. 1–2). Seattle, WA: Morningside Press.

Johnson, K. (2008a). *Morningside mathematics fluency: Math facts* (Vols. 1–6). Seattle, WA: Morningside Press.

Johnson, K. (2008b). Precision teaching. In N. J. Salkind (Ed.), *The encyclopedia of educational psychology* (Vol. 2, pp. 809–813). Thousand Oaks, CA: Sage.

Johnson, K., & Casson, S. (2005a). *Morningside mathematics fluency: Addition and subtraction* (Vols. 1–2). Seattle, WA: Morningside Press.

Johnson, K., & Casson, S. (2005b). *Morningside mathematics fluency: Multiplication and division* (Vols. 1–2). Seattle, WA: Morningside Press.

Johnson, K., Casson, S., Street, E., Kevo, H., & Melroe, K. (2005). *Basic Elements* [Curriculum program]. Seattle, WA: Morningside Press.

Johnson, K., & Layng, T. V. J. (1992). Breaking the structuralist barrier: Literacy and numeracy with fluency. *American Psychologist, 47*, 1475–1490.

Johnson, K., & Layng, T. V. J. (1994). The Morningside model of generative instruction. In R. Gardner et al. (Eds.), *Behavior analysis in education: Focus on measurably superior instruction* (pp. 173–197). Belmont CA: Brooks-Cole.

Johnson, K., & Melroe, K. (2006a). *Teaching computation skills: A diagnostic and prescriptive instructional sequence: Addition and subtraction* (Vols. 1–2). Seattle, WA: Morningside Press.

Johnson, K., & Melroe, K. (2006b). *Teaching computation skills: A diagnostic and prescriptive instructional sequence: Multiplication and division* (Vols. 1–2). Seattle, WA: Morningside Press.

Johnson, K., & Melroe, K. (2009). *Teaching computation skills: A diagnostic and prescriptive instructional sequence: Fractions* (Vols. 1–3). Seattle, WA: Morningside Press.

Johnson, K., & Melroe, K. (2011). *Teaching computation skills: A diagnostic and prescriptive instructional sequence: Decimals* (Vols. 1–2). Seattle, WA: Morningside Press.

Johnson, K., & Street, E. M. (2004). *The Morningside model of generative instruction: What it means to leave no child behind.* Cambridge, MA: Cambridge Center for Behavioral Studies.

Johnson, K., & Street, E. M. (in press). *Precision teaching, progress monitoring, and RTI.*

Johnson, N., Oliff, P., & Williams, E. (2010). *An update on state budget cuts: Governors proposing new round of cuts for 2011; at least 45 states have already imposed cuts that hurt vulnerable residents.* Retrieved from *www.cbpp.org/cms/?fa=view&id=1214.*

Joyce, B., & Showers, B. (1995). *Student achievement through staff development: Fundamentals of school renewal* (2nd ed.). White Plains, NY: Longman.

Joyce, B., & Showers, B. (2002). *Student achievement through staff development* (3rd ed). Alexandria, VA: Association for Curriculum and Development.

Karcher, M. (2009). Increases in academic connectedness and self-esteem among high school students who serve as cross-age peer mentors. *Professional School Counseling, 12,* 292–299.

Kaminski, R. A., & Good, R. H. (1996). Toward a technology for assessing early literacy skills. *School Psychology Review, 25,* 215–227.

Kelley, B. (2008). Best practices in curriculum-based evaluation and math. In A. Thomas & J. Grimes (Eds.), *Best practices in school psychology (5th ed.)* (pp. 419–438). Bethesda, MD: National Association of School Psychologists.

Kho, T. (2008). *Primary mathematics.* Oregon City, OR: SingaporeMath.com.

Kirby, J., Georgiou, G., Martinussen, R., & Parrila, R. (2010). Naming speed and reading: From prediction to instruction. *Reading Research Quarterly, 45,* 341–362.

Kratochwill, T. R. (2007). Preparing psychologists for evidence-based school practice: Lessons learned and challenges ahead. *American Psychologist, 62,* 829–843.

Kratochwill, T. R., Volpiansky, P., Clements, M., & Ball, C. (2007). Professional development in implementing and sustaining multitier prevention models: Implications for response to intervention. *School Psychology Review, 36,* 618–631.

Kurns, S., & Ikeda, M. (2008). Problem analysis. In Heartland AEA 11, *Heartland special education procedures: Module four, decision making practices* (pp. 51–72). Retrieved from *www.aea11.k12.ia.us/spedresources/ModuleFour.pdf.*

Lago, R. M., & DiPerna, J. C. (2010). Number sense in kindergarten: A factor-analytic study of the construct. *School Psychology Review, 39,* 164–180.

Lane, K., Bocian, K. M., MacMillan, D. L., & Gresham, F. M. (2004). Treatment integrity: An essential but often forgotten component of school-based interventions. *Preventing School Failure, 48,* 36–43.

Larson N., Hake J., & Wrigley P. (2011). *Saxon Math* [Curriculum program]. Boston, MA: Houghton Mifflin Harcourt.

Latham, G. (1988). The birth and death cycles of educational innovations. *Principal, 68,* 41–43.

Layng, T. V. J., Ford, V., Leon, M., Shimizu, H., Sota, M., & Twyman, J. S. (2008). *Headsprout Reading Comprehension* [Curriculum program]. Seattle, WA: Headsprout.

Layng, T. V. J., Johnson, K., Twyman, J. S., Ford, V., Layng, M. P., Gilbert, M., & Stikeleather, G. (2002). *Headsprout Early Reading* [Curriculum program]. Seattle, WA: Headsprout.

Layng, T. V. J., Sota, M., & Leon, M. (in press). Thinking through text comprehension: I. Foundation and guiding relations. *Behavior Analyst Today.*

Leon, M., Layng, T. V. J., & Sota, M. (in press). Thinking through text comprehension: II. The programming of verbal and investigative repertoires. *Behavior Analyst Today.*

Levine, A. (2006). Educating school teachers [Electronic Version]. Retrieved April 22, 2008, from *www.edschools.org/pdf/Educating_Teachers_Report.pdf*

Lindamood, P., & Lindamood, P. (2009). *The Lindamood Phonemic Sequencing (LiPS) program* [Curriculum program]. Avila Beach, CA: Gander Educational Publishing.

Lindsley, O. R. (1972). From Skinner to precision teaching: The child knows best. In J. B. Jordan & L. S. Robbins (Eds.), *Let's try doing something else kind of thin* (pp. 1–12). Arlington, VA: Council on Exceptional Children.

Lindsley, O. R. (1990). Precision teaching: By teachers for children. *Teaching Exceptional Children, 22*(3), 10–15.

Loeppke, R. (2008). The value of health and the power of prevention. *International Journal of Workplace Health Management, 1,* 95–108

Louis, K. S., Marks, H. M., & Kruse, S. (1996). Teachers' professional community in restructuring schools. *American Educational Research Journal, 33*, 757–798.

Malecki, C. (2008). Best practices in written language assessment and intervention. In A. Thomas & J. Grimes (Eds.), *Best practices in school psychology (5th ed.)* (pp. 477–488). Bethesda, MD: National Association of School Psychologists.

Marchand-Martella, N. (2010). *Read to achieve pilot study*. Columbus, OH: McGraw-Hill Education.

Marchand-Martella, N., & Martella, R. (2010a). *Read to achieve: Comprehending content area text*. Columbus, OH: McGraw Hill Education.

Marchand-Martella, N., & Martella, R. (2010b). *Read to achieve: Comprehending narrative text*. Columbus, OH: McGraw Hill Education.

Martens, B. K., & Eckert, T. L. (2007). The instructional hierarchy as a model of stimulus control over student and teacher behavior: We're close but are we close enough? *Journal of Behavioral Education, 16*, 83–91.

Matsumura, L., Garnier, H., Correnti, R., Junker, B., & Bickel, D. (2010). Investigating the effectiveness of a comprehensive literacy coaching program in schools with high teacher mobility. *Elementary School Journal, 111*, 35–62.

McDonnell, L. M. (2004). *Politics, persuasion, and educational testing*. Cambridge, MA: Harvard University Press.

McGlinchey, M. T., & Hixson, M. D. (2004). Contemporary research on curriculum-based measurement: Using curriculum-based measurement to predict performance on state assessment in reading. *School Psychology Review, 33*, 193–204.

McIntosh, K., Horner, R. H., & Sugai, G. (2009). Sustainability of systems-level evidence-based practices in schools: Current knowledge and future directions. In W. Sailor, G. Sugai, R. H. Horner, & G. Dunlap (Eds.), *Handbook of positive behavior support* (pp. 327–352). New York: Springer.

McMaster, K. L., Du, X., & Petursdottir, A. (2009). Technical features of curriculum-based measures for beginning writers. *Journal of Learning Disabilities, 42*, 41–60.

McMaster, K. L., & Espin, C. (2007). Technical features of curriculum-based measurement in writing: A literature review. *Journal of Special Education, 41*, 68–84.

McMaster, K. L., Fuchs, D., Fuchs, L., & Compton, D. L. (2005). Responding to nonresponders: An experimental field trial of identification and intervention methods. *Exceptional Children, 71*, 445–463.

Mercer, C. D., & Campbell, K. U. (1998). *Great Leaps reading program, kindergarten–2nd grade*. Gainesville, FL: Diarmuid.

Mercer, C. D., Campbell, K. U., Miller, D. M., Mercer, K. D., & Lane, H. B. (2000). Effects of a reading fluency intervention for middle schoolers with specific learning disabilities. *Learning Disabilities Research and Practice, 15*, 179–189.

Merzenich, M., Jenkins, W., Johnston, P., Schreiner, C., Miller, S., & Tallal, P. (1996). Temporal processing deficits of language-learning impaired children ameliorated by training. *Science, 271* (5245), 77–81.

Meyer, C. (2002). April's mud. In P. Afflerbach et al. *Scott Foresman Reading Street grade 6* (pp. 66–79). Upper Saddle River, NJ: Pearson Education.

Meyers, J., Parsons, R. D., & Martin, R. (1979). *Mental health consultation in the schools*. San Francisco: Jossey-Bass.

Michael, B. (1990). *Volunteers in public schools*. Washington, DC: National Academy Press.

Miller, M. (2009). *Achieving a wealth of riches: Delivering on the promise of data to transform teaching and learning*. Policy Brief, Alliance for Excellence in Education. Retrieved from *www.all4ed.org/files/AchievingWealthOfRiches.pdf*.

Ministry of Education, Singapore. (1997). *Singapore's achievement in the Third International Mathematics and Science Study*. Retrieved from *www.moe.sg/press/1997/st00297.htm*.

Ministry of Education, Singapore. (2000). *Singapore number one in mathematics again in the Third International Mathematics and Science Study 1999*. Retrieved from *www.moe.gov.sg/press/2000/pr06122000.htm*.

Ministry of Education, Singapore. (2004). *Singapore tops the trends in international mathematics and science study 2003*. Retrieved from *www.moe.gov.sg/press/2004/pr20041214.htm*.

Moats, L. (1999). *Teaching reading is rocket science: What expert teachers of reading should know and be able to do*. Washington, DC: American Federation of Teachers. Retrieved from *www.aft.org/pdfs/teachers/rocketscience0304.pdf*.

Montague, M., & Jitendra, A. K. (2006). *Teaching mathematics to middle school students with learning difficulties*. New York: Guilford Press.

Morgan, P. L., & Sideridis, P. D. (2006). Contrasting the effectiveness of fluency interventions for students with or at risk for learning disabilities: A multilevel random coefficient modeling meta-analysis. *Learning Disabilities Research and Practice, 21*, 191–210.

Murray M., Bloomfield K., Russell S., Schifter D., Cochran, K., Economopoulous K., et al. (2008). *Investigations in Numbers, Data, and Space* [Curriculum program]. Upper Saddle River, NJ: Pearson Education.

National Center on Education Statistics. (2007). *Trends in international mathematics and science study (TIMSS)*. Available at *www.nces.ed.gov/timss*.

National Center on Response to Intervention. (2010).

Progress monitoring tools chart. Retrieved from *www.rti4success.org* > "Tools/Interventions."

National Center on Response to Intervention. (2011). *Intervention program evaluations.* Retrieved from *www.rti4success.org* > "Tools/Interventions."

National Council of Teachers of Mathematics. (2006). *Curriculum focal points for prekindergarten through grade 8 mathematics: A quest for coherence.* Reston, VA: Author.

National Institute of Child Health and Human Development. (2000). *Report of the National Reading Panel: Teaching children to read: An evidence-based assessment of the scientific research literature on reading and its implications for reading instruction: Reports of the subgroups* (NIH Publication No. 00-4754).Washington, DC: U.S. Government Printing Office.

National Mathematics Advisory Panel (NMAP). (2008). *Foundations for success: The final report of the National Mathematics Advisory Panel.* Washington, DC: U.S. Department of Education. Available at *www.ed.gov/MathPanel* and *www.2.ed.gov/about/bdscomm/list/mathpanel/ report/final-report.pdf.*

National Reading Panel (2000). *Reading First* [Curriculum program]. Available at *www.2.ed.gov/programs/readingfirst.*

National School Psychology Certification Board. (2010). *Nationally certified school psychologist (NCSP) renewal guidelines and NASP continuing professional development program.* Bethesda, MD: National Association of School Psychologists. Also available at *www.nasponline.org/certification/New%20 NCSP%20booklet.pdf.*

No Child Left Behind (NCLB) Act of 2001, 20 U.S.C.A. § 6301 et seq. (NCLB, 2003).

Noell, G. H., Witt, J. C., Slider, N. J., Connell, J. E., Gatti, S. L., Williams, K. L., et al. (2005). Treatment implementation following behavioral consultation in schools: A comparison of three follow-up strategies. *School Psychology Review, 34,* 87–106.

Okamoto, Y., & Case, R. (1996). Exploring the microstructure of children's central conceptual structures in the domain of number. *Monographs of the Society for Research in Child Development, 6,* 27–59.

Osborne, S. S., & Schulte, A. C. (2001). A school–university project on collaboration and consultation. In V. J. Risko & K. Bromley (Eds.), *Collaboration for diverse learners* (pp. 330–347). Newark, DE: International Reading Association.

Paris, S. G. (2011). Developmental differences in early reading skills. In S. B. Neuman, & D. K. Dickinson (Eds.), *Handbook of early literacy* (Vol. 3, pp. 228–241). New York: Guilford Press.

Phillips, S. (1996). *Sentence combining: A literature review.* ERIC Document Reproduction Service ED 398589. Retrieved from *www.eric.ed.gov/PDFS/ED398589.pdf.*

Prawatt, R. S. (1989). Promoting access to knowledge, strategy, and disposition in students: A research synthesis. *Review of Educational Research, 59,* 1–41.

Rathvon, N. (2008). *Effective school interventions: Evidence-based strategies for improving student outcomes.* New York: Guilford Press.

Rayner, K., Foorman, B. R., Perfetti, C. A., Pesetsky, D., & Seidenberg, M. S. (2001). How psychological science informs the teaching of reading. *Psychological Science in the Public Interest, 2,* 31–74.

Reed, J., Marchand-Martella, N., Martella, R., & Kolts, R. (2007). Assessing the effects of the Reading Success Level A program with fourth grade students at a Title I elementary school. *Education and Treatment of Children, 30,* 45–68.

Rekrut, M. D. (1994). Peer and cross-age tutoring: The lessons of research. *Journal of Reading, 37,* 356–362.

Renaissance Learning. (2009). *Accelerated Math* [Curriculum program]. Wisconsin Rapids, WI: Renaissance Learning. Available at *www.renlearn.com/am*

Reschly, D. J., & Casey, A. (1986). *Behavioral consultation.* Ames, IA: Iowa State University, Department of psychology, Project RE-AIM.

Riccomini, P., & Witzel, B. (2010). *Response to intervention in math.* Thousand Oaks, CA: Corwin.

Ritter, G., Barnett, J., Denny, G., & Albin, G. (2009). The effectiveness of volunteer tutoring programs for elementary and middle school students: A meta-analysis. *Review of Educational Research, 79,* 3–38.

Roach, A. T., & Elliott, S. N. (2008). Best practices in facilitating and evaluating intervention integrity. In A. Thomas & J. Grimes (Eds.), *Best practices in school psychology (5th ed.)* (pp. 195–208). Bethesda, MD: National Association of School Psychologists.

Robbins, J. K. (1996). *TAPS for teachers.* Seattle, WA: Robbins/Layng.

Rogers, E. M. (2003). *Diffusion of innovations (5th ed.).* New York: Free Press.

Rogers, L., & Graham, S. (2008). A meta-analysis of single subject design writing intervention research. *Journal of Educational Psychology, 100,* 879–906.

Rosenfield, S. A. (1987). *Instructional consultation.* Hillsdale, NJ: Erlbaum.

Sadoski, M., & Willson, V. (2006). Effects of a theoretically based large-scale reading intervention in a multicultural urban school district. *American Educational Research Journal, 43,* 137–154.

Schulte, A. C., & Villwock, D. N. (2004). Using high stakes tests to derive school-level measures of special education efficacy. *Exceptionality, 12,* 107–126.

Schultz Center for Teaching and Leadership. (2009). *Fast ForWord longitudinal impact study.* Retrieved from *www.schultzcenter.org/pdf/fast_forword_study.pdf.*

Scientific Learning. (1997). *Fast ForWord* [Curriculum program]. Oakland, CA: Scientific Learning. Available at *www.scilearn.com*.

Seethaler, P., Powell, S., & Fuchs, L. (n.d.). *Help students solve problems with "Pirate Math."* Council for Exceptional Children. Retrieved from *www.cec.sped.org/AM/Template.cfm? Section =Home&TEMPLATE=/CM/ContentDisplay.cfm&CONTENTID=11340*.

Senesac, B. V., & Burns, M. K. (2008). Theoretical soundness, proven effectiveness, and implementation fidelity of the HOSTS Language Arts program among children identified as at-risk in urban elementary schools. *Journal of Instructional Psychology, 35*, 212–221.

Shachar, H., & Shmuelevitz, H. (1997). Implementing cooperative learning, teacher collaboration, and teachers' sense of efficacy in heterogeneous junior high schools. *Contemporary Educational Psychology, 22*, 53–72.

Shapiro, E. S. (2011a). *Academic skills problems: Direct assessment and intervention* (4th ed.). New York: Guilford Press.

Shapiro, E. S. (2011b). *Academic skills problems Fourth edition workbook*. New York: Guilford Press.

Shepard, L., & Smith, M. L. (1983). An evaluation of the identification of learning disabled students in Colorado. *Learning Disability Quarterly, 6*, 115–127.

Shernoff, E. S., Kratochwill, T. R., & Stoiber, K. C. (2003). Training in evidence-based interventions (EBIs): What are school psychology programs teaching? *Journal of School Psychology, 41*, 467–483.

Shinn, M. (2002). *Progress monitoring: Strategies for writing individualized goals in general curriculum and more frequent formative evaluation*. Eden Prairie, MN: Edformation. Retrieved from *http://www.aimsweb.com*.

Shinn, M., Walker, H., & Stoner, G. (2002). *Interventions for academic and behavior problems: II. Preventive and remedial approaches*. Bethesda, MD: National Association of School Psychologists.

Silberglitt, B., & Hintze, J. (2005). Formative assessment using CBM-R cut scores to track progress toward success on state-mandated achievement tests: A comparison of methods. *Journal of Psychoeducational Assessment, 23*, 304–325.

Simmons, D. C., & Kame'enui, E. J. (2003). *A consumer's guide to evaluating a core reading program, grades K–3: A critical elements analysis*. Eugene, OR: Oregon Reading First Center, University of Oregon College of Education. Available at *www.iris.peabody.vanderbilt.edu/rti03_reading/cons_guide_instr.pdf*.

Simmons, D. C., Kame'enui, E. J., Beck, C., Brewer, N., & Fien, H. (2007). *A consumer's guide to evaluating supplemental and intervention reading programs, grades K–3: A critical elements analysis*. Eugene, OR: Oregon Reading First Center, University of Oregon College of Education.

Simmons, D. C., Kame'enui, E. J., Good, R. H., Harn, B. A., Cole, C., & Braun, D. (2002). Building, implementing, and sustaining a beginning reading improvement model: Lessons learned school by school. In M. Shinn, H. Walker, & G. Stoner (Eds.), *Interventions for academic and behavior problems: II. Preventive and remedial approaches* (pp. 537–569). Bethesda, MD. National Association of School Psychologists.

Sin, K. (2006). *New elementary mathematics*. Oregon City, OR: SinaporeMath.com.

Sindelar, P. T., Shearer, D. K., Yendol-Hoppey, D., & Liebert, T. W. (2006). The sustainability of inclusive school reform. *Exceptional Children, 72*, 317–331.

Sota, M., Leon, M., & Layng, T. (in press). Thinking through text comprehension: II. Analysis of verbal and investigative repertoires. *Behavior Analyst Today*.

Sprick, M. M., & Howard, L. M. (1996). *The teacher's encyclopedia of behavior management: 100 problems/500 plans*. Longmont, CO: Sopris West.

Sprick, M. M., Howard, L. M., & Fidanque, A. (2008). *Read Well* [Curriculum program]. Longmont, CO: Cambium Learning Group/Sopris West.

Stanovich, K. E. (1986). Matthew effects in reading: Some consequences of individual differences in the acquisition of literacy. *Reading Research Quarterly, 21*, 360–407.

Stanovich, K. E. (1993). Romance and reality. *Reading Teacher, 47*, 280–291.

Stanovich, P. J., & Stanovich, K. E. (2003). *Using research and reason in education: How teachers can use scientifically based research to make curricular and instructional decisions*. National Institute for Literacy. Retrieved from *www.lincs.ed.gov/publications/pdf/Stanovich_Color.pdf*.

Stecker, P. M., Fuchs, L., & Fuchs, D. (2005). Using curriculum-based measurement to improve student achievement: Review of research. *Psychology in the Schools, 42*, 795–819.

Steege, M. W., Watson, T. S., & Gresham, F. M. (2009). *Conducting school-based functional behavioral assessments: A practitioner's guide* (2nd ed.). New York: Guilford Press.

Stein, M., Kinder, D., Silbert, J., & Carnine, D. (2006). *Designing effective mathematics instruction: A direct instruction approach* (4th ed.). Upper Saddle River, NJ: Pearson Education.

Tallal, P., Miller, S. L., Bedi, G., Byma, G., Wang, X., Nagarajam, S., et al. (1996). Language comprehension in language-learning impaired children improved with acoustically modified speech. *Science, 27*, 81–84.

Therrien, W. J. (2004). Fluency and comprehension gains as a result of repeated reading: A meta-analysis. *Remedial and Special Education, 25*, 252–261.

Thomas, A., & Grimes, J. (2008). *Best practices in school psychology* (5th ed.). Bethesda, MD: National Association of School Psychologists.

Timperley, H., Wilson, A., Barrar, H., & Fung, I. (2007). *Teacher professional learning and development: Best evidence synthesis iteration*. Wellington, NZ: Ministry of Education.

Torgesen, J. K. (2000). Individual differences in response to early interventions in reading: The lingering problem of treatment resisters. *Learning Disabilities Research and Practice, 15*, 55–64.

Truch, S. (1994). Stimulating basic reading processes using auditory discrimination in depth. *Annals of Dyslexia, 44*, 60–80.

U.S. Department of Education. (2010). *Condition of education*. Retrieved from *http://nces.ed.gov/programs/coe*.

Vadasy, P. F., Jenkins, J. R., & Pool, K. (2000). Effects of tutoring in phonological and early reading skills on students at risk for reading disabilities. *Journal of Learning Disabilities, 33*, 579–590.

Vadasy, P. F., Wayne, S., O'Conner, R., Jenkins, J., Firebaugh, M., & Peyton, J. (2000). *Sound Partners* [Curriculum program]. Longmont, CO: Cambium Learning Group/Sopris West.

Vaughn, S., Klingner, J., & Hughes, M. (2000). Sustainability of research-based practices. *Exceptional Children, 66*, 163–171.

Vitale, M., Medland, M., Romance, N., & Weaver, H. P. (1993). Accelerating reading and thinking skills of low-achieving elementary students: Implications for curricular change. *Effective School Practices, 12*, 26–31.

Waldron-Soler, K., Martella, R., Marchand-Martella, N., Warner, D., Miller, D., & Tso, M. (2002). Effects of a 15-week Language for Learning implementation with children in an integrated preschool. *Journal of Direct Instruction, 2*, 75–86.

Walker, B., Shippen, M., Alberto, P., & Houchins, D. (2005). Using the expressive writing program to improve the writing skills of high school students with learning disabilities. *Learning Disabilities Research and Practice, 20*, 175–183.

Walsh, K. (2006). Teacher education: Coming up empty. *Fwd, 3*, 1–6.

Wasik, B. A. (1998). Volunteer tutoring programs in reading: A review. *Reading Research Quarterly, 33*, 266–292.

Wayman, M. M., Wallace, T., Wiley, H. I., Ticha, R., & Espin, C. A. (2007). Literature synthesis on curriculum-based measurement in reading. *Journal of Special Education, 41*, 85–120.

Whimbey, A. (1987). Think Aloud Problem Solving—TAPS: The key to higher order thinking in precise processing. *Educational Leadership, 42*, 66–70.

Whimbey, A., & Lockhead, J. (1999). *Problem solving and comprehension* (6th ed.). Mahwah, NJ: Erlbaum.

Wiley, H. I., & Deno, S. (2005). Oral reading and maze measurements as predictors of success for English language learners on a state standards assessment. *Remedial and Special Education, 26*, 207–214.

Woodward, J., & Brown, C. (2006). Meeting the curricular needs of academically low-achieving students in middle grade mathematics. *Journal of Special Education, 40*, 151–159.

Woodward, J., & Stroh, M. (2009). *TransMath* [Curriculum program]. Longmont, CO: Cambium Learning Group/Sopris West.

Xin, Y., Jitendra, A., & Deatline-Buchman, A. (2005). Effects of mathematical word problem solving instruction on middle school students with learning problems. *Journal of Special Education, 39*, 181–192.

Yell, M. L., & Drasgow, E. (2007). Assessment for eligibility under IDEIA and the 2006 regulations. *Assessment for Effective Intervention, 32*, 202–213.

Ysseldyke, J., & Bolt, D. (2007). Effect of technology-enhanced continuous progress monitoring on math achievement. *School Psychology Review, 36*, 453–467.

Ysseldyke, J., & Tardrew, S. (2003). *Differentiating math instruction: A large-scale study of Accelerated Math (Final report)*. Wisconsin Rapids, WI: Renaissance Learning.

Index

Page numbers followed by *f* or *t* refer to figures or tables, respectively.